Blumenfeld's
DICTIONARY
OF ACTING
AND SHOW
BUSINESS

Blumenfeld's
DICTIONARY
OF ACTING
AND SHOW
BUSINESS

ROBERT BLUMENFELD

AN IMPRINT OF HAL LEONARD CORPORATION
NEW YORK

Published in 2009 by Limelight Editions
An Imprint of Hal Leonard Corporation
7777 West Bluemound Road
Milwaukee, WI 53213

Trade Book Division Editorial Offices
19 West 21st Street, New York, NY 10010

Printed in the United States of America

Book design by UB Communications

Library of Congress Cataloging-in-Publication Data

Blumenfeld, Robert.
    Blumenfeld's dictionary of acting and show business / by Robert Blumenfeld.
        p. cm.
    Includes bibliographical references and indexes.
    ISBN 978-0-87910-363-7
    1. Performing arts—Dictionaries. I. Title. II. Title: Dictionary of acting and show business.
    PN1579.B55 2009
    790.2003—dc22
                                            2008045504

www.limelighteditions.com

To my wonderful family
and to
my loving, supportive friends

And to all those theatricals and show biz folk
who pursue the peaceful occupation
of entertaining others

Contents

Preface

How to Use This Book

Do you know what a "gaffer" does? Or what "dulling spray" is used for? What is the "Alexander technique"? And what does it mean when a director tells you, "Back to one!" or "Stop thinking!" We've all heard such expressions as "less is more" and "tone it down," but what does it mean to "answer back to the camera"? Does a film director want a piece of fruit when he or she asks for a "half apple," or says, "Give me a banana!"? Then why not ask the "gopher," who might just respond with a "raspberry"? What is an "angle-reverse angle shot," and who were the "angry young men"? You've heard of "syndication," but what is it—a kind of musical beat? And what exactly is a "comedy of manners," or a "cup and saucer drama"? Do you know what a "soundie" is? No relation to a "techie"! Can you use a "cough drop" right about now? Hint: It's not something you swallow. And, no, I'm not trying to "gaslight" you.

Acting, the great art of interpreting and playing characters, of bringing fictional creations to life as if they were real, happens of course in the context of show business and the entertainment industry: spoken and musical theater, film, radio, television, recording, new media, and the Internet—all providing a vast number of jobs, and an immense vocabulary to go with them. Show business is global, and its history is millennial: international and historical terms, and the richness of slang, idioms, and expressions, suggest how fascinating is the world of those whose business it is to amuse us. This is all terrific stuff, but if you are a professional actor or want to be one, you have to be practical, as well as starry-eyed, and you owe it to yourself to know as much as possible about the legal documents you sign, hence the information about AEA, AFTRA, SAG, and agency contracts and agreements included here.

A word about the nature of the definitions: In order to make them as clear as possible, I have included the part or parts of speech that categorize the way a single word is used; e.g., the word **broadcast**, used as a noun, adjective, or verb. Also, there are frequent examples of usage to clarify the definitions even further. Where there are phrases, however, parts of speech are not included: the definition should be clear without that information. Alternative words or phrases with synonymous meanings are included at the ends of definitions; e.g., in **clapboard**, **keep take**.

To get the most out of this book, use the index of subjects, which is divided into broader categories: you can then read all the entries in a category, and you will have an overview of the particular field. Used in this way, the dictionary can actually be a concise instructional guide to the rudiments of the art, craft, and business of acting.

The categories in the index of subjects are these:

1. Acting
2. Commercials
3. Dance
4. Directions
5. Drama
   Script and Playwriting Terms
   Genres, Periods, and Schools
6. Expressions, Catchphrases, Idioms, and Slang
7. Foreign-Language and British Terms
8. Jobs and Professions
9. Lights and Lighting Terms
10. Media: Radio, Film, Television, and the Internet
    Technical and Technological Terms
    Genres
11. Music
12. Professional Organizations
13. Recording
14. Rehearsals
15. Show Business
    Terminology
    Contracts
16. Theater
17. Voice and Vocal Technique

Pronunciation Guide, Abbreviations, and Symbols

Pronunciation Guide

Vowels, Semivowels, and Diphthongs

a: like the "a" in *that*.
ah: like the "a" in *father*.
aw: like the long vowel in *law*.
ay: like the diphthong "ay" in *say*.
é: like the French vowel in *café*.
ee: like the "ee" in *meet*.
eh: like the "e" in *met*.
I: like the diphthong "I" in *I'm*.
ih: like the "i" in *bit*.
o: like the short "o" in *hot*.
oh: like the diphthong "o" in *home*.

oo: like the "oo" in *boot*.
oo: like the "oo" in *book*.
ow: like the diphthong "ow" in *cow*.
oy: like the diphthong "oy" in *boy*.
ü: the German umlauted "u" and
   the French "u," pronounced by
   protruding and rounding the lips,
   and saying "ee."
uh: like the "e" in *the*; schwa.
w: like the "w" in *wet*.
y: like the "y" in *yet*.

Consonants

b: as in *bow*.
ch: as in *church*.
d: as in *dog*.
dg: as in *edge* or *just*.
f: as in *off*.
g: as in *go*.
h: as in *hot*.
h: as in German *Ich*.
k: as in *king*.
kh: as in German *ach*.
ks: as in *box*.
l: as in *look*.
m: as in *my*.
n: as in *no*.
n: the nasal final "n" as in
   French *enfant*.

ng: as in *sing*.
p: as in *pie*.
r: the English retroflex or Italian,
   Portuguese, Polish, Russian,
   or Spanish trilled "r."
r: the French or German uvular "r."
s: as in *so*.
sh: as in *shoe*.
t: as in *tea*.
th: as in *thin*.
th: as in *the*.
ts: as in *sits*.
v: as in *very*.
z: as in *zoo*.
zh: like the "s" in *pleasure*.

Abbreviations

abbrev.   abbreviation; abbreviated
adj.   adjective
adv.   adverb
b.   born
BCE   before the common era
Brit.   British
c.   century
ca.   circa
cf.   compare [Latin: confer]
def.   definition
e.g.   for example [Latin: exempli gratia]
esp.   especially
etc.   and so forth [Latin: et cetera]
fr.   from
Hist.   historical
i.e.   that is [Latin: id est]
lit.   literally
n.   noun
n. pl.   plural noun
p.   page
pl.   plural
prep.   preposition
syn.   synonym(s); synonymous
v.   verb
v. i.   intransitive verb
v. t.   transitive verb

Symbols

:   A colon after a vowel in a pronunciation means it is lengthened.
'   An apostrophe following a syllable in a pronunciation indicates that it is stressed.
( )   Parentheses enclose pronunciations.
[ ]   Brackets enclose etymological and other information.

A word in **boldface** within an entry is a cross-reference to another entry.

Acknowledgments

Among those friends who have contributed directly and indirectly to this book are the admirable Christopher Buck; Albert S. Bennett; Michael Mendiola and Scot Anderson; Peter Subers and Rob Bauer; Tom and Virginia Smith; Robert Perillo; Alice Spivak; Laine Goerner; Christopher Layton and Ronald Hornsby; Matthew Deming and Andrew Gitzy; Jay Lesenger; Ian Strasvogel; François Roulmann; Nina Koenigsberg; Jeremy Gage; Tandy Cronyn; John Horton; and my longtime wonderful commercial agent, Tracy Goldblum of Abrams Artists and Associates. The membership departments at AFTRA and SAG were most helpful in giving information, as were Image Metrics technician Justin Talley; Christopher Jones, the Image Metrics production capture supervisor on a Rockstar video game motion capture shoot I did; and Talking Books sound engineers Mikhail Shirokov, Peter Rohan, Jared Lopez, Sunny Basham, and Derek Tague, whose knowledge of comedy and of old-time radio and vaudeville, and their terminology, is truly astounding. And I express my gratitude and thanks for their love and support to my wonderful family, and most especially to my father, Max David Blumenfeld (1911–1994), and to my mother, Ruth Blumenfeld; my brothers Richard Blumenfeld and Donald Blumenfeld-Jones, and his wife, my wonderful sister-in-law, Corbeau, and to my nephew Benjamin and my niece Rebecca. Many thanks are owed to my very helpful copy editor James Barnett; and to the graphic designers of this book, UB Communications, who have done such a beautiful job. I want to thank my publisher, the amicable and erudite Michael Messina, a great theater buff, and project editor Bernadette Malavarca, who have been terrifically supportive and helpful throughout. Lastly, I owe an incalculable debt to all the authors of the books in the bibliography, and to all the people I have worked with as an actor or dialect coach in various theatrical and media venues, who have taught me the specific vocabulary necessary for each kind of job, without even knowing they had done so in most cases.

The Dictionary of Acting and Show Business

A

above *n., prep.* —*n.* **1.** *Archaic* The **upstage** covered balcony, presumably an **acting area**, in an Elizabethan theater. Also called *inner above.* —*prep.* **2.** Upstage of; behind; in back of: *He crossed left above the couch.*

above scale More than the minimum payment (called **scale**) required by the terms of the agreements between unions and producing organizations. Also called *overscale.*

above the line Television or filmmaking costs incurred before production begins; e.g., an author's fee for an adapted novel, salaries for those with credits above the title.
    See also BELOW THE LINE; LINE PRODUCER.

above the title Credits of stars and creative staff shown on screen before the name of a movie or television program appears.

Absolutely, Mr. Gallagher? —**Positively, Mr. Shean!** A **catchphrase** popularized in a song by the famous 1920s vaudeville comedy team Gallagher and Shean [Edward Gallagher (1873–1929); Albert Shean (1868–1949)]; they can be seen singing it on **YouTube**.

abstract set; abstract setting A stage décor that consists of a non-realistic, unidentifiable environment, useful for many kinds of plays.

Academy of Motion Picture Arts and Sciences (AMPAS) A California-based, honorary organization of professionals in the movie industry; membership is by invitation only. The members vote by secret ballot for the annual Academy Awards®, known as the Oscars®, which are given in recognition of outstanding achievement in motion pictures. Called *the Academy*, for short.

Academy Players Directory A book of actors' head shots and information, paid for by those listed under various categories; published by AMPAS in January, May, and September; used for casting purposes; also available via the **Internet**.

Academy of Television Arts and Sciences (ATAS) One of the two principal organizations of television industry professionals; based in Los Angeles. They give the annual Emmy **awards** for nighttime programs.
    See also NATIONAL ACADEMY OF TELEVISION ARTS AND SCIENCES.

accelerated montage The quick intercutting of shots, the length of each shot being shorter as the sequence proceeds, thus creating the impression of exciting, rapid, continuous action; e.g., the shower scene in which Janet Leigh is stabbed in Alfred Hitchcock's *Psycho* (1960).

accent *n.* **1.** A pattern or model of pronunciation; the way in which a language is pronounced, associated with country, region, and/or social class. In theatrical terms, syn. with **dialect**. For more information, see my book, *Accents: A Manual for Actors* (Limelight, 2002). See also INFLECTION; INTONATION; PHONATION; PHONETICS. **2.** The stress or emphasis on a particular syllable. **3.** The strong beginning of a musical **beat**.

accent light A lighting instrument that delineates a small area on a stage set; hence, *accent lighting*.

accessory *n.* **1.** Any device that adds to a lighting instrument's uses, but that is not actually part of the light itself; e.g., a **diaphragm** for a **spotlight**. **2.** Extra pieces that go with costumes (e.g., hats; gloves); **personal props**, such as fans, canes, or watches.

accompaniment *n.* Music performed as background support for a singer or singers or as a background for dance, silent films, etc.: *piano accompaniment*; *orchestral accompaniment*; *choral accompaniment*.

accompanist *n.* An instrumentalist who *accompanies* (i.e., plays along with) singers or dancers, and provides background support.

acoustic *adj.* **1.** Pertaining to sound: *the acoustic qualities of a theater*; i.e., how vibrant the resonance is, and how well sound carries. **2.** Pertaining to an instrument played with its own natural sound; i.e., without electrical amplification: *an acoustic guitar*. **3.** Pertaining to recording from 1890 to 1925, before the days of **electric** recording: singers sang into a huge acoustic horn that amplified the sound being recorded: *acoustic recording*. **4.** Pertaining to a person involved in designing a sound environment, the profession of designing it, and the sound design itself; also, *acoustical*: *acoustic*, or *acoustical engineer*.

acoustics *n.* **1.** The science of sound, studying its nature, production, perception, and effects. **2.** The art and science of arranging and controlling the sound environment in a theater or other space. **3.** The audibility, nature, and quality of sound in a theater or other space.
See also DEAD SPOT; SOUND DESIGNER.

act *n., v.* —*n.* **1.** A large division of a play, musical theater piece, film, or television program. The ancient Greeks had no such divisions, but the Romans invented the act, and their tragedies customarily had five; a system adopted by the Elizabethans. Through the centuries, the number of acts has varied, with plays in three, four, and now usually two acts. **2.** A short play, sketch, vaudeville routine, or other performance piece. —*v. t.* **3.** To perform; to do something with a purpose. **4.** To interpret and play a character. **5.** To be able to be performed; to be *actable*: *Shakespeare's plays act well*.

act all over the place To perform in an undisciplined manner, and not as rehearsed.

act break 1. The interval between the large divisions of a stage play; intermission. **2.** The pause for commercials in a television program.

act curtain 1. The end of an act and the beginning of an intermission, signaled in a proscenium theater by the closing of the **house curtain**. **2.** The climactic last moments of an act in a stage **play**, just before the curtain comes down: *the second act curtain*. Called a *curtain*, for short. **3.** The climactic last moments of an act in a **screenplay**.

acting *n*. **1.** Doing something purposefully; i.e., carrying out an **action**. **2.** The art, craft, and job of interpreting and performing characters; i.e., embodying a fictional person by pretending to live in the character's imaginary **given circumstances**.

acting area The space in which actors perform a play. In **theater in the round** or in three-quarters round, the area may be delimited by light, or may be the entire stage space. On a proscenium stage, there are nine acting areas, beginning at the front of the stage: downstage left, downstage right, and downstage center, also called down left, down right, and down center (abbrev. DL, DR, DC); left center, center, right center (abbrev. LC, C, RC); upstage left, upstage right, and upstage center, also called up left, up right, and up center (abbrev. UL, UR, UC). The stage is also divided into numbered planes that correspond to areas just below the wings (1, 2, 3, or 4), beginning at the front of the stage: *down in one* or **in one** means that a scene is performed in plane 1; *in two* refers to the next plane upstage, and so forth.

acting coach A specialist teacher hired by an actor to help in preparing an audition, or one hired by a film production company to serve as a **dialogue coach**.

acting company The group of actors hired to do a production or to do a season at a repertory theater.

acting edition A published version of a play meant for those who wish to produce and perform it; includes elaborate indications for set and/or lighting design, costume plans, prop plans, and detailed stage directions for actors. Cf. **reading edition**.

acting exercise A practice activity done in an *acting class* to train the actor in a particular skill, and to allow the acting student to acquire knowledge and experience essential for the craft; e.g., Sanford Meisner's *repetition exercise*.
> See also ANIMAL EXERCISES; FREEZE; MASK; MIRROR; SCENE STUDY; SONG AND DANCE EXERCISE; PRIVATE MOMENT; THEATER GAMES; TRUST.

acting in film Performing a role in a motion picture. The fundamental processes of character creation are the same as in the theater, but the actor is not required to project the voice (except in scenes where shouting is necessary) and must speak in natural tones. Also, the actor is not required to sustain a character over an entire evening: the role in a movie is performed piecemeal, sometimes line by line, and usually not in the order in which scenes occur in the story. It is the director and the editor who shape the actor's performance by choosing the takes and by the intercutting they do of various kinds of shots in order to create a scene. But actors should study and know the entire script of a movie the way they would a stage play, so that when any scene is filmed, the actor knows where in the story he or she is, and what emotional pitch and depth are required. For more information, see Michael Caine's excellent book *Acting in Film: An Actor's Take on Movie Making* (Applause, 1990), and *How to Rehearse When There Is No Rehearsal: Acting and the Media* (Limelight, 2007) by Alice Spivak and me.

See also CONTINUITY; LOCATION; SHOOTING IN SEQUENCE; SHOOTING OUT OF SEQUENCE.

acting moment A climactic happening for a particular character at a particular point in time; e.g., Juliet realizing that Romeo is dead, Orgon realizing that Tartuffe has betrayed him.

acting process The way in which an actor gradually brings a character to life in the course of rehearsals; the series of actions taken when proceeding to create a character.

See also PROCESS; SENSORY PROCESS; TOOLKIT.

acting studio. See STUDIO, def. 1.

acting school. See THEATER SCHOOLS.

acting technique 1. The general system, method, way of working, and special skills required in interpreting and performing characters, and the ability to employ them. **2.** An individual tool used in the interpretation of character (e.g., **endowment, playing opposites, substitution**) or in performance (e.g., **timing** an entrance or a laugh).

See also EXTERNAL TECHNIQUE; INTERNAL TECHNIQUE; METHOD OF PHYSICAL ACTIONS; PLASTIC; STAGE TECHNIQUE; VOCAL TECHNIQUE.

acting theory Ideas as to how actors should and do practice their art. E.g., Stanislavsky's **method of physical actions**; Meyerhold's idea of **biomechanical acting**; the Enlightenment encyclopedist and playwright Denis Diderot's (1713–1784) idea that actors do and should imitate emotion, expressed in his treatise *Paradoxe sur le comédien* (The Paradox of the Actor).

action *n.* Something an actor/character does or says purposefully at a specific **moment** in furtherance of an **objective**. An action may be external (in the form of behavior) or internal; e.g., ruminating, making plans or a decision.

Action! "Start acting!" A film director's instruction to actors to begin playing a scene for the camera; used during rehearsals and takes, and often preceded by the warning word "and," followed by a brief pause: "And…action!"

action-adventure film A genre of motion picture, or an individual movie, in which fast-paced, exciting events drive the story of some bold and hazardous enterprise.

action cutting An editing process whereby the impression of continuous, unbroken movement in a scene is created; accomplished by editing the different takes and angles together so that the viewer perceives what looks like one scene, but from different points of view shown in rapid succession.

See also ACCELERATED MONTAGE.

active analysis Stanislavsky's last rehearsal method, never completed. Preserving his use of improvisations before dealing with the text, he shortened the rehearsal period, and emphasized **discovering through doing**.

activity *n.* **1.** Stage business: something the actor does that is not part of the character's main **action**, but is part of the character's physical life, subordinate to the character's principal objective(s); called the **while life** by Uta Hagen. **2.** *Archaic* An acrobatic or juggling **act**, in the Elizabethan theater.

actor *n.* A performance artist who interprets, embodies, and plays a character for an audience; used interchangeably for both men and women.

actor-manager *n.* A star performer who also produced his or her own company, rented theaters, played leading roles, oversaw casting, and staged plays. The actor-managers flourished especially in the 18th and 19th centuries; among the most illustrious were David Garrick, Sir Henry Irving, Edwin Booth, and Sarah Bernhardt.

actor-proof *adj.* Pertaining to a play or role that is so well written it does not matter how poorly it is acted.

Actors' Equity Association (AEA) The principal performing artists' union for actors and stage managers working in the theater; colloquially called **Equity**. Based in New York City, and with offices in major urban centers, the organization was founded in 1913 to combat abuses by producers. Its contracts, which cover more than forty venues, detail salaries, working conditions, terms of employment, and penalties for violations. It provides health insurance, pension, and other programs for qualified dues-paying members. Equity also arranges exchanges of union actors and productions with British Equity, so that outstanding productions and actors who have given notable performances may be seen on both sides of the Atlantic.

Actors and stage managers may join AEA if they have been offered a contract in an Equity production. They must pay an initiation fee. They may also join if they have participated in the **Equity Membership Candidate Program (EMCP)**, earning points toward membership by working in an Equity theater and registering as Equity membership candidates with the union. Members of sister unions affiliated with the **Associated Actors and Artistes of America (4-As)** are also eligible to join Equity.

See also BOND; CONTRACT; DEPUTY; EQUITY RULES; GO TO CONTRACT; SHOWCASE.

Actors Fund of America (AFA) A charitable organization devoted to actors' welfare. The AFA has a retirement home in Englewood, NJ with a fully equipped hospital facility and sponsors an annual health fair for union members, who may get free flu shots and examinations.

actor's process. See ACTING PROCESS; PROCESS; SENSORY PROCESS.

actor's secret A very personal **substitution** that only the performer knows.

See also VAKHTANGOV, EUGENE.

Actors Studio A New York City institution for actors on 46th Street; known esp. as the place where Lee Strasberg taught **method acting**. Actors do projects for presentation and criticism; there is also a director's and playwright's unit (PDU).

actor training The education and formation of professional actors at theater schools and studios.
See ADLER, STELLA; HAGEN, UTA; STANISLAVSKY, CONSTANTIN; STRASBERG, LEE; STAGE TECHNIQUE; THEATER SCHOOLS.

actor trap An onstage obstacle of which the actor must be careful, because of potential physical danger; e.g., **escape stairs** at the upstage end of a raked stage.

actress *n.* A female actor. The word is mostly used when it is necessary to distinguish male from female actors.

actual sound The spoken dialogue and ambient noise recorded during film shooting.

adaptation *n.* **1.** A musical comedy, stage play, or screenplay taken from an existing source; e.g., a novel adapted for the screen. **2.** Changing something from one kind of audio or video format or processing to another; e.g., turning a **hard copy** of a recorded book into an **audio digital download**.

additional dialogue 1. Lines put into a film script after the shooting has been completed, and later dubbed onto the sound track. **2.** Extra lines put into the script during a shoot.

adjustment *n.* **1.** A conscious, deliberate change of **impulse** or **instinct**, sometimes because of a director's instructions to the actor. **2.** A change in the actor's physical positioning on stage or in front of the camera. **3.** An increase or decrease in a SAG or AFTRA actor's pay; e.g., an **upgrade**.

Adler, Stella (1901–1992) Distinguished actor and member of the **Group Theatre**; one of the seminal American acting teachers in the mid-20th c.; and member of the famous Yiddish theater family founded by her father, celebrated actor Jacob Adler (1855–1926). She was an adherent of a classic imaginative approach to the creation of a role and a follower of Stanislavsky, with whom she had studied in Paris in 1934. She founded the school now called the Stella Adler Studio of Acting in New York City in 1949. Her book *The Technique of Acting* (Bantam Books, 1988) is a neat, compact, and clear approach to the art. She emphasizes script interpretation; finding the character's actions and objectives; and the necessity of a broad education in literature, theatrical tradition, history, and culture.

ad lib; adlib *n., v.* [Latin: *ad libitum* (ad lih' bih toom); at will] —*n.* **1.** A spontaneously improvised line or lines, or bit of stage business, added during a performance. **2.** In music, an improvisation during a performance; e.g., a jazz riff. —*v. t.* **3.** To make an off-the-cuff remark or add business during a show. **4.** To **vamp** (def. 5); to improvise on a theme, add to, or otherwise alter music during a performance.

ADR *n.* Acronym, abbrev., and usual appellation for **automatic dialogue replacement**, a technological procedure that has largely replaced the old-fashioned live looping method of re-recording dialogue.

advance man; **advance agent** *Archaic.* The person who went ahead of a touring company and arranged accommodations and other matters, esp. in the days of **vaudeville**.

advance sale The selling of tickets for a show before it has opened.

advance stage manager A stage manager who accompanies a **package** tour, and goes on ahead to the next theater to help prepare the resident company for the tour's arrival.

advance team *Archaic* A group of two or three people that preceded a **circus** by one or more weeks, put up posters, and made arrangements for parades.

advertising *n., adj.* —*n.* **1.** The business of producing commercials and printed advertisements for products or services in order to secure maximum publicity and sales. **2.** Paid publicity announcements, commercials, and other means of securing notice, such as billboards, posters, and magazine or newspaper *ads.* —*adj.* **3.** Pertaining to the business of publicity, and to the publicity itself. Hence, *advertising agency*: a publicity firm, many of which have commercial production departments; *advertising copy*: the text of an advertisement or **commercial**; *the advertising industry*; *advertising slogan*: a **catchphrase**, sometimes sung as a **jingle**, meant to be remembered as associated with a product. Called *ad*, for short: *ad agency*.

AEA *n.* Initialization and abbrev. for **Actors Equity Association (AEA)**.

aerial shot A take photographed from an airplane or helicopter equipped with a specially mounted camera.

aesthetic distance The observed and experienced difference between the reality of life in the world and the life portrayed in a work of art.
See also ALIENATION EFFECT; SCENIC TRUTH.

affective memory The memory of emotions and feelings, called *emotional memory*, and the memory of physical sensations, called *sense memory*. Emotional and sense memories overlap: every sense memory involves an emotional memory; every emotional memory involves the senses. Affective memory is used in **substitution** and **endowment**.
See also EMOTION; SENSORY PROCESS.

afterpiece *n.* A one-act play or musical that is performed after the main event.

after-time *n.* Stanislavsky's term for what happens to the characters when the play is over, shown by the direction the character's lives take as the play is ending.

AFTRA Acronym, abbrev., and usual appellation for **American Federation of Television and Radio Artists (AFTRA)**.

agent *n.* In show business, a talent representative; i.e., an individual or company (*agency*; *talent agency*) whose job is to represent actors or other performers, authors, directors, and others seeking employment. Agents working with performing arts union members must be franchised by the unions. The word is often used in the singular even when an agency is meant: "Who's your agent?" "I'm with Abrams." [Abrams Artists and Associates: a large bicoastal talent agency that employs many agents and works with actors in all areas] The term "I'm with" means that the actor is **signed** to an exclusive contract for representation. Many agencies will work only with signed clients, but some will work with actors on a **freelance** basis; i.e., the agent may submit the actor for a single job or more, but will not necessarily do so regularly. Signed clients usually take priority when it comes to submitting names to the particular *buyers* with whom the agent usually deals; e.g., casting directors. Large agencies have divisions, or departments that deal with specific areas; e.g., commercials, film, or theater. Some agencies also function in a casting capacity: they may hold **in-house** voice-over auditions for their clients. Once an actor is hired, the agent negotiates contracts that include salaries and/or billing, and collects ten percent for doing so, in line with **franchise** agreements.

It is not always easy to secure representation. Actors, particularly at the start of their careers and despite the prolific use of the Internet, usually have to "pound the pavement" and "make the rounds" of the different agencies, dropping off their photos and résumés and a covering letter, or do a large **mailing** of those materials. They then follow up with a postcard with their picture on it and a phone call, which may result in an interview with the agent, and perhaps a submission for a job. Or the agent may call them for an interview.

See also CONTRACT; LEGITIMATE; ROSS REPORTS; VOICE-OVER.

agitprop (a' dgit prahp') *n. Hist.* A form of **political theater**: plays on revolutionary themes for purposes of agitation and propaganda; popular in leftist circles, esp. in the 1930s.

Aha, me proud beauty! [source unknown; perhaps from 1880s melodrama] A line said by a mustachio-twirling villain in melodrama to the cowering heroine whom he has cornered; it had become a comic **catchphrase** by the 1920s.

air *n., v.* —*n.* **1.** A melody; a tune; an opera **aria**. **2.** The amount of time taken up by a pause, whether between actors' lines or as part of a speech: *There's too much air; pick up your cues!* Cf. **drive a Mack truck**. —*v. t., i.* **4.** To broadcast a television or radio program: *to air a show. The show airs on Fridays.*

air date The scheduled broadcast day for a television or radio program.

air-to-air shot A take of something or someone in the sky filmed from a flying plane or helicopter; e.g., another flying plane or a parachutist.

aisle *n.* A passageway between banks of places in a theater's seating areas; used by audience members, and sometimes by actors staged to make entrances. An *aisle seat* (i.e., the seat next to the aisle, or *on the aisle* in the **orchestra** section) is considered by some to be one of the most desirable places to sit in the audience. The full-length *side aisle* is against either wall of the auditorium, going from back to front; the full-length *center aisle* divides the banks of seats down the middle of the auditorium, from back to front. Some theaters also have full-length lateral aisles dividing banks of seats from one side of the auditorium to the other. For safety reasons, the aisles must be kept clear.

See AMERICAN-PLAN SEATING; CONTINENTAL SEATING.

Alan Smithee film A motion picture that the director does not wish to be associated with; the obligatory directorial credit therefore reads "directed by Alan Smithee."

alarums and excursions *Hist.* Military action: an Elizabethan stage direction. Alarums: the offstage sounds of trumpet fanfares, drums, and shouts calling to arms. Excursions: the choreographed movements of soldiers.

aleatory technique Filming without a preconceived plan, capturing indiscriminately everything that happens; e.g., in a nature documentary, or in improvised scenes with actors whose movements are followed by a handheld camera.

Alexander technique A kinesthetic method of relaxation, and of freeing and balancing the body, allowing for efficiency and economy of movement; devised and developed by F. Matthias Alexander (1869–1955). Used as part of actor training in Great Britain and the United States.

alienation effect [fr. German: *Verfremdungseffekt* (feh frehm' doongks eh fehkt') *estrangement-* or *distancing-effect*] Berthold Brecht's term for the achievement of a desirable didactic, politicizing distantiation between an audience and a performance: the **fourth wall** is eliminated, scenic elements are exposed to view, and the actor shows the audience the character, rather than embodying it. The spectators become critical observers of what is happening on stage, as opposed to being passively involved in the show. Also called the *V-effect*; *a-effect*.

See AESTHETIC DISTANCE; ANTI-CULINARY THEATER.

allegory *n.* A story that, while being comprehensible, coherent, and enjoyable in its own right, and acceptable on its own merits as a story, suggests, mirrors, stands for, represents, or signifies another story. E.g., Mikhail Bulgakov's (1891–1940) play *A Cabal of Hypocrites* [also called *Molière in Spite of Himself*: an **allusion** to Molière's title, *The Doctor in Spite of Himself*], which reflects Bulgakov's problematic relations with Stalin: Molière represents Bulgakov; Louis XIV, Stalin.

Alliance of Motion Picture and Television Producers (AMPTP) The organization that negotiates contracts with the unions, including AFTRA, SAG, and the WGA.

allowance *n.* Expense money, contractually provided for.

all right on the night, [it will be] "The performance will go well, even if rehearsals have gone badly"; or "I will remember my lines when I perform, even if I tend to forget them in rehearsal."

11

all-star *adj.* Pertaining to a production with name actors in principal roles.

allusion *n.* A passing, unidentified reference to a work of art, person, event, object, or place expected to be well known to the audience and meant to be germane to the play or film in which it is mentioned.

alone *adj. Archaic* An Elizabethan stage direction, meaning that an actor enters by himself, or is discovered by himself already on stage.

alternate *n., v. —n.* **1.** An actor who takes turns with another actor in playing a role. —*v. t.* **2.** To take turns playing a role.

alternative theater Plays or other performance presentations that are out of the mainstream, and often have a political point of view to advocate; e.g., **street theater**.
   See also BOAL, AUGUSTO; BRECHT, BERTHOLD; GROTOWSKI, JERZY.

All together, please! *esp. Brit.* The invitation to a music hall or vaudeville audience to sing a popular tune or the chorus of a song, along with the performer.

amateur night 1. Esp. in the days of vaudeville, an evening during which amateurs (non-professional, unpaid performers) signed up to do their acts. **2.** A poor professional performance, displaying the deficiencies and ineptitude characteristic of amateurs.
   See also GET THE HOOK!

amber *adj.* A yellow-orange-pink color with variations, common in lighting gels: *light amber*; *medium amber*; *dark amber*; *bastard amber* (i.e., amber with a lot of pink in it).

ambient *adj.* **1.** The quality of pertaining to a particular environment or ambience: *ambient gloom*. **2.** Emanating or arising from the surrounding environment: *ambient light*; *ambient sound*.
   See ROOM TONE.

ambiguity *n.* Conscious conflicting feelings experienced by every character in a problematic situation or relationship.

ambivalence *n.* Unconscious conflicting feelings, which every person and every character experiences in relationships. Finding a character's ambivalences adds depth and dimension to an actor's interpretation.

American Cinema Editors (ACE) An honorary, invitational society of professional film editors; based in Hollywood. They give the annual Eddie® Awards for achievement in film editing, and publish a magazine, *Cinemeditor*. The credit A.C.E. appears on-screen after the name of a member.

American Federation of Musicians (AFM) A union, founded in 1896, with more than 250 local branches in the United States and Canada, where it is known as *AFM Canada*. It represents arrangers, copyists, composers, vocalists, and instrumentalists in all musical fields and live and recorded venues of entertainment.

American Federation of Television and Radio Artists (AFTRA) One of the major performing artists' unions, based in New York City, with offices around the country; founded in 1937 as the American Federation of Radio Artists (AFRA). AFTRA is an open union, which means that there are no membership requirements and anyone can join simply by going to the local branch office and applying for membership; an initiation fee is required. Its contracts, including the **Sound Recordings Code**, cover recorded commercials for radio; some taped television shows, such as certain soap operas; and musicians' recording contracts, among other things. There are also **book recording** contracts, but as of this writing the book recording industry is not completely unionized.

American Guild of Musical Artists (AGMA) The New York City–based union, founded in 1936, that represents classical musicians (both vocalists and instrumentalists) as well as ballet dancers, opera directors, and choreographers.

American Guild of Variety Artists (AGVA) The New York City–based union, founded in 1939, that represents entertainers in various fields, including the circus, nightclubs, and other venues of variety entertainment.

American-plan seating The arrangement of places in a theater auditorium divided by longitudinal center and side aisles, and sometimes by lateral aisles, esp. in large houses (as opposed to **continental seating**). Also called *multiple-aisle seating*.

American Society of Cinematographers (ASC) An honorary association of photographers, camerapeople, directors of photography, and others in related technical areas, with membership by invitation only; based in Hollywood.

American Society of Composers, Authors, and Publishers (ASCAP) A **performance rights organization** of music publishing companies, composers, and lyricists that ensures the observance of copyright laws for the works of its members or their heirs; acts as a clearinghouse for the payment of royalties, and for the authorization and licensing of musical works for performance.

American Theater Wing (ATW) An honorary organization devoted to the interests of the theater and of performers. Its programs include grants and scholarships to aspiring performers, writers, and directors. The ATW, based in New York City, is best known for having created the Antoinette Perry Award®, known as the Tony®, recognizing excellence and achievement in the Broadway theater annually.

amphitheater *n.* An outdoor theater with a semicircle of raked tiers of seats surrounding the stage or acting area; e.g., the ancient Greek and Roman hillside theaters.

amplification *n.* **1.** In **audio**, the enhancement and magnification of sound by means of mechanical equipment; e.g., a **microphone** plugged into an *amplifier*. Wearing personal head or body microphones in **Broadway** musicals is now almost universal, whereas in the old days, singers and actors relied on their own lung power and **vocal technique**. In **outdoor theater**, such as Central Park's Shakespeare in the Park, the actors are similarly **miked**. In most **Off-Broadway** or other small theaters, as well as in opera houses, actors and singers continue to rely on good projection and diction. **2.** In literature and **drama**, a rhetorical device for emphasizing a point or idea by enlarging upon it; e.g., Hamlet's **soliloquy**, "To be or not to be"—expatiating on the reasons for and against suicide—which is an amplification of its first line.

anachronism (uh nak' ruh nihzm) *n.* A chronological anomaly; i.e., something that exists in the wrong historical time frame, as in Shakespeare's *Julius Caesar*, act 2, scene 1, where Cassius says, "The clock has stricken three."

analog *adj.* Pertains to a form of information storage and retrieval. Analog information is stored and played back through the use of a constantly changing, continuous electric current that represents the changing sound waves; e.g., in tape recording, where the tape winds continually as it records, or plays. Cf. **digital**.

anchor *n., v.* —*n.* **1.** [Short for *anchorperson*; *anchorman*; *anchorwoman*] An **announcer** who is the chief **newscaster** or **sportscaster** on a television news show. **2.** A network television show that is a key program meant to attract viewers so that they will continue watching that station. —*v. t.* **3.** To be the main broadcaster of a television news or sports program: *She anchors the evening news.*

ancillary rights Legal claim or provision in some stars' or directors' contracts to a share of the profits derived from the sale of products connected to a motion picture; e.g., action figures, tee-shirts, mugs.

And awa-aa-ay we go! Iconic American comedian Jackie Gleason's (1916–1987) **catchphrase**. One of many he came up with, and said as an exit line at the end of his opening monologue in his first comedy variety series *The Jackie Gleason Show* in the 1950s; accompanied by "traveling" music, and a **soft-shoe** shuffle with appropriate gestures.

and so we say farewell The last line of many a **travelogue** shown as a **featurette** before the main movie. Used so often that it became a risible cliché, delivered archly as a camp **catchphrase**.

angel *n. Slang.* The anonymous financial backer of a theater project.

angle *n., v.* —*n.* **1.** In film and television, the vantage point and position from which a scene or part of a scene is photographed, determined by the camera's point of view, range of field, and perspective. Also called *angle of view.* —*v. t.* **2.** To tilt the camera in a particular direction.

angle-reverse-angle shot A scene of a conversation that alternates between two characters' faces.

angle shots Takes of a scene from different perspectives.

angry young men Alienated British playwrights of the 1950s and '60s who wrote iconoclastic, realistic dramas denouncing the complacency and apathy of society. The first such playwright to be characterized in newspapers as an "angry young man" was John Osborne (1929–1994), whose play *Look Back in Anger* set the tone of the era.

animal exercises The improvisational reproduction of a non-human animal's physical characteristics and behavior, as a way of exploring a character. Devised originally at the **Moscow Art Theatre** school and also developed by Michael Chekhov, they are used both in the classroom and as a tool in rehearsing a play. The following questions are asked: "If my character were an animal, what animal would he or she be?"; "What are the characteristics of that animal that I associate with my character?"; and "How might I incorporate them into my character's physicality?" As classroom exercises, animal improvisations are useful for developing powers of observation and imagination.

animal wrangler A person who trains, handles, and takes care of animals that are used in a motion picture or stage show and is backstage or on the set with them: *dog wrangler*; *lion wrangler*; *monkey wrangler* (i.e., one who handles chimpanzees and other primates). Also called an *animal handler*.
See WRANGLE.

animated feature A full-length **cartoon** film.

animated poster *Hist.* A large flat painted to resemble a political placard. In Soviet theater in the 1920s and '30s, the actors' faces and arms were stuck through cutout holes in the flat as they delivered propagandistic speeches.

animation *n.* **1.** The art and process of making cartoon films; i.e., of creating the illusion that a series of still drawings or inanimate figures have movement and life. **2.** The quality of liveliness, verve, and vivacity that is part of an actor's **stage presence**.

announcer *n.* **1.** A radio or television presenter who introduces programs or people and reads political, sports, or other news or commercial **copy**: *a news announcer*; *a sports announcer*. **2.** *Archaic* In 17th-c. French theater, an actor who introduced the play to the audience.

Answer back to the camera! "Look directly into the camera lens when you speak!" A direction to the actor, who should otherwise generally avoid looking at the camera.

antagonist *n.* The opponent of the **protagonist** (the central character).

anthology film A **documentary** that includes footage from many different motion pictures or other sources; e.g., the MGM series *That's Entertainment* (1974; 1976; 1994), compiled from its own films.

anthology series A weekly radio or television series with a different story and characters in each episode, usually introduced by the same host every time; e.g., the *Twilight Zone* (radio and TV); *Alfred Hitchcock Presents*.

anticipation *n.* **1.** Expecting the next event before the character is in a position to do so, instead of allowing it to happen, and unconsciously communicating that expectation to the audience; e.g., cringing in anticipation of an unexpected blow that the other character has not even started to deliver. One of the cardinal sins in acting. **2.** In a stage performance, the necessary preparation by the stage manager, lighting technicians, and stagehands for a **cue** that is coming up; and by actors waiting for their entrances.

anticlimax *n.* **1.** The disappointing, unconvincing, dissatisfying resolution of a **plot.** **2.** The intentional deflationary rhetorical device of proceeding from high to low, when proceeding even higher is expected by the audience. As M. H. Abrams defines its use in *A Glossary of Literary Terms* (Heinle & Heinle, 1999), an anti-climax "denotes a writer's deliberate drop from the serious and elevated to the trivial and lowly, in order to achieve a comic or satiric effect." In act 1 of Gilbert and Sullivan's *The Mikado,* Ko-Ko is gazing fondly after the departing Yum-Yum:

> There she goes! To think how entirely my happiness is wrapped up in that little parcel! Really, it hardly seems worth while! Oh, matrimony!—[*Enter* POOH-BAH *and* PISH-TUSH] Now then what is it? Can't you see I'm soliloquizing? You have interrupted an apostrophe, sir!

Syn. *bathos,* which means not only anticlimax, but also trite, banal sentimentality.

anti-culinary theater Berthold Brecht's term for the kind of politically motivated, provocative **theater of ideas** he advocated. In his view, most theater was "culinary theater," dispensing easily digested, entertaining pap to a willing, apathetic audience.

anti-hero; **anti-heroine** *n.* The unheroic **protagonist** in a work of literature. In the plays of the **angry young men**, the anti-hero was opposed to the establishment and discontented with the system, while remaining stuck in his or her situation.

antimasque; **antemasque** *n. Hist.* In the 17th c., an extravagant dance entertain-ment presented before a court **masque** or as an interlude within the masque. Also called *antick-masque*; *antic masque*; hence, *antick masquer.*

anti-piracy signal A method of attempting to forestall the illegal duplication of a DVD or VHS tape by means of encoded electronic markers that prevent its being copied.

apart *n.* The **convention** of lines spoken by one actor to another as if in secret, and as if the other actors on stage did not hear them.

aperture *n.* **1.** A camera's adjustable lens opening. **2.** The adjustable opening of a spotlight.

aphorism (a' fuh rihzm) *n.* A laconic, pithy, memorable statement, maxim, or adage, often reducing a situation to a comment on it, or stating a principle or opinion, usually with a moral aspect to it; e.g., Oscar Wilde's dictum, "What is a cynic? A man who knows the price of everything and the value of nothing." (*Lady Windermere's Fan,* act 3).

16

A-picture *n.* A major high-budget **feature film** with stars and high **production values**. The term was coined when the **double feature** was a regular part of cinema programs: the first movie was an A-picture, the second a **B-picture**. Also called *A-movie*.

apostrophe *n.* An address to something or someone who is absent, or believed to be so; e.g., Juliet's speech in act 2, scene 2: *O, Romeo, Romeo, wherefore art thou Romeo?*

appear *v. i.* To act; to perform: *Booth appeared many times as Hamlet.*

applause *n.* Expressions of approval and appreciation for a performance.

apple box [Fr. the fruit crates used as risers in the days of silent film] An eight-inch-high wooden platform on which an actor stands either to raise his or her height, or to place the actor above something. Also called a **riser**.

approach *n.* **1.** Another word for **shot** or **angle**; i.e., the point of view from which a scene is photographed, and whether it is a **medium shot, close-up, long shot**, etc. **2.** The changes of angles and shots used in photographing and then editing a scene. **3.** The actor's or director's initial concept of and attitude towards a play or a role. **4.** The way of beginning to work on a play or a role.

Approach! "Move the camera towards the subject being photographed!" An instruction from the director to the cameraperson. Also heard as "Come in!"

apron *n.* The front part of a proscenium stage.

arc lamp; **arc light** A high-intensity instrument that provides strong illumination from a continual sparking ("arc") of electricity between two poles (e.g., a carbon arc **spot**; a **xenon arc spot**); used in sunlight effects on film studio sets, and in the theater.

arc shot A take in which the camera moves around whatever is being filmed, following the action in a circular or semicircular path; e.g., in Hitchcock's creation of the characters' dizziness in *Vertigo* (1958). The camera movement is called *arcing*.

archival footage Film that has been stored and filed, and is used in documentary or other motion pictures.

archived recording 1. An audiovisual or audio **version** of a live performance that has been taped or filmed for preservation in a library. **2.** A taped or filmed version of an **in-house** industrial, seminar, or meeting kept on file for future reference.

arena *n., adj.* —*n.* **1.** The place where a performance project is presented. **2.** Another word for **theater in the round**. **3.** An ancient Roman outdoor walled structure in the form of an **amphitheater** that served for the presentation of large spectacles. **4.** *Archaic* The area directly in front of and surrounding the stage in an Elizabethan theater. —*adj.* **5.** Pertains to staging in the round, or to a theater in the round, or to its stage: *arena staging*; *arena theater*; *arena stage*.

argument *n.* **1.** *Archaic* Plot summary. **2.** *Hist.* The plot summary spoken as a **prologue** in ancient Roman theater.

aria (ah' ree ah) *n.* [Italian: air] A melodic set piece in an **opera** in the form of a **solo** song expressing the character's feelings.

Aristotle (384–322 BCE) (a' rihs tah' tl) Greek philosopher, aesthetician, and ethicist. Aristotle's *Poetics* (written in 335 BCE) was highly influential for centuries, and was considered by the French and English 17th- and 18th-c. neoclassicists to have laid down sacrosanct, immutable principles to be followed in writing for the theater. All art, in whatever form or mode, is the mimesis of nature, he said. The Greek word *mimesis* (mI mee' sihs) was often incorrectly translated as "imitation": it more properly means "representation" or even "recreation." **Tragedy**, for instance, is the "mimesis of an action which is elevated, complete, and of magnitude": the translation "imitation" for "mimesis" makes very little sense in this context. Aristotle neatly and succinctly defines actors as "mimetic artists [who] represent people in action"; i.e., they play characters. Actors, says Aristotle, use speech to "render the mimesis," hence the importance of a good **voice** and **diction**, since acting, like oratory, is partly dependent on "the right management of the voice to express the various emotions."

See also CATHARSIS; CLASSICAL UNITIES; DRAMA; HAMARTIA; PITY AND FEAR; RECOGNITION SCENE; TRAGIC FLAW; TRAGEDY.

arrange *v. t.* **1.** To put something in order; to plan something, and to effect the plan. E.g., in scoring music; choreographing dances or actors' movements; hanging and focusing lights; or planning and carrying out set-ups in theater, film, or television preparatory to performance, filming, or taping. **2.** To plan the logistics for an activity; e.g., a move to a film location, or a **bus and truck** tour.

arrangement *n.* A **version** of a popular song or other score, always including melody and harmony and orchestrated for different instruments and/or voices than the original composition. E.g., the **vocal score** of a musical comedy, with voice parts and piano reduction of the orchestral **score**; or the reduction for a small ensemble or band of a number from a musical comedy, suitable as dance music. Hence, *arranger*: the person who puts together the written musical arrangements. Cf. **orchestrator**.

art card A placard on which credits are written or printed, for insertion into a film or other media project.

art department The section, division, or team of employees on a motion picture production that is responsible for all its physical aspects: the set; costume, lighting, and other designs; and construction, painting, dressing, and decoration.

art director In film and television, the person responsible for the physical design aspects of the film and the overall design and construction of the set. As head of the art department, the art director oversees the work of the designers and of the set decorator. On location, the art designer coordinates the design elements of the production so that they are in harmony with the studio set design. **Syn.** *production designer*.

art house A cinema that shows foreign films; independent, avant-garde, and experimental features, often in **limited release**; and/or classic motion pictures, usually to audiences of enthusiasts or aficionados.

articulation 1. In diction, the precise formation and utterance of vowel and consonant sounds. **2.** In music, an aspect of **phrasing**: how a singer joins notes together to form phrases.

artificial light Illumination created for a film scene by electric and other means.
See also AVAILABLE LIGHT; NATURAL LIGHT.

artiste (ahr teest') *n.* **1.** A female performing artist. **2.** A performing artist. **3.** A pretentious performer with delusions of grandeur.

artistic director 1. The head administrator of a theater or opera company, in charge of all matters relating to the choosing of projects, the hiring of staff, and of the productions generally. The artistic director of a LORT theater, who works in conjunction with the theater's **board**, may direct some shows, and also serves as a principal fundraiser. **2.** The head administrator of a **ballet** or other kind of dance company.

artistic failure A play or musical panned by the critics, but commercially successful nonetheless; e.g., some Broadway musicals that are popular despite the bad notices.

artist in residence An actor, director, or other artistic professional invited to a university for temporary employment in his or her field and, often, in a teaching capacity as well.
See GUEST ARTIST; RESIDENCE.

arts and entertainment industry The branch of the economy in which artists of all kinds, performers, and those in related professions earn their living.

art song A composed vocal piece meant to be performed in a **concert** or **recital**, combining a sung line with a subtle instrumental accompaniment, usually for piano.

ASCAP Acronym, abbrev., and usual appellation for **American Society of Composers, Authors, and Publishers**.

as cast Stipulation in an actor's contract that the actor will play whatever role or roles are assigned; e.g., in a LORT resident company.

aside *n.* A theatrical **convention** consisting of a brief address to the audience or to the character's self in the middle of a scene; the action is suspended while the aside is delivered.

as if The **endowment** of a character's given circumstances as though they were real; Stanislavsky's "magic *if*." The actor's primary imaginative tool; without it, there is no acting.

assemble *v. t.* To select and put together film takes in the order in which they may be used, so as to prepare a preliminary version of the edited project, called a **rough cut**. Hence, *assembly*: the arrangement of the takes.

assistant director 1. The person who helps a film director (e.g., by overseeing the preparations for a scene while the director is occupied with other aspects of the shooting); abbrev. AD. The assistant director may also direct some scenes under instruction from the director. There are usually several on any high-budget project: the first, second, and third ADs. **2.** In the theater, the person who helps the director by doing various assigned tasks, such as taking notes the director dictates during rehearsals and rehearsing some scenes while the director works on others.

assistant stage manager In the theater and in film, the stage manager's helper, usually assigned specific tasks; abbrev. A.S.M. or ASM. The **Equity** assistant stage manager in a theater is prepared to take over the running of the show in the stage manager's absence. In large theaters, there are several assistant stage managers, in charge of either side of the stage and of various aspects of production; some may also play small roles.

Associated Actors and Artistes of America (4-As) An affiliation of performing arts unions, including **Actors' Equity Association (AEA)**, **American Federation of Television and Radio Artists (AFTRA)**, **American Guild of Musical Artists (AGMA)**, **American Guild of Variety Artists (AGVA)**, **Screen Actors Guild (SAG)**, and the Guild of Italian-American Actors (GIAA). Membership in any one of these unions entitles a performer to join any of the others.

Association of Non-Profit Theater Companies (ANTC) A New York City organization of small theater companies that produce at least two **showcase** productions a year in theaters seating fewer than 199 patrons, and that has special agreements with **Equity** regarding the possible transfer of those shows to paying contracts, as well as rules and regulations governing the use of Equity actors.

at liberty *Slang.* Unemployed as an actor.

atmosphere *n.* **1.** The pervasive feeling, mood, and aesthetic quality that both actors and audiences experience during a performance. **2.** Another word for **background players**.
See also EFFECT SHOT.

at rise An old-fashioned stage direction, pertaining to what the audience sees on stage when the curtain goes up.

attitude *n.* **1.** Psychological disposition towards (or relation to) something; e.g., a character's attitude to his or her situation. **2.** Expressive physical pose, as in a **tableau**: *a graceful attitude.* **3.** In ballet, the dancer's position of standing on one leg, with the other held up behind it and bent at the knee; the arm on the side of the raised leg is curved above the head and the other arm stretched out to the side. **4.** *Slang* Egotistical, defensive way of relating: *He gives the other actors attitude.*

attraction *n.* A featured act, other entertainment, or performer; e.g., in **variety** or **vaudeville**, or at a **carnival** or **sideshow**: *the main attraction.*

audience *n.* **1.** A particular group of spectators. **2.** The collectivity of potential or actual spectators: *the audience for Hitchcock's films*; *meant for an audience of aficionados.*

audience participation Taking part in some way in a performance event at which one is a spectator, whether live in a theater, or by calling into a radio or television **talk show**.
See also CALL-IN; INTERACTIVE THEATER; STREET THEATER.

audio *n., adj.* [fr. Latin (ow' dee oh): I hear] —*n.* **1.** Recorded, amplified, or broadcast sound. —*adj.* **2.** Pertains to the sound aspects of a production; e.g., the recorded or live sound of a television program: *The audio portion of the program was inaudible due to technical difficulties.*

audiobook *n.* A recorded work of fiction or nonfiction meant to be listened to by the public, and available in hard copy or online.
See also BOOK RECORDING; COMMERCIAL EDITION; LIBRARY EDITION.

audiocassette *n.* A length of thin audiotape housed in a small rectangular plastic container, called a *cartridge*, with two spools, on one of which the tape is wound before being wound onto the second spool as it plays or records; *cassette*, for short. The year 2008 was the last in which they were manufactured; largely replaced by the **compact disc** and digital recording and playback devices such as the iPod.

audio download. See DIGITAL AUDIO DOWNLOAD; DIGITAL VIDEO DOWNLOAD.

audio engineer Syn. with **sound engineer**.

Audio Publishers Association (APA) A trade organization of over 200 audio-book publishers and distributors. They give the annual Audie awards to recording artists for excellence in book narration in various categories.

audition *n., v.* —*n.* **1.** A **tryout** for a role. —*v. t.* **2.** To hold tryouts or conduct a **casting session**: *She auditioned twenty actors for the role.* —*v. i.* **3.** To try out for a role by presenting oneself to casting directors, directors, or other potential employers, and doing what is necessary to show them you are the right person for the part.
    The process of casting varies depending on the medium involved. Theater auditions are live; media auditions are usually filmed or taped, although actors read for casting directors in certain situations without being recorded. Film auditions are not always recorded, except in the case of screen tests for a specific role. Auditions can also be conducted on a long distance basis: an actor may audition in New York for a casting director or director who is in a studio in Los Angeles, watching the actor on a live-feed system. Voice-over auditions may be recorded at a casting session in a studio, or submitted by an actor's agent via the Internet,

once the actor has sent his or her recording to the agent directly from the actor's home computer.

Except for most voice-overs, there is usually a series of auditions: after the initial audition, the actor is seen again at a **callback**, of which there may be several. For on-camera commercials, the first audition is taped by a casting director. At the callback, the casting director, the director, and various other people (e.g., representatives of the advertising company and the sponsor) are normally present, and the actor will be given direction by the director.

For a play, there is a similar process: the initial audition is often for a casting director; at the callback, the director will be there, and perhaps other members of the staff as well. For musical auditions, an accompanist will be provided, but the actor may prefer to bring in his or her own.

Alice Spivak describes the process and the different auditions in detail in the book we wrote together, *How to Rehearse When There Is No Rehearsal* (Limelight, 2007).

See also CATTLE CALL; GROUP AUDITION; LIVE-FEED VIDEO AUDITION; OPEN CALL; PREPARED AUDITION; SCREEN TEST; TRYOUT.

auditorium *n.* The area, room, or enclosed space reserved for the audience to a performance in a school, theater, concert hall, or other **venue**.

auditory *n. Archaic* Audience: the Elizabethan term.

Augustan drama [Fr. the ancient Roman Augustan age: a golden period for literature, when Virgil, Horace, and Ovid wrote] English neoclassical plays of the late 17th and early 18th centuries, including the heroic verse dramas of John Dryden, and **ballad opera**; e.g., John Gay's *The Beggar's Opera*.

auteur (oh tuhr') *n.* [French: author] A filmmaker with a unique personal vision and style and ideas who not only directs films, but also has the major hand in editing them and in shaping and/or writing their scripts; e.g., Ingmar Bergman, Federico Fellini, Louis Malle, Jean-Luc Godard, and François Truffaut.

authorial intervention A line or remark put into the mouth of a character that is really the writer's thought or idea, and does not appear to be the kind of thing the character would have said.

autograph hound A collector of live celebrities' signatures, particularly those of star actors. There was one who used to go up to people waiting to get into a Broadway theater for a performance and ask them, "Are you famous?"

automatic dialogue replacement A technological method and procedure of dubbing the dialogue for a motion picture **soundtrack**, whereby an actor records the words in a studio, as with looping, but without having to worry about the **lip sync**, which will be justified later using a computerized process; i.e., the mouth movements and the sounds will be coordinated. Usually referred to as **ADR**. Also called *additional dialogue replacement*.

See also DUB; LOOP.

available light Ambient interior or exterior illumination that may be used when filming a scene; e.g., the lamps in a hotel lobby used for location shooting or natural sunlight for an outdoor scene. Often supplemented with **artificial light**.

avant-garde (a vahnt' gahrd') *n., adj.* [Fr. French military term: forward, or advance guard] —*n.* **1.** An artistic or political practice, project, or movement that is innovative and ahead of its time. **2.** The collectivity of politicians or artists who are the leading innovators of their time: *the avant-garde.* —*adj.* **3.** Pertaining to an artistic or political movement that is ahead of its time, to a particular innovative artistic project, or to the people involved in it: *Impressionist painting and painters were avant-garde in their day.*

avid (ay' vihd') *n.* [Fr. *audiovisual*] An audiovisual recording studio, usually one used for commercials, demos, and voiceovers: *You'll be working in the avid on the twenty-second floor.*

avista *adj.* Pertains to a scene change that takes place in full view of the audience, either on a dimly lit stage (with stagehands in black), or as a choreographed change done by costumed actors on a fully lit stage, or as a mechanical set change, where flies are raised as others are lowered, and scene wagons come on with décors arranged on them. Used in arena staging or on a proscenium stage; often seen in musical comedies, or Shakespearean productions.

award *n.* A prize given to an individual in recognition of outstanding work in his or her field. Among the many film, television, and recording awards are the Oscar®, or Academy Award®, given by the American Academy of Film and Television Arts; the Golden Globe awards, given by the Hollywood Foreign Press Association; the Emmy, presented by the National Academy of Television Arts and Sciences and the American Academy of Television Arts and Sciences; the Indie, awarded by the Independent Film Association; the Grammy, presented annually by the National Academy of Recording Arts and Sciences for outstanding recordings; the Audie, presented annually by the Audiobook Publishers Association (APA); the BAFTA, presented by the British Academy of Film and Television Arts; the Golden Lion, presented at the Venice Film Festival; the Golden Bear, awarded at the Berlin Film Festival; and the Palme d'or (Golden Palm), presented at the Cannes Film Festival. Awards in the theater include the Tony® (or Antoinette Perry Award®), given by the American Theatre Wing in New York City for Broadway shows; the Drama Desk awards, presented annually by the Drama Desk committee; the Theatre World awards, presented by the Theatre World committee of critics; and the Obie (or Off-Broadway) awards, given annually by the *Village Voice* newspaper. In France, the César and the Molière are presented for outstanding work in film and theater, respectively; and in England, the Olivier awards are presented annually for excellence in the theater. Performing arts unions also give annual awards to their own members for various achievements; e.g., Equity's Clarence Derwent and Richard Seff awards and the Screen Actors Guild awards, on which the union membership votes.

23

B

baby *n. Slang* A motion picture camera, to those who work with it.

baby wrangler A person who takes care of babies used in shows or movies and brings them to the film set or waits backstage, handing them to the performer who will work with them. Also called a *baby coach.*

back *n., v.* —*n.* **1.** Short for *backstage: in back; to go back.* **2.** Against the rear wall of a proscenium stage set or the rear wall of the stage itself: *at back.*—*v. t.* **3.** To invest in or help underwrite a production. **4.** To add music to a film.

backing *n.* **1.** A piece of scenery placed behind a door or window on a stage set to mask the backstage area, and to serve as part of the set; e.g., an exterior seen through a window. **2.** Financial underwriting for a show; hence, *backer.*

Back it up! "Start again, just a few lines before where you stopped, repeat what you did, and continue on!" A director's instruction to an actor at a theater rehearsal.

back lighting Illumination from behind actors in a stage performance, or when being filmed. Hence, *to back light*: to design, or install such illumination; *back light*: the lighting instrument itself. In film, such lighting is used to create a romantic effect and to soften the features of some stars.

back lot The part of a film studio complex located behind the administrative buildings. The outdoor sets are there.

back of the house 1. The rear of the auditorium. **2.** The backstage area of a theater.

back projection The system used to display images on a television screen, with the projector (i.e., the cathode ray picture tube) behind it. Also called *back projection system.*

Back to one! "Return to your starting positions; we are going to do another take right away!" A film director's command to actors and technical personnel; also heard as **"Resetting back to one!"**

backdrop *n.* A piece of plain or painted canvas hung from the flies or in the form of a huge standing flat that covers the back of a stage set. Also called a *backcloth.*

backers' audition The presentation of a theatrical project to an audience of potential financial underwriters and investors (backers). Fully staged and performed workshops are often used as backers' auditions, but some presentations are sit-down or staged readings, with songs sung to piano accompaniment for new musicals.

background *n.* In film, the area that is seen on camera behind the actors; hence, *background action*: that which takes place behind the performers.

background music Off-screen instrumental or vocal accompaniment to a scene.

background players Actors who serve to create reality and atmosphere in a scene. In the theater, background players (colloquially called "spear carriers") often understudy as well as playing in crowd scenes. Media background players are protected by either SAG or AFTRA contracts. In film, television, and on-camera commercials, the producers have the right to hire a certain percentage of nonunion extras, depending on the scale of the production. Also called *atmosphere*; *background actors*; *background talent*; *background performers*; *character mimes* (at the New York City Opera); *extras*; *supernumeraries*.
See also ADJUSTMENT; BUMP; CAMERA READY; CATTLE CALL; DOWNSCALE; GOLDEN TIME; RUSH CALL; SCREEN EXTRAS GUILD (SEG); SELECTIONS; SKINS; UPGRADE; UPSCALE.

background presence Syn. with *ambient sound*; **room tone**.

backstage *n.* All the areas of a theater behind the **proscenium** arch (except the stage acting area and the scenery), including the wings, crossover, dressing rooms, shops, and storage areas; or all locations out of the auditorium, front of house, and acting area in a **theater in the round**. Backstage areas in Broadway theaters can be quite extensive, with dressing rooms on several floors, wide wings, and high fly galleries.

backstage musical A film genre of stories, or an individual film, dealing with the lives of performers in theater productions of musical comedies; e.g., *42nd Street* (1933).

back story The events that took place prior to the present-day story being told in the script, and that have led up to it.

back-up schedule In filmmaking, an alternate shooting plan, in case of a **weather delay** or other impediment to carrying out the original schedule.

bad dress rehearsal, good opening The silly idea that if the final dress rehearsal goes terribly, it portends a wonderful opening night performance. Conversely, if a dress rehearsal goes well, it is said to be the unpropitious harbinger of a disastrous opening.

bad laugh An unexpected, undesired, undesirable audience reaction of hilarity to something that is supposed to be taken seriously, or because of an accident at an unpropitious moment.

baggy-pants comic A **low comedian**, esp. in vaudeville and burlesque; often a tramp character or other ne'er-do-well.

balance *n.* **1.** The equalization of sound elements in recording music or the audio for a film. **2.** The adjusted sound levels between on-stage singers and the **pit orchestra** in a **musical theater** piece, so that the instrumentalists do not drown out the vocalists. **3.** The harmony of all elements in the composition of a film shot. **4.** In dancing, the optimal balanced posture necessary to ensure freedom of movement. **5.** In singing, the harmonious working together of all parts of the breathing and vocal apparatus.

balcony *n.* A raised, raked seating area suspended above the orchestra level of a theater auditorium.

balcony rail The lighting **batten** installed below the front edge of a theater balcony; e.g., in a Broadway theater.

bald wig A head covering with a bare pate and hair around its lower sides, meant to make the actor wearing it appear bald.

ballad opera *Hist.* An 18th-c. form from which today's **musical comedy** developed. A story told in dialogue interspersed with popular, well-known tunes drawn from folk ballads or operas, to which lyrics suitable to the story of the play were written; e.g., John Gay's *The Beggar's Opera*, first produced in 1728, and adapted in 1928, by Berthold Brecht and Kurt Weill, as *The Threepenny Opera*.

ballerina *n.* A female ballet dancer.

ballet *n.* **1.** A form of classical theatrical **dance** accompanied by music and using formalized steps, gestures, and movements that are precisely done and smoothly executed in a graceful, flowing, and expressive manner. The ballet originated in Renaissance Italy and was further developed in France in the 17th c. **2.** A theatrical entertainment consisting either of a full-length classical dance piece or drama (e.g., Tchaikovsky's *Swan Lake*), or of a number of either narrative or abstract shorter pieces. **3.** A dance **number** in 19th-c. operettas or operas.
See also RÉGISSEUR.

ballet comedy [French: *comédie-ballet* (ko mé dee' ba leh:')] *Hist.* A 17th-c. entertainment popular at the court of Louis XIV that combined a spoken play with balletic interludes; e.g., Molière's *Le Bourgeois gentilhomme* (luh boor zhwah' zhon tee yuhm'), with music by Jean-Baptiste Lully.

ballet master; **ballet mistress** The person in charge of training the dancers in a ballet company.

balletomane *n.* A person who is enamored of the ballet.

banana *n., v.* —*n. Slang* **1.** A comedian, esp. in vaudeville or burlesque. The *second banana* is the top banana's sidekick. The *third banana* is the put-upon stooge or chump, the fall guy who takes the blame for the actions of the others. See TOP BANANA. **2.** An on-camera walk done in a semi-circular, arcing, curved pattern: *Don't walk to the door in a straight line: give me a banana when you make that cross.* —*v. i.* **3.** In film and television, to walk in front of the camera in a smoothly curved, semicircular pattern. See GIVE ME A BANANA!

band *n.* **1.** A group of musicians who play together: *rock band*; *jazz band*. **2.** The **pit orchestra** and/or onstage musicians that play for a musical theater piece. **3.**

An ensemble of brass, woodwind, and percussion players that performs military music, marches, and other compositions in parades and in concerts in public parks, concert halls, band shells, the circus, or other venues. **4.** An ensemble of percussion, brass, woodwind, and some string players (e.g., a bass player) that perform background or dance music in ballrooms, dance halls, or cruise ships: *a brass band*; *a military band*; *a dance band*.

bandmaster *n.* The conductor and **music director** of a band. Also called a *band leader*.

band part The music and the written score for an individual instrument in a band.

band shell The open concave structure covering over the back of an open-air stage or bandstand, under which the musicians playing a concert sit; it provides an acoustic sounding board off which the music bounces. Also called *acoustical shell*.

bandstand *n.* **1.** A raised open-air platform on which musicians play a concert; it may be surrounded by a decorative fence and surmounted by an ornate canopy. **2.** A small stage or raised platform in a dance hall, cabaret, nightclub, or other public room where musicians play during an event such as a wedding or dance.

bank *n.* **1.** A group of seats in a theater auditorium. **2.** A row of lights that have been hung in place. **3.** A row of light switches or dimmers. **4.** Stored television commercials, **in the can** and ready for broadcasting. **5.** A storage place for data, whether on a computer or as **hard copy**: *data bank*.

Barba, Eugenio (b. 1936) (eh:oo dgeh:' nyo bahr' bah) Italian-born **avant-garde** stage director and theorist, known for his innovative **environmental theater** productions. He spent a year studying with Jerzy Grotowski in Poland before founding the Odinteatret, his experimental company in Norway. His exhaustive, classic book *A Dictionary of Theatre Anthropology: The Secret Art of the Performer* (Routledge, 2006), written with Nicola Savarese, covers world-wide theatrical culture and **performance practice**.

bard *n.* **1.** *Hist.* A medieval poet-singer who wrote, composed, and performed songs and sagas: *the Celtic bards*. **2.** A poet: *William Shakespeare is called the Bard of Avon, or simply the Bard*.

barker *n.* An individual who stands outside a sideshow or other attraction at a carnival, circus, or theater and tries to attract customers by talking in glowing terms about what they can expect to see and experience inside: *a carnival barker*.

barn doors The shutters attached to **lights**. There are usually four of them: one on each side, and one each on the top and bottom. They can be opened and shut to control the amount and direction of the light. Also called *flippers*.

barney *n.* A thick cloth or blanket placed over a film camera to muffle its sounds and to protect the camera in inclement weather; hence, *heating barney*: an electrified camera cover used on winter location shoots.

barnstorming *n.* **1.** Going from small town to small town, performing plays without scenery (mostly in barns), and attracting customers at the last minute; a practice during the depression of the 1930s in rural America. By extension, making political speeches on scheduled stops of a campaign tour; hence, *barnstormer.* **2.** A form of entertainment by airplane pilots, who take off from fields near barns in small airplanes in which they either take passengers on sightseeing flights or do airplane stunts for spectators on the ground.

base payment rate The hourly rate paid to SAG and AFTRA **background players**. See also GOLDEN TIME; SCALE.

base station The central power control equipment of a **PA system**; theater sound system, including the head mikes; or **headset** communications system (e.g., that between a **stage manager** and technicians).

basket *n.* [Short for *property basket*] *esp. Brit.* An open storage container for stage properties.

batten *n., v, —n.* **1.** A long metal pipe, or a bar made of wood or metal, used to hang lighting instruments, scene pieces, or curtains: *a light batten*; *a flyline batten*: one that holds the **line** fastened to a **fly**. They are numbered, beginning with the batten furthest downstage, which is "batten one," and so on to the last upstage batten. **2.** A piece of wood used to reinforce a **flat** or to fasten it to another; or to stiffen a **drop**. —*v. t.* **3.** To fasten together or reinforce flats.

battle scene The confrontation and clash of armed groups; e.g., the combat between opposing forces in Shakespeare's histories, the armies at Borodino in film and television versions of Leo Tolstoy's *War and Peace*.

Bay Area Theater (BAT) agreement The **Equity** contract covering work in non-profit, seasonal theaters seating fewer than 400 people within the nine-county area of San Francisco Bay; it provides for five salary tiers, depending on the size of the theater.

BBC English The distinguished, clear pronunciation and diction once used by trained broadcasters and announcers of the British Broadcasting Corporation (BBC).

beat *n.* **1.** A unit, piece, or bit of a scene. **2.** The beginning of an **action**. **3.** The amount of time during which an action in a scene is played out, resulting in the success or failure of an **objective**: a new beat begins as soon as the previous one ends. **4.** In music, a rhythmic stress, or metrical accent; hence, *downbeat*: the first, strongest beat in a measure, marked off by a bar directly before it in the score. Also, the first metrical accent at the beginning of a musical composition; consequently, the conductor's cue to the musicians to start performing; *upbeat*: the unaccented note or notes before the downbeat. **5.** The rhythm of a piece of music.

beauty shot The take of the product in a television commercial.

bedroom farce A fast-paced **sex comedy** involving lasciviousness, lewdness, and lubricious characters in provocative situations.

before-time *n.* Stanislavsky's term for what happened to the characters before the story began, leading to the events in the story; the **back story**.

behind the scenes Offstage and out of view of the public; hence, by extension, *in secret*.

below *n., prep.* —*n.* **1.** *Archaic* The acting area beneath the upstage balcony in an Elizabethan theater. Also called *inner below.* —*prep.* **2.** In front of; **downstage** of: *He crossed left below the couch.*

below the line Television or filmmaking production costs incurred when a project is actually **in production**; e.g., the price of film stock and set-building materials; the costs of labor, transportation, renting equipment, locations, and craft services; and daily incidental expenses.
See also ABOVE THE LINE; LINE PRODUCER.

below the title Credits that appear onscreen after the name of a project.

belt *v. t.* To sing out loudly and powerfully, using a lot of chest voice: *to belt a song*; *to belt out a song*. Hence *belter*: a singer who belts. This style of singing is often called for in Broadway musicals; it is contrasted with **legitimate singing**.

benefit; **benefit performance** The presentation of a play for which the proceeds are donated to a charity. In the 19th c., the takings went to a performer about to retire, or to the author of the play, who did not otherwise earn royalties.

be on the gate To collect tickets from audience members as they enter.

be up for To be considered for a role: *She's up for Juliet.*

best boy 1. Chief assistant to the key **grip. 2.** Chief assistant to the **gaffer**.

between engagements *Slang.* Unemployed as an actor.

between-time *n.* Stanislavsky's term for what happens to the characters between the scenes, influencing their behavior and feelings in the next scenes in which they appear.

bible *n.* The detailed listing of characters and situations for a television series (e.g., for a soap opera), usually with storylines for six months ahead. Also called *long-term projection*; *series book.*

bicoastal *adj.* Pertaining to actors who divide their time between the east and west coasts of the United States.

bicycle *v. i. Slang* **1.** In acting, to do more than one project at the same time, going back and forth according to schedule; e.g., a stage play and a film. **2.** In acting, to do one project after another, non-stop. **3.** To send audiotapes, videotapes, or DVDs of programs meant for broadcasting (usually programs in **syndication**) from one television or radio station to another; hence, the adjectival phrase *bicycle station*: one of a chain of such stations from which material is shipped.

bidirectional microphone A mike that receives signals from only two frontal directions: right and left.

big head close-up A full-frame shot of an actor's face only. Also called a *choker*.

big screen A **metonymy** for the movies.

big-screen treatment Movie **adaptation** of a novel, play, comic book, etc.

bill *n., v.* —*n.* **1.** A theater program, esp. in vaudeville; playbill. **2.** The management's backstage listing of the **running order** of the acts in a variety or vaudeville show. —*v. t.* **3.** To put a performer, production, or act on the schedule of a theater or vaudeville program: *The theater billed the touring production for a week.*

billing *n.* **1.** The list of **credits**. **2.** The place someone's name occupies on the list of credits, often **in order of appearance**, or in alphabetical order: **top billing**; *star billing.* **3.** Publicity; advertising, as when putting up posters or posting handbills: *Advance billing may ensure a large **advance sale**.*

bill of fare A theater program: *What's on the bill of fare for this evening?*

billy act *Hist.* In vaudeville, a sketch or turn involving a caricatural American Southern mountain character; i.e., a hillbilly. Similar to a *hick act*, with rural characters.

bio *n.* [Short for *biography*] Brief details of the lives and credits of actors, the stage manager, and other creative staff members printed in a theater program; often written by the individual at the management's request.

biomechanical acting Meyerhold's term for precise, perfectly timed movements, gestures, and expressions which become automatic once they have been rehearsed; and which, for him, constituted the essence of the actor's art, as opposed to the psychological approach of Stanislavsky; hence *biomechanics*: the process and techniques of such acting.
    See MEYERHOLD, VSEVELOD.

biopic *n.* [Biographical picture] A film based on someone's entire life story, or on particular events; usually highly fictionalized. Among the more interesting are Abel Gance's unusual silent epic *Napoléon* (1927); Roberto Rosselini's 1966 television film *La Prise du pouvoir par Louis XIV* (The Assumption of Power by Louis XIV; lah preez' dü poo vwahr' pahr loo ee ka to:rz'); and *The Madness of King George* (1994), starring Nigel Hawthorne in the **title role**.

bird *n. Slang* **1.** Disapproval by an audience, expressed with catcalls and whistles—hence, probably, the use of the word—and the throwing of vegetables: *to give someone the bird; to get the bird.* **2.** A communications satellite in orbit around the earth.

bird's-eye shot A take done from above. Also called *bird's-eye view*; *overhead shot*.

birdseye *n.* [Named for its inventor, frozen food magnate Clarence Birdseye (1886–1956)] A spotlight with a back reflector; used in film and television lighting.

bit *n.* **1.** A piece of stage business. **2.** A comic piece of business. **3.** Another word for beat. **4.** A small portion or section of a scene: *Let's do that bit again.*

bit part A small role; a **walk-on** character; *bit*, for short.
  See also COUGH AND A SPIT.

bitten by the bug Seized with the all but incurable desire to become an actor; a victim of *stage fever*; **stagestruck**.

black-and-white [films, television] **1.** Movies made using film stock that can register photographs only in black, white, and shades of gray. **2.** Television broadcasting received on a set that can only display images in shades of black, white, and gray.

black box A **studio** that is painted black; one end of it is used as a stage, **performance space**, or **acting area**. Also called *black room*; *blackbox*; *black box theater*.

black comedy A play or film full of grim, mordant, sarcastic humor about the human condition: *black humor*. E.g., the Coen brothers' *Fargo* (1996) and *No Country for Old Men* (2007), which treat the subjects of blackmail, murder, serial killing, drug running, and psychopathy in a brutal, horrifying, sickening, yet satiric manner. Also called *dark comedy*.

blacklist *n., v.* —*n.* **1.** A secret listing of the names of those barred from employment in an industry. In the early 1950s McCarthy era of Communist witch hunts, those performers, writers, and others in the **arts and entertainment industry** suspected of past or present Communist affiliations were blacklisted by industry executives: *the Hollywood blacklist*. Among those on it were the **Hollywood Ten**. —*v. t.* **2.** To place the names of those barred from employment on a secret list, available only to those who could be expected to keep it secret and to deny jobs to those on it. See *The Way We Were* (1973), *Guilty by Suspicion* (1991), and Woody Allen's *The Front* (1976).

Black Maria (muh rI' uh) *Hist.* Thomas Edison's film studio, the first ever built, in West Orange, NJ. It was on a revolving platform, and was open at one side so it could follow the sun's changing light.

blackout *n., v.* —*n.* **1.** The complete extinguishing of all stage lights, usually at the end of a scene. Hence, *blackout cue*: a lighting cue; *blackout sketch*: a brief vaudeville routine that ends with an abrupt blackout, pointing up its final **punch line**. **2.** A blanket prohibition against the release of certain kinds of news (e.g., war news): *a news blackout*. **3.** A prohibition against broadcasting a television show in a particular area, esp. a sports event that is taking place locally. —*v. t.* **4.**

To extinguish all the stage lights, usually quite suddenly. **5.** To censor (lit. by crossing out material with black ink) or, by extension, to prohibit the spread of certain kinds of material. **6.** To prevent a broadcast from taking place.

blackout drop The opaque curtain or flat lowered behind a **scrim** to ensure the invisibility of whatever is behind it; raised at the moment when the scene is to be revealed.

blacks *n. pl.* The heavy velvet or cotton **masking** curtains at the sides and/or back of a theater **stage** or other **acting area**; so called because they are usually black in color.

bladder *n. Archaic* An air-filled sac, sometimes mounted on a stick handle, used by a medieval **jester** or **merry-andrew** to hit the objects of their mockery.

blank verse Unrhymed poetry, most often in iambic pentameter; the primary verse form in English drama.
   See COUPLET; VERSE TECHNIQUE.

bleeding *n.* The spillover of light into an area that is supposed to be dark.

bleed-through *n.* Intrusive sound from a film heard through the walls in a **multiplex** cinema.

bleep *n., v.* —*v.* **1.** A brief, high-pitched, annoying electronic squeak, played in television broadcasts to replace a word considered obscene. —*v. t.* **2.** To censor words by inserting such a sound over them. Also called *blip*.

block *v. t.* **1.** To plan the schema of actors' movements and positions on stage or in front of a camera; hence, *to block out*; *to block the moves*. **2.** To direct the actors' movements in rehearsal, telling them when and where to move: *to block the actors*.

blockbuster *n.* [Fr. the term for a powerful WW II bomb] A huge box-office hit; hence *summer blockbuster*: a film, often a major fantasy or action-adventure movie, released during the hot summer months and expected to be a **tentpole** for its studio.

blocking *n.* **1.** The schema of actors' movements on stage or in front of the camera. **2.** The moves themselves. **3.** The director's planning and staging of the actors' moves. Blocking is sometimes **set** very early in theater rehearsals, depending partly on the time allowed for rehearsal, and partly on the director's way of working. Actors may be allowed to improvise their own *organic blocking*, subject to the director's approval.

blocking rehearsal A play, television, or film **rehearsal** focused on the director giving the actors their moves; hence, *to block in*: to give an actor moves when putting the actor into a scene. Also called a ***staging rehearsal***.

blood and thunder Pertains to esp. sensationalistic 19th-c. **melodrama**, with its endless scenes of gory murder and frightening storm effects.

blood effects Various special effects involving the use of materials that look like blood. E.g., *fake blood* (made from non-toxic liquids, such as corn syrup and food coloring); *blood capsule* (a thin-walled tiny container held in the mouth until needed; when the actor bites down on it, the red powder inside mingles with saliva, and creates the effect of blood flowing out of the mouth); *blood hit* (a capsule containing liquid, shot at an actor wearing concealed protective armor, creating the effect of the actor's having been hit); *blood sacks* used with a **squib**; *blood knife* (a real or dummy prop containing a groove with a narrow tube leading to a bulb of fake blood in the handle, squeezed when the knife is used); hoses concealed inside a costume and attached to pumps that force the fake blood to the surface in accident or homicide scenes. Also called *special blood effects*.

blood tub *Archaic Brit.* A theater where melodramas were performed.

blooper *n.* A mistake made by a film or television actor (or a technician) during a take.

blow *v. t. Slang.* To forget, misspeak, or otherwise **flub** a line of dialogue.

blower *n. Slang* A **microphone**.

blue pencil The censor's instrument, used to cross out unacceptable material; also used as a verb: *He blue-penciled every other line in the script.*
See CENSORSHIP.

blue-rinse audience A group of spectators, mostly old ladies attending matinees, who have used hair rinses that give a slight blue tint to their white or gray hair. Also called *blue-rinse crowd*.

bluescreen process A **special effects** method in which a scene is shot against a blue backdrop, so that later a computer-generated background can be supplied by **compositing**, with the actors superimposed on it.

bluescreen shot A take of a scene in front of the specially constructed blue background cloth used in the bluescreen process. Actors may have to pretend to be caught in the middle of a raging tempest in stormy seas, or to be fleeing from the falling lava of an erupting volcano.

Boal, Augusto (b. 1931) (ow goosh' too bwahl') Influential Brazilian stage director and theorist, directly political in his approach to theater. He wrote *Theatre of the Oppressed*, published in English in 1979, in order to provide a dramatic voice for the masses and to present his ideas on the oppressive nature of theater, which he perceives as a political weapon, serving to reinforce the existing social system and acting therefore as an instrument of oppression. In this situation, the artist must learn anew to create, and must give us a new view of humanity and of what it means to make moral choices.

board *n.* **1.** Short for *lighting board* or *sound board*; i.e., the **console**, or computerized control panel for a theater's audio or lighting, or for the audio in a recording studio. **2.** A group of people that includes both policy makers and honorary members connected with a particular theater or other arts organization.

boards *n. pl. Slang* The stage. Hence, *to tread the boards*; i.e., to perform.

body brace A harness worn by a cameraperson to steady a handheld camera during a take. Also called *body frame*; *body pad*.

body double An actor physically similar to another actor, for whom he or she stands in during certain shots; e.g., in long shots, or with back to the camera. Cf. **stunt double**.

body language Physical position, facial expression, movement, and gesture that communicate an actor's feelings and attitudes to the audience, without a word being said.

body makeup artist A technician who works in film or television applying prosthetics and/or using paint and powder to alter the physical appearance of an actor. The union body makeup artist does not work on the arms or face of the performer: that is the domain of the union **makeup artist**.

body mike A microphone worn by an individual actor during a performance; usually hidden somewhere in the costume.

Bogart, Anne (b. 1951) Award-winning American theater director, who teaches at Columbia University. Co-founder of the Saratoga International Theatre Institute in 1992 with Tadashi Suzuki; with Tina Landau she wrote *The Viewpoints Book: A Practical Guide to Viewpoints and Composition* (Theater Communications Group, 2005), expounding her theory of **viewpoints**: all characters have a point of view, and each viewpoint has its parameters, which must be explored and recreated.

Boleslavsky, Richard (1889–1937) (boh leh slahv' skee) Influential Polish-born film director; acting teacher in New York and Hollywood with his partner Maria Ouspenskaya (1876–1949) (oo' spehn skah' yah), both of whom chose to stay in the United States instead of returning to Soviet Russia with the **Moscow Art Theatre**, which had been touring in 1928. He remained faithful to Stanislavsky's ideas, and taught his system to a generation of actors. His brief, useful book *Acting: The First Six Lessons* (Routledge, 1987) is still available. The six lessons are on concentration, memory of emotion, dramatic action, characterization, observation, and rhythm.

Bollywood *n.* [Fr. Bombay; Hollywood] *Slang* The film industry of India, one of the largest in the world.

bomb *n. Slang* **1.** A play or film that is an ignominious failure; hence, *to bomb*: to fail utterly. **2.** *Brit.* A huge success (like a bomb that explodes on target).

bond. See EQUITY BOND.

boo *n., v.* —*n.* **1.** A shout of anathema, pronounced as it is spelled. —*v. t.* **2.** To express one's disapproval and dislike by shouting "boo."

boob tube A television set, in front of which one often finds a **couch potato**, who may sometimes **channel surf**. Also called an *idiot box*.

book *n., v.* —*n.* **1.** The complete text of a musical comedy or operetta. **2.** That part of the script of a musical comedy or operetta that includes the spoken dialogue. **3.** The prompt copy of the script used by the stage manager. **4.** A model's album of head shots and posed photographs, to be shown to agents, photographers, and potential employers. **5.** A photographer's album of work; to be shown to agents or potential employers; sometimes left at an agent's office so the agent can show it. —*v. t.* **6.** To be hired for a particular job, esp. in the media: *She booked the job.* **7.** To hire someone to do a job in entertainment and related fields; e.g., modeling or photography: *He booked the actor.* **8.** To buy tickets to an entertainment event: *to book seats.* **9.** To schedule a film at a particular cinema; e.g., at an art house: *They booked the film for two weeks.*

book flat. See FLAT.

booking *n.* An engagement for a job.

booking agency A company that arranges tours and schedules professional engagements for variety acts, star musicians, and performing artists of all kinds.

book recording An area of the arts and entertainment industry that employs actors to record works of fiction and nonfiction for commercial release, or for libraries, or as a public service for the blind. There are various contracts between AFTRA and certain production companies, or such public service organizations as the American Foundation for the Blind, but the book recording business is not completely unionized. However, AFTRA members can unionize a job by having the production company go through a **paymaster** or talent payment company, with the producer making the usual percentage contribution to the AFTRA health and pension fund, provided the paymaster is a union **signatory** and the company pays union **Sound Recordings Code** scale. It is up to the reader to do a thorough job of preparing the text before a session, whether recording in a **home studio** or working with a sound engineer and, in commercial venues, with a director as well. In a home studio, an actor who is assigned a book records it on a computer, using recording software, and then sends the recording via the **Internet** to the producers. The narrator acts as **sound engineer** and **recording artist** rolled into one. For more, see my book *Acting with the Voice: the Art of Recording Books* (Limelight; 2004).

   See also AUDIOBOOK; CHARACTER VOICES; COMMERCIAL EDITION; CORRECTIONS SESSION; LIBRARY EDITION; MICROPHONE; MICROPHONE TECHNIQUE; READING TECHNIQUE; SIDE ANNOUNCEMENT; SOUND RECORDINGS CODE.

book show A musical comedy, with its spoken dialogue and storyline, as opposed to a variety show or musical revue.

boom *n.* **1.** A microphone attached to the end of a long pole; used out of camera range to record dialogue, it may be handheld or mounted on a stand or truck.

During recording, the *boom operator* of a handheld mike may follow the actors as they move. Also called a *fishpole*. **2.** The hydraulic lift on which a camera may be mounted, enabling it to move smoothly up and down. **3.** A light on a long pole, held over the head of a subject being filmed or taped.

boom stand A pole with an adjustable horizontal arm to which a microphone is attached; used in recording studios to extend the mike over the stand holding the copy or book.

bootleg *v., adj. Slang* —*v. t.* **1.** To make an illegal copy of a video, film, DVD, music CD, or the like, in order to sell it; i.e., to commit the crime of **piracy**. —*adj.* **2.** Pirated; stolen: *a bootleg copy.*

booth *n.* **1.** A small, enclosed room located in the back of a theater auditorium from which lighting technicians run a show, receiving their cues through headsets by the stage manager. Also called *control booth*; **lighting booth. 2.** A small, curtained-off area constructed backstage; used for quick changes. **3.** A small, enclosed, soundproof room used for recording.
    See SOUND BOOTH.

border *n.* A piece of scenery hung horizontally above the set in a proscenium theater, framing the scene in some way; e.g., a blue sky border, a **cloud border**, a **foliage border**.

born in a trunk To come by theatrical aspirations naturally, by virtue of presumably having first seen the light of day backstage while one's theatrical parents were on tour: costumes for touring companies were stored backstage in trunks, ready for travel.

Borscht Belt The Catskill mountain resort hotels where mainly Jewish comedians used to do their acts from the 1920s through the '60s, until most of the hotels went out of business. Many of the comedians were vaudeville performers who went on to do radio, television, and film work. Also called *Borscht Circuit.*
    See also STAND-UP COMEDY.

Boston version A **burlesque** act from which any obscenity or ribald reference has been excised, in deference to presumed New England puritanical, censorial attitudes.

bottom of the bill The last act in a vaudeville or music hall running order.

boulevard theater Highly popular French comedies, farces, dramas, and melodramas that originated in 19th c. theaters (now gone) located near a number of streets, called boulevards, in the fourth arrondissement of Paris. Such pieces are still being written, and are performed in theaters all over the city.

bounce *n.* **1.** Stray light that creates a glare. Also called *spill.* **2.** Television broadcast signals from a satellite, meant for **satellite television**.

bow *n., v.* —*n.* **1.** An inclination of the body in acknowledgement of the audience's applause at the end of a performance. **2.** A debut in the theater: *He made his bow* *as Hamlet.* —*v. i.* **3.** To take a **curtain call**. **4.** To make a theatrical debut: *She bowed as Juliet at the Old Vic.*

bowdlerize (bohd' luhr Iz) *v. t.* [Fr. the name of the squeamish, puritanical clergyman Thomas Bowdler (1754–1825), who published a censored edition of Shakespeare's plays] To delete or excise material considered unpleasant, violent, or, esp., sexually suggestive, from a literary or theatrical work. Hence, the adj. *bowdlerized*: *bowdlerized Shakespeare.*

bowl *n.* An open-air amphitheater; e.g., the Hollywood Bowl.

box *n.* A small, intimate theater seating space, containing only a few seats, divided by partitions from other such spaces, and entered through a private door. The ring of boxes is the lowest of the raised seating areas in a theater or opera house, just below the first **balcony**.

box office 1. The small room with a window or windows open to the public where admissions tickets to an entertainment are purchased; usually located in the front of a theater, stadium, or movie house. Seating charts and selling plans are computerized for easy management of sales. Many box office personnel are members of **IATSE**. **2.** *Slang* A **draw**: *Tom Cruise is box office.*

box office draw A name actor or other well-known artist who is expected to attract audiences.

box office manager The person in charge of hiring and overseeing the personnel who sell tickets; of keeping the accounts of receipts, returns, and sales; and of dealing with customers when necessary. Also sometimes called the *treasurer.*

box office poison A famous name whom audiences are expected to shun.

box set A stage décor in a proscenium theater with three walls and a ceiling, usually representing a room, and with the **fourth wall** open at the proscenium arch.

B-picture *n.* A low-budget, inferior film with minor stars; originally, such a movie shown as the second half of a **double feature**.

bravo (brah' voh) *n.* [Fr. Italian: brave man] A shouted expression of approval. Technically, "Bravo!" refers to an individual man only; "Brava!" [Italian: brave woman!] is meant for a woman; "Bravi!" (brah' vee) for men; and "Brave!" (brah' veh) for women.

bravura *n., adj.* —*n.* **1.** High-spirited brilliance and florid showiness. —*adj.* **2.** Pertains to a spirited, florid performance.

bread-and-butter job An actor's work outside the field of show business that is a fairly steady source of income; it usually allows actors time to audition. Also called a *day job.*

break *n., v.* —*n.* **1.** A brief pause in the work of rehearsal or technical set-ups; hence, *to take a break.* Proper breaks after an hour (5 minutes), an hour and a half

(10 minutes), or two hours (15 minutes) are required by **Equity rules**. SAG and AFTRA have required breaks during filming and taping. **2.** The date on which a film opens nationally or in a particular market. **3.** A lucky opportunity or chance for an actor to be noticed; hence, *break-through role*: *Juliet was her big break*. **4.** A good deal; e.g., a *money break* in a contract negotiation, where the producers agree to a salary increase. **5.** The accidental interruption of a television or radio broadcast, due to technical difficulties or uncontrollable meteorological conditions. —*v. t.* **6.** To open a film nationally or in a particular market. —*v. i.* **7.** To end a workday in the theater or the media: *to break for the day* (e.g., as in a stage manager's announcement: *OK, folks, we're broken*). Cf. **wrap**.

break a fall When taking a tumble on stage or in a film, to land first on one leg and one arm, allowing the relaxed body to crumple to the floor, all in one smooth move; a technique used in **stage combat**, certain death scenes, etc.
See STAGE FALL.

Break a leg! [Origin obscure; possibly from a translation of the German phrase used by actors before a show: *Hals und Beinbruch* (hahls' *oo*nt bIn' brookh'); lit., neck and leg-break] "Good luck!" This is said by actors and other show folk to each other before a show, because of the **superstition** that wishing someone "good luck" is sure to bring about bad luck. Had it not first been heard of in the 20th c., the phrase might have come from the Elizabethan theater: the Elizabethan bow was done by bending slightly at the waist, with the right hand held over the heart, while simultaneously moving the right leg slightly behind the left, and breaking it (i.e., bending it, at the knee). The same superstition prevails in other countries. In Italy, actors say, "*In bocca al lupo*" (ihn bo:k' kah ahl loo' po) [Into the mouth of the wolf, i.e., the audience], to which the response is "*Crepi il lupo!*" (kreh' pee ihl loo' po:) [May the wolf drop dead!]; in France, they say, "*Merde!*" or "*Merde ce soir!*" (mehrd' suh swahr') [Shit; shit this evening]; and in Germany, as well as in opera houses worldwide, actors and singers say, "*Toi toi toi*" (toy' toy' toy'), presumably fr. the first syllable of German *Teufel* (toy' fuhl) [Devil].

breakaway *n.* Anything prepared so that it can easily come apart, without injury to the actors; e.g., a partially severed balcony railing that breaks during a **fight scene** in a **western**, as the actor tumbles off the balcony.

breakaway costume An actor's stage clothing, of which the entire outfit or some part of it is fastened with **Velcro** so that it can easily come apart; e.g., for a **quick change** or in a **fight scene**.

breakaway prop A property that is put together in such a way as to allow it to be easily broken, with minimal danger; e.g., a bottle made of **sugar glass**.

break character To drop temporarily out of the part one is playing; e.g., during a rehearsal.

break down To **distress** a set or costumes; i.e., to make them look shabby and worn.

breakdown *n.* **1.** Short for **cast breakdown**. **2.** The complete, detailed listing of every shot in a motion picture or television project, and all the requirements for that shot. The listing is then further broken down and arranged in the order the scenes are to be taken, so that such aspects as **location** can be taken into account when scheduling.

break in To refine a new act or routine in a variety, vaudeville, or music hall show by performing it a number of times to see what works; hence, *break-in time*: the period during which this is done.

break into To launch one's career: *She broke into movies when she was very young.*

breath control The management of the intake and outflow of air from the lungs, helped by diaphragmatic breathing: an important part of **vocal technique**.
See also DIAPHRAGM.

breath cut The preparatory intake of air just before speaking or singing that may be recorded, and must be edited out by starting the recording again, or later during the editing process.

Brecht, Berthold (1898–1956) (beh:' tolt br*ehht*') Celebrated German playwright and theoretician. Brecht's ideas on theater were linked to his political ideas as a Communist: he thought theater as it existed—demanding the audience's rapt attention and eliciting manipulated responses—was a manifestation of bourgeois capitalism and called unconsciously for the basic acceptance of the prevailing social norms and system. He felt that the actors should create a distancing or **alienation effect**, so that the audience would not simply be able to sit back and enjoy the spectacle being presented.
See also ANTI-CULINARY THEATER; EPIC REALISM.

breeches part Syn. with **trousers role**, esp. in **opera**. Also called *pants part*.

bridge *n.* **1.** A narrow, maneuverable, hanging platform (or **catwalk**) used by technicians hanging lights for a proscenium stage. Also called a *lighting bridge*. **2.** In music, a brief transitional section between two important parts of a musical **number**, symphony movement, etc. **3.** A transitional passage or brief scene in a drama; e.g., the conversation between Prospero and Ariel at the end of act 1, scene 2 in Shakespeare's *The Tempest*. **4.** The concealed, raised platform in back of a **marionette** stage, on which the puppeteers stand during the show.

bridging shot A piece of film edited into a movie between scenes, and used as a transitional moment. Also called a *bridge shot*.

bring down the house To elicit such merriment, laughter, or applause that a show must temporarily stop.

bring up 1. To raise the intensity of light or sound levels. **2.** To turn on the stage or house lights in a theater or film studio.

British Academy of Film and Television Art (BAFTA) U.K. counterpart of AMPAS. The members vote for the annual BAFTA awards, honoring achievements in motion pictures and television.

British Actors' Equity Association The London-based union of professional actors working in all fields, founded in 1930. Usually called *Equity*; *British Equity*.

British Film Institute (BFI) U.K. organization that keeps national film archives, shows programs of motion pictures, offers filmmaking courses, and promotes the art of film.

broad *n., adj.* —*n.* **1.** A wide-angle floodlight. —*adj.* **2.** Unsubtle, unrestrained, risqué, as in **low comedy**, sex farces, and the style of playing of low comedians: *broad comedy.*

broadcast *n., v., adj.* —*n.* **1.** Transmission over the airwaves of a radio or television program; usually from a studio. Hence, *studio broadcast.* News programs are often transmitted from a location, using equipment on specially outfitted trucks; hence, *live broadcast*; i.e., one in which the transmission is simultaneous with what is happening. **2.** The transmission, or transmitted program itself. —*v. t.* **3.** To transmit a radio or television program over the airwaves so that it can be received on a radio or television set. Hence, *broadcasting*: the act and process of transmission; *broadcasting service*: a radio or television channel. **4.** To announce or read the news or otherwise speak, perform, or present material on television or radio. **5.** *Slang* In acting, to over-project subtext, intention, and emotion; to overact: *She broadcast that moment so it practically hit you over the head.* —*adj.* **6.** Pertaining to television or radio transmissions: *broadcast quality*: the acceptable level of sharpness needed for transmission; *broadcast television standard*: the technical method, specifications, and format of transmissions.

broadcaster *n.* **1.** A radio or television **announcer** or other person whose job is to speak, present, or introduce a program. **2.** An organization that transmits programs; e.g., a radio or television station. **3.** A machine that transmits receivable signals over the airwaves.

broadcast journalism 1. News gathering, writing, and reporting as practiced on radio or television. **2.** Television or radio news shows.

Broadcast Music Incorporated (BMI) A **performance rights organization** that gives performing licenses for the vast stock of copyrighted music under its control, for which it collects royalties on behalf of composers, songwriters, and music publishers.

Broadway *n.* **1.** A north-to-south avenue in Manhattan; called "The Great White Way" because of the lights that illuminate it at night. **2.** New York City's main commercial area of theaters, located in midtown Manhattan. **3.** The centerpiece of the American theater industry, particularly devoted to big spectacle musicals. **4.** A **synecdoche** for the theater and show business in their more glamorous aspects.

Broadway League of Theater Producers The organization that negotiates contracts with Actors Equity, IATSE, and musicians' unions for Broadway and Off-Broadway productions.

Bronx cheer [Fr. *Bronx*, a borough in New York City; home of Yankee Stadium, where such a "cheer" may have originated] A vocal expression of disapproval made by sticking the tongue between closed lips and emitting air in a sound similar to breaking wind. **Syn. *raspberry*.**

Brook, Peter (b. 1925) Much honored English director and author known for his ground-breaking approach to directing actors and staging plays, inspired by Grotowski, Brecht, and Meyerhold, among others. He wrote the influential, iconoclastic *The Empty Space: A Book About the Theatre: Deadly, Holy, Rough, Immediate* (1968), which begins with two lines that have become famous: "I can take any empty space and call it a bare stage. A man walks across this empty space whilst someone else is watching him and this is all I need for an act of theatre to be engaged."

brush-up rehearsal A repetition of a play meant to refresh the actors' memories. Following a hiatus, the actors are called for a brief rehearsal around a table or sitting in the green room, where they may do a **line rehearsal**, or on stage, where they may go through blocking as well. Scenes or the whole play may be done. Fights and dance numbers in musicals are usually brushed up daily, often shortly before the curtain. Individuals normally brush up dance steps or other moves on their own. Called a *brush-up*, for short.

buddy film A subgenre of motion picture that features the relationship and activities of two friends or partners, or of two people thrown together by circumstance; e.g., *Butch Cassidy and the Sundance Kid* (1969), *Thelma and Louise* (1991), and *The Shawshank Redemption* (1994).

buff *n.* A knowledgeable devotee of a particular form of entertainment, or of the work of particular artists: *a movie buff; an opera buff; a theater buff; a Gilbert and Sullivan buff.*

build *n., v.* —*n.* **1.** The momentum and thrust in the arc of a scene. —*v. t.* **2.** To develop the playing of a scene so that **dramatic tension** is created, leading up to its climax. **3.** To construct and put materials together; e.g., scenery. —*v. i.* **4.** In writing, performing, and directing, to develop the throughline of a film, play, moment, beat, or scene so that it has a forward and mounting movement: *The play builds to a satisfying climax.*

bump *n., v.* —*n.* **1.** A one-time extra payment to a SAG or AFTRA background player for an additional service; e.g., a costume change for another scene. —*v. t.* **2.** To bring up theater stage lights suddenly; hence, *bump cue*, meant to reinforce the **button** by brightening the illumination at the end of a musical comedy number. **3.** To thrust the pelvis forward or back, as in the *bump and grind* movements of a **striptease artist**; the grind being a gyrating movement of the pelvis.

41

bunch light *Archaic* Illumination from a number of instruments, giving a flood-light effect; e.g. in the 19th c., a group of gas flames inside a single reflector.

bunraku (boon' rah' koo') *n.* A Japanese form of classical **puppet** show that began in the 17th c.

burlesque *n., v.* —*n.* **1.** A satirical piece or play that parodies or mocks an existing play or persons; e.g., Rowan Atkinson's *Blackadder* television series, a burlesque of historical drama. **2.** A form of theater that combines vaudeville comedy sketches, musical numbers, and ladies who strip for the audience, esp. in a *burlesque house.* —*v. t.* **3.** To **parody** or lampoon an existing play or persons.

burletta (buhr let' uh) *n.* [Fr. Italian: little joke] *Hist.* A late 18th- and early 19th-c. English three-act farce with at least five songs, to get around the licensing laws that allowed spoken plays to be performed only at certain patent theaters.

burn *v. t.* **1.** To superimpose captions or subtitles on a film. **2.** To make a compact disc.

burn gag A carefully controlled, dangerous movie stunt requiring special training and skills, in which an actor (usually a stuntperson) wearing a *burn suit* (syn. with **fire suit**)—i.e., a fireproof costume—is set on fire. Also called *fire gag.*

bus and truck A **tour** of a theatrical production in which the actors and other personnel travel in buses, while the scenery, costumes, and other necessary equipment are transported in trucks.

business *n.* Physical tasks the actor performs as part of the action: *stage business.*

business manager The person who handles the accounting and makes out checks for a theater company.

Business Theater and Events Agreement The contract under which **Equity** actors perform at trade shows, product launching and other promotional events, and live industrials. Formerly called the *Live Corporate Communications or Industrial Contract.*

busker *n. Brit.* A street entertainer who "busks"; i.e., performs songs, dances, or a comedy routine in hopes of receiving money from patrons waiting on a theater queue (line) to purchase tickets or to enter for a performance.

busy *adj.* **1.** Full of action and life, with too many distracting things going on in the background; e.g., a street scene in a film. **2.** Doing too much; said of an actor who makes many gestures and movements in the course of saying lines.

button *n. Slang.* **1.** The last, climactic note and moment of a musical number, delivered sometimes with a finalizing movement or gesture, so that the audience knows it is time to applaud. **2.** A joke's **punch line**, delivered in such a way as to cap the joke, and make the audience laugh: *to put a button on it.*

buzz *n.* **1.** *Slang* Exciting, excited gossip and rumor surrounding the release of a major feature film, the premiere of a new play or musical, or the activities of an individual actor or star: *Hollywood buzz*; *Broadway buzz.* **2.** An annoying, low-pitched static hum coming from a television or radio.

buzz track The **soundtrack** of ambient noise or **room tone**, parts of which may be inserted or mixed into the main soundtrack of a motion picture.

buyout *n.* In commercials and other venues, a one-time-only flat-rate fee paid to the actor, with no residuals to be paid thereafter.

by-play *n.* Another word for **subplot**, or secondary action that accompanies the main action of a story, and may either reflect it or be a complete contrast to it; e.g., the love stories of the lower-class characters in Shakespeare's *As You Like It*.

C

cabaret (kab 'uh ray') *n.* **1.** A French nightclub, with entertainment in the form of singing and dancing. **2.** A show at a nightclub or in a public room set aside for entertainment; covered in many cases by an **Equity** cabaret contract.

cable television Audiovisual broadcasts from a closed-circuit system that go through fiber-optic or coaxial cables that are connected to the home television sets of subscribers. Thousands of channels are available, including premium channels such as HBO and Showtime that provide work for actors in their original series and movies. The pay scales for actors doing commercials and programs for cable are different from those for **national network**. Called *cable*, for short.

call *n., v.* —*n.* **1.** A notification to actors and staff requiring them to appear for work at specific times. Theater calls are given orally, and posted on a bulletin board; i.e., the callboard in the rehearsal studio or backstage at a theater. Call sheets are distributed on film or television sets: the time of each person's required arrival is listed. **2.** The time when personnel must report: *the call time; union call;* i.e., the time when union stagehands and technicians, members of IATSE, must report for work. They are "on the clock" at the appointed call time. **3.** A warning that a theater performance is close to curtain time: the calls are half hour; fifteen minutes; five minutes; places. In the theater, calls are given over a **PA system**, or by an assistant who goes round to the dressing rooms, in which case the actors should reply "thank you" to indicate that they have heard them. All actors are supposed to begin getting ready by the half hour call at the latest. "Places" indicates that the actors should take their positions for their first entrances, usually five or ten minutes before the curtain goes up. **4.** A **cue** to technicians during a performance for a change in the lighting, the lowering or raising of a fly, and so forth. —*v. t.* **5.** To notify or summon actors or staff to report for work. **6.** To give the cues while running a show. During the performance, the stage manager wears a headset through which he or she communicates to *call the show.*

callback *n.* Any **audition** for a project after the initial one.

callboard; call board Conveniently located bulletin board on which the **sign-in sheet**, notifications of calls, certain notices by unions, and other pertinent pieces of information are posted. In a theater, it is usually outside the dressing room area. In a film studio, it is usually inside the entrance, or in the production office nearby.

call boy *Archaic* A young male who made the rounds of actors' dressing rooms to give them the pre-performance calls. Called a *prompter's boy* in the 18th c.

call-in *n.* An **audience participation** television or radio **talk show** that broadcasts phone conversations with viewers or listeners who telephone to express their views.

call letters The four (sometimes, three) alphabetical symbols designating an individual television or radio station, used for station identification; beginning with the letters W or K, assigned regionally by the FCC.

call man *Hist.* In the 18th c., the person hired by theater management to go round to the actors' lodgings and give them their rehearsal and performance calls for that day or the next.

call sheet The schedule of times when people must report to work for a film shoot, either on the set or for transportation to the studio or location. It includes a list of scenes to be shot, the shooting order, the sets or locations, and any special equipment. The call sheet, prepared at the end of the shooting day by the first and second assistant directors, is subject to approval by the **production manager**. It is posted on the callboard, and copies are handed out.

call time The moment when a performer or crew member must report to the set for a shoot or to the theater for rehearsal, performance, or a **work call**.

camcorder *n.* A portable, handheld video camera with a built-in audiovisual recorder and playback machine. Also called a *video camcorder*.

cameo *n.* A small but choice role in a play or film; hence, *cameo appearance*, usually by a well known actor.

camera *n.* A machine or apparatus for photographing, taping, or filming. In **film** and **television**, the typical cumbersome camera is mounted on a heavy pedestal base on which it can be rolled or transported, together with its own battery pack. There are two basic kinds of television cameras: *live*, i.e., those used for direct broadcasting transmission; and *film*, i.e., those used to broadcast recorded material. Digital cameras are sometimes used on commercial shoots and still digital cameras on photo shoots.

camera leading The backward movement of a camera during a take, with the actors walking towards it.

camera left The side of a set to the left of the camera, as viewed from behind it, looking towards the set. An actor moving camera left moves to his or her right.

camera log The detailed listing of shots taken or about to be taken by a particular camera for a film or television shoot.

cameraperson *n.* The individual who operates the camera during shooting or taping, as well as his or her assistants: the first assistant cameraperson; the second assistant cameraperson, and so forth. Also called *camera operator*.

camera rails Tracks laid down for camera movement during a **tracking shot**.

camera ready Prepared for the shoot. Said of a set, and of an actor in costume and makeup. Background players may be told to report camera ready for their **call time**.

camera rehearsal A full dress **run-through** of actors' moves just prior to doing a **take**, to make sure that a shot is correctly framed and to check camera movements and blocking.

camera report A detailed listing of all the shots taken during a particular shooting session.

camera right The side of a set to the right of the camera, as viewed from behind it, looking towards the set. An actor moving camera right moves to his or her left.

camera test 1. An actor's audition for a media project: **screen test. 2.** A rehearsal for the camera just before shooting or taping, to make sure it is functioning correctly.

camera work Syn. with **cinematography**.

camp *n., v., adj.* [Origin obscure; perhaps fr. *scamp*: a playful scalawag; earliest documented use, 1909, when camp was first associated with the homosexual world] —*n.* **1.** A combination of pose; flip humor; and arch, ironic remarks displaying a knowing attitude; e.g., the humor in some plays by Oscar Wilde or Noël Coward. *Low camp* is ostentatious and banal, as in the case of some drag queens who wear garish makeup and costumes; *high camp* is a more sophisticated show of cleverness and wit. **2.** Certain forms of performance art; e.g., parodies of opera and ballet done by men in **drag**. —*v. i.* **3.** To indulge in such parody or flip humor: *to camp it up*, as Dame Edna, Divine, and Liberace did in their performances. —*adj.* **4.** Pertaining to such behavior. Hence, also *campy*: *a camp remark*; *a campy performance*.

campaign *n.* [Short for *advertising campaign*] A plan and schedule for the release of print work and the airing of commercials for a product.

Canadian Actors' Equity Association The principal performing artists' union for theater people in Canada; based in Toronto. Usually called *Canadian Equity*.

candle snuffer 1. A small hollow cone, open on one side, attached to a long handle; used for putting out tapers. **2.** *Hist.* From the Renaissance until **gas lighting** began in the 19th-c., a person whose job was to put out the lights after a performance, using such an implement, and to relight those that went out during a show, often to great applause.
    See also DECORATOR.

candy butcher *Hist.* The person in a cinema who walked around with a tray suspended on shoulder straps and sold candy and other snacks to audience members before the movie was shown. Called a *butcher*, for short.

canned applause A **recording** of people clapping and expressing approval vocally; inserted at strategic moments into the **soundtrack** of a pre-recorded television show.

canned laughter A recording of people laughing inserted into the broadcast version soundtracks of sitcoms and other comic shows. Adding laughter done by hired actors to a **laugh track** of actual studio audience laughter is called *sweetening*.

cans *n. pl. Slang* **Headphones**.

capacity *n.* The number of places in a theater auditorium or other performance space: *The house was filled to capacity* (i.e., all seats were occupied).

cape and sword play [Fr. Spanish: *la comedia en capa y espada* (lah ko meth' ih yah ehn kah' pah ee eh spah' tha)] *Hist.* A 17th-c. Spanish genre of melodramatic comedy that involved love and honor, aristocratic characters, and their clever and wily servants.

caper film A movie that revolves around the commission of a crime, esp. a bank robbery or other elaborate escapade.

capper *n. Slang* The last joke in a **running gag**, often in a series of three and expected to get the biggest laugh.

captions *n. pl.* Printed subtitles shown at the bottom of a screen, either as translations of a foreign film's dialogue, or for the benefit of the hearing-impaired.

carbon electric arc light. See ARC LIGHT.

carnival *n.* **1.** A public festive event: *a winter sports carnival*. **2.** A traveling show with a variety of entertainments that sets up in fields or other places, usually just outside a town, and provides such amusements as rides, games of chance, weight-lifting contests, and **sideshow** attractions. See also BARKER; CIRCUS.

Carnovsky, Morris (1897–1992) Distinguished **Group Theatre** actor and acting teacher at Brandeis University. Blacklisted during the McCarthy era, he resumed his career at the American Shakespeare Festival in Stratford, CT, where he was famous for his King Lear, Shylock, Prospero, and other leading roles. *The Actor's Eye* (Performing Arts Journal Publications, 1984), written with Peter Sander and with a foreword by John Houseman (1902–1988)—a brilliant actor and the first head of the theater department at the Juilliard School—provides a practical **Stanislavskian** approach to the actor's art. Carnovsky's system involves three simple concepts that subsume a world of complications: the **action**, the object, and the self. The self is the character: who you are as a person. The object is that at which the character's desires are directed; the term may mean a general **objective** or specific objects; e.g., Prospero's magic wand or the map that Lear uses to divide up his kingdom. The action is what the character does to fulfill the objective.

carpenter *n.* In the theater, a person who constructs scenery, as well as a back-stage crew member who maintains it.

carry *v. t.* To have the main burden of keeping a play, movie, or scene going and of holding the audience's attention: the leading players' job.

cartoon *n.* An animated **feature** or short film made with drawings of characters, three-dimensional computer-generated or **motion capture** figures, or claymation figures.
See also CELLULOID; CHARACTER VOICES; ROTOSCOPING.

casino *n.* An entertainment establishment where legalized gambling takes place; e.g., those in Atlantic City, NJ or Las Vegas, NV. **Equity** contracts cover the live shows that are presented in such venues, and provide for seven salary tiers, depending on seating capacity.

cast *n., v.* —*n.* **1.** The actors who are members of a theatrical or cinematic company; hence, *cast list*: a list of such actors. **2.** *Hist.* In the 18th c., the particular type of role an actor played: *His cast was the young aristocratic hero.* —*v. t.* **3.** To hire actors and distribute the roles in a play or film, usually after the *audition process* (also called *the casting process*); actors may be cast by request of a director or producer.

cast against type To hire an actor to play the kind of role that he or she would not ordinarily play or would not usually be considered right for. Cf. **play against**.

cast breakdown The list of parts in a project, together with brief character descriptions; sent to casting personnel and agents.

cast commercial A **promo** for a television show, using actors who are in it.

casting call 1. Syn. with *casting session*. **2.** Syn. with *audition*. **3.** A notice in a trade paper, on a union bulletin board, or elsewhere giving detailed information about an audition; a **casting notice**.

casting couch The sofa in the office of a show business employer or casting person used for sexual purposes when an actor who wants a part in a particular project returns the favor of sex for a role and career promotion. The term is common; the piece of furniture presumably is not.

casting director The person who screens actors for directors and producers by holding auditions, at which they give some direction to the actors. They recommend actors for callbacks, when the actor will see the actual project director. Commercial auditions are recorded by the casting director, and the tape is given to the decision makers. For soap operas, the soap's casting director casts extras, under-fives, and some day players.

casting notice A public notification appearing in trade papers and posted on union bulletin boards and web sites, giving details about auditions; a **casting call**.

casting session 1. The scheduled period of time during which a director, casting director, or other personnel audition actors: *a four-hour casting session*. **2.** The actor's individual audition time with the casting personnel.

cast of thousands Advertising come-on referring to the crowds of background players in a spectacular epic film.

cat calls Boos and shouts expressing disapproval of a performance.

catchphrase; catch phrase *n.* A sentence or phrase that has caught on with the public. In show business, the trademark of a particular performer, esp. a comedian, who has become identified with a phrase he or she repeats over and over; e.g., in Ricky Gervais' television series *Extras*, where the character he plays in a sitcom repeats the line, "Are you 'avin' a laugh? Is 'e 'avin' a laugh?" In the days of vaudeville and radio comedy, there were any number of such phrases: Jack Pearl (1894–1982), playing the champion liar Baron Munchausen on radio in the early 1930s, would tell an outrageous, obviously untrue story, which his straight man would then question. Pearl's reply would be, "Vas you dere, Charlie?" **Syn.** *tag line*; *catchword*.

See the index, p. 351, for a list.

catharsis (kuh thahr' sihs) *n.* [Fr. Greek: *katharsis* (kah *th*ahr' sees)] Aristotle's undefined term for the emotional relief felt by an audience and actors when the feelings of **pity and fear** are relieved by the resolution of a **tragedy**; hence, its general meaning: the purging or relief of upsetting emotion.

cattle call A mass open audition; e.g., when casting extras for a film. Actors line up outside the room where the casting takes place, and, having handed in their pictures and résumés, file past the decision makers, who cast based on looks.

catwalk *n.* A long overhead walkway, sometimes in a system of such walkways, located above a stage in the **flies** of a theater, or over the floor of a soundstage in a film or television studio. Technicians and stagehands can walk along it to hang and check lights, secure or loosen ropes, hang sound equipment, and so forth. Cf. **bridge**.

celebrity wrangler A person who works for the organizer of a publicity or other gala social event and whose job is to arrange for the appearance at the event of a well-known star or other famous person. The wrangler also arranges for transportation and other needs, and looks after the celebrities once they have arrived.

celluloid *n., adj.* —*n.* **1.** The thin, transparent coating that forms the base layer of a film strip. **2.** Each separate clear, transparent plastic sheet on which an **animated feature** character or scene is drawn. Called an *animation cel*; *cel*, for short. A three-dimensional effect is created by photographing the cels (drawings on **celluloid** sheets, arranged on transparent glass trays, laid flat, and photographed from above) of hand-made drawings of décors with the two-dimensional, properly shaded drawings of characters superimposed on them. See also ROTOSCOPING. —*adj.* **3.** A **metonymy** for film: *a celluloid heroine*.

censorship *n.* The regulation and/or suppression of the contents of literary or journalistic works; of dramatic, cinematic and television entertainment material; or of anything spread about or broadcast for public consumption. Material is examined by censors to see if it meets certain criteria; objectionable content is deleted, or entire projects banned. In the early days of television, toilets could not be shown, and married couples had to be seen sleeping separated, in twin beds, usually with a night table between them.

See BLACKLIST; BLACKOUT; BOSTON VERSION; BLEEP; BLUE PENCIL; BOWDLERIZE; FEDERAL COMMUNICATIONS COMMISSION (FCC); HAYS CODE; LICENSE; MPAA RATINGS; TELEVISION RATINGS.

center *n.* Michael Chekhov's term for the place in the actor/character's body where the character lives emotionally. It may be located anywhere on the body: Juliet's center might be her heart; Hamlet's, his head.

center line The dividing line on a theater stage going down its center, from upstage to downstage.

center stage Syn. with **stage center**.

central casting A mythical place where stereotyped actors are given stereotypical roles; *right out of central casting* (i.e., a perfect generic representative of a type): the bluff British colonel; the pert and perky chambermaid; the prim and proper spinster schoolteacher; and so forth. The term comes from an actual Hollywood company called the Central Casting Corporation, a casting service that supplied the movies with crowds of appropriate extras from 1925 to 1976, when it went out of business.

chain pocket The sewn compartment at the bottom of a **house curtain** or other large drapery, containing a length of chain, for purposes of weighing down the curtain.

chamber theater [Fr. chamber music] Small-scale plays involving only a few actors and minimal technical and scenic demands; and the intimate playhouse where they are presented. In Sweden, August Strindberg (1849–1912) wrote such dramas as *Miss Julie* for his own chamber theater.

changes *n. pl.* [Short for *costume changes*] The different costumes required in the course of a play or shoot.

changing booth A small, makeshift dressing room in the wings where costume changes may be effected, e.g., a **quick change**.

channel *n.* **1.** The broadcasting frequency assigned by the FCC to a radio or television **station**, represented by a number. The channel can be accessed by tuning into it; i.e., by turning to it on a numbered dial, or pressing a remote control channel selector button. **2.** A television station. **3.** The path an independently processed sound signal takes when being recorded onto a preservative medium. Audio recording equipment can often record more than one channel at a time; e.g., a two-channel tape recorder.

channel surf To use a television's remote control to go from channel to channel, looking for something interesting, and pausing occasionally to watch part of a broadcast.

chanteur; chanteuse (shan toor'; shan tooz') *n.* [French: male singer; female singer] A cabaret or nightclub singer.

character *n.* **1.** A created, fictional person, whether a written, literary creation or one created through an actor's **improvisation**, as in **commedia dell'arte**. **2.** The personality, moral fiber, distinctive attributes, and qualities of an individual. **Aristotle**

50

defines character as "that which reveals moral choice—that is, when otherwise unclear, what kinds of thing an agent chooses or rejects (which is why speeches [in a drama] in which there is nothing at all the speaker chooses or rejects contain no character)."

character actor; **character actress** Actors playing parts other than that of the leading man or woman or the juvenile leads; also, an actor who plays roles that are far from him or herself (e.g., an eccentric, or a young actor playing an old person).

character biography The life history of the fictional person the actor plays. Many actors write out a biography for their characters, most of which is either clear from the text of the script, or can be deduced logically from it.

character creation In acting terms, bringing to life a theatrical personage, using the actor's own psychology and physicality.

character development The revelation of character and its nuances as they change in the course of a play or film: a job shared by writer, director, and actor.

character makeup Cosmetics, hairpieces, or prostheses that alter an actor's facial features, helping to create the illusion of a different personage. Cf. **straight makeup**.

character part Any role aside from that of the leading actors.

character psychology The workings of a fictional person's mind and personality: "Why do I, the character, want what I want?" Characters are treated by all concerned in their creation (actors, writers, directors, etc.), as well as by the audience, as if they were real human beings, with true concerns, foibles, and an interior emotional life, which is actually the one the actor imparts to a character. For more information on how to use psychology and psychoanalysis in character creation, see my book *Tools and Techniques for Character Interpretation: A Handbook of Psychology for Actors, Writers, and Directors* (Limelight, 2006).

character type. See TYPE.

character voice(s) Alterations of an actor's normal speech sounds and intonation patterns, so as to sound vocally like another, distinctive person; e.g., for a **cartoon** or a **book recording**. In book recording, a man reading a woman character plays the intentions and uses the higher end of the normal range, adding a slight amount of breathiness to the voice. A woman reading a male character plays the intentions and uses the lower end of the range, without trying to imitate a man's voice. The high and low ends of the voice are used to create various **voice qualifier** sounds; e.g., a "creaky" voice; a hoarse or gruff voice; the voice of someone who is old, feeble, or sick.

characterization *n.* **1.** The author's particularized portrait of a fictional person, including psychological and physical traits. **2.** The actor's particular interpretation and physical and psychological embodiment of the character. The Nurse in *Romeo* *and Juliet* is characterized by Shakespeare as an understanding, sympathetic, earthy person with a bawdy sense of humor. But she can be played as older or younger, more or less conscious of bawdiness, and as having more or less refined manners. These aspects of characterization are up to the actor and director.

charges *n. pl.* Accusations of misconduct against an actor by fellow actors or by management. If officially lodged with the union, they may result in disciplinary hearings, and if the person is found guilty, in such penalties as a fine, or even in dismissal from the union, in severe cases. Sometimes, the mere threat of "bringing charges" is enough to cause the performer to reform his or her conduct.

chase film A subgenre of motion picture, or an individual movie in which one of the major pieces of action is the pursuit of one or more characters by other characters. Also called a *chaser*.

chaser *n.* **1.** Bulbs placed in a line or around a border that go quickly on and off in order, one after the other, appearing to chase each other along; used on advertising billboards or theater marquees. **2.** *Slang* Another name for a baby follow spot. **3.** Music played after a show, as the audience is leaving, esp. in vaudeville. **4.** Another word for **exit music**.

cheat *v.* —*v. i.* **1.** In the theater, for an actor to adjust his or her position in order to give the audience a better view. Hence, *cheat down*: to turn slightly downstage; *cheat up*: to turn slightly upstage; *cheat center*; *cheat left*; *cheat right*. **2.** In film or television, to play away from the camera, or to look in a particular direction. Hence, *cheat right*; i.e., to turn the head in that direction. —*v. t.* **3.** In film or television, to place an object (e.g., the product in a television commercial) in the best place for the camera angle; hence *cheat shot*: *Cheat that vase a little to the left!*

cheater cut A scene from the previous episode of an old-time movie **serial** inserted at the beginning of the new episode.

check list 1. The stage manager and assistant stage manager's lists of all tasks that have to be done for the **preset**. **2.** The property person's listing of all the props, except actors' personal props; used during the **preset**.

Check the gate! "Look into the camera lens frame in order to make sure no dust or dirt has gotten into it that might have interfered with the clear taking of a shot!" In film and filmed television commercials or programs, this is the director's instruction, and is usually carried out by the first assistant cameraperson; it is often the last technical job done before moving on to the next take.

Chekhov, Michael (1891–1955) Russian-born actor, acting teacher, and theorist. Perhaps the most innovative, influential extension of Stanislavsky's **system** is the imaginative and simultaneously practical approach of MAT actor Michael Chekhov (playwright Anton Chekhov's nephew), which he taught in Hollywood, where he eventually went after leaving the Soviet Union. Chekhov's *To the Actor on the Technique of Acting* (revised and expanded edition, Routledge, 2002), one of the best in the canon of books on acting, details his methods of work. Probably his most famous technique is the **psychological gesture**. Lisa Dalton's *From Russia to Hollywood: The 100-Year Odyssey of Chekhov and Shdanoff* (Singa Home Entertainment DVD, 2004) is an informative documentary in which many of the actors who studied with Chekhov and George Shdanoff (1905–1998)— another Russian émigré, who taught Chekhov's methods—are interviewed, as well as Shdanoff himself. Leslie Caron talks about the Michael Chekhov use of images: a quick and witty character, who may be very pleased with herself and in a humorous, cheerful mood, might see the **image** of lines dancing before her eyes like a butterfly. This makes the character funny without the actor's even trying to be so, as her droll demonstration shows.

See also CENTER; RADIATE.

Chekhovian (cheh koh' vee uhn) *n., adj. —n.* **1.** An actor devoted to performing the plays of the Russian writer Anton Chekhov (1860–1904). **2.** A scholar who studies the life and works of Anton Chekhov. **3.** An adherent of the philosophy of life and psychological views expressed in Chekhov's works; a devotee of his plays. —*adj.* **4.** Pertaining to the works, and to the bittersweet, melancholy, compassionate, perhaps somewhat pessimistic view of life exemplified in Chekhov's short stories and plays.

chemistry *n.* The intangible quality of the attraction and connection between two romantic leads that makes their relationship believable to an audience.

chest shot A take of an actor's torso from the breast area up.

chest voice The lower register of a person's vocal range, the vibrations of which are felt in the upper chest when a performer speaks or sings.

chew the scenery To overact; to over-emote.

chiaroscuro *n.,* (kyah' roh skoo' roh) [Fr. Italian: light-dark] The interplay of sharply defined light and shadow. Originally a technique in painting, chiaroscuro is also used in theater lighting and filmmaking; e.g., in such black-and-white masterpieces as Orson Welles's *Citizen Kane* (1941) and Carol Reed's *The Third Man* (1949).

Chicago Area Theater (CAT) agreement The **Equity** contract that covers employment in theaters seating 900 or fewer located within Chicago, IL and the area within thirty-five miles of the city.

chick flick A movie made with an audience of women in mind, esp. those under thirty, because it deals with women's life issues and relationships; e.g., *Sex and the City* (2008), based on the television series, or *Divine Secrets of the Ya-Ya Sisterhood* (2002); or because it has a feminist sensibility; e.g., *Thelma and Louise* (1991); or for the dismissive, male chauvinist, anti-feminist reason that it is a light **romantic comedy**.

child actor Any actor who is less than eighteen years of age. The employment of child actors is regulated by child labor laws, such as Coogan's Law, named for the famous child actor Jackie Coogan (1914–1984), and by union rules. Parents, guardians, chaperones, or others in charge of the child's welfare must be present on the set, and in long-term projects, a studio teacher or tutor is hired to continue the child's education.

children's theater Plays performed by adult actors for children. **Actors' Equity Association** Theater for Young Audiences (TYA) contracts cover most employment in children's theater. Also called *theater for youth*; *theater for young audiences*.

child wrangler A person who takes care of child actors hired to do a play, opera, or film during rehearsals and performances, as well as publicity appearances. The child wrangler keeps the children entertained, supervises them, and cues them to go onstage, or takes them to the film set. The job, which is more than just babysitting, is called *child wrangling*: an important aspect of stage managing in productions that use groups of children, as some large-cast Broadway musicals do. A tutor or studio teacher may also function as a child wrangler. Also called a *child coach*.

chitlin' circuit [Fr. *chitterlings*: pork intestines cut into small pieces, boiled or fried; a popular southern U.S. food] *Hist.* From ca. the late 1800s to the 1960s, in the days of segregation, a series of entertainment venues in the eastern, midwestern, and southern United States where it was safe for African-Americans to perform; e.g., the Cotton Club and the Apollo Theater in New York; the Fox Theatre in Detroit; the Howard Theatre in Washington, D.C; and the Second Whispers Restaurant in Greenville, Miss.

choices *n. pl.* Selection among various possibilities for interpreting the character as a whole, as well as for playing each moment or beat in a scene.

choragus; **choregus** (ko ray' guhs) *n., pl.* choragi (–gI) *Hist.* **1.** The leader and trainer of the **chorus** in ancient Greece. **2.** A rich citizen appointed with others, on a rotating basis, to help underwrite the expenses of productions at the **Dionysia**.

choreographed facials Expressions done simultaneously as part of a number in a musical comedy, or by all the actors at once in a farce; e.g., jaws dropped open and eyebrows raised in surprise.

choreographer *n.* A person who devises, arranges, stages, and rehearses dances.

choreography *n.* **1.** The art of devising, arranging, and staging dances; hence, *to choreograph*: the act of doing so. **2.** The dances, taken as a whole, in a ballet, musical comedy, opera, operetta, etc.: *Agnes DeMille's choreography for* Oklahoma; *Marius Petitpa's (1818–1910) original choreography for Tchaikovsky's* Swan Lake. **3.** The order of steps in a particular dance: *the choreography of the minuet.* **4.** The movements and blocking of actors, esp. in crowd scenes; hence, *choreographed movement.*

chorister *n.* A member of a chorus, esp. one that performs classical music.

chorus *n.* **1.** A group of characters, usually of one type, such as citizens, soldiers, or officials, who comment on the action in ancient Greek tragedy. **2.** The ensemble performers who sing and/or dance as a group in a musical theater piece. In **Gilbert and Sullivan**, the male and female choruses play groups of characters (e.g., the crew of sailors (male), and Sir Joseph's sisters, cousins, and aunts (female) in *H.M.S. Pinafore*), and they usually have all kinds of opinions about what is going on. **3.** A group of singers who sing together, either by themselves or in choral pieces; e.g., in liturgical music performed at church services by a choir or as part of a larger ensemble, as in Handel's *Messiah*, written for instrumentalists, solo singers, and a chorus of men and women. There are men's choruses, women's choruses, and children's choruses, such as the famous American Boys' Choir or the Boys' Choir of Vienna. **4.** A piece of music sung by the chorus: *the "Hallelujah" Chorus.* **5.** The **refrain** of a song; or of a number in a musical theater piece.

chorus contract The **Equity** contract covering Broadway chorus workers; also known as a "pink" contract.

chorus master The person who rehearses and conducts the chorus during performances of classical choral works; or who rehearses the opera chorus.

cigarette girl *Archaic* The young lady who walked around nightclubs or movie theaters and sold packs of cigarettes from a tray suspended on shoulder straps.

cineaste (sih' nee ast) *n.* [Fr. French: *cinéaste*; film director] **1.** Someone professionally involved in filmmaking, esp. a film director. **2.** An enthusiast or aficionado of the cinema.

cinema *n.* **1.** *Brit. esp.* A movie house. **2.** The art of motion pictures: *the art of the cinema.* **3.** Motion pictures, collectively: *the cinema.*

cinema organ *Archaic* The large keyboard instrument with pipes, stops, and pedals used for playing live music to accompany silent films.

CinemaScope *n., adj.* —*n.* **1.** *Trademark* 20th Century Fox's name for their widescreen motion picture process. Other trademarked widescreen processes include *Cinerama* and *Todd-AO.* **2.** By extension, any widescreen film process; usually spelled with lowercase letters: *cinemascope.* —*adj.* **3.** Pertains to such a process, or to a widescreen film: *a cinemascope movie.*

cinematographer *n.* An expert artist and scientist who must understand everything from the art of color and the artistic composition of a shot to the precise angle and distance of the camera and the necessary amount and kind of light needed for a scene. **Syn.** *director of photography*, for a motion picture.

cinematography *n.* **1.** The art of photographing motion pictures, including framing and composing shots and dealing with equipment, light issues, color palette, and so forth. **2.** The element or nature of photographic composition in a movie: *beautiful cinematography.*

cinéma vérité (sih né mah' vé: *r*ee té') [French: lit., cinema truth; truth cinema] An improvisational style of filmmaking, meant to simulate candid, unposed, unrehearsed, spontaneous reality; used in both documentaries and fictional narrative motion pictures. Typically, a **handheld camera** is used, as well as **available lighting** or deliberate **flat lighting**. The **long take**, in which the camera keeps rolling, is also a hallmark of this style, which began after World War Two with the French **New Wave cinema**.

See also ALEATORY TECHNIQUE.

cineplex Syn. with **multiplex**.

circle *n.* **1.** *Brit. esp.* The first raised seating area in a theater above the orchestra; the mezzanine or balcony. At the Metropolitan Opera, the balcony above the **grand tier** is called the *dress circle*, and the topmost balcony is called the *family circle*. **2.** Short for the **Stanislavskian** term "circle of **concentration**."

circle theater Syn. with *arena theater*; **theater in the round**.

circuit *n., adj.* —*n.* **1.** A chain of theaters owned by one company, e.g. the Keith circuit. In the days of vaudeville, performers were booked into each successive theater on the circuit; colloquially called a **wheel. 2.** The tour route from one chain theater to another. **3.** A series of particular entertainment venues: *the talk-show circuit*; *the Borscht circuit*. **4.** A chain of cinemas. —*adj.* **5.** Pertaining to the theaters in a chain: *a circuit theater*.

circular file An agent's wastepaper basket, where (according to some cynical actors) most head shots wind up, particularly those that arrive in unsolicited droves.

circumstances *n. pl.* The factors and situations that condition a character's life. **Given circumstances**—a term Stanislavsky borrowed from the poet Alexander Pushkin—are those supplied by the author. Emotional circumstances are internal, and include **character psychology** and relationships. Physical circumstances include time, place, the weather, the temperature, and the character's state of physical health or physical condition. Stanislavsky included production elements (staging, scenery, lighting, costumes, etc.) as circumstances the actor had to deal with.

circus *n.* A form of **variety** entertainment that usually travels from place to place with its equipment, tents, seating, menagerie of trained animals, and performers. The main tent is called the *big top*, which is also a **metonymy** for circus. The tents are set up and the audience sits in tiers of seats surrounding an arena that may contain one or more rings: *a three-ring circus*. The performances are presided over by a **ringmaster**, who is an **emcee**. There may be a publicity parade through town at which performers and circus elephants file down the main street to the enjoyment of the onlookers. Circuses include high-wire acts, trapeze and other acrobatics displays, clowns, bareback horse riding, and other trained animal acts. A large circus may also travel with a **sideshow**.

civilian *n. Slang.* Anyone not professionally involved in show business.

clap *v. t.* To strike one palm against the other repeatedly, making a loud sound, for any of several purposes, e.g., to applaud a performance; as a sarcastic expression of disapproval, clapping two or three times in a slow rhythm; or as a signal to a servant.

clapboard *n.* A slate with two boards, called *clapsticks*, hinged together on one side and attached horizontally to its top. The number of the scene and of the particular take, as well as other pertinent information (date, director, title, cameraman) is written on it in chalk, erasable marker, or removable tape; or, in a current version, in electronic lights on a screen. The clapboard is filmed at the beginning and end of every take, a procedure essential for editing. It also serves to mark the synchronization of the sound with the picture: when the person holding the slate bangs the clapsticks together at the beginning of the take, this is the first sound heard. At the end of the take, the clapsticks are banged together again, and the clapboard is held upside down to signify the end. Also called *clapper board*; *clapstick board*; *number board*; *production board*; *sync slate*; **slate**; *take board*.

claque *n.* Hired audience members who support a particular actor with vociferous applause and/or boo a rival actor whom they are employed to denigrate; hence, *claquer*: a member of a claque.

classic *n., adj.* —*n.* **1.** A memorable, distinguished, and enduring work of art, viewed as setting a standard for excellence. —*adj.* **2.** Pertaining to such an excellent or definitive work: *a classic example of Gothic architecture*; *a classic novel*; *a classic of musical composition*; *a classic motion picture*; *a classic performance*.

classical drama The plays of ancient Greece, including the tragedies of Aeschylus, Euripides, and Sophocles, and the comedies of Aristophanes; and of ancient Rome, including the tragedies of Seneca and the comedies of Terence and Plautus: *classical comedy*; *classical tragedy*; *Senecan tragedy*.
See also AMPHITHEATER; ARENA; ARISTOTLE; COTHURNUS; DIONYSIA; DITHYRAMB; EMELIA; EXODUS; HUBRIS; KORDAX; MASK; PARADOI; PARADOS; SATYR PLAY; SOCK AND BUSKIN; SIKKINIS; SKENE; STASIMON; THEATRON.

classical unities The three principles that must be applied to the writing of a play, according to late 17th- and early 18th-c. neoclassicists, who based this idea on their interpretation of **Aristotle**. They are: *unity of action* (there must be a single story), *unity of time* (the play must unfold either within the actual time its events would take, or at least during the space of one day), and unity of place (everything must unfold in one place). Also called *the three unities*.
See also NEOCLASSICAL DRAMA.

classicism *n.* A 17th- to early 19th-c. school of artistic and intellectual thought, literature, and theatrical presentation that paid homage to Aristotle's aesthetics and to the values of ancient Greece and Rome; more accurately called *neoclassicism*.

clay animation A technology for animated films that uses pliable three-dimensional figures made from modeling clay. Also called *Claymation*, fr. the trademarked name of the technique invented at the Will Vinton Studios in Portland, OR.

Clear frame! "Move away from where we can see you through the camera!" In film, this is a command to someone by a director to move out of camera **range**.

Clear yourself! "Move so we can see you through the camera without interference!" In film, this is a direction to an actor to move so as not to be partially hidden; e.g., if something is casting an unwanted shadow on the actor's face.

cliché *n.* A hackneyed, worn-out, overused phrase, mannerism, or stereotype. In acting terms, this word applies to a stereotyped, banal characterization; to conventional behavior that is supposed to be typical of a situation or physical condition; and to mannerisms supposed to be typical of a character **type**, such as a fop or an old person; in other words, to generalized, **mechanical acting**.

click *v. i. Slang* To be successful with the audience: *His performance clicked.*

cliffhanger *n.* **1.** A film with situations of imminent danger; the audience is kept in **suspense** when, just at the critical moment, the film cuts to another scene. **2.** The end of an old-time movie **serial** episode in which a suspenseful situation remains unresolved, meant to ensure that the spectator will return the following week to see the next episode.

climax *n.* The culminating, or highest, most exciting point of a play or film, after which it soon comes to a conclusion.

clip *n.* [Short for **film clip**.] A brief excerpt from a film, usually meant to be used for publicity purposes.

clip lights Small low-wattage lamps, usually blue in color, clamped to strategic places backstage (e.g., over an entrance to the stage set, or in a **crossover**) and aimed downwards; used during a performance, allowing personnel to see their way.

cloak and sword play *Hist.* A 19th-c. swashbuckling costume melodrama.

cloakroom *n.* The facility in a theater or other venue where patrons may leave their outer wear, umbrellas, packages, etc. during a show, usually requiring a tip to the attendant, who hangs up the coats and gives patrons numbered tickets needed for retrieval.

close *v. t.* **1.** To end the run of a show. **2.** In vaudeville, to be the last act before intermission, or before the final curtain: *to close the first half.* **3.** To draw nearer together as a group, in order to tighten the stage picture: *to close it up.* **4.** To face upstage, fully or partially, with one's back to the audience.

closed rehearsal A rehearsal at which only those involved in the production may be present: no visitors allowed.

closed set A soundstage or location décor from which everyone but the director, actors, and crew involved in a project or a particular take is excluded. Used where secrecy is deemed essential; in the shooting of nude, sex, or other scenes requiring as much intimacy and privacy as possible; or simply to maintain a level of comfort, creativity, and relaxation for all concerned, without the feeling that anyone is being judged by an outsider while a project is in gestation.

close shot A take of an object that is in near focus, but not as near or as detailed as in a close-up, or as far away as a **medium shot**; abbrev. CS in screenplays.

closet drama 1. A play that reads better than it performs; or one that is meant to be read rather than performed. **2.** Such plays, taken collectively as a whole. Also called *literary drama*; *armchair drama*.

close-up *n.* A camera shot that focuses directly on an actor's face, or on any particular object that is in frame to the exclusion of other people or objects; abbrev. CU in screenplays. Close-ups of each principal actor are generally shot after any establishing, master, long, and medium shots. For certain close-ups, a tape will mark the spot on the camera lens frame that the actor is to look at; the mark may be slightly above, below, or to either side of the lens.

closing credits The list shown at the end of a film or television program of the names and positions of cast, crew, staff, and others.

closing notice Notification posted by the management on the callboard of a theater that a show will end its run; hence, *to post notice*. **Equity rules** provide for at least a week's notice to be posted; sometimes two.

cloud border A long, narrow, horizontal piece of scenery painted to look like the sky and hung at the top of a proscenium set.

cloud machine A projector that throws the image of the sky and still or moving clouds onto a backdrop or **cyclorama** on a proscenium stage; used to simulate any kind of meteorological condition. Also called a *cloud projector*.

clown *n., v.* —*n.* **1.** A **circus** performer whose job is to provoke laughter through **slapstick** comedy that is usually done as a form of **mime**. Clowns have their individual, distinctive makeups, costumes, and character specialties, and the art of clowning has a long history. **2.** A comic, esp. a slapstick or **knockabout** comedian. **3.** The character of a fool, jester, or wry philosophical type, who comments on the action and may give advice to other characters, or serve as a **foil**; e.g., Feste in Shakespeare's *Twelfth Night*, the Fool in *King Lear*, Jacques in *As You Like It*, or Arlecchino (Harlequin) in **commedia dell'arte**. —*v. i.* **4.** To joke, act foolishly, or perform in a slapstick manner, whether as part of a circus act or other entertainment, or in real life: *to clown around*.

club *n.* **1.** A performance venue for cabaret, musical acts, singers, and variety entertainment. **2.** A place of entertainment where patrons may dance, purchase refreshments, and/or see performers. **3.** A society, association, organization, or gathering of individuals with common interests as well as the place or building where they meet or go to relax. Yearly dues are paid by members, as well as separate charges for refreshments. Two famous actors' clubs are the Garrick in London and the Players' Club, located in Edwin Booth's house on Gramercy Park South in New York City.

club circuit The series of nightclubs, jazz clubs, rock clubs, etc. that book cabaret entertainers and bands.

club date A **booking** for a singer, comedian, or other performer at a cabaret, etc.

clutter *n.* **1.** Television commercials and announcements broadcast during the breaks in a program. **2.** A page full of print advertisements.

coach *n., v.* —*n.* **1.** A specialist in a particular field who teaches or helps actors preparing for auditions or rehearsing for performance. May be hired by an individual actor or by the management of a production: **acting coach**; **dialect coach**; **dialogue coach**; **voice coach**. —*v. t.* **2.** To teach a performer a particular skill, or generally to help an actor prepare for auditions or performances.

coaching *n.* **1.** The job or act of teaching or helping actors: *private coaching*; *production coaching*: working with actors on a specific area during rehearsals. **2.** Short for *coaching session*.

Coast, the Center of the media industry; i.e., Los Angeles. The West Coast of the United States is always meant.

cold reading The oral interpretation of a hitherto unseen or minimally prepared text; e.g., **sides** or **copy** at an audition or a play read aloud at its first rehearsal.

collective creation The theatrical entertainment devised jointly by the actors in a theater company, usually an improvisational group.

color cover Wearing the same color costume as a **principal** when standing in.

color [films; television] 1. Movies photographed using **stock** that is sensitized to the spectrum of colors. **2.** Television broadcasting received on a TV that displays images using the spectrum of colors.

colorized version A **black-and-white film** that has been tinted either manually or by computer, frame by frame.

color wheel 1. A disc-shaped frame into which gels of different colors can be fitted, each one in a round hole the size of the **spotlight** on which it is used; the wheel can be rotated on the spotlight so that each gel may be used in turn. **2.** A circle on which colors are arranged in the order of the spectrum; used by artists and costume and lighting designers.

comeback *n.* **1.** Appearance in a play or film after having been out of the limelight for some time or after having appeared in one or more flops: *Her comeback was a great success.* **2.** A witty rejoinder in conversational **repartee**.

come back To proceed to the backstage area, esp. the dressing rooms: *I'll come back to see you after the show.*

comedian *n.* **1.** An actor who performs in comedy. **2.** A funny, droll, amusing actor. **3.** A performer who does a comic act in various venues, including comedy clubs, television, nightclubs, and cabarets: *a stand-up comedian.*

Comédie Française (ko mé dee' fro:n seh:z') The French national theater company, founded by Molière's troupe in 1680 and devoted to the presentation of classic drama and comedy. Its home is the Théâtre Français (té a' truh fro:n sé') in Paris.

comedienne *n.* **1.** An actress who performs in comedies. **2.** A female stand-up comic.

come down 1. To descend from the stage into the auditorium. **2.** To lower the intensity of something; e.g., a luminaire or a performance.

comedown *n.* A demotion to playing a lesser role: *It was a comedown to play Osric after having played Hamlet.*

comedy *n.* A play or film that has a happy ending and deals in a light-hearted, witty way with the situations it portrays; meant to provide amusement and to provoke laughter.

comedy of character A play, film, or television show that depends for its humor on the specific persons involved in the situations, as opposed to one that relies more on plot; e.g., such television sitcoms as Jackie Gleason's *The Honeymooners, I Love Lucy, The George Burns and Gracie Allen Show*, and *The Golden Girls*.

comedy of humors *Hist.* A Jacobean subgenre, popularized by Ben Jonson (1573?–1637), dealing with what we would now call psychological humor; i.e., the humor that arises from people's personalities, foibles, etc. It was based on the medieval medical and physiological concept of the four humors (biophysical elements that make the body function as it does): blood, phlegm, black bile, and yellow bile. These humors were thought to determine a person's temperament, which could be sanguine, phlegmatic, melancholic, or choleric, depending on which humor was dominant.

comedy of ideas A play that revolves around a debate concerning politics, philosophy, religion, and the like, but in a humorous way. Characters often represent different points of view in the debate; e.g., in the plays of George Bernard Shaw.

comedy of intrigue A play in which the plot is all-important, and the characters—memorable though they may be—less so than the situations in which they are involved, as in some of the 19th-c. farces of Georges Feydeau.

comedy of manners A play that deals with upper-middle-class or upper-class mores, usually in a sophisticated, witty, sometimes even arch style. The setting is always in a society stratified by class, and class differences and behavior are readily apparent; e.g., many Restoration plays, the satiric comedies of Molière, the late 19th-c. comedies of Oscar Wilde, and some of the 20th-c. plays of Noël Coward, (e.g., *Private Lives*).

See DRAWING-ROOM COMEDY.

comedy of morals Comic plays that deal with ethical issues in an amusing way; e.g., Molière's *Tartuffe*, Oscar Wilde's *An Ideal Husband*.

comedy quartette *Hist.* A team of four vaudeville comics: the first comedian; the straight man; a tramp, who was usually drunk; and a sissified schoolboy dressed in a beribboned, broad-brimmed straw hat and wide lace collar.

comedy team Esp. in vaudeville, a pair of comedians who do an act together: one is the straight man, the other the comic.

Come up and see me some time! Brooklyn-born playwright, screenwriter, and stage and film star Mae West's (1893–1980) sexy **catchphrase**, first used in her Broadway play *Diamond Lil* in 1928 but made more famous in her films.

comic *n., adj.* —*n.* **1.** Another word for comedian, esp. one who does a stand-up or vaudeville act. —*adj.* **2.** Funny, amusing, eccentric, hilarious.

comic relief An amusing or droll interlude in a serious drama or tragedy, meant to relieve tension. Often in the form of a **subplot** in which the secondary characters are supposed to be funny, and that may mirror or contrast with the main dramatic story.

coming attractions The trailers that advertise future offerings of films to be shown at a cinema.

coming-of-age film A motion picture that deals with the rites of passage of the young as they grow from adolescence to maturity; e.g., *Rebel Without a Cause* (1955), *The Graduate* (1967), *Get Real* (1999).

command performance The public or private presentation of a play, opera, or other entertainment project at the behest of reigning monarchs or other heads of state.

commedia dell'arte (ko meh:' dee ah deh lahr' teh:) [Italian: comedy of art] An Italian form of improvisational comedy and comic plays based on standard, **formulaic** scenarios using stock characters, such as Harlequin, Columbine, Pantaloon or Pantalone, Punchinello, and Scaramouche; it began in the late 16th c. Many of the characters wore masks or half-masks. The term *commedia dell'arte* was not actually heard until the 18th c., when the Venetian playwright Carlo Goldoni (1707–1793) used it to refer to scripted plays that he had written—many of which were based on well known commedia stories—as opposed to the *commedia dell'improviso* (ihm' pro vee' zo) or comedy of improvisation. For full information, consult John Rudlin's admirable *Commedia dell'Arte: An Actor's Handbook* (Routledge, 1994).

See also CLOWN; HARLEQUINADE.

comment *v. i.* To let the audience know in some way during a performance what the performer thinks of either the character, the play, the other actors, or the direction.

commercial *n.* A recorded television, radio, or Internet advertisement, as opposed to one that appears in print. Most commercials are thirty seconds long, and the timing is exact; some are sixty seconds or fifteen seconds long—the latter usually being shortened versions of a thirty-second **spot**. Commercial **residuals** can be a lucrative source of income for actors. Agreements regarding residual payments for cable TV and Internet commercials are the subject of sometimes acrimonious negotiations. Radio commercials are covered by AFTRA contracts and television commercials by SAG contracts. Producing organizations must be signatories in order for union members to do their commercials.

See also AGENT; BUYOUT; COMMISSION; CONFLICT; FOREIGN DISTRIBUTION; LEGITIMATE; NATIONAL NETWORK; LOCAL SPOT; PUBLIC SERVICE ANNOUNCE-MENT; PLUS TEN; PROMO; WILD SPOT.

commercial edition The version of an **audiobook** meant to be sold in bookstores or online, for which the narrator is paid at AFTRA's commercial book rates for union members. As opposed to a **library edition** or a recording made as a service to the blind, for which there are special agreements.

commercial singer A vocal artist who sings in radio and television commercials; another term for **jingle singer**.

commercial theater The **venue** where actors and staff work for pay, and producers hope to make a profit.

See also NONPROFIT THEATER.

commission *n.* A percentage of the money earned by a performer and paid to an **agent** or **personal manager** for services rendered in securing a job: *agent's commission*. The usual contractual commission for franchised agents is ten percent. For commercials, the agent takes ten percent of the original session fee, and ten percent of each residual check. If the session fee is **scale**, the agent is not allowed to take a commission, but many actors will give them ten percent anyway, for good will. If a client is **signed** with an agent, ten percent commission is usually due for anything over scale, even if the actor secured the job. A special clause for any necessary exceptions to this rule should be put into the contract the performer signs with the agency. Personal managers often take at least fifteen percent, so the actor who employs both pays twenty-five percent commission—worth it, if the job is well compensated.

See also FRANCHISE; SCALE PLUS TEN; SIGNATORY.

commune *v. i.* Stanislavsky's term for the communication that takes place between actors involved in rehearsing and performing a play, when the actors are in harmony with each other and on the same wavelength.

communication *n.* In theatrical terms, the giving and receiving of ideas and emotions from one actor to another and, in turn, to the audience.

See also LISTEN AND RESPOND; TAKE IT OFF.

compact disc A small, round, coated, plastic, digital **record** played on a CD player or computer, using a **laser** light; abbrev. CD.

company *n.* **1.** Short for **acting company**; *ballet company*; *dance company*. **2.** The personnel, including actors and **backstage** staff, involved in a particular production.

company manager The chief backstage administrator in a theater or on a theater tour in charge of backstage personnel and the acting company. The company manager's jobs include keeping records, making sure the show runs smoothly and as rehearsed, giving out the weekly paychecks, and handling complaints.

compose *v. t.* **1.** In film and television, to frame or arrange a shot. **2.** To write music; hence *composer*: the person who does this. **3.** To put together and organize written material: *to compose a letter*.

composite *n.* **1.** An actor's **head shot** with two or more photos of the actor in it. **2.** Two or more photographs or images in a film combined into one image; hence *composite shot*: a take in which this has been done manually or digitally, as in the **bluescreen process**.

compositing *n.* **1.** The computerized **special effects** process of combining visual elements from different sources into a single scene, the result being as if they were indeed all part of the same scene; used in the **bluescreen process**, to supply the live action shots with a background. The pre-digital technique of compositing by using **superimposition** is as old as silent film. **2.** The act and job of putting together the visual elements for a scene; hence, *compositor*: the person who does this.

composition *n.* **1.** In film and television, the framing, arrangement, and position-ing of all the elements in a shot. **2.** A piece of music: *a musical composition*. **3.** The act of composing music. **4.** A short piece of writing (e.g., an essay) or the act of composing it.

comps *n., v. Slang* —*n.* **1.** [Short for *complimentary tickets*] A free ticket given away by the management of a production. Actors and staff will often be allowed comps for certain performances as part of their contracts (e.g., previews and opening night) or when a producer wishes to **paper the house**. —*v. t.* **2.** To give away free tickets; e.g., to critics reviewing a show, who are always "comped."

computer-assisted lighting system In the theater, the control for stage illumina-tion, using software designed to store light cue data, with the duration of cues, fade time, changes of color, etc., as well as the provisions for manual operation of cer-tain cues by the technician, who runs the computerized system during rehearsals and shows. Also called *computer lighting system*; *memory lighting system*.
See also INTELLIGENT LIGHTING.

concentration *n.* Focus on the task in hand: one of the primary elements of acting, allowing the actor to relax and to feel private, and therefore involved.

Stanislavsky talked of a *circle of concentration*, and the **privacy** that the actor builds around him or herself while rehearsing and performing.
See also FOURTH WALL; PUBLIC SOLITUDE.

concept meeting A **preproduction** gathering of director, designers, and other staff and production personnel to discuss basic ideas about the nature of the presentation of a theater or film project. Cf. **production meeting**.

concert *n.* A public performance of instrumental, orchestral, choral, or vocal music; dance; or of a **spoken arts** event, by one or more individuals: *a jazz concert*; *a rock concert*; *a classical music concert*; *a poetry concert*. Classical music concerts usually take place in a specially built *concert hall*, such as Carnegie Hall, but also sometimes in such outdoor venues as the Hollywood Bowl or New York City's Central Park.

concert film A motion picture of a live musical event; e.g., a recital, a classical orchestra concert, or a rock band performance.

concession *n.* A refreshment bar or souvenir stand at an entertainment venue; e.g., one located in the front lobby and/or upstairs lobbies of a theater: a *concession stand*; hence, *concessionaire*: the person in charge of the stand. Sometimes run by an outside company that rents it on a contract called a "concession," whence the name for such a stand.

condenser mike See MICROPHONE.

confidant *n.* A supporting character who is the friend and adviser to a principal character (e.g., Horatio in *Hamlet*), sometimes acting as the voice of moderation and reason (e.g., Philinte in Molière's *The Misanthrope*), or a servant in whom the master confides, and who is his **foil** and counterweight (e.g., Leporello in Mozart's *Don Giovanni*). Cf. **sidekick**.

confidentiality agreement A legal document signed by actors and others in which they consent to keep secret any information about a product they may be involved in advertising, or a project they may be doing. Such an agreement is signed at an audition for a commercial, or on the set when an actor has been booked for a commercial, video game, or other project. Also called *non-disclosure agreement*.

conflict *n.* **1.** Confrontation and struggle; antagonistic desires and needs that lead to struggle. Conflict, it is often rightly said, is the heart of every drama: if there is nothing to fight for or against, there is nothing of interest for either the actors or the audience to be concerned with. See also AMBIGUITY; AMBIVALENCE; PLAYING OPPOSITES; SUPPRESSION; REPRESSION. **2.** Incompatible interests; e.g., with regard to a **commercial**: *a conflict of interest*. If an actor has made a commercial that is still running, he or she is then precluded from advertising a similar product (e.g., a car or a breakfast cereal) unless and until the actor is **released** by the producers of the first commercial. A *conflict sheet* must be signed, often at the **audition**, in which the actor affirms that there is no such conflict of interest. See also FIRST REFUSAL.

console *n.* **1.** A lighting or sound control **board**. **2.** A **video game** unit.

constructivism *n.* An approach to play production (and esp. scenery) that uses abstract pieces resembling those seen at building sites, factories, or children's playgrounds.

See MEYERHOLD, VSEVELOD.

contact list 1. In the theater, the list of names and addresses of all the personnel involved in a production. Also called *contact sheet.* **2.** In film, the list of all the companies involved in supplying everything from food to lumber or lighting equipment for a particular project.

contact sheet 1. In the theater, the list of the personnel's names and addresses. **2.** A large photographic sheet onto which all the shots from a roll of film are printed in their original, small negative size. An actor can select head shots by viewing the photos taken during a **photo session** through a **loupe**. In film, a director, editor, and cinematographer can see shots of a scene in order and begin to make editing decisions.

continental seating Arrangement of theater places in a mass block, without a longitudinal center aisle to create left and right banks of seats, as opposed to **American-plan seating**; typical in European theaters. Also called *continuous-row seating.*

continuity *n.* One of the most important jobs in film. A combination of the consistent placing of props and other scenic elements every time a scene or part of a scene is shot and the repetition by actors of their physical positioning, movements, and gestures, even if they read the lines differently in every take.

continuity supervisor The person in charge of continuity. Also called *continuity clerk*; *continuity girl* (in the old days, the position was almost always held by a woman); *script clerk*; *script girl*; *script supervisor*.

continuous action Apparent seamlessness in the ongoing, sequential events in a scene, edited from takes done from different angles, distances, and points of view; a **convention** accepted automatically by viewers.

contract *n.* In actors' show business terms, a renewable written legal agreement between a performer and a talent agency securing representation for the actor and commissions for the agent, usually for between one and three years; or between the performer and the producer of a project providing for AEA, AFTRA, or SAG terms of employment, working conditions, salary, any other incremental expenses (e.g., rental of the actor's own wardrobe) and for regular contributions by the producer to the union's pension and health funds. General contract terms are arranged between the unions and producing organizations; such items as salaries, fees, wages, and allowances for expenses are often negotiable, at least for well known actors. Each contract has its own booklet of rules and conditions. No actor should start work without signing a contract. In the theater it should be signed at the first rehearsal, if not before. In the media, it should be signed soon after the actor arrives on the set. The actor should at least see that the contract is there to be signed (even if that is done later in the day) or be assured by a union representative that the contract is on its way. Take nobody else's word: notify your agent, who may advise you what to do, and call the union if the situation is at all unclear, and/or if the contract is not there. A contract is sometimes sent well ahead of time to agents so that they can go over its provisions, and the actor may sign it in the agent's office; the agent will then send it back to the producer.

For a listing of union contracts, see the index, p. 371.

contract player An actor who has a legal arrangement with a studio to perform in its film projects. In the days of the **studio system**, the producers had a **stable** of such actors "under contract," who worked regularly.

control board. See BOARD; CONSOLE.

control booth. See BOOTH.

control room Soundproof room in a film, radio, or television studio from which audio and video aspects of production or broadcast are monitored by various expert technicians and engineers seated at consoles and supervised by the director and the *chief engineer*, in charge of technical matters. Communication with the floor is effected through headsets or by means of a loudspeaker system. *Brit.* **Gallery**.

convention n. Any cinematic, playwrighting, and performance practice or device that the audience accepts, choosing to ignore its essential unreality, such as the **aside** or the **soliloquy** in stage plays: *a theatrical convention*; *a dramatic convention*. In musical comedy or comic opera, the chorus singing en masse, and the alternation of musical numbers and dialogue scenes, are theatrical conventions; musical numbers in which the characters express their feelings and emotions are themselves a convention. In film, the convention that we can see a single scene from more than one angle or direction or **point of view** as it is proceeding is essential, as are the cinematic conventions of **action cutting** and **continuous action**.

cook *v. t. Slang* **1.** To be in fine fettle when performing: *That actor was cooking tonight!* **2.** To **wash** part of the stage with esp. bright lights.

cool fogger A **fog machine** that uses dry ice to create the effect of mist.

copy *n.* Lines; script, esp. television and radio commercial scripts; or books prepared for recording.

copyholder *n.* In book recording, the person who follows the book along with the reader; a job done by the director of the recording, or by the **sound engineer**. Also called *monitor*.

copyist *n.* The person who copies out the parts for each instrument in an ensemble. Also called *music copyist*.

copyright *n.* Legal ownership of an artistic property by its creator, his or her immediate heirs, his or her estate, or someone to whom such ownership is assigned, entailing the right to license, distribute, or otherwise dispose of the property in question. The U.S. copyright law of January 1, 1978 provides for the lifetime ownership of such a property, and keeps the copyright in force for seventy years after its creator's death.

See also MUSIC RIGHTS; PERFORMANCE RIGHTS ORGANIZATION; PIRACY; PUBLIC DOMAIN; STAGE RIGHTS.

copyright performance *Brit.* The presentation of a theater piece, usually not fully mounted or rehearsed, to insure the author or authors' legal rights to the property, esp. in the 19th c. when plays and musical theater pieces were pirated and unauthorized productions were mounted; e.g., in the case of early **Gilbert and Sullivan** comic operas.

copywriter *n.* The person at an ad agency who writes the text for ads and commercials.

corrections session Scheduled time for fixing errors made during a book recording. Also called *pick-up session.*

costar *n., v.* —*n.* **1.** A leading performer who has equal **billing** with another leading performer. —*v. i.* **2.** To have equal billing with another leading performer.

costume *n., v.* —*n.* **1.** Clothing worn by an actor for a performance. Costumes may be designed and manufactured for a particular project, rented from the actor or from a costume storage company, or purchased ready-made. **2.** In the pl., a theater's **wardrobe** department, and its personnel. When a **dress parade** is due to start, the director or stage manager might say to an assistant, "Can we have costumes out here, please?" In other words, "Will the wardrobe people who can deal with costume problems please come into the auditorium?" —*v. t.* **3.** To clothe an actor for a character; to supply such clothing.

costume call A summons to the theater for actors to try on their wardrobe for the first time, so that they can begin to get used to the clothing, and so that adjustments may be made. Often held before a **dress parade**.

costume designer The artist-craftsperson who draws the designs for clothing to be worn by the actors during performances, selects the fabrics and accessories, supervises and sometimes participates in the sewing and construction of the clothing, and oversees the actors' costume fittings. The costume designer must be an expert in drawing, painting, materials, tailoring, and in period styles and art.

See also STYLIST.

costume film A motion picture set in an era other than the contemporary one.

costume fitting A **session** in which actors are measured for wardrobe or try the clothing on in preliminary, intermediate, and final stages. A separate fee is paid to the actor, apart from the regular salary, and the times when an actor may be called are contractually provided for. Photographs of the actors in costume are taken, and filed for reference purposes. In a film, it may be necessary to use such photographs for purposes of **continuity**; e.g., in order to make sure that the actor looks the same in two halves of a scene that may be shot days apart. Also called *wardrobe fitting*.

costume parade Syn. with **dress parade**.

costume play A drama written or set in a period other than the present day.

costume plot The list of costumes for a theater production in the order in which they are used, including when and where costume changes are to be made.

costume rehearsal A **rehearsal** that takes place when actors are first given more or less complete **wardrobe**. The focus of the rehearsal is on dealing with the costumes, and on any difficulties that may be encountered, particularly in the case of period plays or films.

costume shop The atelier where the costumes for a play or film are manufactured. Directed by a shop manager and employing cutters, drapers, stitchers, and other craftspeople.

costumier; costumer *n.* **1.** A supplier of clothing for productions. The costumes may be ready-made and taken off a rack, or manufactured from designs supplied by the **costume designer**. **2.** A person who measures performers for **wardrobe** during a **costume fitting**. **3.** A person who sews and puts together costumes.

côté cour/côté jardin (ko: té koor'; ko: té' zhahr dan') [French: court, or courtyard side; garden side] The charming French designations for **stage left** and **stage right**, respectively; often called *cour* and *jardin*, for short. Before the French Revolution, stage left was called *côté de la reine* (ko: té duh lah reh:n') [queen's side], and stage right, *côté du roi* (ko: té dü rwah') [king's side].

cothurnus (ko thuhr' nuhs) *n., pl.* —ni (–nI) [Latin; fr. Greek: *kothornos*] *Hist.* A calf-length, heavy, laced boot worn by tragedians in ancient Greece and Rome to give them stature, limiting their movement enormously, and requiring athletic strength. **Syn.** *buskin.*
　　See SOCK AND BUSKIN.

couch potato Someone who sprawls on a sofa, munching snacks and watching the **boob tube** for hours on end.

cough and a spit *Brit.* A **bit part**. Also heard as *two lines and a spit*.

cough button A cutoff switch on a radio station microphone. Pressed to stop the sound for an instant when an announcer has to clear his or her throat, cough, or make any extraneous sound. Also called a *cough drop*.

Council of Resident Stock Theaters (CORST) An organization of seasonal theaters that employs **Equity** actors working under resident dramatic and musical **stock** contracts.

Council of Stock Theaters (COST) Agreement The **Equity** contract that covers employment in non-resident dramatic and musical theaters; there are five salary tiers.

count *v. t.* **1.** In dancing, to go numerically through the choreographed steps in order, usually silently to oneself. When a choreographer is staging a dance number, he or she will count the steps out loud while rehearsing with the dancers. **2.** In music, to go numerically through the beats, usually silently to oneself, in order to make an entrance at the right time: *to count the beats*. In early rehearsals, a conductor will count the opening upbeat and downbeat out loud, and the orchestra or band will start playing, or the singer singing on the correct downbeat.

counter-cross; **counter** *v. i.* To move in the opposite direction, away from an actor who is making a **cross**: *counter left*; *counter right*.
   See also DRESS, def. 6.

counter-throughline *n.* That which opposes the **throughline** of the action leading to the fulfillment of the **superobjective**.

counterweight system The arrangement of lines, ropes, pulleys, sandbags, etc. that hold flies and other scenery in place to battens or rails.

count the house *Slang.* To **walk through** a performance, not paying much attention to the task in hand. It was apparently the practice of some 19th-c. actor-managers to look at the audience during a long speech, calculating the box office receipts by counting the number of spectators present in the auditorium.

coup de théâtre (koo' duh té ah' truh) [French: theatrical master-stroke; *coup* means blow, strike, hit, etc. depending on the context] **1.** A striking, thrilling theatrical effect; a *dramatic stroke* or *dramatic coup*. In the 1963 production of *The Tempest* at the Stratford Shakespeare Festival in England, Prospero commandingly raised his magic staff to bring on the storm. Lightning flashed, and part of the back wall of the set fell away in a jagged pattern and with a loud crash. **2.** In playwriting, a startling, thrilling plot development or turn of events that takes the audience unawares. **3.** In acting, a virtuosic moment in a performance.

couplet *n.* A set of two rhymed lines. In verse drama, often in iambic pentameter; and frequently used at the end of a scene in Shakespeare; e.g.: *The time is out of joint; O, cursed spite,/ That ever I was born to set it right!/ Nay, come, let's go together. [Exeunt.]* (*Hamlet*, act 1, scene 5)

courtroom drama A play or motion picture that revolves around a legal case, and unfolds almost entirely in the course of a trial at law.

court theater A playhouse located in a castle, palace, or other royal venue and meant for the limited audience of royalty and other aristocrats who attended plays there. Drottingholm in Sweden has a working court theater where operas are presented; on visiting tours of the theater, 18th-c. stage technology is demonstrated.

cove *n.* A cover or concealment for luminaires installed in the **house**.

cover *n., v.* —*n.* **1.** Syn. with **understudy**. **2.** Short for *cover charge.* —*v. t.* **3.** To understudy: *He covers the role of Laertes.* **4.** To conceal a mistake during a performance; e.g., to **stall** during a **stage wait**. Hence, *to cover for*: *She covered for him when he missed his entrance.*

cover charge In nightclubs or cabarets, the cost of entertainment. Some clubs have a two-drink minimum plus a cover charge. Called a *cover*, for short.

cover girl The female **model** on the cover of a magazine.

cover set A duplicate or replica of an exterior film décor or part of it, ready for use either in case of inclement weather, or as a background for close-ups and other shots.

cover shot 1. A take of a scene already considered satisfactory, done "for safety" in case part of it should turn out to be unusable. Also called *insurance shot*; *protection shot*. **2.** A take of optional transitional material, used to give a unifying effect to a scene.

cowboy shot A take of a person from the knees up, as in old-fashioned American westerns.

crab dolly A small, wheeled truck that can move right or left, forwards or backwards, on which a camera is mounted; used to follow the action during a take.

crack up To **break character** by bursting into laughter at what the actor finds irresistibly funny. *Brit.* To corpse.

craft service(s) The company that provides food and drink during a shoot, catering meals and servicing snack tables. Employees of the company often work in conjunction with members of the film or television crew assigned to catering and craft service jobs.

craft union A labor organization for those who work in a particular field requiring special knowledge and skills; e.g., organizations of stunt performers, **IATSE**.

crane shot A take of a scene in which the camera is placed overhead on the platform of the movable arm of a crane (a motorized vehicle meant for raising, lowering, and moving materials by means of a long, projected arm mounted on a swivel). There are three seats on the platform: for the director, cameraperson, and camera assistant.

create *v. t.* **1.** To engender; to bring something into being that was not there before; e.g., a work of art. Hence, *creative arts.* **2.** To originate or to be the first person to play a particular role: *Richard Burbage created Hamlet.*

creative mood; **creative state** The condition and feeling of having a desire to engender something; e.g. the actor's feeling, desire, and readiness to rehearse or perform, brought about by a combination of concentration, relaxation, and inspiration.

71

creature shop A factory or atelier where monsters, robots, and other non-human characters, and working models of them, are manufactured.

credit union A private, federally insured bank run by a union or other organization for its members only; e.g., the Actors Federal Credit Union.

credits *n.* The listing in a theater program, film, television broadcast, or video game of the personnel involved in the show. Each individual has a *credit*: an acknowledgement of the particular job done.

See also BILLING.

creeper *n.* An actor who gradually moves too close to the camera during a take, and is off his or her **mark**.

crew *n.* The backstage workers in a theater, some of whom are hired as temps to load in scenery and equipment, some of whom will work the show; the technicians and production workers behind the film and television camera; and the stagehands. Professional crew employees are members of the International Alliance of Theatrical Stage Employees, Moving Picture Technicians, Artists and Allied Crafts of the United States, Its Territories, and Canada (**IATSE**).

critic *n.* A person who reviews a performance event by analyzing, judging, and evaluating it; a **reviewer**: *a film critic*; *a music critic*; *a theater critic*. Ideally, critics have training and background in the fields for which they review events. In Great Britain, the Critics Circle was formed in 1913 as an informal, honorary organization that saw to the professional interests of its members and allowed them to meet as a kind of **club**. The New York Drama Critics Circle presents the annual Drama Critics Circle awards for theater.

croon *v. t.* To sing in a low, soft, evenly modulated, soothing, mellow voice, drawing out the sounds almost seductively, using more of the head voice than the chest voice. The opposite of **belt**. Hence, *crooner*: the song meant to be delivered in this manner; and the vocalist who sings this way; *crooning*: the style and act of singing in this manner, associated with certain male pop singers; e.g., Perry Como; Bing Crosby, and many others. Made possible once the voice could be amplified electrically, and did not have to be projected. It is still used in pop singing, musical comedy, and nightclub acts.

cross *n., v.* —*n.* **1.** A move from one place to another on the stage or in front of the camera. —*v. i.* **2.** To make a move from one place to another, symbolized by "X"; e.g., XR: cross, or crosses right.

cross angle A shot with actors' profiles or other subjects seen either on the right or left side of the screen, while the main focus of the shot is what is past or beyond them. Also called a *raking shot*.

cross-cutting *n.* A film editing **technique** that consists of assembling two scenes that take place simultaneously at two different locations and alternating takes from each, maintaining the viewer's impression of simultaneity; similar to **parallel film editing**.

cross-fade *n., v.* —*n.* **1.** In the theater, the slow dimming of the lights in one scene as the lights for the next scene simultaneously come up. **2.** In film, a scene that dissolves as another comes up simultaneously on the screen to replace it; similar to **dissolve.** —*v. t.* **3.** In the theater, to dim the lights for one scene slowly as the lights for the next scene are coming up. 4. In film, to dissolve one scene as the next one comes onto the screen.

crossover *n.* The space behind a proscenium set that allows people to go from one side of the stage to the other. In some theaters, it is very narrow, and in all theaters, extreme quiet is necessary during a performance. Some stages are so small that they have no crossover, and in some theaters the crossover is under the stage.

crotch lights The luminaires placed on a **light tree** two to three feet above the stage floor.

crowd *n. Slang.* **1.** The audience: *We had a good crowd this evening.* **2.** *Brit.* The acting company of which one is a member: *He toured with a good crowd.*

cue *n., v.* —*n.* **1.** A signal for someone to take a particular action; e.g., for the lighting technician to lower or raise the lights. For actors, a cue is an incorporated part of the dramatic action. It means any of several things: an **entrance** cue may be the signal that the actor is supposed to start performing, or to enter; a **line cue** is the signal to deliver the next line; a **light cue** may indicate a move to a certain place: *Your cue to move is when the lights go on.* The cue to enter may be a hand signal from a stage manager, a **cue light** going off, or a word or phrase the actor waiting to make an entrance hears from a character on stage. **2.** A conductor's hand signal to a musician to make an entrance (i.e., to begin singing or playing). —*v. t.* **3.** To give someone a signal to do something immediately; *cue the lights*: signal the lighting technician to adjust the lights; *cue the actor*: give the actor a cue; *cue a singer*: signal a singer to begin.

cue card 1. A large paper board on which an actor's lines are written. Used for on-camera television **commercial** auditions, where they are placed either below or to one side of the camera, and during television broadcasts, when a stagehand holds them up for the performer. Also unkindly called an *idiot card*. **2.** In the theater, the written listing of scene change assignments for crew members. Also called a *cue sheet*.

cue light 1. A small lamp, often blue in color, placed just outside an entrance to the stage set; it is turned off, if lit, or on, as a signal to an actor that it is the moment to enter. **2.** A backstage light used to warn a crew member that a task is imminent. Sometimes a system of two lights of different colors; e.g., green as a warning, and red as a go.

cue line The words spoken by an actor at the end of a speech, automatically signaling the other actor that it is his or her turn to speak. Cf. **line cue.**

cue lines To drill dialogue; i.e., to help an actor by going over his or her text, giving the cues or cue lines, and prompting the actor when there is a lapse of memory.
See also RUN LINES.

cue-to-cue *n.* A specific kind of **technical rehearsal** or **lighting rehearsal**, in which only the cues are rehearsed, so that when one lighting, sound, or effects cue is fully dealt with, the rehearsal immediately skips to the next, without a full scene being rehearsed by the actors, until all the cues have been dealt with in order. Sometimes, actors are not called for a cue-to-cue; at other times, their presence is necessary; e.g., when rehearsing follow spots.

cue track A recorded sound track made during a take, to be used later as a guide when looping or dubbing. The cue track records every sound heard during a take, including those interfering with the desired sound of the dialogue; e.g., a dog barking during an outdoor location shoot.

cult classic A movie or television show that has developed a following of fans; e. g., *The George Burns and Gracie Allen Show*, *The Rocky Horror Picture Show* (1975). Hence, *cult film*; *cult movie*.

cup and saucer drama *Hist.* A particular kind of 19th-c. realistic play in which tea was served, and the characters sat around discussing social issues; e.g., Thomas William "Tom" Robertson's (1829–1871) problem plays, such as *Caste*: POLLY *meantime has poured out tea in two cups, and one saucer for* SAM, *sugars them, and then hands cup and saucer to* HAWTREE. (act 3)

Curses! Foiled again! [Source unknown] The quintessential, stereotypical line said by an oft-defeated, mustachio-twirling villain in a melodrama.

curtain *n.* **1.** The huge cloth drapery that masks a proscenium stage, separating it from the audience. Also called a *house curtain*. **2.** Any drapery that serves for masking on a stage; e.g., **tabs** or **blacks**.

Curtain! The direction from the stage manager to the stagehand in charge of the curtain either to open or close the curtain. As a warning that the direction is imminent, the stage manager may say, "And . . . curtain!" or "And . . . curtain open!" or "And . . . close curtain!" Alternatively, the stage manager might say, "Bring up [or bring down] the curtain!" or "Raise [or lower] the curtain!" Also heard are, "Curtain going up!"—syn. with "Curtain up!"; and "Curtain going down!"—syn. with "Curtain down!"

curtain call The summoning of actors to give an acknowledgement at the end of the performance of the audience's appreciative applause, and the acknowledgement itself. Many curtain calls are staged, or choreographed, particularly in the case of musical comedies. All actors must report for a curtain call unless they are specially exempted.

curtain line 1. The very last spoken line in a play, just before the closing of the curtain. **2.** The line across a stage that marks where the house curtain separates the stage from the audience.

curtain music Live or recorded instrumental music played just before the beginning of a play, signaling that the curtain is about to open.

curtain raiser 1. A short play, operetta, or sketch that is performed before the main performance event of the evening. **2.** The opening act in a vaudeville variety show.

curtain speech A brief, informal discourse delivered to the audience either before or after a show by someone from the management or by a performer in the show, standing in front of the curtain or on the set. E.g., that typically given by the manager of an Off-Off Broadway company telling the audience something about the play they are about to see, and appealing for a charitable contribution.

curtain time The scheduled moment for the beginning of a performance. The curtain is often held beyond the scheduled time, to allow for late audience arrivals. Announced for eight o'clock, the real curtain time on Broadway is 8:10.

custard-pie *adj.* Pertains to the kind of **slapstick** comedy routine, or *pie-throwing humor*, seen in vaudeville and silent films, in which a custard pie is thrown by one actor at another, the other actor throws a pie back, and so forth.

cut *n., v.* —*n.* **1.** Something deleted, eliminated, or excised from a script, score, film, etc. —*v. t.* **2.** To eliminate something from a script or score. **3.** In film or tape editing, to separate or sever one piece of film or tape from another and to attach or splice it to another piece of film or tape. **4.** In film editing, to proceed directly from one scene to the next without any fade, cross-fade, or other form of transition. **5.** *Archaic Slang* To make a **record**: *cut a record*.

Cut! "Stop what you are doing immediately!" The command given when a film or television scene is finished, or when the director feels it is not going well: the camera stops rolling and the actors stop acting, after a brief pause. During a radio or television talk show, the command to cut is signaled by a single finger drawn across the throat, like a knife, often accompanied by a mouthing of the instruction, "Cut!"

Cut and hold! "Actors, stop what you are doing, but don't move off your marks, and maintain your positions! Crew, put your equipment on pause!" In film, this direction is usually given when there is a technical glitch that is expected to be solved quickly and expeditiously, so that filming or taping can resume immediately.

cutaway *n.* An inserted shot that takes the audience away from the immediate main action in a scene to some other place or time; the main action resumes just after the cutaway shot. A cutaway may be a brief **flashback**; or **flash**, e.g., from the main action of firemen fighting to rescue someone in a burning building, to the people inside. **2.** A man's formal tailcoat, often used as part of a costume in drawing-room comedies. **3.** A drawing, model, or cross-section of something (e.g., a **set piece** of a room masked by a removable wall) with at least part of its outer layer removed to reveal its insides.

cut in To interrupt another actor's lines by speaking or doing something, whether as part of the writing or playing or because of jumping a cue.

cut-in shot A brief sequence inserted into a scene, amplifying the action and calling attention to something, e.g., a gun or a knife in a fight scene, or a hand reaching for a weapon; a letter that is being read, so that the audience can read it, too. Called a *cut-in*, for short.

cutter *n.* **1.** The assistant to the film editor. **2.** *Archaic* A film editor. 3. The expert craftsperson in a **costume shop** who cuts the cloth into patterns for sewing together.

cutting room The fully equipped studio where film and television editing is done; the editing room. The cutting room floor, as all actors know, is where the discarded film or tape of unused portions of their performance—or of an entire performance that has been excised—traditionally winds up, as the editor cuts it out of the roll and throws it on the floor, from which it will be swept up and sent to a landfill.

cut to An indication of a transition in a film script, telling the reader what the next scene or shot will be.

cycle *n.* The thirteen-week period of time during which a commercial is shown or is **on hold**; a new cycle requires payment to the actor, either of a **holding fee** or, eventually, of **residuals**.

cyclorama (sI' kluh ra' muh) *n.* A gently curved backdrop that stretches across the entire back of a theater set, masking the back walls of the stage from the audience. Flats or other set pieces may be placed **below** it. Called a *cyc* (sIk'), for short.

D

daikon (dī' kon') *n.* [Japanese: white horseradish-turnip, often pickled] *Slang* The Japanese term for a **ham** actor.

dailies *n. pl.* The unedited film scenes shot on one day and developed immediately for viewing the next by the director, cinematographer, editor and, often, the actors. Before the director moves on to the next scene, the dailies must be approved, and decisions made about whether reshooting is necessary. Also called *rushes*.

dance *n., v.* —*n.* **1.** The art of moving in a choreographed or improvised rhythmic pattern, usually in time to music; hence *dancer*: one who practices the art of the dance. **2.** A particular pattern of steps done in a preset, consecutive series; e.g., *minuet*; *waltz*. **3.** The music to which such a pattern is executed by the dancers, or listened to as music by itself: *a waltz by Johann Strauss*; *a dance suite*. **4.** Choreographed movement in a musical theater piece, or in a ballet, modern dance, or other program. —*v. t.* **5.** To move or step in a rhythmic, choreographic pattern, often to music.
    See also BALLET; CHOREOGRAPHY; INTERPRETIVE DANCE; MODERN DANCE.

dance band Group of instrumentalists who play at social events, weddings, and in dance halls or other venues.

dance belt An athletic supporter with a wide, elastic waistband worn by male dancers and by actors in **tights**; e.g., in a Shakespearean play.

dance captain The member of a musical comedy chorus appointed to be in charge of the dance numbers, and to make sure they are maintained as rehearsed.

dance hall A public room, building, or other establishment where people pay an admission fee to dance to the music of a live band or to recorded music played by a **disc jockey**; sometimes, dance partners are available for hire, and, often, refreshments may be purchased.

dark *adj. Slang* **1.** Closed. **2.** A permanent or temporary closing of a theater: *The theater was dark while they loaded in and set up the scenery.* **3.** Pertaining to the particular day or days during the run of a show when there is no performance scheduled and the cast and staff have their contractual day off: *The theater is dark on Monday. Monday is our dark day.* **4.** Pertaining to ironic comedies of disturbing morbidity; i.e., **black comedy**.

date movie A film considered pleasant viewing for a couple on an evening out; often, a **romantic comedy**.

day for night 1. In film, the technique of shooting a nighttime exterior scene during daylight hours, using a special blue filter—called a **night filter**—that allows it to seem as if the scene is taking place at night. **2.** The shooting itself: *day for night shooting.* **3.** The shoot or shot using such technology: *a day for night* *shoot*; *a day for night shot*. Such filming is a central aspect of François Truffaut's *Jour pour nuit* (Day for Night; 1973), where you can see the technique in action.

day-out-of-days schedule The contractually arranged day or number of days out of a weekly shooting schedule on which an individual performer may be called.

day player In film and television, an actor who is hired by the day for one or more days to play a small role of five lines or more; a category in AFTRA and SAG contracts. Cf. **under-five**.

day shoot Filming that starts early in the morning, and may go until dusk.

daytime drama Taped, ongoing television series plays, broadcast mornings and afternoons, but not during evening and primetime hours. Also called *daytime serial*; *soap opera*.

dead-hung *adj.* Pertains to lighting instruments or scenery that remain in the same position throughout a performance, as opposed to luminaires that will move up or down, or **flies** that will be raised and lowered during a show.

deadpan *n., adj.* [Fr. a combination of "dead" and "pan," 1920s slang for *face*] —*n.* **1.** Subtly understated, dry, but pointed comedy and comic playing or performing, in which a comedian uses an impassive, neutral expression (without showing a change of emotion) when uttering a joke, reacting to something, or doing funny bits of business. —*adj.* **2.** Pertains to the facial expression, type of comedy performing, or comedian just described: *a deadpan expression*; *deadpan comedy*; *deadpan performance*; *a deadpan comedian*. E.g., Buster Keaton, with his hang-dog look and poker face.

dead spot 1. A poorly lit, small area of a stage. **2.** An area in an auditorium where the sound is poorly heard.

deaf theater Plays performed in sign language by deaf actors, such as those presented by the National Theater of the Deaf (NTD), who tour the United States and other countries with their productions. They perform in a heightened, theatrical version of American Sign Language, while hearing actors on stage in costume simultaneously translate the dialogue and act as the characters' voices; the majority of the audience is hearing. Sign language is not international, and every country has its own deaf theater using the national sign language.

debut *n., v.* —*n.* **1.** A performer's first job in a particular venue: *a Broadway debut*; *a film debut*. —*v. i.* **2.** To make a first appearance in a particular venue: *She debuted on Broadway in a musical comedy.*

decelerator *n.* In falling stunts, a cable worn attached to a special harness, and controlled by technicians who play the cable out gradually. The stuntperson attached to the decelerator falls slowly until the cable stops, on the director's **"Cut!"** **Wire removal** digitally eliminates all trace of the cable, and the fall can be speeded up in the **final cut**.

deck *n. Slang* [Fr. nautical terminology; hence, the 19th-c. slang term *main deck*: the part of the stage seen by the audience] **1.** The stage area, esp. **backstage**. In the theater, an actor waiting in the **wings** for an entrance is **on deck**. **2.** A temporary platform built over the permanent stage floor; e.g., a **level** designed as a **playing space**. **3.** A waiting area. An actor waiting to enter for a commercial audition may be told, "You're on deck"; i.e., "You're next." **4.** The console of a reel-to-reel tape recorder: *tape deck*.

deck cues The signals given to backstage crew and technicians working on deck; e.g., those for the shifting of scenery.

declaim *v. t.* To intone or deliver a speech in a technical, rhetorical manner, as opposed to acting it realistically; hence, *declamatory*, pertaining to this kind of delivery. Once a neutral term, meaning the actor's delivery of a text, *declamation* came to be perceived as what Racine, in his preface to *Brittanicus*, called "discourse marked by affectation."

deconstruction *n.* Taking apart; breaking something down into its components, so they can be analyzed and understood. This is the basis of the Stanislavsky **system**: a play and a role are first deconstructed, then reconstructed so that they can be brought to life as a whole, based on the understanding gained from the deconstruction.

décor *n.* Film or theater **set**.

decorations *n. pl. Archaic* **1.** In 17th-c. French theater, all the scenery, props, costumes, and any other visual elements of a production. **2.** In 18th-c. English theater, **stage properties**; also, the ornamental features of the theater auditorium.

decorator *n. Archaic* In 17th c. French theater, the person in charge of the scene painters, and also of certain stage managerial jobs, such as maintaining order backstage during a performance, and supervising the candle snuffers.

deferred payment An arrangement whereby actors agree to work on a film project for nothing, or for a minimum covering their expenses. The actors sign a SAG **waiver**, stipulating that if the project moves on to a venue where the producers make money, they will give the actors proper compensation.

delayed reaction **1.** A response that takes time to form in someone's mind: a useful tool in acting certain moments or characters. **2.** Syn. with **slow take**.

delivery *n.* The way in which a speech or part of a speech is uttered; the general manner in which an actor recites his or her lines: *Her delivery of the lines was excellent*.

Delsarte, François (1811–1871) (frawn swah' dehl sart') Highly popular, very influential French acting teacher and theorist, who thought he had discovered the science of how actors could be real and psychologically truthful in their performances. He felt that all emotion, all nuances of feeling, and all ideas could be expressed on stage by using beautiful elocution and specific, meaningful gestures and poses, which, however calculated and studied they might be, must appear to be spontaneous and natural. His elaborate system described in minute detail the movements associated with each emotion. Delsarte began to write a book, but had only finished five chapters by the time of his death. They were published in *Delsarte System of Oratory* (Edgar S. Werner, 1882), which also contains lengthy writings by some of his disciples.

demo *n.* [short for *demonstration*] **1.** A commercial made to be shown to the people in charge of buying a product's publicity campaign from an advertising agency. Actors are paid a contractual *demo rate* for making them; if the shoot lasts more than a day, each day is paid for at the same demo rate. Also called *in-house commercial*; *non-broadcast commercial* (i.e., one not meant to be shown on the air). **2.** A CD made by a band, providing samples of its music for agents, record producers, and clubs that might **book** them for a **gig. 3.** An actor's or director's reel of work samples on videotape or DVD; or an audiocassette or CD of an actor's voice or **voice-over** work. Also called a *reel*, esp. for video demos: *a director's reel*; *an actor's reel*.

Actors' demos are compiled from actual work done on camera or in voice-overs. The CD or a download of it via the Internet is sent to agents when the actor is seeking representation and expedited by the actors or their agents on demand to potential employers. Every actor needs one for each area of interest: film, television shows, commercials, voice-over work in commercials, book recording, film narration, and cartoon or **character voices**. Whenever the actor does a job, he or she should obtain a copy of the finished project for use in making up a demo. If the actor does not have the facilities to make a demo at home, there are many professional studios that will compile demos from the different video and audio work the actor supplies them with. The studio will also insert opening video or audio titles and credits, as well as music. In the case of actors starting out in the voice-over field, a demo of material that the actor has not actually done professionally may be made in a studio with the help of a sound engineer, who can even insert sound effects and music taken from the studio's library. It may then be uploaded into a computer, and sent out over the Internet as necessary. Any beginner's demo will eventually be replaced by one made of samples drawn from actual performances. It is best to keep a demo fairly short, no more than six to ten minutes long: film or television scenes of a few minutes each; voice-over demos of no more than five minutes. Few potential employers or agents look at or listen to more than the first few minutes, so put the material first that shows you off to greatest advantage.

denouement (day noo mo:*n*') *n.* [French: unknotting] The resolution of a story.

depth of field The range of focus on the area seen through the camera, including primary objects of focus and background (some of which may be in sharp primary focus, some of which may be slightly blurred). What can be seen as a sharp, clearly defined image varies with the **focal length** of different lenses. When an actor remains in focus no matter where he or she moves, the actor is within the depth of field. Also called *depth of focus*.

deputy *n.* A volunteer who acts on behalf of members as a liaison between unions and the management of a production company; e.g., a **set deputy** on an AFTRA or SAG shoot. The **Equity** deputy is employed as a member of the acting company, and is elected by his or her fellow actors. Every week, the deputy must file a report with the union of hours worked; and deal with any problems that arise between the management and the acting company or any individual in it by calling in union officials to settle matters, if the problems cannot be settled in any other way. The deputy is not empowered to act on his or her own, except perhaps in an emergency. It is an excellent idea for actors to serve as deputy on at least one show; it is a perfect way to learn the ins and outs of the contract one has signed, and to gain an understanding of labor-management relations.

design *n., v. —n.* **1.** A plan and graphic representation, drawing, rendering, sketch, blueprint, or schema of a physical aspect of a production; e.g., that for a décor or set, showing what it will look like, and the logistical plans for its construction; or a plan and graphic representation of costumes, and the patterns and logistical plans for their construction; or for the placement of lighting and sound equipment, and the plans for the intensity of sound and light. **2.** The general, overall look and appearance of sets and costumes, and other physical aspects of a production. —*v. t.* **3.** To conceive, create, and devise plans for the physical aspects of a production, and to concretize the plans for those aspects by providing drawings, schematic renderings, or other graphic representations of them; e.g., the plans for sets, costumes, lighting, or sound.

design conference 1. A preliminary **preproduction** gathering between the director and designers of a project to discuss concepts and proposals. **2.** A periodic **production meeting** between director and designers to discuss problems and progress. Cf. **concept meeting**.

designer *n.* An artist-craftsman who plans the look and logistics for an aspect of production involving his or her field of expertise, and supervises the people putting the designs into effect; e.g., a **costume designer**, a **lighting designer**, a **scenic designer**, a **sound designer**.

Desist! Cease your hilarity! *Hist.* Popular English music hall entertainer George Robey's (1869–1954) **catchphrase**, used in any number of situations. Another famous catchphrase of "the Prime Minister of Mirth": "Desist, refrain, and cease!"

detective film A genre in which the principal emphasis in a mystery story is how an investigator solves a crime, rather than the crime itself; the detective may be a member of a regular police force, or a private "consulting" detective like Sherlock Holmes.

deus ex machina (day' *oos* ehks mah' kee nah) [Latin: god from the machine] An artificial, tacked-on, facile, improbable plot resolution. The expression comes from ancient Greek and Roman theater, when a god entered, perhaps lowered by mechanical means onto the stage, in order to solve the problem presented by the play.

deuteragonist (dyoo' tuhr ag' uh nihst) *n.* **1.** An actor of secondary or supporting roles. **2.** *Hist.* A supporting actor, or the role he played, in classical tragedy.

dialect *n.* Syn. in theatrical terms with **accent**. For linguists, a dialect is a version of a language, including its accents, vocabulary, and grammar. We all speak a dialect, and we all speak that dialect with an accent. Although the terms "accent" and "dialect" are used interchangeably in the world of show business, accent is usually what is meant.

dialect coach An expert who teaches an actor how to do a particular accent.

dialect comedy act A comic vaudeville turn in which the performers used accents. Among the most usual were Irish, Yiddish, Italian, and African-American. Such acts usually mocked and denigrated the groups involved, but some were more authentic in their **ethnic humor**.

dialect part A role requiring the use of an accent.

dialogue *n.* **1.** The lines in a script that are spoken by the actors. **2.** A conversation on stage or screen between two or more characters. **3.** The part of a musical comedy book or operetta libretto that consists of spoken conversation.

dialogue coach In film, someone who works on lines with an actor and gives advice on how to say them, as well as on other acting points, such as subtextual interpretation. A dialogue coach may also be a dialect coach. Cf. **acting coach**.

diamond horseshoe The broadly curved first tier of boxes, in which the wealthy sit on the opening night at the opera.

diaphragm *n.* **1.** The muscular partition separating the chest and abdominal cavities; with the action of this partition, achieved through the use of the abdominal muscles, the flow and force of air can be controlled by singers and actors using good **vocal technique**. **2.** The flexible membranous disk against which sound waves vibrate in a **microphone** or loudspeaker. **3.** A large device (similar to the **iris** in a camera) consisting of a circle of opaque, overlapping, thin metal flaps that may be manipulated to create a central opening, allowing the diameter of a light beam to be controlled; it is fitted onto a spotlight, esp. a **follow spot**. Also called *iris*; *iris diaphragm*; *iris shutter*.

diction *n.* **1.** Clarity of speech, i.e., the clear **articulation** of the vowel and consonant sounds; articulation: *Her diction was excellent.* **2.** A writer's way of expressing ideas, choice of words, and grammatical construction: *Shakespeare's diction is the most beautiful in the English language.*

die *v. i. Slang* **1.** To be received with glacial silence or some other indication of displeasure and dislike by the audience: *The play died; I died out there on stage tonight.* **2.** To cease to function, said of audiovisual equipment: *The microphone died in the middle of the speech.*

digital *adj.* Pertains to a form of information storage and retrieval and to electronic **recording** and broadcasting technology. Digital recording and playback are discontinuous; i.e., done by means of constant, almost instantaneous coded stops and starts, as opposed to **analog** recording and playback, which are continuous.

digital audio download A recorded book, piece of music, or other sound data material that is received from the **Internet** from a **web site**, often for pay, as an **electronic sell-through**; and stored in a computer. **Piracy** is a problem, not easily dealt with. Downloads from web sites are an increasing source of income for music and book recording companies and for Internet retail outlets, and the subject of negotiations between performing arts unions and producing organizations and companies. Also called *audio download*.

digital television 1. Audiovisual **broadcasting** and broadcasts using advanced, high definition digital technology. As of February 17, 2009, all television broadcasting is digital in the United States. **2.** The home monitor-receiver for such broadcasts.

digital video download A film, music video, or other audio-visual entertainment that is received from the **Internet** from a **web site**, often for pay, as an **electronic sell-through**, and stored in a computer. Sometimes available free, or else pirated. Also called *video download*.

digs *n. Slang esp. Brit.* [Short for *diggings*; fr. the temporary huts around gold rush sites] Temporary lodgings; a room or rooms rented by the day or for longer periods in a boarding house or other residence that receives actors who are **on the road**.

dimmer *n.* The switch by which theater lights can be made softer or brighter.

dinner theater A performance venue, often a chain of theaters, that provides a buffet meal before a performance, sometimes with coffee or other beverages served by waiters. The show is performed **in the round**, while the patrons surrounding the **acting area** continue to drink their coffee and eat their desserts. Some dinner theaters are nonunion; some are **Equity**. A hilarious example is provided in the film *Soapdish* (1991), where Kevin Kline performs a scene from *Death of a Salesman* in a dinner theater in Florida.

Dionysia (dI' uh nihsh' ee ah) *n. Hist.* An annual ancient Athenian theater festival in honor of the god Dionysus (dI' uh nI' suhs).

direct address Speaking to the audience, thus acknowledging that they are there, and breaking the **convention** of the **fourth wall**; e.g., in an **aside** or **soliloquy**.

direction *n.* **1.** An instruction from a director to an actor to perform something in a certain way, to make a particular move, and so forth. **2.** The art of mounting or staging plays or other performance projects, or of making a film or television project. **3.** The job and act of overseeing a play, film, television production, or other entertainment project.

See also STAGE DIRECTION(S); TAKE DIRECTION.

director *n.* The person who oversees all aspects of a production in any entertainment venue, and is in charge of telling the story.

See also TAKE DIRECTION.

director's chair A folding armchair with a back canvas panel and canvas seat on a metal or wooden frame with crossed legs, and a bar for resting the feet, if it is the high version of the chair; used esp. on shoots.

director's cut A filmmaker's ideal version of his or her motion picture, usually different from the commercially released film, and including deleted scenes, and perhaps some that are differently arranged. Such versions are sometimes available on DVD.

Directors Guild of America (DGA) The Hollywood-based union, founded in 1959, that represents film and television directors, assistant directors, production managers, and film and television stage managers.

director of photography The person in charge of the shooting of a film or television program, usually with a cameraperson and assistants whom he or she directs; abbrev. DP. In conjunction with the director, the director of photography chooses camera angles, shots, and colors; i.e., the overall color palette for the project, as well as individual colors. The cinematographer determines the look of the film as much as the director, who has final approval of everything that is selected. **Syn. cinematographer**.

direct sound Audio recorded during an actual shoot. Also called *actual sound*.

disaster film A genre of motion picture in which some manmade or natural catastrophe or cataclysm, such as an earthquake or a tidal wave, is at the center of the movie.

disc jockey 1. A person who selects and plays recorded music on a radio broadcast, comments on it, and chats informally; abbrev. DJ (dee' dgay), a usual appellation. **2.** A person who selects and plays recorded music at a dance hall or discotheque.

discotheque *n.* A large **dance hall** or **nightclub** where recorded music played by a DJ or live **band** is often blasted through loudspeakers. Special light effects, sometimes using strobes, and other entertaining features, such as dancers performing on a stage or on the drinks bar, are part of the scene.

discovered *adj.* Said of a character or characters revealed as the curtain rises or the lights go up: a stage direction that originated in Elizabethan published plays.

discovering through doing Finding the character in rehearsal. This is one of Stanislavsky's basic principles: an actor can only truly understand the character's motivations and desires by carrying out the planned actions in rehearsal.

discovery shot A take during which something not seen at the beginning of the take is revealed as the camera moves to focus on it. Discovery shots are also named by the kind of take; e.g., **pan** discovery shot, **zoom** discovery shot.

Disney World agreement The **Equity** contract that covers performers employed at the Walt Disney World thematic amusement park in Orlando, FL.

dissolve *n.* The simultaneous, gradual fading out and disappearance of one scene as another begins to appear and gradually fades in, taking over the screen.
See also CROSS-FADE.

distress *v. t.* To work with sets or costumes so as to make them look old, shabby, decrepit, rundown, and worn.

dithyramb (dihth' ih ram; —ramb) *n. Hist.* Ancient Greek dramatic poem in praise of gods or heroes, given as a dramatic presentation; said by **Aristotle** to be the origin of **tragedy**.

diva (dee' vah) *n.* [Italian] Originally a neutral term, meaning female opera star; now derogatory, applied to men and women actors who are egotistical, spoiled, pampered, and demanding. Cf. **prima donna**.

divertissement (dih vuhr' tihs muhnt) *n. Archaic.* An entertaining interlude in the middle of a longer entertainment; popular in 17th- and 18th-c. European theater.

divo (dee' vo:) *n.* [Italian] A male opera star.

doctor act *Hist.* A salacious **vaudeville** routine in which a ludicrous, usually myopic doctor examines patients with the help of a particularly buxom nurse, while constantly looking down the bosom of her scanty uniform. Exemplified hilariously in the film of Neil Simon's hit Broadway comedy, *The Sunshine Boys* (1975); and, in a variant, in the American vaudeville comedy team Smith and Dale's "Dr. Kronkheit and His Only Living Patient," filmed as a **soundie** in 1941 [Joe Smith (1884–1981); Charlie Dale (1885–1971); Kronkheit (krahng' kIt): fr. Yiddish; German, *Krankheit* (krahnk' hIt): sickness, disease].

docudrama *n.* A play based on real facts and documents, such as Moisés Kauffmann's 1997 Off-Broadway hit *Gross Indecency: The Three Trials of Oscar Wilde*. Docudramas often contain direct quotations from documentary sources, as well as invented dialogue.

documentary film A genre of nonfiction movie, or an individual film, concerning real events, people, and issues, using actual source material, interviews, and so forth; or concerning some endeavor or area of knowledge and activity; i.e., nature, or travel. Called a *documentary*, for short.

Dolby *n. Trademark* [Short for *Dolby Noise Reduction System*; named for its inventor, sound engineer Ray Dolby (b. 1933)] An electronic system for the reduction of extra noise, the equalization and balance of sound, and the modulation of high frequencies during audio recording and playback. Also called *Dolby NR*.

dolly *n.* **1.** A small platform mounted on wheels, used to transport something. **2.** In filmmaking, such a platform with a camera mounted on it, so that it can roll alongside actors during a take; hence, *dolly shot*, also called a *trucking shot* or *tracking shot*; *dolly in*: to move into a shot to focus more closely on the subject; *dolly out*: to pull back in order to widen the area filmed; *dolly man*: the person who operates the dolly. It may have special wheels that enable it to roll along tracks laid down for both interior and exterior sets and locations, or it may have ordinary wheels and be used without tracks.

See also CRAB DOLLY; TONGUE.

dolly zoom shot A take in which the **tracking shot** includes the use of a **zoom**.

domestic drama/tragedy A play, film, or television program set generally in a middle-class milieu, and dealing with everyday problems. The genre has its roots in the **comedy of humors** and in Molière's domestic farces, and was popular in the 18th c. A forerunner of **melodrama**, these plays had aristocratic villains and servant heroes; e.g., Beaumarchais' *The Marriage of Figaro*. Also called *bourgeois drama*.

Don't just do something—stand there! An ironical twist on the desperate plea, "Don't just stand there—do something!" It is directed sarcastically at an actor who wants to **hog the stage**.

door *n.* The general entrance to a theater auditorium, which may, in fact, have several large contiguous doorways through which the audience is admitted: *We took in a lot of money tonight at the door.*

double *n., v.* —*n.* **1.** An actor who plays more than one part in a stage show; common in musical comedies, with many minor characters that do not appear together on stage. **2.** An actor who resembles another actor physically, and is used in certain shots; e.g., those with a character's back to the camera, or in long shots. —*v. i.* **3.** To play more than one part in a stage show. **4.** To do the job of a **body double** or **stunt double**.

double bill 1. A theatrical entertainment in two halves, presenting two different, often unrelated pieces, each of which is not by itself long enough to constitute an entire program. **2.** Syn. with *double feature*, in a movie theater.

double feature 1. A program at a movie house showing two films for one admission price, one after the other. Art houses still sometimes show double features; e.g., two films by a particular **auteur**. **2.** *Hist.* A popular program from the 1930s through '50s, consisting of an **A-picture** followed by a **B-picture**, both films being preceded by cartoons, coming attractions, and shorts.

double scale Twice the minimum payment required in union contracts.

double take A comic bit, in which a look of neutrality or blank incomprehension is instantly followed by a second look of surprised comprehension. Done in three beats: a look at someone or something, a turn away, and an instant look back.

doubletalk *n.* Gibberish combining real words with nonsense syllables and words; used by some comics as part of a comedy routine. The satiric mock-lectures of the brilliant "Professor" Irwin Corey (b. 1914)—"The World's Foremost Authority," as he billed himself—included a different kind of doubletalk involving long, florid, convoluted clauses that went nowhere, and said nothing, but sounded profound and erudite.

down *n., adj.* —*n.* **1.** Short for **downstage**: *down in one*, said of a scene performed in **plane** 1. —*adj.* **2.** Low in energy; dispirited; slow; said of a performance or of an actor: *The show was down tonight.* **3.** Pertains to a light below its fullest level of intensity.

down angle A shot or take of a scene from above.

downgrade *n., v.* —*n.* **1.** A change from a higher to a lower salary category in a SAG or AFTRA venue of employment. —*v. t.* **2.** To put a performer into a lower contractual category, with a consequent lowering of salary, esp. in commercials or films. An actor can be hired as a principal to play a small part in a commercial, and downgraded to extra status if that part has no lines and the actor is not recognizable: the actor will not receive residual payments, since background work is done on a **buyout** basis.
See also OUTGRADE; UPGRADE.

download *n., v.* —*n.* **1.** Any data received from another computer or web site; such data can then be stored in the receiving computer; e.g., a **digital audio download** of music or a recorded book. —*v. t.* **2.** To receive data on a computer.
See also UPLOAD.

download to own An audio or audiovisual entertainment project available for purchase on the Internet; bought as an **electronic sell-through**. Unions have negotiated with producers to secure performers' rights to residuals for such sales.

download to rent A subscription to a pay web site that allows the temporary viewing of an entertainment project through **streaming**, but not a permanent download. Unions have negotiated with producers to secure performers' rights to residuals for such rentals.

downscale *v., adj.* —*v. t.* **1.** To render something less luxurious, and to make it appear lower on the economic ladder; e.g., when decorating an interior location set. —*adj.* **2.** Dressed in ordinary clothing; e.g., when doing a crowd scene as a background player. **3.** Pertains to a lower- or middle-class economic milieu.
See also UPSCALE.

downstage *n.* The forward part of a proscenium or three-quarters round stage, nearest the audience.; abbrev. D or DS. Called *down*, for short.

down time The pause or period of time taken between shots, or when it is necessary to stop a take in order to deal with technical problems involving equipment: to reset lights or camera angles, to deal with makeup and wardrobe problems, or to change locations altogether. Down time, however little it may be, is the actor's opportunity to rehearse or to go over lines.

draft *n.* A version of a script or other written material: *first draft*; *final draft*.

drag *n.* [Conjecturally, fr. 1870s theater slang, in the days when women's long skirts dragged on the ground] Women's dress worn by a man; men's dress worn by a woman. Playing roles in drag is as old as theater: in ancient Greece, men played women using special costume pieces, and women were not allowed on the European stage until the 17th c. The old-style British Christmas pantomime would not be complete without more than one *drag role*: the fairy godmother or a witch played by a man; the **principal boy**. In cabaret and nightclub shows, female impersonators may lip sync women's recorded voices; some clubs are devoted entirely to this form of entertainment. The plots of some of Shakespeare's plays (e.g., *As You Like It*) depend on women disguised as men, as does the **denouement** of Verdi's *Rigoletto* (ree' go leh' to:). And the stories of such works as *Charlie's Aunt* or Gilbert and Sullivan's *Princess Ida* hinge on men disguised as women. In opera, there are male roles composed for women—called breeches, pants, or **trousers roles**—such as the title role in Rossini's *Tancredi* (tahn kreh:' dee), and Octavian (ok tah' vee ahn') in Richard Strauss's *Der Rosenkavalier* (deh ro:' zehn kah' vah lee'uh). In the ballet, the role of the Wicked Stepmother in Prokofiev's *Cinderella* is danced by a man. Men have sometimes played Lady Bracknell in Wilde's *The Importance of Being Earnest*, although the role was not actually written as a drag role. On the other hand, the riotously funny Dame Edna, played by Australian actor Barry Humphries, is an example of a true drag role, which he did to great acclaim in the theater as well as on television. Albin (ahl ba*n*') in *La Cage aux Folles* (lah kazh' o fo:l') makes his living doing a drag act in the nightclub that the play is named for, and also disguises himself as his partner's son's mother.

    See CAMP; LIP SYNC; TROUSERS ROLE.

drag queen A female impersonator; i.e., a man who dresses as and assumes the perceived mannerisms of a woman.

drama *n.* **1.** Another word for **play**. "Dramas are so called because they represent people in action," writes **Aristotle**: the word "drama" has its etymological root in the Greek verb *dran*, meaning "to do" or "to act." **2.** The branch of literature that comprises plays.

drama school. See THEATER SCHOOLS.

dramatic *adj.* **1.** Pertaining to plays: *dramatic monologue*. **2.** Pertaining to the theater as a whole: *the dramatic repertoire*. **3.** Histrionic, theatrical, striking, or startling: *a dramatic temper tantrum*; *a dramatic moment*; *a dramatic contrast*. **4.** Displaying, exhibiting, or containing qualities appropriate for work in the theater: *dramatic skill*. **5.** Vivid, lively: *dramatic colors*.

dramatic cycle A series of plays that present one story; e.g., Shakespeare's **histories**, which tell the story of the English monarchy from Richard II to Richard III in eight plays covering several centuries.

dramatic form 1. The genre and subgenre to which a play belongs. **2.** Syn. with **dramatic structure**.

dramatic irony The juxtaposition of contradictions or contradictory elements of which some characters in a play or film are unaware until developments force awareness on them. The Duke of Vienna in disguise in Shakespeare's *Measure for Measure* is in a position of dramatic irony: the audience knows he is in disguise, but the other characters do not, until he reveals himself to them. The device can be used to create suspense; e.g., in James Whale's movie of Mary Shelley's *Frankenstein* (1931): the blind man, not realizing what he is dealing with, befriends the monster played by Boris Karloff.

dramatics *n.* **1.** Theater, and theatrical studies and activities in schools and clubs. **2.** Amateur theater presentations.

dramatic structure The way in which a play or film is put together and tells its story; e.g., in the following order: exposition, **inciting action**, episodes and events, climax, resolution; or, in film, using the **three-act structure**.

dramatic tension The conflict and clash of characters, creating suspense in the unfolding of a story as it builds to a climax.

dramatic time Syn. with **stage time**.

dramatis personae (dra' muh tihs puhr soh' nee) [Latin: persons in the drama] The list of characters in a play; the cast list.

dramatist *n.* Syn. with **playwright**.

Dramatists Guild of America (DG) An organization of professional playwrights based in New York City that provides for its dues-paying members legal services, spaces for play readings, events at which directors and playwrights may meet, and other events and services, including an annual directory of agents and play contests. The DG has contracts that it suggest its members use when a production is offered; e.g., the **minimum basic agreement**. Unlike unions and other guilds, it has no legal power to insist that its contracts be signed with producing organizations, but a DG member will not work without such a contract.

dramatize *v. t.* **1.** To adapt an original story or an extant literary source, such as a novel, for stage or screen; i.e., to turn it into a drama. Hence, *dramatization*: the act of doing so, and the adapted work itself. **2.** To exaggerate a situation when describing it. **3.** To behave in an exaggerated way, as if one were in a play.

dramaturge *n.* **1.** A professional literary/theatrical adviser to the playwright and/or director of a project. The dramaturge may give advice on structure, writing, and/or elements of staging, but does not do any rewrites, although he or she may suggest some. Cf. **play doctor**. **2.** *Archaic* Originally, an alternative word for **playwright**.

dramaturgy *n.* **1.** The art of writing plays. **2.** The profession, job, and practice of advising a playwright and/or director on the structure, story, writing, and other literary or theatrical elements of a particular project.

draper *n.* The skilled craftsperson in a **costume shop** who assembles clothing, draping pieces over a dressmaker's **dummy**.

draw *n.* *Slang* An actor whose mere name is expected to attract paying customers.

drawing-room comedy A play featuring repartee, witty badinage, and airy persiflage, as well as a complicated story set in a middle or upper-class milieu; sometimes referred to as **high comedy** or **comedy of manners**. There are often scenes in a drawing room, as in Oscar Wilde's *An Ideal Husband* and *The Importance of Being Earnest*.

dream sequence A film scene of a character's dream or reverie.

dress *n., v.* —*n.* **1.** Costume; clothing: *modern dress*; *medieval dress*. **2.** Short for **dress rehearsal**. —*v. t.* **3.** To finish a set by placing props and furniture in their assigned positions or by adding scenic details, as when an artist works to **line** scenery. **4.** To arrange items on the set of a play, television program, commercial, or film. In the media, this is the job of a set decorator, or **set dresser**, who works with assistants. In commercials, it is often a prop person who dresses the set with the product; i.e., places it in the optimum position for the camera. **5.** To establish or alter the look of a particular prop, item of furniture, or set piece, such as a door or window; e.g., *to dress the windows for night* (i.e., to make it look as if it were nighttime outside). **6.** To adjust the stage picture by making a **counter-cross**: *to dress the stage*.

dress circle 1. The first tier of boxes in a theater. **2.** The second or third balcony up in some opera houses; at the Metropolitan Opera, it is just above the **grand tier**.

dress parade A showing of costumes by actors wearing them to the stage director and other personnel, so that any problems may be discerned; takes place as part of a regularly scheduled rehearsal. With stage lights on, the actors either file across the stage, stand in a line, or are called individually. Also called *costume parade*.

dress rehearsal A fully costumed and lit practice repetition of a play before it is open for performance in front of a public audience; there is usually more than one. An invited audience is sometimes in attendance: an **invited dress**. The dress rehearsal is supposed to simulate performance conditions, and is usually not to be interrupted. The director, coaches, and designers take notes, which are given to the actors or staff members after the rehearsal. A *full dress rehearsal* is held after one or more *technical-dress rehearsals*, which may be interrupted at any time to make adjustments to lighting, sound, and so forth. Also called a *dress*, for short.
See TECHNICAL REHEARSAL.

dresser *n.* The backstage wardrobe person who helps actors in and out of their costumes; e.g., during a **quick change**. Stars often had and have their own personal dressers, such as Margo Channing's (Bette Davis) dresser, Birdie Coonan (Thelma Ritter), in *All About Eve* (1950). Ronald Harwood's *The Dresser*, about a touring Shakespearean company during World War Two, concerns the sensitive title character's relationship with the venerable, hammy Shakespearean actor with whom he has toured for years. The 1983 film adapted from the hit play stars Tom Courtenay, reprising the **title role** he created on stage, and Albert Finney as the actor known to us only as Sir.

dressing room The backstage space where actors put on costume and makeup. Stars have their own individual dressing rooms, supporting cast members often share dressing rooms, and the chorus usually has two dressing rooms: one for men, one for women, in accordance with **Equity rules**.

drive a Mack truck Said when a pause is too long, or actors are not picking up their cues: *You could drive a Mack truck through it* (i.e., through that pause). A phrase heard from a stage director in theater rehearsals and sometimes said of a slow performance.

drive-in *n., adj.* —*n.* **1.** An outdoor movie theater, into which people drive their cars, park them, and see a film. —*adj.* **2.** Pertaining to such a **venue**: *a drive-in theater*.

drop *n., v.* —*n.* **1.** A curtain that may be lowered. **2.** A large painted **flat** or other piece of scenery that may be lowered; e.g., a **fly**. —*v. t.* **3.** To lower a flat. **4.** To lower the volume of one's voice momentarily, so that it ceases to be projected. Many actors have to be told in rehearsal not to drop their voices at the end of a line, a common habit that makes for inaudibility and monotony. **5.** To omit a line or more of dialogue accidentally.

dry; **dry up** *v. i. Slang.* To forget one's lines in the middle of playing a scene; to go blank. *Brit.* To blank.

dry-for-wet A film scene that is supposed to take place either underwater or during a storm or shower, but that is shot in a dry location or on a dry studio set; e.g., as a **bluescreen shot**. The effect of the deep sea, swimming pool, or rain will be supplied later, often using computer-generated effects that are superimposed onto the filmed scene. Cf. **wet-for-wet**.

dry tech A **technical rehearsal** of a play in which no actors participate and only the director, designers, stage managerial staff, crew, and technical personnel are needed, to run the lighting, sound, scenery, and effects cues, often in a **cue-to-cue**.

dual role Two separate roles played by the same actor; e.g., Rudolf Rassendyl, the English traveler who is a distant cousin of the King of Ruritania, and the kidnapped king, whom he resembles, both played by Ronald Colman in the 1937 Hollywood film version of Anthony Hope's *The Prisoner of Zenda*.

dub *v. t.* **1.** To **loop**; to record dialogue that replaces the original soundtrack. Hence, *dubbing session*: the scheduled time when this is done. Dubbing may be done for a foreign film intended for domestic distribution or done in the language of the film by the actor who originally recorded it: *to dub a film*; *to dub dialogue*. In any case, the dubbing must be synchronized with the on-screen actor's mouth movements. In the old-fashioned procedure, the actor watches the screen while speaking simultaneously, helped by a running timer just above or below the screen; this has been largely superseded by **automatic dialogue replacement. 2.** To combine and put together the sound tracks of recordings of dialogue, sound effects, music, and so forth so as to be able to make one master recording, from which the final full soundtrack for a film, television program, or commercial will be made; to **mix. 3.** To copy all or part of a recording.

duct tape [So called fr. its use in sealing heating and air-conditioning ducts] A wide, vinyl, cloth-reinforced, water-resistant adhesive ribbon with many uses in engineering, photography, and show business; e.g., as **spike tape**, for fastening lighting cables down onto a stage floor, or for temporarily fixing a broken **prop**. Also called *duck tape*; *gaff tape*; *gaffer tape*; *gaffer's tape*.

dues *n. pl.* The fee paid to a **union, club,** or other organization for continued membership. Dues to AEA, SAG, and AFTRA are paid twice yearly on a graduated scale that depends on the performer's income; there are minimum and maximum payments.

dulling spray A chemical aerosol mist that dries as an *anti-reflection coating* on the surface it is applied to. Used by photographers and stage, film, or television **set decorators, set dressers,** or **property masters** to prevent shine and eliminate the glare from such surfaces as a glass window or **mirror**. Sometimes, black or gray spray paint, applied and wiped down, may serve the same purpose.

dumb show A mimed presentation of a play, without spoken dialogue; e.g., the play within the play in *Hamlet*.

dummy *n.* **1.** A ventriloquist's doll, with a movable jaw and often, movable eyes. **2.** The tailor's form on which a **draper** or costumer drapes clothes. **3.** Short for *dummy prop*.

dummy prop A fake or phony nonworking stage property that resembles or replicates the real thing.

duologue *n.* **1.** Dialogue for two characters. **2.** A scene, sketch, or play for two characters.

dutch angle A tilted position of the camera so that it can shoot a scene from a nonstandard point of view; e.g., the interior of an overturned car after an accident, seen on a diagonal.

DVD *n.* Acronym, abbrev., and usual appellation for *digital versatile disc*: a round, flat, coated disc on which a film, television show, or other entertainment is recorded. Played with a laser, like a CD. The name was changed from *digital video disc* because the disc can also retain interactive video games and has Internet access capabilities.

dynamic mike. See MICROPHONE.

E

early retirement The fiction—or the reality—that a performer has stopped working before the age of 65, and can begin collecting a union pension, provided he or she is vested; i.e., has worked enough under union auspices to have earned the right to collect it. Early retirement may begin at age 57; the pension will be less than if the performer waits until retirement age. AEA and AFTRA do not require officially retired performers to report income they earn under union auspices, but SAG sets a limit on how much a performer may earn without reporting the income. If the amount of earnings exceeds the limit, the performer must report it, and will not receive the pension payment for the month in which the income was earned; but this applies only to session fees, not residuals.

earprompter *n.* An audio playback device that fits in an actor's ear. Lines are fed to the actor during a take; especially useful during a phone conversation scene.

ecdysiast (ehk dihz' ee ast) *n.* A striptease artist. Also called an *exotic dancer*.

echo *n.* A reminder to the audience of something that happened earlier in a script.

echo chamber A booth, room, or other enclosed space that is constructed especially to refract and reverberate sound. It was used for special sound effects in films, such as the hollow laughter of a creature or the echo in an underground vault or cave—effects that are now usually created electronically. Also called *echo box*.

edit *n., v.* —*n.* **1.** The finished job done by a film editor: *a good edit*. —*v. t.* **2.** To **cut** and shape a film or recording; hence, *editing*: the job of doing this.

editor *n.* The person who puts music or spoken arts recordings into their final versions, or who assembles film or television scenes into their final order, inserting shots, under the supervision of the film's director—who may be his or her own editor.

educational theater 1. Drama at a university, college, or other institution of learning. **2.** Plays presented by drama department students as part of their training.

educational television Broadcasts of programs such as those that teach people how to read, or of high school or college courses. Documentary programs, while educational, do not fall under this category.

Edwardian drama The theater of the early 20th c., named for the reign of King Edward VII of England (1901–1910) and lasting until World War One. It includes realistic, well-made plays by Sir Arthur Wing Pinero; the fantasies and comedies of Sir James Barrie; the **New Drama** of Granville-Barker; plays by George Bernard Shaw; and, in Ireland, the plays of W. B. Yeats, John Millington Synge, and Lady Gregory.

effect shot A take inserted into a scene in order to create **atmosphere**, such as the ominous ocean waves and views of icebergs in all the film versions of the *Titanic* story.

effects *n. pl.* [Short for *stage effects*; *lighting effects*; *sound effects*; *special effects*] Special, artificially created acoustic and/or visual simulations in a film or play; e.g., thunder, lightning, and rain *(storm effects)*; or the effect of moonlight shining through trees in a garden, created by using a **gobo**. You can see 18th-c. storm and other stage effects demonstrated at the **court theater** of Drottingholm, Sweden. **Sound effects** in the theater and on the radio that are now done electronically used to be produced by a variety of mechanical devices or simple machines; e.g. a **rain drum**. Visual effects were also done by machine; e.g., a **cloud machine**, a **snow machine**. A lightning effect was created when the lighting technician turned the lights sharply on and off, or rapidly opened and closed the flap on a lantern once or twice, or used a special **flash box**. In film, **special effects** are usually computer-generated, with sound effects produced by **foley** techniques.

effects film A motion picture of which one of the main attractions is its use of **special effects**.

effects filter A device attached to a camera to create a soft, hazy light, also accomplished through **back lighting** or by shooting through gauze.

effects light Any of a number of lighting instruments used in the theater to create special effects; e.g., a water wave light, a flame effect light, a color changer light, a **strobe** light.

effects track The separate channel on which sound effects are recorded for later insertion into the finished soundtrack of a film or television program.

eight-by-ten; **8 × 10** *n. Slang* An actor's **head shot**, the dimensions of which are eight by ten inches. Also called a *glossy*.

eighteen to play younger A young adult who appears young enough to play a teenager; e.g., as an extra playing a student in a high school scene. A phrase seen in casting notices for SAG or AFTRA projects.

electric *adj.* **1.** Pertaining to a musical instrument connected to amplifying equipment requiring electricity or electronics: *electric guitar*; *electric keyboard*. **2.** Striking; dynamic: *an electric performance*. **3.** Pertaining to the kind of **analog** recording technology using microphones, electric amplification, and other electric recording equipment, beginning ca. 1925 and completely superseding **acoustic** recording by 1933.

electrician *n.* In theater and the media, the trained craftsperson in charge of installing, removing, and maintaining the cables, wiring, and switches for lights and sound equipment.

electronic sell-through (EST) Purchase on the Internet of an entertainment project that the customer possesses as a **download to own**.

elevator shot A take done from a platform that moves up or down, with the camera mounted on it, following the action.

elevator stage A platform that is either an entire stage or part of one, and that can be raised or lowered. Sometimes, an elevator stage is used to effect a spectacular entrance; it can also be used to lift heavy scenery, furniture, and equipment up to stage level.

Elizabethan drama The theater of the English Renaissance, during the reign of Queen Elizabeth I (1558–1603), including the tragedies, comedies, and histories of William Shakespeare and the plays of Christopher Marlowe.

ellipsoidal *n.* Short for *ellipsoidal* **spotlight**.

ellipsoidal reflector spotlight The most common kind of **spotlight**, along with the **fresnel**, with a smooth, full lens, and internal shutters than can change the dimensions of the light beam; a **gobo** may be attached to it. One of the most well known brand names for such a spotlight is **Leko**, often used generically for any such spotlight.

elocution *n.* **1.** Manner or way of speaking: *The actor's elocution was elegant, and the diction perfect.* **2.** The study of oratory, **diction**, **speech**, and **vocal technique**.

emcee *n., v.* —*n.* **1.** A pronunciation of the letters M.C., standing for master (or mistress) of ceremonies. —*v. t.* **2.** To act in the capacity of a master or mistress of ceremonies: *He emceed the show.*

emelia (eh meh' lee ah) *n. Hist.* In ancient Greek **tragedy**, a dance by the **chorus** to illustrate their emotional reaction to the events of the story.

emotion *n.* [Fr. Latin: *emovere* (eh: mo:' weh reh): a movement outward] Desire, want, and **feeling** aroused by external and/or internal stimuli: responses to those stimuli arising from the depths of the unconscious. The word is usually not applied to purely physical responses, such as feelings of hunger, but to psychological responses. For instance, a person may respond to hunger with pleasurable anticipation of a meal about to be served, or with disgust at some dish that he or she dislikes. For purposes of the theater, Stanislavsky distinguished *primary emotion*, which involves an immediate, visceral reaction to something that happens, from *secondary emotion*, which is remembered emotion from a situation that has been dealt with and assimilated into the unconscious, from which it can be recalled. The latter is what the actor wants to use in interpreting a character.

emotional memory; **emotional recall**. See AFFECTIVE MEMORY; SUBSTITUTION.

encore *n., v.* [French: again] —*n.* **1.** The repeat of a **number**, usually at the request of the audience, who shout "Encore!" The French, however, do not use this word in the theater: instead, they shout "*Bis!*" which means the same thing. —*v. t.* **2.** To repeat a number.

end slate The indication, written on a clapboard, that a scene or take is finished. The clapboard is held upside down in front of the camera by the second assistant cameraman, who claps the boards together.

end title The final word(s) in a film, showing that it is over; e.g., "The End."

end titles Syn. with **closing credits**.

endowment *n*. The projection of physical or emotional qualities onto an object or person in order for the actor endowing the object or person to relate in a personal, real way: *He endowed the empty suitcase, which was supposed to be packed, with heaviness.* All acting is endowment: to treat the **given circumstances** as real is to endow fictitious life with reality.

See also "AS IF."

enfant terrible (ah*n* fah*n* teh *r*ee' bluh) [French: terrible, terrifying child] In show business, a star actor or a theater or film director who is narcissistic, egotistical, insistent, and demanding. Some in the category of the **monstre sacré** were also *enfants terribles*.

engage *v. t.* To hire an actor for work in the theater; hence, *engagement*: a job in the theater.

See also LIMITED ENGAGEMENT.

ensemble *n., adj.* [Fr. French: together] —*n*. **1.** The complete company of actors involved in any particular production. **2.** The chorus in a musical theater piece. —*adj*. **3.** Together as a group: *ensemble acting*; *ensemble playing*, of paramount importance in the theater.

enter *v. t.* To come onto the stage or into a scene in a film or television show.

entertain *v. t.* **1.** To amuse; to divert. **2.** To provide the means for amusement and diversion; e.g., a dinner for invited guests. **3.** To perform in public. **4.** To consider an idea: *Hamlet entertains the notion of revenge.*

entertainer *n*. A performing artist, one of whose jobs is to amuse the public.

entertainment *n*. **1.** Amusement; diversion; performance piece. **2.** Something that occupies and distracts the mind in an agreeable, pleasurable manner.

entertainment industry The area of the economy that deals with amusing people and occupying their leisure time, and in which performing artists of all kinds, as well as those in related professions, make their living.

entr'acte (o*n*' trakt) *n*. [French: (o:*n* t*r*ahkt'); lit. between-act; interval] Intermission; interval between the acts of a play.

entrance *n*. **1.** The way into a place, or onto the stage. **2.** Coming into a scene, whether in film, television, or the theater. **3.** Coming onto the stage by oneself or with others; or into a scene in progress: *to make an entrance*. The entrance must be carefully prepared, and the actor should ask the following questions:

1. Where have I just come from?
2. How did I get there?
3. What have I just been doing?

4. What condition am I in physically, mentally, and emotionally?
5. What is the first thing I want when I make my entrance?
6. What or whom do I expect to find when I come into the scene?
7. What am I doing? What action am I performing?

environmental theater Dramatic presentations that surround the audience with a particular ambience. In one production in Norway at the Odinteatret, Eugenio Barba began the evening with the audience seated at dining tables set with china and silverware, and the actors poured wine for the audience.

See also GROTOWSKI, JERZY.

epic film A motion picture that recreates a mythological or historical story with a vast, panoramic canvas; e.g., the films based on Tolstoy's *War and Peace*, the many films about *King Arthur*, and the *Lord of the Rings* series.

epic realism The theater of Berthold Brecht, in which vast sweeping events are acted out and are always to be perceived as real; e.g., *Mother Courage and Her Children*, which takes place during the devastating religious Thirty Years War.

epic theater Historical pageants, mythological dramas, or sweeping panoramic plays on any subject, sometimes in an outdoor setting. One of the most famous theater companies in Europe in the latter half of the 19th c. produced spectacular historical pageant plays for which they were much admired: the Meiningen Company, founded by its artistic director (a son-in-law of Queen Victoria) Georg II, Duke of Saxe-Meiningen (1826–1914) (saks' mIn' ihng uhn), assisted by its most famous actor, Ludwig Chronegk (1837–1891) (kron' ek). The company was known for realistic characterizations and scenery, accurate costumes, and the fluid handling of crowd scenes. It had a great influence on Stanislavsky's thinking.

epigram *n.* Originally, a short, witty, or amusing poem or couplet, like Benjamin Franklin's well known rhyme from *Poor Richard's Almanac*: "Early to bed, early to rise, makes a man healthy, wealthy, and wise." But in contemporary terms, an epigram is a concise witty phrase that has a twist to it: an unexpected, but satisfying ending, as in Oscar Wilde's well known **one-liner**, "I can resist anything except temptation."

epilogue *n.* **1.** A short, concluding speech at the end of a play, sometimes telling the audience what will happen to the characters. **2.** The character who gives the speech.

episode *n.* **1.** In **Stanislavskian** terms, a part of a drama involving events that may take place over one or more scenes. **2.** An individual radio, television, or Internet program that is one of a series. See also WEBISODE. **3.** In ancient Greek **tragedy**, an event in the story.

episode film A motion picture that tells several basically unconnected stories; e.g., *Dead of Night* (1945), in which several travelers on a train pass the time by telling each other horror tales. Also called *omnibus film*.

episodic television Programs that are made as a series, one episode at a time, usually lasting an entire season, or seasons. The audience gets to know and expects to see regular casts of principal characters, and there are usually guest appearances by stars, and featured recurring roles.

See also MINISERIES; NIGHTTIME DRAMA; PILOT SEASON; SITUATION COMEDY.

equestrian drama A spectacle or show involving the use of horses; e.g., the ancient Roman spectacle *Troy*, which recreated the Greek siege of Troy as its central event.

Equity *n*. A commonly used short name for **Actors' Equity Association (AEA)**.

Equity bond The money deposited with Equity by producers, serving as a guarantee that members working in a production will be paid if the producer defaults. The producers must "post a bond" with Equity in the amount of two weeks' worth of each member's weekly salary and health care and pension credits, except in the case of certain **guest artist** contracts. Seasonal theater contracts are not subject to a full bond, whereas a single production is.

Equity card A wallet-size rectangular piece of laminated paper showing that someone is a member of AEA. It is carried by all members of the union, and must be presented on request; e.g., for admittance to the Equity lounge, the union hall where actors can meet, sit, and talk, and which in New York is also used for **open calls**.

Equity deputy. See DEPUTY.

Equity Membership Candidate Program (EMC) A method of joining **Actors' Equity Association (AEA)** by registering with the union as a candidate and accumulating points by working in participating Equity theaters; one point (or credit towards membership) is earned per week. Fifty points are required for eligibility; twenty-five if the candidate is a member of a sister union (e.g., AFTRA or SAG).

Equity 99-Seat Plan The California equivalent of a New York **showcase**. The plan operates according to a strict code, whereby a showcase theater may seat no more than ninety-nine audience members. Also called a *waiver production*.

Equity rules The regulations negotiated with producing organizations, covering terms of employment and working conditions in more than forty live performance venues.

Equity showcase The AEA-authorized public presentation of a play by actors who are not paid, for a limited number of performances, in a theater that may seat no more than ninety-nine people and that operates under the **showcase code**. Theaters with more seats are reserved for paying venues.

erudite theater Plays presented by amateurs for an elite audience; e.g., at the **court theater** of King James I of England (ruled 1603–1625).

escape artist An **illusionist** who is an expert at getting out of such constraints as chains, handcuffs, ropes, and sealed trunks or other containers. The most famous escape artist of modern times is undoubtedly the daring escapologist and stunt artist Harry Houdini (1874–1926).

escape film A motion picture that tells the story of a breakout from an untenable situation; e.g., *The Great Escape* (1963), about a breakout from a POW camp in World War Two.

escape stairs Steps at the edge or back of some raised part of the set, down which the actors may **exit**; e.g., from an upper story in an apartment house set, or at the back of a raked set, from which it would be dangerous to step down onto the stage floor. In some cases, there is an escape **ramp** instead of escape stairs.

establish *v. t.* To set the scene, or some element in it, for the audience. In the theater, this may be done through the use of scenery and lighting, or through the expository speeches of the characters. In film, the director chooses shots and takes that will set up the scene or situation.

establishing shot A take that sets up some aspect of a scene or a story. An establishing shot may tell the audience where something takes place: a New York city block, or a dusty street in a western town. Or it may tell the audience whom the story concerns, or what the weather is like: a character's face or storm clouds are seen. It creates **atmosphere** as well, telling us how we are to feel about what we see. Also called *orientation shot*.

establishing stock shot A take that uses **file footage** to set up the location of a scene for the audience; e.g., the Houses of Parliament seen in an aerial shot.

ethnic humor 1. Inauthentic outsider jokes that mock groups and cultures; e.g., many of vaudeville's dialect comedy acts. Sigmund Freud thought that when people laugh at insulting, inauthentic ethnic jokes it shows that they are shocked, and also that they understand the nature of the prejudice, even if they don't subscribe to it. Also, their laughter may involve a narcissistic impulse to feel superior. **2.** Authentic sociocultural jokes about a group that arise from the group itself and from its culture.

ethnic theater, film, radio, and television Authentic plays, movies, and programs emanating from and devoted to the lives, activities, life situations, and problems of a particular societal group that shares a distinctive background, history and culture—which may include a religion and/or language—different from that of the mainstream majority culture that surrounds it. Ethnic entertainment in the United States includes, for instance, those important contributions to the creative, interpretive, and performing arts of Native-American, African-American, Asian-American, and Hispanic-American writers and artists that concern their own groups. Often, the entertainment may be performed in the group's language; e.g., Spanish-language theater, Yiddish theater and film, and Italian-American theater at the turn of the 20th c. Some language-specific ethnic venues have been so large that they have necessitated the formation of performers' unions; e.g., the Hebrew Actors Union and the Guild of Italian-American Actors (GIAA).

ethnic type A vague, elastic (not to say outmoded) casting category, usually referring to anyone who is not of northern European ethnic background.

euphemism (yoo' phuh mih' zuhm) *n.* The substitution of an unobjectionable or sensitive term for an objectionable, blunt, or potentially unpleasant one. In Edward Albee's *Who's Afraid of Virginia Woolf?*, the idea of euphemism as a form of squeamish censorial puritanism is made fun of when the toilet is referred to as "the euphemism."

eurythmics (y*oo* rihth' mihks) *n.* Rhythmic games, dances, exercises, and gymnastics intended to inculcate a sense of movement and **rhythm**; first designed by the Swiss musician Émile-Jacques Dalcroze (1865–1950) as a method of experiencing music viscerally through movement exercise. Eurythmics had an influence on public education and on education for the theater. The exercises are useful not only for musicians, but also for **actor training**; e.g., for developing the actor's sense of tempo and rhythm.

event *n.* Stanislavsky's term for an important, key happening in a drama.

exclusive *adj.* Pertains to the condition of working with only one actor's talent representative or **agent**, as opposed to freelancing with many: *exclusive contract*.

exclusivity *n.* **1.** The condition, written into a performer's **commercial** contract, that allows the performer to advertise only one particular brand-name product, and no other similar product. **2.** The condition of being signed with one agent, as opposed to freelancing.
See CONFLICT; CONFIDENTIALITY AGREEMENT; SIGNED.

executive in charge of production A supervisor who coordinates logistics for one or more of a company's entertainment projects, esp. in television.

executive producer The person at the helm of a particular film project with ultimate responsibility for it, who makes sure all areas and aspects of the production are coordinated.

Executive Speech Prompter *Trademark* A small **videoprompter** that sits on a desk or podium, so that lines can easily be read by a speaker.

exeunt; exeunt omnes (ehks' ee *oo*nt om' neh:s) [Latin] Stage directions: they leave; they all leave.

exit *n., v.* [Latin: he or she leaves] —*n.* **1.** A character's departure from a scene. **2.** The way out of a theater set leading to the **backstage** area. —*v. t.* **3.** To leave the stage. **4.** A stage direction: he or she leaves.

exit line A character's last words before leaving the stage; esp. refers to a line meant to be punched, done with a flourish, or delivered as a parting sally.

exit lights The lamps over a theater auditorium's doorways; they are illuminated in the dark during a performance.

exit music A sprightly theme played as a performer is leaving at the end of a routine; often a **signature tune**. Also called a **chaser**.

exodus *n. Hist.* The concluding section of an ancient Greek **tragedy**; it always followed the chorus's last utterances.

exotic dancer Euphemism for a striptease dancer. **Syn.** *stripper*; *ecdysiast*.

expectation(s) *n.* What a character thinks will happen next, or awaits as a result of some action.
See ANTICIPATION.

experimental film 1. A motion picture that does not rely on the usual camera and editing techniques, but uses innovative methods. **2.** Such motion pictures, collectively.

experimental theater Play productions that are innovative and do not rely on presenting material in the standard way. Experimental theater may present new or classic scripted plays in unusual stagings and performances, or may be improvisational.
See BARBA, EUGENIO; BOAL, AUGUSTO; BROOK, PETER; GROTOWSKI, JERZY; SILLS, PAUL.

exploitation film A motion picture full of gratuitous violence or torrid sex scenes, meant to attract the maximum number of customers.

exploration *n.* That part of the **rehearsal process** where actors delve into the character's motivation and the playing of specific moments, with the help of a director. Eventually, decisions will be made as to how specific scenes and moments are to be played, and the process of exploration will then end. New ways of playing moments will be discovered organically in the course of performing, but the basic architectonics and dynamics set up in rehearsal will continue to inform the way the actors play.

explosion scene An event involving bursting vehicles, buildings, oil wells, and the like; created by special effects at the filming location, or computer-generated.

exposition *n.* Setting up and laying out the background details necessary for the understanding of a story, for the benefit of its audience. The art of exposition is a very difficult and complicated one, and must seem to occur in a natural way. For instance, it is usually ludicrous for one character in a play to tell another something he or she already obviously knows. Exposition may not always be used at the very beginning of a story, and certain expository details may only be clear later on. In other words, exposition may take place at different points in a story. Some stories begin *in medias res* (ihn meh' dee ahs rehs') [Latin: in the middle of things], so that exposition must perforce await a convenient time. And some exposition is indirect; i.e., shown through actions, or implied in a plot development without being directly stated.

exposure scene The moment in a drama when hidden motivations or secrets are revealed. E.g., the scene in Sophocles' *Oedipus the King* where Oedipus's unwitting crimes are brought into the open; the scene in Molière's *Tartuffe* where the perfidy of the title character is revealed to Orgon, whose wife Tartuffe has been attempting to seduce; or the scene in act 3 of Chekhov's *Uncle Vanya*, where Vanya walks in on Astrov and Yelena as they are kissing.

expressionism *n.* An **avant-garde** artistic movement lasting from about 1910–1925 in the German theater and cinema, prizing the individualistic expression of emotion. Eschewing psychological characterization, the expressionists used long speeches, unnatural situations, and strange dialogue. In film, expressionism is exemplified by director Robert Wiene's (1873–1938; vee' nuh) *The Cabinet of Dr. Caligari* (1920), a bizarrely photographed, surrealistic horror film about a traveling magician who has trained his assistant to commit murders.

exterior *n.* In film or theater, any scene that takes place outside; abbrev. EXT in screenplays.

external technique Those ways of working on a character that have to do with the character's **plastic**. In what has been called the *outside-in approach* to character creation, the actor begins with the externals of appearance, physicality, and ways of moving and speaking, before working on internal motivations—a so-called *technical approach*. The justification for this comes from the Stanislavskian idea that what the character does is of paramount importance, but the results can be unsatisfactory, shallow, and superficial; and the approach contradicts the idea that everything a character does has a psychological motivation that the actor must find before performing an action.

See also PLASTIC.

extra *n.* Syn. with **background player**.

extravaganza *n.* An elaborate, spectacular show with a large cast; e.g., some operas and musicals, the *Ziegfeld Follies*, the Radio City Music Hall presentations.

extreme close-up A shot that focuses tightly on and magnifies a particular object; e.g., an actor's eye or several petals of a flower in a vase. Abbrev. ECU or XCU. Also called *tight close-up*; abbrev. TCU.

extreme long shot A take from very far away, usually used for exteriors, aerial shots, and sometimes in an **establishing shot**; abbrev. ELS.

extreme sightline The farthest view of backstage areas from any particular theater seats; used for placing masking so that such views are concealed even from those seats.

eye line In film, the direction in which an actor is looking. A director must make sure that the actor is looking in the same direction in all takes of a scene, so that editing is possible.

F

façade *n.* False front representing a building exterior. In movie sets, façades are often used to construct entire streets on an outdoor set; e.g., parts of Warsaw in the World War Two era, meticulously recreated for Roman Polanski's *The Pianist* (2002).

facial lifts Concealed attachments that raise and pull back the skin, smoothing out wrinkles, making an actor appear younger; esp. useful when playing a character at different ages. With computer-generated special effects, the same differences in appearance can be achieved digitally.

fade *n., v.* —*n.* **1.** A film shot in which the images gradually grow paler until they disappear. **2.** A film shot that dissolves into another. —*v. t.* **3.** To do such a shot. **4.** To adjust the lights gradually in the auditorium or on stage: *fade the lights*; hence *fadeout*: the process of dimming; *to fade out*: to dim the lights out; *to fade in*: to bring the lights up.
    See also CROSS-FADE; DISSOLVE.

Fade to black! Turn off all the lights on stage gradually until they are out! Also heard as "Go to black!"

fair booking agency *Hist.* A **booking agency** that secured employment for vaudeville and variety acts at county and country fairs, during the Depression of the 1930s in the U.S. Instead of working for a **commission**, the agency would pay the performer a flat fee, and then negotiate with the fair manager for as much as they could get over the fee; this was called working on an "over and above basis."

fall season Autumn television schedule, with its **lineup** of new programs, and new series of old programs that have been carried over.

false proscenium Part of a set design, or of the structure of the proscenium stage, consisting of a frame or flats inside the proscenium arch.

false start Beginning to move or to speak before a cue is given. When an actor starts to say a line while another actor is still speaking, and then repeats the line when the actual cue comes, that actor has not been listening.

family show A television program or stage piece that is mild enough in its sexual overtones or use of violence to be suitable for people of all ages.

fan *n., adj.* [Short for *fanatic*] —*n.* **1.** A person who is devoted to a celebrity. **2.** A person who loves and enjoys a particular form or work of art or entertainment, or a particular artist: *a folk music fan*; *an Offenbach fan*. **3.** Someone who follows and enjoys a sport and/or a sports team. —*adj.* **4.** Pertaining to the adoration of a celebrity; hence, *fan magazine*: a gossipy periodical with details of celebrities' lives; *fan letter*: a missive from an adoring fan; *fan mail*: the collectivity of such missives; *fan club*: an organization devoted to a particular celebrity.

fan dance A risqué specialty act in which a young lady gyrates to music while using two huge ostrich plumes to tantalize the audience. Hence, *fan dancer*; e.g., the movie star Sally Rand (1904–1979), who did her celebrated fan dance at the 1933 Chicago World's Fair.

fantasy film A movie set in some fictitious world or place, and often involving strange creatures and supernatural events.

farce *n.* A fast-paced comedy that involves unlikely, far-fetched, and extreme situations, which are nevertheless plausible. Supporting characters are often eccentric, with quirky character traits. Sexual innuendo, broad physical humor, wordplay, chase scenes, slapstick bits, mistaken identity, frustration, and misinterpretations of people and events are some of its elements. Among the masterpieces of farce are Molière's satires, Chekhov's vaudevilles, and the absurdist plays of Ionesco.
    See also FRENCH FARCE.

farceur *n.* A comic actor who plays in farce, and specializes in the slapstick humor and fast-paced playing necessary for the genre.

farewell performance The final appearance by a singer, actor, or other well known artist: *The opera singer gave her fifth farewell performance.*

fast change Syn. with **quick change**.

fast cutting The rapid replacement of one shot by another, so that the transitions between images are quick; used to create suspense in such scenes as car chases, rodeo stunts, races, and other action scenes.
    See also ACCELERATED MONTAGE.

fauteuil (fo: tuh'ee) *n.* [French: armchair] **1.** An individual armchair in a row of unattached orchestra armchairs, esp. in older European theaters and concert halls. **2.** An armchair in a theater box.

favored nations [Fr. an international trade agreement term] A clause in a contract between a producer and an individual actor that stipulates that if another actor is offered more favorable terms (specified in the clause), esp. a higher salary, the actor signing the contract with the favored nations clause will receive those same terms. The phrase, commonly misunderstood, does not mean that every actor in a company receives equal pay: there is no such thing as a favored nations contract.

feature *n., v.* —*n.* **1.** A special **attraction** or quality. —*v. t.* **2.** To offer as a special attraction: *The circus featured a daring lion-taming act. The film features several name actors.*

feature film A full-length motion picture at least eighty-five minutes long meant to be shown in movie houses: *a feature-length film.* Also called a *theatrical film.*

featured player An actor with a prominent role.

featurette *n.* A short film, e.g., a **travelogue**; a DVD bonus about the making of the movie.

Federal Communications Commission (FCC) A U.S. government board that oversees, regulates, and licenses radio and television broadcasting, assigns broadcast frequencies, exercises a certain amount of **censorship** over words considered obscene, and decides which body parts may be viewed by the television audience.
See also BLEEP.

Federal Theater Project (FTP) *Hist.* A U.S. government organization, lasting from 1935 to 1939, that provided employment for theater artists nationwide, as part of the New Deal program to help overcome the Depression. Called *the Federal Theater*, or *FTP*, for short.
See also LIVING NEWSPAPER.

feed *n., v. Slang* —*n.* **1.** [Short for *feed line*] The straight line or lines in a comedy routine or joke. —*v. t.* **2.** To deliver the straight, or feed, line(s) setting up a comedian's **punch line**.

feedback *n.* **1.** [Short for *acoustic feedback*] Sound emanating from an audio system and going back into that system, resulting in a loud, sharp whistle or squeak; e.g., as a result of a person speaking too loudly into a mike, so that the sound of the voice bounces from the loudspeaker back into the mike again, causing an instantaneous, extra reverberation from the loudspeaker. **2.** Comments to an actor about his or her performance from someone not involved in the production; e.g., a friend who has seen it.

feed lines to To assist actors at rehearsals by giving them the beginnings of lines, esp. when an actor calls, "**Line!**"

feeling *n.* **1.** A sensory impression, which may give rise to **emotion**: *a feeling of hunger.* **2.** An affective state or condition that includes emotions. **3.** A general idea, intuition, impression, or notion about something: *Hamlet feels that someone is spying on him and Ophelia.*

feel the part To get inside a role with emotion because the actor identifies so completely with the character.

female impersonator A male performer who assumes and plays the persona of a woman and performs in **drag**; similar to a **drag queen**.

feminist theater Plays dealing with women's rights, sociocultural roles, and life conditions, including experimental improvisational plays done by women's theater groups and scripted plays, often written by women; e.g., the comedies and dramas of Wendy Wasserstein (1950–2006).

festival *n.* A gala, celebratory event taking place periodically and seasonally at a particular venue; e.g., **film festival**, **music and opera festivals**, **theater festival**.

Festspielhaus (fehst' shpeel hows') *n.* [German: festival playhouse] A theater specially built for festival performances; e.g., the Bayreuth Festspielhaus constructed for the performances of Wagner's operas.

fight captain The person in charge of maintaining, brushing up, and rehearsing stage combat during the run of a show; usually one of the people involved in the fights.

fight director The person who choreographs and rehearses stage or film combat scenes.

fight scene An film or stage episode involving pugnacious behavior between individuals or groups.

figurative language The use of words in other than an everyday, standard, communicative way in order to amplify and create meaning in both literature and ordinary discourse. Understanding figurative language and figures of speech is particularly necessary when the actor is doing Shakespearean and other verse plays, or the witty comedies of such writers as Oscar Wilde or George Bernard Shaw.
See also APHORISM; EPIGRAM; EUPHEMISM; METAPHOR; METONYMY; PATHETIC FALLACY; PUN; SIMILE; SYNECHDOCHE; VERSE TECHNIQUE.

file footage Archived film shots of locations, people, or objects that are used in such takes as an **establishing stock shot**, or in documentaries. Also called *found footage*.

fill *v. t.* To complete casting: *fill the roles*.

fill light 1. A lighting instrument used to provide a softening effect for shadows in areas on a stage that are directly and brightly illuminated. **2.** The illumination so provided.

film *n., v.* —*n.* **1.** A long, light-sensitive, emulsion-coated, acetate-based plastic ribbon on which photographic images are registered as negatives when the strip in a **camera** is exposed to light. The film is then developed so that the positive images can be seen when printed, or shown on a screen. **2.** A motion picture. —*v. t.* **3.** To photograph a motion picture, scene, or anything in motion.

film clip A brief excerpt from a motion picture, often used for publicity on talk shows.

film cycle A series of movies that tell a continuous story; e.g., *The Lord of the Rings* trilogy, the *Star Wars* hexology.

film editing The process of putting together a motion picture from the various shots and recorded tracks by assembling them into a whole.

film festival Gala, celebratory event taking place periodically and seasonally, centered around the exhibition of selected motion pictures. The ***Ross Reports'*** *Film Casting and Production Directory* for 2008/2009 lists more than 280 film festivals for the United States alone, with more than eighty of those in California. Festivals are attended by the filmmakers, actors, and others involved in the chosen movies; by people in the motion picture industry; and by the general public. Festivals, which may last for a week or more, are very good places for actors to be seen, and to meet and mingle and **network**. Some of the most prestigious are the Cannes Film Festival and Market in France; Robert Redford's Sundance Film Festival in Utah; Germany's International Berlin Film Festival; Italy's Venice Film Festival; and the New York and Tribeca Film Festivals, both in New York City.

filmgoer *n.* A spectator who attends the cinema.

filmic *adj.* Having qualities associated with or appropriate to a **movie**; cinematic.

film industry The branch of the entertainment industry in which professional motion pictures are made, involving all those employed in it. Also called *the movie business*.

filmization *n.* A movie adaptation of a novel, story, play, etc.

film noir (nwahr') [French: black film] An American genre of crime movies that deal with nearly inextricable, painful situations; made generally through the 1940s and 50s; e.g., *The Maltese Falcon* (1941), Alfred Hitchcock's *Strangers on a Train* (1951).

filmography *n.* **1.** The partial or comprehensive listing of the movies of a director, actor, cinematographer, or other industry professional. **2.** A list of the films in a particular genre.

film rating system See MPAA RATINGS.

film residual Payment to actors and/or other personnel for the showing of a motion picture on television or the Internet.

filmspeak *n.* The jargon and the vocabulary of terms used specifically in the movie business.

film strip A length of a finished movie containing a scene or part of a scene.

final call The last notification to actors and crew that a theater performance is about to begin: "Places!" *Brit.* "Beginners!"

final curtain The end of a play.

final cut The completed version of a movie.

finale *n.* The concluding section of an act in an opera, operetta, or musical; or of a movement in a symphony, concerto, or other musical composition.

find the light To check where the light is brightest, followed immediately by moving into the **hot spot**; an actor's technique.

fire curtain The proscenium-size protective screen behind the proscenium curtain of a theater; formerly wire-mesh asbestos, now usually steel. Also called *safety curtain*.

fire effect In film or television, a controlled incendiary event; e.g., a burning building, or a person wearing special protective clothing that is set alight.

fire gag Syn. with **burn gag**.

Fire in the hole! A warning from the motion picture technician in charge of pyrotechnics that an explosive device is about to be detonated.

fire suit A protective, flameproof, fire-resistant, or inflammable costume or full-fitting body garment, and fire-retardant underclothing and socks, worn by performers in stunts involving the use of fire. Also called *burn suit*.

first balcony The raised seating area immediately above the orchestra in a theater auditorium that has more than one **balcony**.

first hand The chief assistant to the **costume shop** manager.

first night Official opening performance of a play; or of a motion picture or other show. Also called the *premiere*; *opening night*.

first-nighter *n.* A theatergoer who habitually attends the premieres of plays.

first position 1. The starting **mark** for an actor or camera at the beginning of a take. The film director will say, "First positions!" or "**Into positions!**" meaning that the actors are to take their places. **2.** In ballet, the placement of the feet in a line, heels touching each other, with the arms forming a graceful semicircle.

first refusal [Short for *right of first refusal*] Reserving an actor's services for a particular **commercial** (or other project) on a particular day; the producer who has put the actor **on hold** has the right to that actor's services before another producer, who might want to use the actor on the same day: *to be put on first refusal. You're on first refusal.* If the actor on first refusal is put on hold for a second commercial for the same date, the actor is said to be on "second refusal." The phrases have no legal force, but are conventionally agreed upon and honored.

first-run *adj.* Pertaining to the original release and initial showing of major feature films: *a first-run movie*.

first team The cast of actors playing the roles in a film, as opposed to their stand-ins, i.e., the **second team**, used to help in camera placement and lighting arrangements before the shooting begins: *Let's have the first team back in*, i.e., the setup has been completed—a frequently heard instruction from a director.

first unit The film crew that shoots the **principal photography**.
    See also SECOND UNIT.

fitting *n.* **1.** Short for **costume fitting**. **2.** Syn. with **wardrobe call**. **3.** [Short for *fitting rehearsal*] A television rehearsal for purposes of adjusting camera angles and positions (e.g., for a political convention), in which stand-ins for reporters and interviewees rehearse positions for the cameras, which go through their moves.

flash *n.* A brief, dramatic cut-in of a sequence into a film scene; e.g., the intermittent brief flashback images of the concentration camp in Sidney Lumet's *The Pawnbroker* (1965), a brilliant way of showing how the character played by Rod Steiger is haunted by the past.

flashback *n.* A scene or sequence in a film showing events that happened in the past, prior to the present-day events being depicted.

flash box A metal container that holds *flash powder*, ignited to produce a quick, bright, momentary light, creating the effect of lightning on stage.

flash-forward *n.* A sequence that shows a future event that may or may not occur; e.g., a vision of the future seen in a dream. Also called a *flash-ahead*.

flat *n., adj.* —*n.* **1.** A large, movable piece of film, television, or theater scenery, varying in size, and often made of canvas, mounted in frames, and painted. In the theater, flats are secured to the stage floor and to each other by stage braces and clamps. A flat, so called because it is literally a flat surface, may be painted to represent the walls of a room, with openings for doors and windows (*door flat*; *window flat*) or it may be painted to represent a three-dimensional environment; e.g., a forest. A *book flat* consists of two flats of the same size, hinged together so that they can open out and stand on their own in a "V" shape. A **flipper** is a kind of book flat: a narrow flat attached to a wide flat, so that the two may stand upright. —*adj.* **2.** Colorless, drab, vapid, unvaried, dull: *His performance was flat. That film fell flat.* **3.** Even, level, unvarying.

flatbed editor A motion-picture editing table with the film reels laid out horizontally on plates, and an attached monitor on which the film can be seen synchronously with its soundtrack. Also called *flatbed editing machine*.

flat lighting Illumination that washes over a film set evenly and creates a boring lack of contrast; seen in some amateur independent films, or deliberately used in **cinéma vérité**.

flat rate A fixed, set fee, contractually negotiated, that is paid to a performer or other employee: *a flat-rate deal.* No other monies, overtime, penalties, residuals, or royalties will be paid.
   See also BUYOUT.

flea pit A rundown, shabby, dirty, third-rate theater or **road house**.

flick *n.* [Fr. *flicker*: the shaking, unsteady, rapidly wavering light effect seen in old films projected at the wrong speed] *Slang* A movie.

flicker generator An electronic device used in the theater to create a fire effect by causing several strategically placed luminaires to send out a shaking, wavering light all at the same time.

flies *n.* **1.** The area above the stage, where scenery and lights may be hung and stored; reached along a **catwalk**, called a *fly gallery*. Scenery can be flown in (i.e., lowered) or flown out (i.e., raised from and to the flies) and attached to the **grid**. Also called the *fly loft*. —*n. pl.* **2.** [Pl. of **fly**] The scenery itself, stored above the stage.
   See also LINE; TAKE IT IN; TAKE IT OUT.

flipper *n. Slang* **1.** A narrow **flat** attached to a wide flat. **2.** A **set piece** or part of a stage floor that can be rapidly moved, or flipped, into its place.

float(s) *n. Hist.* In the 17th c., footlights made from oil lamps with lit wicks floating in them, put out in rows across the front of the stage.

flooding *n.* The act and process of widening the light beam emanating from a **spotlight**, esp. a **fresnel**, in which the lamp inside the housing can be moved back. Cf. its opposite, **spotting**.

floodlight *n.* **1.** A type of **luminaire** that covers a general area, and is not focused on a small portion of the stage or film set. **2.** The individual instrument that does this. It is usually gelled and combined with other lights that may soften its impact. There are two kinds: *standard*, which cannot be focused, and *focus floodlights*, which can be adjusted. A *wide-angle floodlight* is sometimes called a **broad**. Cf. its opposite, **spotlight**.

floor *n.* **1.** The area on a studio or location set where filming takes place. **2.** The playing area of a theater stage. **3.** The area of a television studio where taping takes place.

floor plan 1. A schematic, outline drawing of a stage set from above, with the wall flats, backing, crossover, windows, entrances, and places for furniture or other items indicated. Also called *ground plan*; *scene plan*. **2.** A schematic drawing of the layout of a television studio, with the set(s) indicated; e.g., for a soap opera. **3.** The layout itself.

floor show Entertainment at a nightclub.

flop *n.* A failure; an abysmal flop is a *floperoo*.

flourish *n. Archaic* A horn or trumpet fanfare: an Elizabethan stage direction, usually indicating the entrance of royalty or some other important personage(s).

flub *v. t.* To **blow** a line; to misspeak.

fluff *n., v. Slang* —*n.* **1.** Froth and bubbles; the lightest of superficial **light entertainment**; **schlock**. —*v. t.* **2.** To misspeak; to deliver an inaccurate version of a line. **3.** To arouse the male star of a pornographic film immediately before a take.

fluffer *n.* The person whose job is to arouse the male star so he can perform properly during a **pornographic film** shoot.

fluid camera Constant, continuous, smooth movement of the photographic apparatus during filming, as in a **tracking shot** or a **pan**; hence, *the fluid camera technique*.

fly *n., v.* —*n.* **1.** A piece of scenery (e.g., a large **flat**) that can be lowered and raised, and is stored above a stage in the **flies** by means of a system of ropes and pulleys attached to a **grid**; hence, the term *flying scenery*. —*v. t.* **2.** To raise or lower a piece of scenery.

Fly coming in! A warning to everyone on stage that a piece of scenery is being lowered.

fly ladder A ladder against the stage wall that allows personnel to ascend to the grid and the fly loft.

fly lines; flylines The ropes by which flies are raised or lowered.

flyman *n.* The theater crew member in charge of raising and lowering the flies.

foam latex A rubbery chemical substance used in the manufacture of prosthetic makeup pieces, or to serve as a false covering in such grisly effects as the cutting of a throat.

focal length 1. The reach of the light beam from an **ellipsoidal** spotlight, determining where it will be positioned to best effect. **2.** The measurement from a camera lens's optical center to how far it can keep a subject within a clear range; its **depth of field**. The focal length varies with the type of lens used; e.g., the varifocal **zoom** lens.

focus *n., v.* —*n.* **1.** The concentration and clarity of view of a **camera** trained on an object that is **in frame**: *in focus; out of focus.* **2.** The adjustment of a **lighting instrument**, i.e., the amount of light spread, and the direction in which it is aimed; hence *focal point*: the place at which the beams of light are directed. **3.** An actor's **object of attention**; something an actor is looking at, relating to, or concentrating on. **4.** The central **event**, incident, or **theme** in a scene: *The focus of the scene is the troubled relationship of Hamlet and Ophelia. The focus of the last scene is the duel between Hamlet and Laertes.* **5.** The central theme of a play, film, etc.: *The focus of* The Graduate (1967) *is the loss of innocence.* —*v. t.* **6.** To train a camera on a particular spot, making sure that everything in frame is clearly seen: *to focus the camera.* **7.** To adjust a lighting instrument, training the light onto the area to be illuminated: *to focus lights.* —*v. i.* **8.** To concentrate, to the exclusion of anything extraneous; e.g., when an actor concentrates on an object of attention. Hence also, *to be focused*, i.e., concentrated: *She was focused on the action she had to play.*

fog filter A translucent, semi-transparent device that creates the effect of mist when fitted onto the front of a camera lens.

fog machine In theater and film, a mechanical device that generates smoke in order to create a hazy atmosphere, which can be used either for the smoke from a fire, or for mist and fog; e.g., the simple *smoke pot* used in the theater for burning kerosene, mineral oil, or special chemicals, of which safe, nontoxic, nonirritant compounds have been developed, and the more elaborate *smoke gun*, used in films to create the effect of mist rising from the ground. Smoke and fog are also created by immersing dry ice in hot water in a *cool fogger*, also called a *rumble pot*. Also called *smoke machine*.

foil *n.* A character in a drama or film who has qualities and personality traits that contrast with those of the **protagonist**, serving to bring out the protagonist's virtues and worthiness.

foliage border A long, narrow, horizontal piece of scenery on which the over-hanging branches of trees are painted; it hangs above a proscenium set.

foley *n.* [Named for pioneer sound effects editor Jack Foley (1891–1967)] Sound recorded on a separate **soundtrack** for insertion into the soundtrack of a motion picture. The film is run at the same time the recording is made, so that the *foley engineer*, also called a *foley artist*, can coordinate and synchronize the desired effect with the visual image. Such sounds as a door slamming, glass breaking, glasses clinking, a car crash, or an explosion are usually recreated and recorded in a *foley studio* by a skilled sound effects artist. An expert actor will watch a film and simultaneously record such sounds as someone out of breath and panting, or a lion roaring, or a dog barking. On the *foley stage*, tap dancers for a musical number will simultaneously watch and dance, as their steps are recorded and synchronized with the dancers on the screen; they may be the same group that did the filmed dance.

follies *n. pl.* [Used as a singular or pl. n.] *Hist.* A lavishly staged revue, or series of revues, featuring dance numbers, songs, and comedy routines and, esp., gorgeous young women in spectacular costumes slowly and seductively walking down staircases. Popular in the early 20th c. in the U.S.; e.g. the *Ziegfeld Follies*, produced from 1907 to 1931 by Florenz Ziegfeld (1867–1932).

follower *n.* Stanislavsky's term for the character who is led along in a scene. A character may be a follower in one scene and a **leader** in another.

follow shot A take in which the camera (handheld, moving on tracks, or mounted on a vehicle) goes along beside a subject as it moves; e.g., an actor or actors playing a scene, or animals in a nature **documentary**.
   See TRACKING SHOT.

follow spot A **luminaire** worked by a trained technician, called the *follow spot operator*; used to track a performer's movements during a stage show.
   See also SPOTLIGHT; TROMBONE; XENON ARC SPOT.

fool *n. Hist.* A medieval court **jester**.

foot *n.* **1.** The lip of a proscenium stage, i.e., the very front of the **apron**. **2.** In verse, the alternation of strong and weak stresses in a predetermined, recurring pattern. See VERSE TECHNIQUE.

footage *n.* Any length of film; often, film that has been used to shoot something: *footage of the campaign rally*.

footlights *n.* A row of masked, shielded bulbs, placed on the floor along the foot of a proscenium stage to illuminate the actors from below; the metal shielding may be for each individual light, or may run unbroken behind them along the stage floor. Footlights, considered old-fashioned, are little used anymore, except to create a period effect.

forecaster *n.* Syn. with **weathercaster**.

forced call An obligatory shooting session to which the performer must report, even though it is within less than the amount of **turnaround** time contractually permitted between sessions; overtime and penalties are paid by the production company. A forced call occurs in circumstances involving time constraints; e.g., when a particular location must be used within a certain period.

foreground *n.* The filmed space in front of the actors; i.e., the area between the actors and the camera. Anything that takes place in front of them is called *foreground action*.

foreground music Vocal or instrumental pieces performed on-screen as part of a film or television program; e.g., that played by a **dance band**. Also called *direct music*; *source music*.

foreign distribution The sale of a commercial, film, or television program to any place outside the country in which it was made, perhaps entitling actors to **residuals**. Some commercials are made in the United States specifically for a foreign market, and may only be shown in that market, unless the contract is renegotiated; the actors are often paid a **buyout** fee, which precludes residuals. In other cases, residuals must be paid, but it is nearly impossible to monitor the showings of such commercials or shows.

foreshadowing *n.* The prefiguring of some future event in a play or film by something that happens, or by an indication in the dialogue.
    See also PLANT.

forestage *n.* **1.** The front part of the stage, including the stage **apron**. **2.** The stage **apron**.

foreworks *n. pl.* Norwegian dramatist Henrik Ibsen's (1828–1906) term for the preliminaries involved in writing a play; e.g., the outline and first sketches.

formalism *n.* **1.** Adherence to the idea of designing generalized scenery or stages that could serve for productions of any kind of play, using non-representational shapes or forms; hence, *formal stage*; *formal setting*. **2.** A movement in the Russian theater during the 1920s and '30s, exemplified in Vsevelod Meyerhold's productions, which used **symbolism** in the scenic and directorial presentation of plays.

formulaic *adj.* **1.** Participating in the conventions of a particular genre in an unoriginal way; clichéd. **2.** Repeating a pattern that has been done many times already.

found footage Syn. with **file footage**.

4-As *n.* Short for **Associated Actors and Artistes of America (4-As)**.

four-camera technique Using four cameras simultaneously to shoot a scene; esp. useful in filming and editing stunt sequences; often used in sitcoms. Called *four-camera* for short.

four-wall set Movie décor constructed with four movable partitions, each of which can be placed in such a position as to allow a camera to shoot a scene at different angles.

fourth wall [A term fr. the proscenium stage set with three walls; the front of the stage constituted the missing "fourth wall."] An imaginary partition or, by extension, any imaginary setting between the actors and the audience. In order to develop a sense of **privacy** or **public solitude**, the actor may place imaginary objects on the wall of a room; or, if the scene is on a ship's deck, may imagine the ocean. The concept can be used for a three-quarters arena stage or in the round, where fourth walls are on all sides of the playing area; or in shooting a film using the **bluescreen process**.

frame *v. t.* To compose a shot by focusing through a viewfinder on a particular area, which is then *in frame*.
    See also ANGLE; BALANCE.

franchise *n.* **1.** The legal right granted to a talent agency by performing arts unions to represent union members, upon signing an agreement that stipulates the rules the agency must abide by; hence, *a franchised agency*. **2.** A series of lucrative theatrical films licensed for showing on television and in other venues; released on VHS and DVD; and giving rise to products such as action figures; e.g., the *Indiana Jones* franchise.

freak show The exhibition of unusual, often physically abnormal people or animals, esp. as a **sideshow** attraction at a **circus** or **carnival**; hence, by extension, a derogatory, dismissive term for an outlandish show or event of any kind.

freedom *n.* The actor's liberty to make choices in rehearsal, and to play moments spontaneously in performance, while remaining true to what has been **set**.

freelance *n., v., adj.* —*n.* **1.** An independent contractor; a worker without fixed employment who is free to take job after job; e.g., a book recording artist. —*v. i.* **2.** To work as an independent contractor. **3.** To work with several commercial or legit agents, as opposed to being **signed**. —*adj.* **4.** Independently contracted; employed on a job-to-job basis: *a freelance worker*.

freeze —*v. t.* **1.** The television convention of holding the final image on-screen at the end of a telefilm or program motionless, to finalize the ending. —*v. i.* **2.** To stop what one is doing, and hold one's position without moving; or to assume a particular position and hold it. **3.** To be a victim of a sudden attack of nerves during a performance.

Freeze! "Stop what you are doing, be completely still, and hold the exact position you stopped in without moving at all!" In the theater, this direction is used for a **tableau** that the director has created on stage. In a film, the director may say "Freeze!" to all the actors on a set in order to create the special effect of an actor vanishing from the scene. The actors remain static and still, while the actor who is supposed to disappear walks out of frame. The direction to resume normal action is then given. When the final edited scene is shown, with the actor's leaving cut out of it, the actor appears to have vanished like a ghost. There is a well known **theater game** in which actors move around until they hear the teacher's command, "Freeze!" The actors must stop and may not move again until told to do so; they are supposed to take account of how they feel in the frozen position.

freeze-frame A still picture in a film that results from printing one shot as many times as necessary to achieve the effect of a stationary picture. Such shots may be edited into a scene in order to create a dramatic effect when the freeze-frame shot suddenly gives way to live action. **Syn.** *stop-motion*; *stop-motion photography*.

French farce A **bedroom farce** or **sex comedy**; e.g., those by Georges Feydeau (1862–1921) and others who wrote for **boulevard theater**. Feydeau's plays are now considered classics, and are performed at the **Comédie Française**.

French hours On a SAG shoot, a system of fluid mealtimes, with food constantly available, but without set meal breaks for the entire company at once. Cf. **non-deductible meal (NDM)**.
See also MEAL PENALTY.

French scene. See SCENE.

fresnel (fruh nehl') *n*. [Named for Augustin-Jean Fresnel (1788–1827), the French scientist who invented the grooved lens that gives this light its particularity.] A soft **spotlight** that focuses diffused light with a blurred outline on a particular area of the stage; one of the most generally used luminaires in the theater. Its focus may be made wider or narrower by moving the lamp inside the luminaire forward or back. Fresnels are usually arranged in rows, and function together.

fright wig A hairpiece with unruly shocks sticking wildly up and out in every direction, looking as if its wearer were terrified; worn by circus clowns and low comedians.

Fringe *n. Brit.* London's equivalent of Off- and Off-Off-Broadway; hence, *fringe theater*; *fringe festival*: presenting productions of all kinds.

fringe benefits Monies paid out for other than actual salary payments (e.g., obligatory contributions by a producer to a union's health and welfare fund) and other forms of compensation not covered by wages and fees, such as comps, or the free use of a company vehicle.

front credits The listing of lead performers and creative staff that appears at the beginning of a film or television program.
See also ABOVE THE TITLE; BILLING.

front car mount Support structure for holding a camera or cameras fastened securely onto the forepart of a vehicle, so that the cameraperson can film the vehicle's interior. Cf. **rear car mount**.

front lighting Lights illuminating an actor or object from in front of the actor or object; hence *front light*: the lighting instrument so used, in theater and in film.

front lot The area of a movie studio complex where its main entrance is located, with security booths manned by guards; the administrative offices, parking facilities; studios, soundstages, outbuildings for wardrobe and makeup, etc.
   See also BACK LOT.

front projection An image on a screen, flat, or other piece of scenery that comes from a projector located somewhere in front of the screen. Cf. its opposite, **rear projection**.

full body shot An inclusive take or view of an actor from head to foot.

full house A theater or cinema in which every seat is occupied; a sold-out house.

full shot A take of a performer's entire body, or of some other subject photographed so that all of it can be seen. Also called a *full-frame shot*, because the subject fills the frame.

furniture plot The listing of the furniture used in each act of a play, in the order in which it is needed, together with notes on its exact placement.

fustian *n.* A bombastic, ranting style of performing, esp. in melodrama; **ham** acting.

futurism *n.* An early 20th-c. artistic movement, popular esp. in Italian film; e.g., A. G. Bragaglia's *Perfido Incanto* [(pehr' fee do ihn kahn' to) Perfidious Enchantment; 1906]. His principal tenet was that technology holds the key to development in the arts. Computer-generated special effects are an example of the kind of thing the futurists had in mind.

G

gaffer *n.* Chief electrician and supervisor of the lighting crew in a theater or film studio.

gaffer tape Another name for **duct tape**; esp. used in photography, theater, and the media. Also called *gaff tape*; *gaffer's tape*.

gag *n. Slang.* **1.** A **joke**. **2.** A **bit** of comic business. **3.** An **ad lib. 4.** In film, a **stunt**.
See also PUNCH LINE; RUNNING GAG; SIGHT GAG.

gala *n.* A special, glamorous evening, usually at high prices; e.g., an awards ceremony banquet, the reception held at the premiere of a film, or a performance and reception given to benefit a charity: *a charity gala*; *a gala performance*.

gallery *n. Brit.* **1.** The uppermost tiered seating area in a theater auditorium; at the Metropolitan Opera, it is called the *family circle*. Also called the **gods**. **2.** A television **control room**.

game show A radio or television program on which competing contestants play games of skill or chance for prizes.

gangster film A genre or individual movie that portrays crooks, con artists, and assorted violent criminals and criminal capers of all sorts.

garden cloth A stock **fly** painted with trees, bushes, flowers, etc. used upstage as a **backdrop** to an outdoor scene, or behind the windows of an interior. *Brit.* Garden drop.

gas lighting *Hist.* The system of stage and theater illumination using coal gas instruments, from 1817 (when it was introduced at London's Drury Lane theater) until the late 1880s, when electric lighting superseded it. The first theater to use electric illumination was the Savoy in London, in 1881; it was built by D'Oyly Carte esp. to produce **Gilbert and Sullivan**. The gas lights were hot and could be smoky, and added to the stuffiness of theater auditoriums.

gaslight *v. t.* [Fr. the film *Gaslight* (1944), in which the fortune hunter (Charles Boyer) tries to drive his unsuspecting wife (Ingrid Bergman) insane. He dims the gas lights in the house, and when she remarks on it, tells her she is imagining things.] To try to manipulate someone into believing he or she is losing all grip on reality.

gate *n.* **1.** The hinged frame of a camera lens; it swings out to one side, like a gate. See also HAIR IN THE GATE; CHECK THE GATE! **2.** The opening of a projector. **3.** The aperture of a spotlight. **4.** In an **audio** system, an electronic circuit activated by increasing or decreasing the power sent to it. **5.** A theater box office's receipts.

gauze *n.* Thin, small-meshed, muslin cloth placed in front of a camera lens, to help diffuse light and blur the edges of whatever is photographed. It was much used in old-time films to soften a star's features, and to create an ethereal, romantic, or dream-like quality.

gay and lesbian theater, film, and television Authentic entertainment dealing with the situation of the lesbian, gay, bisexual, and transgender (LGBT) community. Among notable playwrights and theater artists who have dealt with gay subjects are Paul Rudnick, Mart Crowley, Tony Kushner, Terence McNally, and Harvey Fierstein, whose outspoken Broadway hit *Torch Song Trilogy* was made into a film in 1988. Frank Marcus's drama dealing with homophobia directed against lesbians, *The Killing of Sister George*, was also made into a movie, in 1968. Jerry Herman and Harvey Fierstein wrote the Broadway musical based on the 1978 French stage play and film *La Cage aux Folles*. Martin Sherman's play *Bent*, filmed in 1997, brought to public notice the Nazis' persecution and extermination of homosexuals. There have been many gay, lesbian, and transgender films; e.g., the heartbreaking *Boys Don't Cry* (1999) and the brilliant, funny, moving *Transamerica* (2005), both about transgender issues, and the English **coming-of-age film** *Get Real* (1999). Television has had the long-running sitcom *Will and Grace*; *Queer as Folk* and *The L-Word*, both on Showtime; and HBO's *Six Feet Under*, which featured gay characters. There are two gay television networks: Here! and Logo.

gel *n., v.* —*n.* [Short for *gelatin*; from the days when gels were manufactured from animal products] **1.** A colored plastic sheet that is cut, shaped, and then fastened in a frame to a light; **amber** and pink are common colors; hence, *gel frame*: the device into which a gel is inserted for attachment to a light. Gels act as filters to create soft or atmospheric lighting effects, and to eliminate the harsh white glow of unfiltered lights. —*v. t.* **2.** To place such plastic sheets in position on lights. —*v. i.* **3.** To solidify a performance: *Her performance really gelled at the last rehearsal.*

general area mike One of several microphones placed at the lip of the stage, hung from the flies, or placed strategically on the set; hence, *general area miking*: the system of placing mikes strategically; used sometimes in opera houses and in large theaters, even where the actors use head or body mikes.

See also SOUND DESIGN.

general manager Syn. with **company manager**.

general release Nationwide distribution of a motion picture; larger than **wide release**.

general understudy An actor who covers several roles in a production; esp. common in **Broadway** musicals, where a **chorus** member may also be a general understudy.

genre *n.* [French: type; kind; sort] **1.** Different categories within a particular art; e.g., impressionist painting, baroque music. **2.** In theater and film, the type or form of theatrical literature, including tragedy, farce, and comedy. Each type of comedy (e.g., drawing-room or romantic comedy) is also considered a genre, although it is more properly a subgenre.

George Spelvin Fictitious name used in theater programs for an actor doubling a role; the female version is Georgiana Spelvin. *Brit.* Walter Plinge.

Georgian drama 1. Plays written and performed during the reigns of the four Georges who ruled England from 1714 to 1830; e.g., the comedies of Richard Brinsley Sheridan and Oliver Goldsmith. **2.** The theater of the post-World War One period until the onset of World War Two, named for the reign of King George V of England (1910–1936); e.g., the early plays of Terence Rattigan and Noël Coward and, in Ireland, the plays of Sean O'Casey.

gesture *n., v.* —*n.* **1.** A purposeful, expressive movement of the arms, hands, and/or head. **2.** Such movements, taken collectively: *The actor must study gesture and movement.* —*v. i.* **3.** To make a purposeful movement with part of the body.

get it across [the footlights] To **project** a moment, song, scene, relationship, or an entire character clearly, so that the audience understands the import.

get the bird To receive disapproving catcalls and rotten eggs and vegetables during a performance, esp. in vaudeville and British music hall.

Get the hook! An expression of disapproval, called out from the audience, esp. in vaudeville and burlesque, meaning that the stage manager should use the large crook on the end of a long staff designed for the purpose of pulling a performer off the stage.
See AMATEUR NIGHT.

get the show on the road 1. To prepare for and start a **tour**. **2.** To organize things properly for a rehearsal or performance, and then to begin rehearsing or performing.

get up 1. To mount the scenery for a show: *Let's get that flat up!* **2.** To mount a production: *We got the show up in record time.* **3.** *Hist. Brit.* In the 18th c., to prepare a role: *He got up Hamlet.*

get-up *n. Slang* An outfit; costume and makeup: *Get a load of her in that get-up!*

gig *n. Slang* A job, esp. in the performing arts; a **booking**.

Gilbert and Sullivan 1. The writing team that composed the comic operas. **2.** [Short for *Gilbert and Sullivan comic opera*] The comic operas of Sir W. S. Gilbert (1836–1911), who wrote the libretti and directed the productions, and composer Sir Arthur Sullivan (1842–1900), produced by Richard D'Oyly Carte (1844–1901): a musical theater phenomenon that took the Anglophone world by storm in the latter part of the Victorian era; hence, *a Gilbert and Sullivan fan.* Although there are still professional productions from time to time, Gilbert & Sullivan is now largely the preserve of American and British amateur companies. Also called *G & S.*
See also COPYRIGHT PERFORMANCE; LEADING COMEDIAN; NAUTICAL DRAMA; PATTER; SAVOYARD; SAVOY OPERAS; WHAT, NEVER? HARDLY EVER!

Gilbertian (gihl buhrt' ee uhn) *adj.* Pertaining to the topsy-turvy, paradoxical, whimsical wit exemplified in the G & S comic operas and other works of Sir W. S. Gilbert.

gimbal stage (dgim' buhl; gim' buhl) A huge platform mounted on a controlled, mechanized fulcrum or swivel; hence, *gimbal set*: an enclosed or open, full- or small-scale replica décor, controlled and manipulated by a series of hydraulic lifts and tubes (on large gimbal stages); built on the platform for use in scenes requiring that the set be in some kind of motion; e.g., the deck of a ship at sea or land that shakes because of an earthquake. On a smaller gimbal stage, the set is manipulated by stage crew using poles and projecting rods. The direction and speed of the motion on both small and large gimbal stages is adjustable. They have been used for a very long time: in 1951, the effect of Fred Astaire dancing on the walls and ceiling of his hotel room in *Royal Wedding* was achieved by the use of a gimbal stage, as were the action scenes in *Air Force One* (1997). Called a *gimbal*, for short.

gimmick *n.* **1.** In scripts, a plot device that draws attention to a turn of events; e.g., in **French farce**, where people who know each other enter and exit through doors, just missing seeing each other. **2.** A magician's secret device used in performing a magic trick; a gizmo or gismo. **3.** A means of drawing attention to oneself by unusual actions, dress, and the like: *One of Liberace's gimmicks was his array of glittering costumes.*

give [a performance] 1. To present a play: *They're giving Hamlet tonight.* **2.** *Brit.* To perform a particular role: *He's giving his Hamlet tonight.*

Give me a banana! "Walk in a single, continuous, gentle curve that makes a semicircle!" A director's instruction to an actor who must walk in front of the camera.

Give me three in a row! An instruction from a **voice-over** casting director to an auditioning actor, to record a piece of copy three times in a row, doing a variant reading each time and taking a pause between the readings.

give the axe to 1. To fire someone. **2.** To kill a project. **3.** To be eliminated from the television lineup of programs.

given circumstances Those situations supplied by the writer as part of a character's life, condition, characteristics, and background, as well as those that pertain to a particular production, i.e., the director's interpretation of a play; the actor's **approach** to a role; the sets, lighting, and costumes.

glasses *n. pl. Hist.* In 18th-c. theater, mirrors placed behind candles to reflect and refract their light, esp. in the auditorium.

global rule one The first law of any union member in the performing arts unions: to work only under a union contract. Also called *rule one.*

glossy *n. Slang* An actor's shiny head shot.

120

glowtape; glow tape *n., v.* —*n.* **1.** Specially coated adhesive that shines in the dark; used to outline steps and other danger points on stage, as a help during a **blackout** to actors exiting, and scene shifters changing a set while the curtain is up: spikes for furniture may also be glowtaped. —*v. t.* **2.** To put down such tape where necessary.

See also LED.

go *n.* Permission to proceed; e.g., with a light cue in a tech rehearsal: *That's a go.*

Go! "Do what you are supposed to do immediately!" This direction is a **cue** from the stage manager to actors or various technicians; often heard by itself, or combined with another word; e.g., "Go, curtain!", "Go, lights!" Directed to an actor, who must time an entrance, it means, "Enter now!"

goal n. What a character is aiming at or going for; **objective**; another translation of **zadacha**.

go back 1. To proceed to the backstage area, esp. the dressing rooms: *He went back to see her after the show.* **2.** In rehearsal, to start again, repeating what has just been done, then continuing on, as in the instruction, "**Take it back!**"

go blank To forget a line; also heard as "to draw a blank"; to **dry**. *Brit.* To blank.

gobo *n.* **1.** A flat metal disc or template with a shape or shapes cut out of it; e.g., leaves on a tree, the interstices of a gothic window. It is placed in a frame fastened onto a light, often a **fresnel**, so that when the light shines through the template, a visual effect is created either on the stage floor or on some part of the scenery. **2.** In film, a metal template placed on a camera, or a cloth or screen with a cutout template placed in front of a camera, to create various light effects. **3.** A shield for either a microphone or camera, to prevent the intrusion of extra sound or light.

gobo rotator A disc-shaped frame that holds a gobo, and whirls it around slowly or quickly to create an effect (e.g., snow or rain); an effect wheel.

go down To move downstage.

God bless you both! *Brit.* A wry phrase uttered out of the side of a performer's mouth—so as to be audible to others on stage—by someone bowing to an audience that has responded so unappreciatively to a joke that apparently only two people were laughing.

god light The shaded lamp on a conductor's music stand that shines on the score, and allows the conductor to be seen by the orchestra.

god mike The microphone connected to a theater's **PA system**, used during rehearsals by the stage manager or director to communicate instructions to the entire company at once, or to summon needed personnel who may be anywhere in the house or backstage.

gods *n. pl. Slang Brit.* **1.** The seating area at the topmost balcony in a theater, where the seats are cheapest. Also called *paradise*, as in Marcel Carné's **classic** film *Les Enfants du paradis* [(leh: zo*n* fo*n*' dü pah *r*ah dee'); *The Children of Paradise*; 1945]; *peanut gallery* in the U.S. **2.** The occupants of those **gallery** seats.

golden time In a SAG or AFTRA contract, any hours after a performer has been working for sixteen hours straight (including meal breaks). Each hour is paid for at a full daily base rate; i.e., if a background player is earning $115 per day, each hour of golden time will be paid at $115 per hour.

Goldwynism *n.* An oft-quoted paradoxical remark, verbal quip, or quiddity made by or attributed to Academy Award–winning Hollywood producer Samuel Goldwyn (1879–1974) of MGM. Among the most famous: *A verbal contract isn't worth the paper it's written on. They stayed away in droves. Include me out.*

good side Most photogenic angle from which to photograph an actor's face; sometimes insisted on by self-conscious stars, who would only allow themselves to be filmed from what they thought was their good side.

go off 1. To make an exit. **2.** To say the wrong line or do the wrong thing, out of confusion.

go on 1. To perform: *My understudy went on when I was ill.* **2.** To proceed onto the stage; to make an entrance.

go on cold To perform with little or no rehearsal. Cf. **wing it.**

gooseneck *n.* A microphone attached to a flexible arm placed on a rostrum, used by public speakers; the arm may be bent, and adjusted to the speaker's height.

gopher; gofer *n.* The **production assistant** assigned to "go for" coffee or fetch something else for the director or other personnel.

gothic film A motion picture set in an eerie, old-fashioned mansion, castle, or in some other out of the way place, involving mystery and sometimes terror; e.g., Conan Doyle's Sherlock Holmes thriller *The Hound of the Baskervilles* and Bram Stoker's *Dracula*, both remade many times for cinema and television, and Alfred Hitchcock's *Rebecca* (1940) and *Psycho* (1960).

go to contract To be moved from a non-paying **showcase** to a commercial venue, i.e., when a **producer** picks up an **Equity showcase** for a commercial production.

go to series To be picked up for production, i.e., when **network** producers order (buy) a season of programs from those producing a promising **pilot.**

go up 1. To move upstage. **2.** To forget one's lines in the middle of a performance.

go up for To audition.

grain *n.* The **Stanislavskian** term for the **spine** of a scene, the main **theme** of a play, or the life drive of a character: the motivating germ or seed that grows into **action.**

grammar *n.* **1.** In acting, the framework of the **system**: *Stanislavsky provided a grammar for acting, and a vocabulary as well.* **2.** In film, the set of conventions, shots, and takes that form the basis of the art and craft of filmmaking: *the grammar of film.*

Grammy [Fr. *gramophone*]. See AWARDS.

grand drape 1. A decorative valance that hangs in the upper part of the proscenium arch, concealing the top of the **house curtain**, the upper reaches of the stage, and the **flies**. **2.** An occasional term for house curtain. Also called the *main rag.*

grand finale The spectacular concluding section of an opera, musical comedy, circus show, or other entertainment, bringing all the performers on stage for an elaborate final appearance.

Grand Guignol (gr*aw*n gee nyol') [Fr. the name of the Paris theater that specialized in the presentation of lurid melodramas; *guignol*: glove puppet, or puppet show] Grisly, ghastly, gory 19th-c. **melodrama** full of murders, mayhem, torture, and sensationally horrifying special effects; also used as an adj.: *a Grand Guignol play*. Contemporary examples include Stephen Sondheim's Broadway musical *Sweeney Todd: The Demon Barber of Fleet Street*, directed by Harold Prince and made into a superb film by Tim Burton in 2007; the vampire theater sequence and other episodes in the film of Anne Rice's *Interview with the Vampire* (1994), starring Tom Cruise.

grand master A central control switch that overrides all other switches controlling a particular system; e.g., a **dimmer** system. A *group master* controls a particular set of switches within a system. Also called a *master switch*; *master handle*.

grandstand *n., v.* —*n.* **1.** The tiered seating area in a sports stadium, at a county fair or rodeo, or lining a parade route. —*v. i.* **2.** *Slang* To make a play for applause; i.e., to **play to the audience**. Hence, used as an adj., *a grandstand play.*

grand tier The first balcony above the tier of boxes, esp. in an opera house.

grant *n.* Monies awarded after being applied for by playwrights and others so that they can afford to pursue their artistic projects.
  See also WEB SITE.

grass cloth A large or small mat with artificial green grass, hay, or moss on it; used on stage to recreate a full lawn, a sparsely planted heath, or any other outdoor area.

grave trap [So called because it is used for the gravediggers' scene in *Hamlet*] The downstage trapdoor on a proscenium stage.

grease-glass technique Taking a scene through a lens smeared with Vaseline, in order to create a blurred effect.

greenroom; **green room** *n.* [Etymology obscure: perhaps fr. the (conjectural) Elizabethan practice of actors vocalizing in a room filled with green plants, for moisture] A meeting place or lounge where the actors can relax, wait for their entrances, and listen to the play on the **Tannoy**.

greenscreen shot A take using the *greenscreen process*; identical to the **bluescreen process**, but using a green background. The actors perform in front of it, and a background is later supplied.

grid *n.* The series of crisscrossed metal rods and tubes located just below the ceiling of a theater stage, in the **flies**, or above a film studio floor. Scenery and lights are hung on the grid. Ropes, pulleys, and levers are used to attach, lower, raise, and generally handle the scenery in a theater. The grid can be approached along a **catwalk**.

grip *n.* Stagehand in a theater, or on a film or television set, assigned to various crews (lighting, sound, camera, construction, etc.) to do any and every general task as necessary. Grips lay dolly tracks for tracking shots, assist other members of the crew in installing and positioning lights or cameras, and so forth. Each film crew has a **key grip**, who is in charge of the grips on that crew, and a **best boy**, who is the assistant to the key grip. In the theater, grips shift scenery manually, and do such jobs as walking up a flat; hence, *gripping*: moving scenery by hand.
    See also WALK UP A FLAT.

Grotowski, Jerzy (1933–1999) (yeh' zhih: gro tof' skee) Innovative, highly influential, avant-garde Polish theater director, theorist, writer, and teacher who went beyond Stanislavsky's ideas of psychophysical actions and Meyerhold's biomechanics to develop his own system of actor training and **environmental theater**. The so-called "rich" theater was one in which the politics of acceptance of normative social values prevailed, while he wished in his "poor" theater, with its direct relation of actor and audience, to propagate the values of basic human relations and revolutionary social reforms (in accord with Brecht's ideas), as he makes plain in his seminal book *Towards a Poor Theatre* (Odin Theatrets Forlag, 1968), a compendium of lectures and actors' exercises. His theater was his experimental laboratory; hence the term *laboratory theater*. Grotowski's semi-ritualistic plays were acted in various realistic, semi-realistic, and abstract settings in which a symbol or piece of furniture could stand for a place. The audience did not sit in a mass, but in various places on the set, so that they were often part of the action; e.g., in *Kordian*, which takes place in a mental hospital. Some spectators sat in the bottom half of bunk beds while the doctors dealt with patients placed directly above their heads or right in front of them.
    See also THEATER OF SOURCES.

ground cloth A huge canvas that is used to cover a theater's stage floor. Also called *stage cloth*.

ground plan Schematic outline drawing of a stage set. Also called **floor plan**.

ground row 1. A painted scenic border placed on the stage floor, to mask the bottom of a backdrop or a light. **2. Strip lighting**, usually placed upstage on the floor, to light a backdrop from below.

groundling *n. Hist.* A playgoer who stood in the area surrounding the stage of an Elizabethan theater; a standee. Also called a *penny stinkard*; the admission price for standees was one penny.

group audition Casting session in which several performers try out at the same time. Dance and chorus auditions may be held as group auditions: the choreographer will teach the dancers a number of steps, which they do for the casting personnel.

Group Theatre *Hist.* An influential New York theater company and collective, founded in 1931 by director Harold Clurman, producer Cheryl Crawford, and actor Lee Strasberg and lasting until 1941; known for its productions of plays by Irwin Shaw and Clifford Odets and for its realistic, **Stanislavskian** approach to acting; forerunner of the **Actors Studio**. Among its famous members: Stella Adler, Morris Carnovsky, Sanford Meisner, and director Elia Kazan.

guarantee *n.* A clause in a written contract that provides for unbreakable terms (e.g., salary, profit sharing, and billing); usually provided for stars and other key personnel.

guest artist An actor, director, or other theater professional invited and employed as a temporary member of a theater company to direct or perform in a particular play, or on a university campus to teach and/or perform. Guest artists working professionally in nonunion companies are covered by special **Equity** guest artist contracts.

guest director A stage director invited to do a production; e.g., at a **LORT** house where the **artistic director** does most of the projects. Hence, *guest direct.*

guest star A name actor who appears in a television series for one or more episodes, but who is not a regular member of the cast; billed as "guest star," "special guest star," or "special appearance by." Some guest stars are actually regulars who started their job in the series after it was already running.

guild *n.* An organization of professional craftspeople and artists. **Syn.** *union.*

gunfight scene Episode in which the performers engage in combat using any kind of firearm. In science fiction films, the gunfight scenes are often made using computer-generated special effects. Dummy bullets and guns are used where there is a live exchange of gunfire. Every safety precaution has to be taken; even dummy bullets and blank cartridges can cause damage. Also called a *shooting scene.*

gypsy *n. Slang.* Broadway musical comedy performer, esp. a member of the **chorus**. It is a time-honored custom to give the performer with the most Broadway credits temporary custody of the *gypsy robe* in order to ensure the success of a Broadway musical that is about to open. The robe, which is a gown decorated with emblems from each show for which it has been used, is given away by its previous possessor during a backstage ceremony in the new production's theater.

H

hack *n.* A bad professional actor who indicates, indulges in **mechanical acting**, and is content with clichés and stereotypes: *a hack actor*.

Hagen, Uta (1919–2004) (hah' gehn) Distinguished American actor and acting teacher; worked with her husband Herbert Berghof [(buhrg' hof); 1909–1990] from 1957 on at the influential school he founded, the HB Studio, to train generations of actors in their version of the Stanislavsky system. She emphasized the necessity of detail, of the actor's knowing everything about the character, and taught the importance of objects and how to use them effectively to portray **relationship** and character. Her first book, *Respect for Acting* (written with Haskell Frankel; Macmillan, 1973) remains one of the best books on the subject ever written, and her second, *A Challenge for the Actor* (Charles Scribner's Sons, 1991) is also highly informative.

See also LAND; OBJECT; RECEIVE; SEND; SPECULATION; WHILE LIFE.

hair in the gate A cameraman's phrase, meaning "There is some substance in the camera's **gate**." The gate must be absolutely clean—not a hair in it—when the camera is filming.

hairdresser *n.* The person who cuts, arranges, and styles performers' hair and/or headpieces. Hairdressers are more often used in the media than in the theater, except in cases where elaborate wigs or styling are necessary, as in a fully produced Restoration comedy or in opera. Hairdressers have their own supplies, tools, and kits, which are rented by film producers for a weekly fee. In the theater, each actor is sometimes required to report for a haircut once a week. Those hairdressers who do not deal with wigs are usually called *hairstylists*.

See also WIGMAKER.

hairpiece *n.* A partial wig that serves to conceal the wearer's baldness. A hairpiece may be required for a role, or the actor may wear one to conceal thinning hair. Also called a *toupee* or, in slang terms, a *rug*.

half-apple *n.* A box or crate four inches high, i.e., half as high as an **apple box**.

half hour 1. The time at which actors must report for work in a stage production, one half hour before the official announced **curtain time** at the latest. **2.** The stage manager's **call**, indicating that this time has arrived.

half-hour series Television programs, such as sitcoms, that are transmitted in thirty-minute broadcasts. The programs themselves are actually between twenty to twenty-five minutes long, to allow time for commercials.

half-price booth In New York and other cities, a **box office** located in a public area that sells a number of tickets at a discount for many, but not all, productions on the day of a performance. A board has the available shows posted on it.

halogen light A long-lasting lighting instrument that emits a bright light from a tungsten filament surrounded by inert halogen gas; used gelled in the theater, and as a small lamp illuminating the text for a reader in **book recording** studios. Also called a *quartz-halogen lamp*, fr. its quartz bulb; *tungsten-halogen lamp*: fr. its long-lasting filament.

ham *n., v., adj.* [Etymology uncertain; two of the more interesting guesses: **a.** Refers to the cheap ham grease amateur actors used at the beginning of the 19th c. as a medium in which to dissolve makeup powder; **b.** Refers to 19th-c. amateur actors themselves, the word "amateur" being pronounced with an initial "h" (hamateur) mocking the habit of snobs who, in an ignorant attempt to sound upper-class, inserted an "h" that did not exist; "hamateur" was eventually shortened to "ham."] *Slang* —*n.* **1.** A bombastic actor who indulges in histrionic vocal effects and exaggerated playing. —*v. i.* **2.** To perform in an overdone, inept manner; to **indicate**: *to ham it up*; *hamming.* —*adj.* **3.** Pertaining to an amateurish actor, and to the way such an actor performs: *ham actor*; *ham acting.*

See also DAIKON.

hamartia (hah mahr' tee ah) *n.* [Greek: error; mistake; fault] Aristotle's word for a hero's **tragic flaw**.

hand *n.* A **metonymy** for applause: *Let's give them a big hand!*

hand and rod puppet A three-dimensional figure with long, thin, wooden or metal poles attached to its arms and legs; worked form below by a concealed puppeteer who manipulates the rods with one hand, and uses the other, inside the puppet's head opening, to nod or shake the head. Cf. **rod puppet**.

hand cue A manual signal; e.g., **"Wind it up!"**; **"Stretch it out!"**; **"You're on!"**

handheld camera A portable, non-stationary movie camera; sometimes held with the support of a **body brace**.

handheld shot A take filmed with a portable camera, carried during shooting.

hand mike [Short for *handheld microphone*] A wireless or wired **microphone** used by emcees, singers, or stand-up comics; it may stay on its **mike stand**, from which it is detachable: the comic, singer, **emcee** or other performer may carry it and move freely.

See also TRANSCEIVER.

hand model A performer whose hands are so **photogenic** that they are used in **close-up** shots in commercials or in print advertisements.

hand prop Any object, such as a fan or a cane, that is used personally by actors and carried onto the stage, or is ready in place on the set. These props may be kept with the actor's costumes in the dressing room, but are often stored in their own specific places on a **prop table** conveniently located backstage, and the actor puts them back there when they are not in use. The term does not apply to such props as plates and forks in a dinner scene, but only to personal props that are used for a specific character.

hand puppet A miniature figure of a person, animal, or object with an opening at the bottom of its long cloth costume, so that the figure can be held over the arm and manipulated by the puppeteer. Also called a *glove puppet*.
   See also GRAND GUIGNOL; MARIONETTE; PUPPET.

hanging plot A schematic drawing showing where each rope or flyline has been fastened and what it holds fast, and giving all the details of each crew member's tasks regarding scenery.

happening *n.* A spontaneously held, unexpected, but planned performance event that may take place anywhere, in any public arena; e.g. in the middle of a meeting of some kind. It seems to erupt from nowhere, and may attempt to involve audience participation, or it may be an arts show with artists in different fields performing a **multimedia** event.
   See PERFORMANCE ART.

happy talk The inane chatter and banter that anchorpeople on television news shows indulge in when not reporting current events, sports, or the weather.

hard break The obligatory stop for commercials, esp. on a TV news show, where a newscaster may even be cut off in the middle of a sentence when the timer kicks in.

hard copy A book, CD, DVD, video or audio cassette, printed manuscript, or other material that can be held in the hand, read, or inserted in a machine for playback (as opposed to material stored and accessed in a computer). Cf. its opposite, **soft copy**.

hard sell 1. In commercials, a fast-paced, obnoxious, loud-mouthed, aggressive sales pitch; some actors specialize in this kind of delivery. **2.** Someone who resists sales pitches.

harlequinade (hahr' luh kwihn ayd') *n.* **1.** *Hist.* A popular 18th-c. form of entertainment, based in **commedia dell'arte**, and using such commedia characters as Harlequin and Columbine. **2.** *Archaic* The second part of a British **pantomime**, featuring commedia characters, esp. in the Victorian era.

have your lines down 1. To know your words perfectly. **2.** An instruction from a director; e.g., "Have your lines down by tomorrow!"

having had In film, an indication on a **call sheet**, when there is a late call, that a proper meal break will be taken after six hours, and that it might be a good idea to eat before arriving for the shoot, "having had" a meal: *12 p.m., having had*.

Hays code *Hist.* A set of criteria for puritanical self-censorship that Hollywood imposed on itself in 1930 with regard to the sexual content of films. The code was named for and administered by Will Hays (1879–1954), a former government official who became the first president of the Motion Picture Producers and Distributors of America (MPDA), later renamed the **Motion Picture Association of America (MPAA)**.

hazard pay In the theater and the media, extra monetary compensation for participating in dangerous activities required for the performance (e.g., stunts involving **wire flying** in stage productions of James M. Barrie's *Peter Pan*, or movie stunts such as a **burn gag**).

head camera A miniature camera fastened onto a cap/helmet on an actor's head by means of a clamping strap, and extended in front of the face by means of two thin wire arms to which it is fastened. Attached to a long wire cable that feeds into a display monitor, it photographs facial expressions registered on a computer during a **motion capture** or **performance capture** shoot; there are miniature lights on either side of it, lit during takes.

headliner *n. Archaic* The most important featured act or performer in a vaudeville or music hall show. *Brit.* top liner.

head mike A microphone worn on an actor's head during a performance to amplify the sound of the voice; sometimes hidden in a wig, headdress, or hairpiece, but more often, seen by the audience, because narrow tubing with the microphone at its end extends around the actor's face.

head-on shot A take of something coming directly at the camera.

head-on, tail-away shot A take of something or someone moving directly towards the camera and filling up the frame, followed by a take of something or someone moving directly away from the camera.

headphones *n.* An electro-acoustic listening device consisting of two earphones, i.e., miniature speakers through which sound is sent to the ear, attached to a band worn on the head; either wireless or plugged into equipment. Also called *earphones*; *headset*.

headroom *n.* The space from the top of an actor's head to the upper part of the frame in a film or television shot.

headset *n.* A compact, wireless or wired communications device consisting of a tiny microphone and earphones attached to a band worn on the head. Used for communication; e.g., between stage management and lighting technicians during a stage show.

head shot 1. An actor's photograph, either full-face or in three-quarters profile, used to present to agents, or to casting personnel at auditions. Also called a *glossy*; an *eight-by-ten*; *picture*; *pic*. See also COMPOSITE. **2.** In film, a take in which the actor's face fills the frame; e.g., a **close-up** or **extreme close-up**.

head voice The higher register: the upper range of the voice, the vibrations of which are felt mainly in the **mask**.

heavy *n., adj.* —*n.* **1.** The principal villain of a piece. —*adj.* **2.** Said of a play that is upsetting, serious, lugubrious, and hard to take.

heavy properties Furniture and other weighty set pieces used on stage.

here, today, now, this very minute The watchword of the **Moscow Art Theatre** actors who worked with Stanislavsky: every moment in a play happens for a specific reason and at a specific place and time, and the actor must know exactly where, when, and why.
    See also SPECIFICITY.

Here's another fine mess you've gotten me into. A **catch phrase** popularized by the comedy team of Laurel and Hardy in the 1930s. Looking tragic and injured, Oliver Hardy (1892–1957) addresses this reproach to Stan Laurel (1890–1965) in many of their films, but it is usually Hardy who is responsible for the mess!

hero *n.* **1.** A male **protagonist**. **2.** An exceptionally courageous man who would brave the most terrible adverse circumstances and fight to overcome them.
    See also TRAGIC HERO; TRAGIC HEROINE.

heroic acting *Hist.* In the 19th-c., the bombastic, stentorian declamation and noble poses used in such plays as Shakespeare's *Henry V*; it can be heard in acoustic recordings; e.g., *Great Shakespeareans*, with, among others, Herbert Beerbohm Tree, Arthur Bourchier, and Lewis Waller (Pearl, Gemm CD 9465; 1990).

heroine *n.* **1.** A female **protagonist**. **2.** An exceptionally brave, courageous woman; e.g., Joan of Arc, portrayed in many plays and films.

hiatus *n.* In television, the break between seasons.

high-angle shot A take done from far above whatever is being filmed.

high comedy Witty, jocular plays dealing with the upper strata of society and their romantic problems; e.g. **comedy of manners**, **drawing-room comedy**.

high-definition television (HDTV) 1. An advanced television broadcasting and receiving technology that provides sharper, clearer images than heretofore. **2.** A set capable of receiving such broadcasts.

hireling *n. Archaic* An actor engaged for performances who was not a regular, shareholding member of an Elizabethan acting company.

historical film A genre of motion picture, or an individual movie that tells a tale based on real past events; e.g., the **biopic** *Mrs. Brown* (1997), starring Judi Dench as Queen Victoria and *Reds* (1981), about the Russian Revolution of 1917. Many films that purport to be based on history are almost entirely ahistorical fiction.

history plays; **histories** Dramas that are based on real past events, as in the Shakespeare plays called by this name. Also called *chronicle plays*.

histrionics (hihs' tree on' ihks) *n*. Hysterical, overly dramatic behavior; theatrics; self-indulgent, extravagant acting. British and **French farce** would not exist without histrionic or hysterical types; e.g., Basil Fawlty, played by John Cleese in the television series *Fawlty Towers*. Histrionic characters include Mrs. Bennett in Jane Austen's often-filmed *Pride and Prejudice* and Blanche in *A Streetcar Named Desire*.

hit *n*. A hugely successful entertainment project; a **rave**; a **smash**.

Hit the lights! "Turn on the illumination!" A direction heard in a film or television shoot.

Hit the mark! The direction to a film or television actor to arrive at a designated spot. Also heard as "Hit your mark!"

Hit your mark and say your lines! "Speak as soon as you arrive at the **mark!**"

hog the stage To behave in an inappropriate, egotistical, overbearing, scene-stealing manner, drawing attention to oneself; also, *hog a scene*; *hog the limelight*.

hokum *n*. **1.** Clichéd, **mechanical acting**; indicated, obvious emotion; hence, *hokey*: pertaining to a **stock response**, or an unconvincing piece of acting or business. **2.** An obvious, predictable, contrived, unconvincing stage effect; **smoke and mirrors**, e.g., the machinations of the wizard in *The Wizard of Oz* (1939).

hold *v. t.* **1.** In theatrical terms, to pause. **2.** To prolong a moment or a pause, either deliberately (to allow the audience to laugh, or in order to create a dramatic effect) or unintentionally (when an actor has missed an entrance, causing a **stage wait**). **3.** To keep the audience's attention: *to hold the audience*. **4.** To pause momentarily during the **stop and start** of rehearsal in order to make an adjustment, whether technical (e.g., to change the position of a piece of furniture) or to confer with an actor or staff. **5.** To arrange for and carry on a rehearsal, meeting, conference, or other gathering. **6.** To keep a camera steadily trained on whatever is being filmed or photographed. **7.** In film or television, to put a performer or crew member **on call** for a particular shoot day. **8.** To put an actor on **first refusal** status for a commercial. **9.** To keep a commercial, film, or television show **in the can**, while awaiting its possible showing. **10.** To pay a commercial actor a **holding fee**.

hold for a laugh A technique of comic **timing** that consists of an actor's waiting until the laughter following a funny line is beginning to subside before he or she comes in with the next line. **Syn.** *time a laugh*.

hold over To continue the **limited run** of a show beyond its originally scheduled time, because it has proved so popular; or to run a show that was about to close, but continued to sell tickets, requiring the management to rescind its **closing notice**; or to schedule a performer for more time than his or her original booking; e.g., in a vaudeville show. Hence, *holdover*: such a show or performer.

hold the stage 1. To be popular and to continue to be revived and performed periodically: *Shakespeare's plays still hold the stage.* **2.** To keep the audience's attention during a performance.

holding area 1. The place set aside for **background players**, and, sometimes, for principals, on a film, television, or commercial shoot to relax in while they wait to be called to the set. **2.** The place on a location shoot where principal actors wait for their entrances, when they are not in their trailers. **3.** The backstage area where children in a large production wait for their entrances, supervised by the **child wrangler**.

holding fee The money paid for each thirteen-week **cycle** during which a commercial is not being shown. The producer who pays the holding fee reserves the right to begin showing the commercial again at any time, and pays the actor for contractual **exclusivity**, which ceases at the end of a cycle, if the producer does not pay the next holding fee.

Hollywood *n.* **1.** The section of Los Angeles devoted to the art of making motion pictures; many studio complexes are actually in other districts, such as Culver City. **2.** A **synecdoche** for the entire motion picture industry. **3.** A designation for the mythological place associated with the glamorous life of movie stars and their satellites: *the city of dreams*; *the dream factory*; *movieland.*

Hollywood Area Theater (HAT) Agreement The **Equity** contract covering employment in theaters seating fewer than 500 in the county of Los Angeles; there are four categories of such theaters, and seven salary levels based on box office receipts.

Hollywood Ten, the A group of writers and film directors who were blacklisted during the McCarthy era, after having been jailed for contempt of Congress because they had refused to answer questions in 1947 for the congressional House Committee on Un-American Activities concerning Communist activities in the movie industry, and their own possible Communist affiliations: screenwriters Dalton Trumbo, Samuel Ornitz, Albert Maltz, John Howard Lawson, Ring Lardner, Jr., Lester Cole, and Albert Bessie; directors Edward Dmytryk and Herbert Biberman; and producer Adrian Scott. Some of them worked under assumed names. See *One of the Hollywood Ten* (2000), in which Jeff Goldblum plays Herbert Biberman.
    See BLACKLIST.

Holocaust film A movie set in the World War Two era concerning the events, repercussions, and aftermath of the Nazi genocidal slaughter of the Jews, as well as events leading up to it in the 1930s and the Nazis' wholesale murder and persecution of other groups; e.g., Stephen Spielberg's *Schindler's List* (1993), Roman Polanski's *The Pianist* (2002), and Louis Malle's *Au revoir les enfants* (1987; o *r*uh vwah*r*' leh: zo*n* fo*n*')—all three based on actual events.

home studio A fully or partially equipped room, recording booth, separate area in someone's house, or an outbuilding nearby on the owner's grounds that is specially used for audio or, occasionally, video recording; e.g., by some musicians, film composers, or actors who do **book recording** and send the product to their employers via the Internet; or who do **voice-over** auditions at home for Internet transmission to casting people.

homework *n.* **1.** The actor's preparation for a play rehearsal, e.g., script and character analysis; studying the director's notes; planning actions and moves. **2.** Working on and memorizing lines for a film, sitcom, soap opera, or other media project.

honeywagon *n. Slang* The mobile **trailer** van that contains dressing and makeup rooms, and the toilets for all personnel, used on location.

hoochy-koochy show [Etymology uncertain] A routine performed as an **attraction** at a **sideshow** by a woman or group of women, involving sexual teasing, lots of bumping and grinding, and minimal stripping.

hood roll A very dangerous stunt in which the stuntperson jumps onto the left or right front of a stationary or moving vehicle and then tumbles off it on the other side, rolling off on his or her shoulders.

hoofer *n. Slang* A dancer, esp. a chorus dancer in a Broadway musical.

hook *n.* **1.** A large metal crook on a long handle, used to haul performers off the stage in the old vaudeville days, when the audience was booing so much that the performance could not continue. The hook was much used on **amateur night**. **2.** The **plot device** that engages an audience.

horror film A famously popular movie genre or individual film that provides the audience with chills, thrills, and shudders as stories involving monsters such as vampires or werewolves (or real-life stalkers and killers) unfold in gory detail; e.g., the many Dracula and Frankenstein films.

horse opera A mocking term for a **western**.

host *n.* The **emcee** or **presenter** of a television or radio show; hence, **talk show** host; **quiz show** host; **game show** host.

host theater A theater that invites visiting companies or productions; e.g., the Metropolitan Opera House in New York City, where the American Ballet Theater, or such visitors as the Bolshoi Opera from Moscow or the Rome Opera Company, perform when the opera is not in season.

hot actor A performer who is much in demand, and very popular with the public.

hot prop **1.** In film and television, any stage property that is in place and ready to be used. **2.** In film and television, something that can be heated, e.g., an appliance such as a hotplate or stove that will be used for cooking. **3.** In film and television, a loaded gun or explosive device that is primed and ready for use. Also called a *live prop*.

hot set A décor that is complete, and **camera ready**. Nothing on such a set is to be touched or moved except on the express orders of the director, and nobody is to go onto the set until filming is actually going to take place.

hot spot The place on the stage where a light beam falls at its brightest; the place that the actor has to look for when he or she wants to **find the light**.

hot ticket A hit show for which it is difficult to obtain seats.

house *n.* **1.** The theater auditorium: *The house is now open*; i.e., it is time to admit the audience. *The house was filled*; i.e., all the seats in the auditorium were sold: *a sold-out house.* **2.** The audience: *The house was very good*; i.e., either many seats were sold, or the audience was very responsive and appreciative.

house board A glassed-in case on the wall of a theater; e.g., on Broadway, where posters and cast pictures for its current production are displayed.

house crew The personnel who work in the front of the house, including the ushers, box office people, and concessionaires.

house curtain The huge cloth drapery that hangs in the proscenium arch. It is either raised and lowered, drawn from one side, or made in two halves and drawn to either side. Also sometimes called the ***grand drape*** or just the ***curtain***, for short.

house left The side of a theater auditorium that is to the spectator's left as he or she faces the stage.

house lights 1. The illumination in a theater's auditorium. **2.** All the lighting in a film or television studio, except that used for illuminating the set.

House lights out! The direction from the house manager or stage manager to turn down or lower the illumination in the auditorium.

House lights up! The direction from the house manager or stage manager to turn on the illumination in the auditorium.

house manager The person in charge of overseeing all activities in a theater that have to do with the lobby and the auditorium, and with making sure the backstage area is kept clean and sanitary. The house manager's duties include notifying the stage manager that the audience is seated and that the show can commence, and overseeing intermissions.

house right The side of a theater auditorium that is to the spectator's right as he or she faces the stage.

house seats Places in a theater auditorium for which tickets are set aside by the management. They may be given away by special invitation, or placed at the disposal of the actors (sometimes on a rotating basis), who may offer them to friends and relatives. But the house seats are not free to the actors, who must guarantee payment; invitees purchase them, unless the actor chooses to pay.

housing *n*. **1.** The metal shell or casing surrounding, containing, and protecting an individual lighting instrument. **2.** The protective metal container or casing for a microphone. **3.** Lodging for actors at LORT and repertory theaters, summer stock theaters, or any theater away from the actor's home town requiring a long stay. Housing is either provided by the theater contractually or rented to the actor for a minimal fee.

How different, how very different, is the home life of our own dear Queen! Apparently, an actual remark made in all seriousness by a Victorian English matron after a perfervid, histrionic performance by Sarah Bernhardt as Cleopatra in Shakespeare's *Antony and Cleopatra*. The remark became a **camp** ironic **catchphrase**, referring to the sexual scandals surrounding notable political figures.

hubris (hyoo' brihs) *n*. [Greek: overweening, god-defying pride] A combination of the sense of complete entitlement to whatever the **tragic hero** desires and a blindness to the consequences of his actions. The needs of others are ignored, and the tragic hero goes self-confidently forward to his own destruction, deflecting warnings from the gods or from other people.

See also TRAGIC FLAW.

humorist *n*. **1.** A writer of comic performance material or amusing, funny literature. **2.** Another word for **comedian**, particularly one who writes his or her own act.

hurry music Fast-paced instrumental **incidental music** played during action or chase scenes in a **melodrama**.

I

iActor.org A free web site for **Screen Actors Guild (SAG)** members only, sponsored by the union: an online casting directory that features SAG talent exclusively; www.iactor.org.

IATSE (yah' tsee) Usual appellation for International Alliance of Theatrical Stage Employees, Moving Picture Technicians, Artists and Allied Crafts of the United States, Its Territories, and Canada: the **union** to which **crew** members, stagehands, technicians, and other allied professionals belong.

Ibsenism (ihb' suhn ihzm) *n.* Adherence to the sociopolitical ideas of the Norwegian playwright Henrik Ibsen; and to his ideas on playwriting and the theater.

ice show A musical and figure-skating spectacular done entirely on ice skates; e.g., shows based on Walt Disney cartoons.

illusion *n.* **1.** A deceptive appearance; e.g., in feats of legerdemain, where the hand deceives the eye. In the theater, actors create the illusion of real life being lived spontaneously before the eyes of the spectators. **2.** A false belief thought to be true, because it might be: *He is under the illusion that he is God's gift to the stage.*

illusionist *n.* A performing **magician**, esp. one who does elaborate appearing and disappearing tricks involving machinery or **smoke and mirrors**; e.g., in *The Illusionist* and *The Prestige*, both released in 2006.
　See also ESCAPE ARTIST.

image *n.* **1.** A picture that the mind imagines and visualizes: *Hamlet sees the image of his father in his "mind's eye."* **2.** A picture; e.g., one recorded on film or in a photograph.

imagination *n.* The creative faculty of the mind that allows us to conjure up and see images; i.e., to see pictures of things that are not there before us in external reality, though they may be of things that exist in the external world. As Freud noted, reality and fantasy are not differentiated in the deep recesses of the unconscious, which is why we experience dreams as real. Therefore, to imagine that something is real is essentially to perceive it and to feel it as real, so that the body reacts as if it were in a real situation. This is true of past events, as well: all the emotions experienced at the time of the event are reawakened; hence, the value of **substitution** as a rehearsal tool. The senses remember, too. Taste and touch and smell come alive again, physically as well as in the imagination; hence, the value of **affective memory** and **endowment** as actors' techniques.

Imax *n.* A surround-screen process for showing a motion picture on a screen 70 feet high and 135 feet wide; 9 speakers are used.

imitation *n.* Aping or mimicking someone or something.

immediacy *n.* The present urgency of the moment, and of the immediate objective.

impersonation *n.* A portrayal of another person, usually a celebrity, done by an actor who *impersonates* that individual. Impersonations are complete characterizations; e.g., the depictions of Truman Capote by Robert Morse in Jay Presson Allen's stage play *Tru*, Philip Seymour Hoffman in the film *Capote* (2005), Toby Jones in *Infamous* (2006), or Helen Mirren's Queen Elizabeth II in *The Queen* (2006).

impresario *n.* A producer, esp. of ballet, opera, or visiting foreign companies.

impression *n.* An **imitation** of someone using salient features of that person's physicality; i.e., gestures, movement, facial expressions, and vocal mannerisms.

impressionism *n.* A late 19th- and early 20th-c. French school of music, theater, and cinema inspired by the impressionist painters and by **symbolism**, exemplified in the films of Abel Gance and others and in such operas as *Pelléas et Mélisande* by Claude Debussy (1862–1918), with a libretto by Maurice Maeterlinck (1862–1949), whose plays, such as *The Blue Bird*, produced by Stanislavsky at the **Moscow Art Theater**, are moody, murky, and mysterious, evocative and abstract, rather than concrete.

impromptu *n., adj.* —*n.* **1.** A genre of presentation in which the actors pretend to be improvising, although they are using scripted lines, e.g., Molière's *The Impromptu of Versailles*. —*adj.* **2.** Extemporaneous, on the spur of the moment: *an impromptu concert*.

improvisation *n.* A form of **performance art** in which the actor invents lines and actions in a situation that is either original (e.g., in-class exercises meant to promote spontaneity) or, as in Stanislavsky's **rehearsal technique**, based on scripted material. As a rehearsal technique, improvisations are meant to allow the actor to come alive in the situation, without relying on words that might induce a certain artificiality of feeling. Historically, improvisation was associated with the **commedia dell'arte** genre, in which actors would invent dialogue based on plot situations and the stock characters they were playing. American improvisational theater groups include Chicago's Second City and the comedy teams that grew out of it, such as Mike Nichols and Elaine May. Their hilarious, innovative improvisations were recorded on a Grammy Award–winning record in 1962. Called *improv*, for short.

impulse *n.* The spontaneous, organic desire to do something, arising from the situation the character is in at the moment.

in character Behavior, speech, movement, and gesture that are consonant with the personage the actor is playing: *to be in character*; *to play in character*. Cf. its opposite, **out of character**.

incidental music A score composed to accompany selected moments or scenes in the production of a play, to serve as a background to it, to *underscore* the action, and to create an atmosphere or mood; e.g., Felix Mendelssohn's music for Shakespeare's *A Midsummer Night's Dream*.

inciting action The compelling incident in a story that propels it forward; e.g., Hamlet's decision to avenge his father's murder.

independent *adj.* **1.** In the world of film and television, not legally bound to, an employee of, or associated with a major studio, producing organization, or major distributor; hence, *independent casting director*; *independent distributor*; *independent filmmaker*; *independent director*; *independent producer*. **2.** Not financed or backed by a major studio, although in many cases a studio will take over the sponsorship of the production: *an independent production*.

independent contractor A **freelance** worker.

independent film A motion picture not made under the auspices of a major studio or producing organization.

indicate *v. t.* Imitating feelings and emotions; showing what an emotion or an action is like, rather than feeling or doing it; one of the cardinal sins in acting, except in particular comical or farcical situations; e.g., when a character might be doing bad acting on purpose; **mechanical acting**.

indirect action Events that take place offstage, either before the play began or between the scenes, influencing what happens to the characters; e.g., the sale of the cherry orchard in Chekhov's play. In ancient Greek tragedies, violent happenings, such as the murder of Agamemnon in Aeschylus's *Agamemnon*, took place offstage; it was considered unseemly to show them to an audience.

indoor location A real interior used as a set for a **shoot**.

indoor set 1. A designed décor representing an interior, constructed in a film or television **studio**. **2.** An actual interior used on **location** as a décor for a shoot.

indulgence slip A piece of paper inserted in a theater program announcing a change of cast for the evening.

industrial *n.* [Short for *industrial film*; *industrial show*] A live, filmed, or taped project or show that deals with aspects or an aspect of a particular business or profession, used for publicity, training, or educational purposes; e.g., those made to inform and educate medical doctors. Some industrials are **in-house**: they are made by and for a particular company. AEA contracts cover live industrials; SAG and AFTRA contracts cover recorded industrials.
   See BUSINESS THEATER AND EVENTS AGREEMENT; NON-BROADCAST/INDUSTRIAL AGREEMENT.

industrial felt A heavy material with a matte nap finish used in making props, costume hats, and sometimes in scenery; e.g., as **backing**.

inflection *n.* The rising and falling pitch patterns of an utterance. Inflection and intonation patterns vary in different languages and in regional and foreign accents.
   See also DIALECT; VOCAL TECHNIQUE.

In five... four... three... two... [one]! The command in a television taping for the actors to begin performing, usually accompanied by a hand cue: the word "one" is not said. Sometimes preceded by the words "We're on."

infomercial *n.* A long commercial giving a lot of information about the product or service it is designed to sell; sometimes made with a studio audience of **background players**, who watch demonstrations.

in frame Within the parameters set up by where a camera has focused.

ingénue (a*n'* zhuh noo') *n.* A young actress with an air of innocence or naivety who plays a young lady character with similar characteristics. The character is also referred to as an ingénue; hence, *ingénue role*.

in-house *adj.* **1.** Describes a project developed internally by a company for its own use: *an in-house training film*; *an in-house industrial*. **2.** For a company's private internal use only: *in-house use*. **3.** Not for public broadcast; e.g., in the case of a demo commercial. **4.** Open only to clients of a particular agency; *an in-house audition*: some agents function as casting directors for voice-overs.

ink *v. t. Slang.* To sign a contract.

inky *n. Slang* A small lighting instrument that uses an incandescent bulb.

in one Short for **scene in one**; i.e., a scene played on the forestage.

in-ones *n. pl.* The set of **legs** placed in the wings immediately behind the proscenium arch.

in order of appearance A listing of the character's names in a program, beginning with the first character the audience will see.

in production Said of a film in the process of being prepared and/or shot, or of a theater piece in the process of being rehearsed and/or performed.

in sequence Pertains to a film shot in the order in which the scenes were written. See SHOOTING IN SEQUENCE.

insert *n., v.* —*n.* **1.** A sequence or brief close-up of something put into a scene to add information and focus the audience's attention on a particular aspect of what is happening. These sequences are shot separately from the main take on a specially prepared *insert stage* in a studio. **2.** A piece of paper containing an announcement, such as an **indulgence slip**, an advertising flyer, or the like, put into a theater program. —*v. t.* **3.** To edit such a sequence into a scene. **4.** To put separately printed material into a theater program.

inspiration *n.* A sudden, compelling desire to take action, aroused and stimulated by spontaneous creative thoughts, emotions, and ideas. As Stanislavsky and others have pointed out, actors cannot rely on inspiration alone to get them through eight performances a week.

instinct *n.* In acting terms, the general overall **feeling** or feelings the actor has about what the character is like psychologically, emotionally, and morally.

instrument *n.* **1.** A device used for playing music: *a stringed instrument.* **2.** The actor's mind, body, and voice. **3.** The singer's voice. **4.** The dancer's body. **5.** An individual light: *a lighting instrument.*

insurance coverage Arrangement made by a studio or production company with its insurance company to indemnify a production or project against loss: *production insurance coverage.* Coverage usually includes not only physical damage to or loss of equipment, costumes, the soundstage, and the like, but also the loss of a star. Stars must have their own insurance coverage against anything that might cause them to leave a project.

intelligent lighting Computerized system of theater stage illumination, whereby each luminaire can change color, turn, refocus, or move up and down for each automated **cue**.

See also COMPUTER-ASSISTED LIGHTING SYSTEM.

intention *n.* The subtextual meaning of a line; the reason for which the line is said, which is a determining factor in how it is delivered. Finding and interpreting the intention is one of the actor's most important tasks.

intensity *n.* **1.** The level of sound, whether soft or loud. **2.** The brightness of lighting, whether low or high. **3.** The amount and quality of emotional or vocal energy with which a song is sung, a part is played, or a particular line is delivered.

interactive theater Plays involving **audience participation** in some way; e.g., the Broadway musical of Charles Dickens's last, unfinished novel, *The Mystery of Edwin Drood*, where the audience votes on who committed the unsolved murder.

intercut *n., v.* —*n.* **1.** An alternation of takes in the same scene, such as that of a telephone conversation, where the audience sees each speaker in back and forth sequences. —*v. t.* **2.** To edit a scene by using alternating sequences.

interior monologue 1. The running stream of thoughts in a character's head that goes on constantly. Also called *imaginary monologue; inner monologue; internal monologue.* **2.** In film and television, a character's thoughts heard as a **voice over**.

interlude *n.* **1.** A brief entertainment presented between the acts of a play. **2.** A brief instrumental piece of music played between the acts of a play or the verses of a song. **3.** *Hist.* An entertainment presented between the courses of a medieval or Renaissance banquet, or a comic sketch performed between the acts of a medieval mystery or morality play; hence, a farcical sketch or short play.

intermezzo (ihn' tuhr meh' tsoh) *n.* **1.** A musical interlude; e.g., the piece composed to be played between the two short acts of Pietro Mascagni's *Cavalleria Rusticana.* **2.** *Archaic.* Music played as the audience returns to their seats after the intermission. **3.** *Hist.* In Renaissance Italy, a comic entertainment performed as an interlude between the acts of a tragedy, in order to lighten the mood.

intermission *n.* **1.** The interval between the acts of a production, during which the lights in the auditorium come up and the audience is free to wander about, returning to their seats on a signal that the intermission is over. **2.** The interval between the two halves of any entertainment; e.g., a concert or sports event. *Brit.* **interval**.

internalize *v. t.* To absorb a personalized **motivation** or **emotion**, and to feel it inside, making it part of the acting **score**; hence, *internalization*: the process of doing so. A **result** arrived at organically in a play rehearsal, or achieved more quickly in film acting by using **substitution**. An internalized emotion is read by the audience without any necessity for the actor to **indicate** it. Cf. **own**.

internal technique The set of tools the actor uses to create the character's mentality and psychology, fused with the actor's own mind and feelings. The basic Stanislavsky idea is that every **action** a character takes is the result of an inner psychological process, whence his term **psychophysical action**.
See ACTOR'S SECRET; AFFECTIVE MEMORY; AMBIGUITY; AMBIVALENCE; ENDOWMENT; MOTIVATION; PLAYING OPPOSITES; REPRESSION; SUBSTITUTION; SUPPRESSION; UNCONSCIOUS.

International Phonetic Alphabet (IPA). See PHONETICS.

Internet *n.* The world wide web (www) and other functions of the global cyberspace network, including email. Aside from being a huge encyclopedia and shopping mart, the Internet increasingly represents employment for performers. For instance, in 2008, television's Independent Film Channel (IFC) launched its first web-only weekly series, *Luncheon*, which airs on the channel's **web site** and features reportage on various new web sites and independent entertainment projects. Commercials, movies, book recording, and various other performance projects are now made directly for the Internet, for which pay scales and conditions are the subject of controversy and negotiations, as actors' unions try to assure fair play and fair pay for their members. In addition, movies meant for theatrical release, audio and audiovisual musical performances, recorded books, printed books, and commercials made for other media are often available on the Internet, where the buyer can pay to download them. Many are downloaded free of charge, and some are pirated; i.e., illegally downloaded without having been paid for. One of the main issues in the 2007 WGA strike concerned the financial rights and compensation that should be due to writers if their projects are used on the Internet; the result was a recognition of such rights. Called *the net*, for short.

Internet Broadway Database (IBDB) An exhaustive **web site** with information on all past and current Broadway productions, and all the people involved in them.

Internet, Interactive, and New Media Commercial contracts Agreements by Screen Actors Guild (SAG) with producers covering employment by its members in these areas, and establishing salary levels, residual payments, etc.

Internet movie A motion picture made for showing on the world wide web, and viewed on a computer screen.

Internet Movie Database (IMDb) An invaluable, exhaustive, constantly updated **web site** with information on American and foreign films, and all the people involved in them.

interpolation *n.* Inserted material not written by the author or composer for the particular project; e.g., an interpolated **aria** that may have been written for another opera, as in the Metropolitan Opera production of Offenbach's *La Périchole*, in which an air from *La Grande Duchesse de Gérolstein* was inserted.

interpret *v. t.* To analyze and make clear one's individual understanding of a work of art, music, or literature; a role one is playing; or a script one is filming.

interpretation *n.* **1.** In acting, the art and act of analyzing and understanding a character. **2.** The specific conception, analysis, and performance by an individual actor of a character, resulting in a particularized, personalized **characterization**: *Olivier's interpretation of Hamlet*; i.e., his conception, analysis, and performance of the role.

interpretive arts 1. Those aesthetic occupations involved in analyzing and making clear to others one's understanding and view of artistic, literary, theatrical, musical, or filmic works, e.g., theater, literary, or movie criticism; essays or books by literary or art critics. **2.** Often seen as syn. with **performing arts**.

interpretive dance The translation of the mood set up by music, things, places, or ideas into rhythmic movement; important esp. in **modern dance**.

interval *n. Brit.* The **intermission** taken between acts in a theater, between two halves of a concert, etc.

in the aisles In a state of near collapse from laughing so hard: *rolling in the aisles*.

in the can [Can: short for *canister*] Completely finished and done. Said of a film that has been completely shot, and is now ready for release; or of film stock that contains a complete take, and has been taken from the camera and placed in its protective metal container, awaiting processing and development; or of a commercial that is **on hold**.

in the moment Concentrating on and involved in what is happening, as opposed to thinking about what is coming up, or anticipating the next moment.

in the round [Short for **theater in the round**] Pertains to plays presented in **arena** staging.
See also DINNER THEATER.

in the running Being considered for a role: *She's in the running for Juliet*. Cf. **be up for**.

in the spotlight 1. Within the small area illuminated by a light that focuses narrowly on the performer. **2.** *Slang* In the public eye.

intonation *n.* The melodic or pitch pattern of a language or of an individual utterance; very important in working on an **accent**: *intonation pattern*. Each language has its own pitch patterns that may tend to carry over into a new, learned language.
    See also DIALECT; INFLECTION.

Into positions! "Get on your marks!" A direction to actors to go to their starting places, or to assume opening poses, because filming or taping is about to start. Also heard as **First positions!**

introducing *v. t.* [Present participle of *introduce*] Presenting for the first time. A film credit signaling the debut of a young actor in a leading or featured supporting role.

introduction *n.* **1.** A short **overture** played before the curtain rises, or a brief piece of music played just after it rises. **2.** A brief piece of music played before the main section of a number, song, etc., that is part of the number and leads directly into it. Called an *intro*, for short.

invade minimum; invade scale To take an agent's **commission** on the lowest rate of pay for a job: a practice prohibited to franchised agents working with AEA, SAG, or AFTRA clients. Of course, agents do not do this, but on some **commercial** contracts the actor earns **scale plus ten**, thus allowing the agent to earn a well-deserved commission. The term "invade scale" is esp. used for work in the media; the term "invade minimum" esp. for work in the theater, where agents may not collect a commission from actors working for Broadway or Off-Broadway minimum.

invited dress [Short for *invited dress rehearsal*] A dress rehearsal of a play to which the producer, director, actors, and other personnel may invite guests. Also called a **public rehearsal**.

in voice In good vocal shape for a performance; usually said by or of singers.

invoice *n., v.* —*n.* **1.** A bill for services rendered and/or for out-of-pocket expenses incurred in the performance of a job. Often, an invoice must be sent by an **independent contractor**, such as a **dialogue coach**, to a **producer** who will then pay the contractor. —*v. t.* **2.** To send such a bill.

in your head Intellectually or mentally playing a character, as opposed to viscerally and spontaneously feeling the part and playing the moments organically; the opposite of **organic** acting.
    See STOP THINKING!

iris *n.* **1.** A device consisting of a circle of overlapping, thin, opaque metal flaps placed in back of a camera lens, which remains closed until it is opened for an instant, creating a narrow hole that allows the light passing into a camera's aperture to register a negative image on film. **2.** Another name for the **diaphragm** used on a spotlight.

irradiation *n.* A late **Stanislavskian** term for the actor's energy in performance, given out or projected to other actors and to the audience, and received back or taken in again.

isolation exercise A common actor's movement or acting exercise. One version consists of lying flat on one's back, eyes closed, and concentrating first on the feet, and then shifting the concentration to the thighs, and so on, in order to feel the emotional and physical sensations and to become aware of the body as the actor's instrument.

It must be the landlady. *Brit.* Said by a touring performer of an audience that has responded with such a sparse laugh at a joke that the landlady of the **digs** where the performer is lodging is the only one to have laughed. Cf. **God bless you both!**

J

Jacobean drama [Fr. Latin *Jacobus*: James] The theater of the reign of James I (1603–1625), who followed Queen Elizabeth I on the throne; it includes the plays of John Webster, Francis Beaumont and John Fletcher, and the later plays of Shakespeare.

See ERUDITE THEATER; REVENGE TRAGEDY.

jazz singer A vocalist of popular music whose style includes occasional improvised wailing sounds like that of a clarinet or other instrument, and improvised melodic and rhythmic variations of a tune, much in a jazz style.

jerk harness A protective contraption consisting of straps and padding that a stuntperson wears underneath a costume while doing a stunt during which the stuntperson will be pulled off something (e.g., a moving motorcycle, a horse, or a bull in a rodeo) by someone operating the line to which the jerk harness is attached. Also called *jerk suit*; *jerk vest*.

jester *n. Archaic* A medieval court **fool** who dressed in cap and bells and **motley** and carried a **zany** and/or a bladder; a **merry-andrew**.

jingle *n.* A facile, catchy melody or **theme** played and/or sung in a **commercial**, and meant to be remembered as associated with a particular product; hence, *jingle singing*; *jingle writer*: a composer of jingles; *jingle singer*, also called a **commercial singer**: a person who records jingles, and is expected to know how to sing in various styles, from **legit** to rock, and in different voices, from a smooth lyric voice to a gravelly "beer" voice. Jingle singers may be represented by agents, working with a **music contractor**, or they may obtain work through their own contacts.

job in To hire an actor who is not a regular member of a company to do a role in a particular show; hence, *jobber*: an actor hired to come into a company.

join *n., v. —n.* **1.** The line between a wig, hairpiece, or prosthetic makeup device and the face, blended with care so that it does not show. **2.** The fastening of two flats. *—v. t.* **3.** To blend the prosthetic makeup device, wig, beard, or other hair line with the rest of the makeup. 4. To fasten two flats together; e.g., using a **stage clamp**.

joke writer A person who thinks up gags for a stand-up comic or television show, and writes witty, funny, amusing brief anecdotes, witticisms, droll one-liners, wisecracks, or skits. Also called a *gag writer*.

journey *n.* The forward development and arc of a character's life in the course of his or her story, step by step; where the character goes, and how he or she gets there.

journeyman actor 1. An apprentice actor. **2.** A **working actor**. **3.** An **Equity** member in a LORT or stock company who does utility roles, and works for **scale**. **4.** *Hist.* In the Elizabethan theater, an actor hired to play minor roles.

145

juice *n. Slang* **1.** Electricity: *Turn on the juice backstage!* **2.** Energy: *to get the juices flowing*; e.g., in a performance on stage or in front of a camera.

jukebox musical A stage or screen musical comedy whose score consists of the popular songs of a particular performer or singing group; e.g., *Mamma Mia* (1999; filmed in 2008), *Jersey Boys* (2005).

jump *v. t.* To be **off cue**, speaking at the wrong time before an actor has finished his speech: *He jumped a line.* Cf. **cut in**.

jump cut An abrupt, rapid transition of one image to another, used sometimes for shock value in a **horror film**; e.g., in Hitchcock's *The Birds* (1963), where we suddenly see the damage inflicted by the birds after having seen them flying towards the camera.

justification *n.* Logical, plausible **motivation**; appropriate reasons for particular actions, and for specific interpretations of both the character as a whole and of individual moments. Sometimes, an actor will be directed to read a line or do a movement that is not in accord with the actor's ideas, but that the director feels is necessary. It is part of the actor's job to **take direction**, i.e., to do what the director asks and to justify the new reading or action.

juvenile *n.* The part of an adolescent or young adult of either gender, and the actor who plays the part: *She was the juvenile lead.*

K

kabuki (kah' boo' kee') *n.* A form of traditional Japanese theater founded in the 17th c. and still very popular, with commercial troupes in many Japanese cities. Its characteristics include standardized characters wearing stylized makeup; presentational choreography and acting, using traditional movements and gestures; gorgeous, flowing costumes; and stylized scenery. All parts are played by male actors; "women-style" roles and the actors playing them are both called *onnagata* (on' nah gah' tah).

kathakali (kah' thuh kah' lee) *n.* A classic Indian form of mime-dance-drama originating in the 17th c; performed by actors in exquisite costumes and elaborate makeup, with vocal and instrumental music played by four musicians.

keep *v. t. Slang* To remember and retain a particular **moment** or **move** so that it can be reproduced every time; hence, a director's instruction, "Keep that!"

keep take A shot that a film director wants saved, for possible use in the **final cut**; the take is safeguarded when the camera people are directed to **"Print it!"** Also called a *hold take*; *keeper*; *print take*.

key grip The chief **grip** on a particular crew, in charge of the other grips.

key light The main lighting instrument, creating the brightest light for a particular area.

kick-off *n. Slang.* **1.** The first day on a film shoot. **2.** The first day of **principal photography**.

kids *n. pl.* A common term for performers, esp. in musical theater, applied even to older adult actors and especially to the **chorus**: *Tell the kids to come on stage!*

kill *v. t. Slang* **1.** To get rid of: *Kill the light(s)!* (i.e., "Turn out the light(s)!"); *Kill that vase of flowers!* (i.e., "Remove that vase of flowers from the set!"). Also heard as *eighty-six*. **2.** To ruin totally: *He killed the joke.*

kinescope (kih' nuh skohp) *n., v., adj.* —*n.* **1.** A recording machine used in the early days of television. —*v. t.* **2.** To make a recording using such a machine. —*adj.* **3.** Pertaining to such a machine: *a kinescope recording.*

kitchen sink drama Realistic plays set in a working-class milieu; a term first applied to the plays of London dramatist Arnold Wesker (b. 1932), whose drama *The Kitchen* (1959) actually takes place in a restaurant kitchen.

klieg light (kleeg') A powerful carbon arc light used in illuminating film studio sets.

knee shot A take of an actor from the knees up, often seen in old-time westerns.

knockabout *n., adj.* —*n.* **1.** Rough and tumble physical action; **slapstick**. —*adj.* **2.** Entertainment in which the humor consists of many physical gags: *a knockabout farce.*

knock 'em dead To be received with tremendous acclaim for a terrific show.

kordax (ko:r' daks) *n. Hist.* In ancient Greek **comedy**, a **chorus** dance involving mime as well as dance movements that could be grotesque and obscene.

kudocast *n. Slang* The television broadcast of an entertainment **awards** ceremony.

L

lab *n.* [short for *laboratory*] In the film world, the establishment or facility where film stock that has been used to shoot a movie is developed and processed.

laboratory theater. See GROTOWSKI, JERZY; STUDIO THEATER.

land *v. t.* **1.** *Slang* To be cast in a role: *She landed the lead role.* **2.** *Slang* To hit home; to elicit the desired reaction: *The joke landed.* **3.** Uta Hagen's term for the reception and absorption of a character's line by the actor to whom it is delivered. See also RECEIVE; SEND.

landmark film A **classic**, pioneering motion picture, recognized as such by the National Film Registry of the Library of Congress; e.g., the first talking film, *The Jazz Singer* (1927).

lap dissolve 1. In the theater, the cross-fading of lights, as one scene goes into another. **2.** In film, syn. with **dissolve**.

laser *n.* [Short for *light amplification by stimulated emission of radiation*; l*aser light*; *laser beam*] The light inside a CD or DVD player that reads and plays the material with its pinpoint beam, without making actual physical contact with the **compact disc** or **DVD**. Hence, *laserdisc*: a flat, plastic, audiovisual **record** played by using a laser beam; *laser technology*: that using laser lights for audiovisual playback, recording, or projection; *laser optical media*: any medium that uses laser technology.

last night The final performance of a show.

last position The place on a studio or location set where a performer ends up as a scene finishes. Also called *last mark*; *final mark*; *final position*.

latency *n.* In recording, the time it takes for a recording artist's voice, relayed back from the computer, to be heard in his or her **headphones**; it should be simultaneous with what the artist hears as he or she is speaking into the **microphone**. When the audio signal lags, even by a millisecond, the artist hears the voice echoing in the headphones.

late-night television TV broadcasts shown from 11 p.m. to 5 or 6 a.m.: *a late-night rerun*; *a late-night talk show*.

latex *n.* A rubber product, usually in liquid form, that can be placed in a mold to form prosthetic makeup devices, which are then glued on, painted, and blended with the rest of the makeup. It can also be used directly on an actor's face to create scars, wrinkles, and wounds.

laugh line The final words of a joke. Also called the *punch line*.

laugh track Laughter recorded on a separate soundtrack and inserted at strategic moments into the soundtrack of a television sitcom; **canned laughter**.

lavalier (la' vuh leer') *n.* A **body mike** used on television broadcasts and affixed to a lapel or collar. Also called *lav*; *lapel mike*; *lap microphone*.

lay an egg To fall flat: *That joke laid an egg.*

layover *n.* Time during a road **tour** when there are no performance or travel days scheduled; hence, *to lay over*; *to be laid over*.

lazzo (lah' tso:) *n., pl.* lazzi (lah' tsee) [Italian: trick] A trick, standard bit of comic business and comedic embellishment of various moments in **commedia dell'arte** plays. Lazzi were originally improvised; the most successful were standardized.

lead *n., adj.* —*n.* **1.** The principal part in a play. **2.** The actor who plays a principal part. **3.** The insulated end of the wire attached to a light and proceeding from it. —*adj.* **4.** Pertaining to the principal part, or to the actor playing it: *lead role*; *lead actor*; also, *leading*: *leading role*; *leading man*; *leading woman*.

leader *n.* **1.** The **Stanislavskian** term for the character who causes a scene to take place because of a strong desire to fulfill an objective. A character may be a leader in one scene and a **follower** in another. **2.** The short strip, which cannot be recorded on, at the beginning of a tape or roll of film.

leading comedian The actor who plays the most important comic role in a play or in a repertory season, or plays a **line** of comic roles, esp. in comic opera or operetta; e.g., the line of patter-song roles in **Gilbert and Sullivan**, such as the Major General in *The Pirates of Penzance*.

lead sheet A list, in order, of the musical cues in a show, used by the music director in place of a full score.

League of American Theatres and Producers (LATP) The organization, founded in 1930 and based in New York City, that serves as the representative of Broadway and Off-Broadway producers in contract negotiations with **Actors Equity Association**.

League of Resident Theatres (LORT) The organization of regional American theater producers, founded in 1965 and based in New York City, that represents the network of resident theaters in contract negotiations with **Actors Equity Association**. Aside from the many regional theaters, there are also LORT theaters in New York City itself. Salary levels on a scale from A to D depend on the size of the **resident theater**.

learning lines Syn. with **memorizing lines**.

LED; L.E.D. (ehl' ee dee') *n.* Acronym for *light-emitting diode*, a tiny, but powerful lamp used as an indicator on control panels, for LCD (liquid crystal display) television or computer backlighting, and in some flashlights. A low-voltage LED is often used in the theater in place of **glowtape**; e.g., to illuminate **escape stairs** at the upstage end of a raked stage.

left *adj.* **1.** The side of the stage to the actor's left as he or she faces the audience: **stage left**; abbrev. L. **2.** The side of a movie or television set seen to the left from the camera's point of view: **camera left**.

leg *n. Slang* **1.** Part of a **tour**: *The first leg of the tour lasted for two months.* **2.** A full-length vertical drape or border hung on either side of a proscenium stage just inside the proscenium, usually topped by a horizontal drape. The *legs* form a kind of proscenium within the proscenium, and mask lights that are on a **light tree**.

legs *n. pl. Slang* Box office appeal. A play, or esp. a film, that attracts a wide audience and is expected to have a good **run** is said to "have legs."

legit *adj. Slang* Commonly used short form of *legitimate*: *legit agent*; *legit singing*.

legitimate *adj.* **1.** Valid, worthy, artistic, respectable; e.g., the theater, film, or television, as opposed to commercials. At one time, only the theater was considered a legitimate area of endeavor for actors; film and radio were thought of as not respectable or artistic, and a similar snobby attitude prevailed at first towards television. **2.** Spoken theater and drama, as opposed to musical theater: *legitimate theater*. **3.** Pertains, usually in its shortened form, to those agents who submit actors for jobs in the media or the theater, as opposed to *commercial agents*, who deal with commercials: *a legit agent. Who are you signed with for legit?*

legitimate singing The vocal technique and aesthetic style used by a singer trained to place the **voice** in the **mask**, and to control the changing muscular tensions involved in the shifts between the **chest voice** and the **head voice**; heard in classical music, opera, operetta, Broadway musical comedy, and some popular music: *She belts, but she also sings legit.* Called *legit singing* or *legit*, for short. Cf. **belt**.

Leko (lee' koh) *n. Trademark* [Short for *Lekolite*] A type of **ellipsoidal reflector spotlight** named for its inventors, Joseph Levy and Edward Kook; often used as a generic appellation for such a spotlight.

leotard (lee' uh tahrd') *n.* [Named for its inventor Jules Léotard (1839–1870), a French acrobat known as "the daring young man on the flying trapeze" fr. the song written about him in 1867 by English lyricist George Leybourne and composer Gaston Lyle] A skintight, formfitting garment with or without sleeves that covers the torso, but not the legs, allowing freedom of movement. Worn by acrobats, gymnasts, and dancers, esp. for rehearsal and classes. There is also a full-body version, called a *unitard*.

less is more An oft-heard paradoxical statement from a director to an actor meaning that over-emoting or histrionics are not as effective or telling as playing a moment simply.
See also TONE IT DOWN.

let it out 1. In acting, to allow free rein to suppressed emotions, sometimes held in because of an actor's inhibitions. **2.** The instruction given by an acting teacher in class, or by a director in a rehearsal, to release pent-up emotions. **3.** To widen or enlarge a costume; or part of a costume; also, *let out*: *Let it out at the waist. Let out the waist.*

letter of agreement (LOA) The **Equity** contracts that cover employment in various situations, including those in certain non-Equity companies, and some small, non-profit theaters devoted to developing new projects and playwrights.

level *n., adj.* —*n.* **1.** The **intensity**, strength, loudness, or volume of sound. **2.** The intensity, brightness, or strength of a light setting. **3.** A platform: *The scene was staged on the second level.* —*adj.* **4.** Even with: *The picture frame was level with the top of the window.* **5.** Flat and even: *a level tone of voice*; *a level playing area.*

level check A test by a sound engineer during a **recording session**, just before recording begins, to hear, and to see on a recording computer's screen, the highs and lows of a performer's voice, so that the **microphone** and recording equipment may be adjusted.

library edition The version of an **audiobook** recorded specifically for distribution to libraries, and not to be sold otherwise. Specific AFTRA rates apply, but library editions are sometimes released commercially even though they are not supposed to be; it is very difficult to secure the requisite **upgrade** for the **reader**.

library shot A piece of archival or file film footage that is used to establish place.

libretto (lih breh' toh) *n.* [Italian: little book.] The text, or **book** of an opera, comic opera, or operetta; hence, *librettist*: the writer of a libretto.

license *n.* **1.** *Brit. Hist.* Permission granted by the Lord Chamberlain's Office to produce and perform a play; the office censored material until censorship was abolished in 1968. **2.** A liberty taken by or allowed to a performer: *The star had license to change the blocking.* **3.** A liberty taken by a writer; i.e., a deviation from the rules, strict forms, or facts: *artistic license*; *dramatic license*; *poetic license.* **4.** Distortions of history, as in Shakespeare's *Richard III* or the Showtime series *The Tudors*; *historical license.*

light check A control for brightness done by a lighting technician with a *light meter* before a take, to see how hot the light is on a particular actor or area in case the lights have to be adjusted in some way.

light comedian A comic actor who plays in **drawing-room comedy** and light comedy, and whose specialty is charming, witty **repartee** rather than physical humor.

light comedy An amusing play or film that depends on witty dialogue rather than physical business, and does not have much depth or point, but abounds in laughs; e.g., Neil Simon's *Barefoot in the Park*, Noël Coward's *Hay Fever.*

light cue 1. A signal to a lighting technician to change the lights. **2.** The level at which the lights are set for a particular moment in a stage production. Also called a *lighting cue*. **3.** A signal to an actor to enter, to do some particular bit of business, or to make a move or a cross. See also TAKE IT OFF.

light entertainment Publicly presented amusements and diversions of an undemanding, relaxing nature; e.g., the circus, magic shows, sports events, variety, television sitcoms, reality TV, quiz shows, or pop music concerts.

lighting *n.* Illumination of the stage or of a film, commercial, or television set.
See the index, p. 358, for lighting terms; and see COMPUTER-ASSISTED LIGHTING SYSTEM; INTELLIGENT LIGHTING.

lighting booth The small, enclosed space at the back of a theater auditorium from which lighting cues are run during a performance.

lighting designer The person who arranges the placement of lights for a production, determining their color and the number of lights used, as well as where they are focused. Lighting design in the theater is facilitated by using a **computer-assisted lighting system**. The designer works in conjunction with an *assistant lighting designer* and with the project's director.

lighting director 1. In film, syn. with lighting designer. **2.** In television, the person who oversees the placement and focusing of lights in a studio.

lighting state The particular level at which the lights have been set for a light cue.
See also PRESET.

lighting supervisor The person in a television studio in charge of arranging and hanging lights, setting levels under instruction from the lighting director or designer, and maintaining the lighting instruments.

light plot The complete plan for the layout of a production's lighting, including the light cues and the placement and angle of each lighting instrument and where it is focused on the stage.

light rehearsal A run-through of the lighting cues only, for the benefit of the lighting technicians and the director of a production, going from cue to cue and checking and adjusting the lights as necessary. Actors are not usually involved, except in the case of follow spots, but the stage crew are there to change the sets.

light tree A tall metal pole or vertical stand steadied on a wide base, sometimes with several horizontal branches arranged vertically, used for hanging lighting instruments in the wings or elsewhere on a stage. Also called a *light stand*; *lighting tree*.

lights *n. pl.* Instruments or devices designed and used for the purpose of providing illumination; stage lighting instruments are also called *luminaires*. During a theater show, the stage manager, on **headset**, will **call** the lighting cues to the technician: "Stand by for cue one! Go, cue one!" The lights that are fixed in a particular pattern before moving on to the next one are "in **cue**": *in cue one*. Commonly used lighting instruments include the **arc light**, the **floodlight**, the **follow spot**, **footlights**, the **fresnel**, and the **spotlight**.

For a full list of lights and lighting terms, see the index, p. 358.

lightning box A mechanical or electrical device used in the theater to create rapid bursts and flashes of lightning.

like *prep. Archaic* Disguised as. An Elizabethan stage direction: *Ariel like a water-Nymph* (Shakespeare, *The Tempest*, act 1, scene 2).

limelight *n.* **1.** A **follow spot** with an extremely white, hot light; *lime*, for short, esp. in the 19th c. The villain in a **melodrama** often appeared in lurid "green lime"; i.e., in the greenish light of such a follow spot. Hence, the ironical 19th-c. **catchphrase** "Green lime, please," said surreptitiously when an actor was over-doing it. **2.** *Slang* The glare of publicity; hence, *in the limelight*.

limited contract A contract that limits the amount of time during which an actor will remain with a particular production; e.g., one signed by a star who has film or television commitments. Cf. **run of the play contract**.

limited engagement 1. A play or other presentation that runs for a specific period of time. **2.** A run for which the performer has signed a **limited contract**.

limited release Distribution in only a few venues of a motion picture not expected to have wide appeal, in order to restrict financial loss; e.g., foreign films shown in art houses in large cities only.

limited run A specified number of performances or weeks of performances for a play or other entertainment; e.g., foreign productions scheduled for a run of several weeks, or a production starring a movie or television celebrity who has other commitments.

line *n., v., —n.* **1.** A single sentence, phrase, or word of **dialogue**; hence, *lines*: an actor's dialogue, taken as a whole. **2.** A rope, cord, cable, or other means used backstage for hanging something, or for tying something down and keeping it in position, e.g., *fly line*: a rope used to lower and raise **flies**. **3.** The kind of part or role an actor usually plays. Also called *line of business*; *line of roles*: *That part is not in her line*. Cf. **cast**; **walk**. **4.** A facial wrinkle; e.g., one emphasized or added using theatrical **makeup**. *—v. t.* **5.** In making up the face, to emphasize or add wrinkles; surround the eyelids with a thin line, using eyebrow pencil, liner, or mascara; or to extend or shape the eyebrow. **6.** To **dress** a set by painting in archi-tectural details (e.g., interstices on a brick wall) using a straight rule and brushes. **7.** To sew material for an inner layer inside a **costume** or costume piece, in order to add weight, make it fall well, or make it more comfortable to wear; hence, *lining*: the material sewn in; and the act of sewing it in.

Line! "Please tell me what my next line is!" This is the request from an actor who is **off book** to whoever is **on book** in a rehearsal; also heard as "Line, please!" and "What's my line?"

line cue The actor's signal to speak, as soon as the other actor has stopped or on a **word cue**, signaling the actor to interrupt or overlap the other actor's lines.

line producer The person in charge of budgetary matters for a film or TV show that is **in production**. The line producer deals with costs that are **above the line** in the **pre-production** phase, and with **below the line** costs in the **production** and **post-production** phases, receiving reports from the **production manager** during film shooting.

line reading An actor's particular interpretation and expression of a bit of dialogue: the way of uttering it, including inflection, stressed words, and tone.

line rehearsal A brush-up rehearsal without movement or blocking that consists of reciting the words of a play. Also called a *line-through rehearsal*.

lineup *n.* Schedule of television programs; e.g., for a network's **fall season**.

lip sync (lihp' sihnk') [Sync: short for *synchronize*; *synchronization*] **1.** To mouth spoken lines or vocal music simultaneously with a recording without uttering sound, timing the mouth movements so that it looks as if the speaker is saying or singing the words. **2.** To have or do a job dubbing or looping: *I'm lip syncing for a movie today*.

listen and respond To hear not only the words, but also the intentions in what another actor is saying, and to react and reply accordingly: an elementary acting technique.

literary agent A writer's business representative. The literary agent negotiates contracts and tries to place an author's work with a publisher or a play, teleplay, or screenplay with a producer.
    See also PLAY AGENT.

literary manager The head of a theater company's play-reading department. The literary manager's duties include reading and evaluating scripts with a view to recommending them for possible future production and/or delegating that duty to one or more play readers, who report to the manager, who reports to the **artistic director**. The job may include putting on staged readings of scripts that might be considered for production.
    See also PLAY READER; STAGED READING.

liturgical drama Plays on religious themes: **miracle play**; **mystery play**. Also called *ecclesiastical drama*.

live *adj.* **1.** Present and in person: *live theater*, as opposed to television or movies; *live action* done by people, as opposed to animated figures; *live music*; *a live broadcast*. When television was in its infancy, it was usually live; i.e., performed and broadcast simultaneously. **2.** Functioning, with the electricity turned on: *a live mike*; *a live wire*.

live action-animation Using both real actors and animated figures in combination in a film scene.

155

live-feed video audition A casting session for a commercial or other media project done via a camera hookup to a distant location. An auditioning actor may be in New York, receiving instructions from a director in Los Angeles.

live prop Syn. with **hot prop**.

living allowance A contractually determined amount of expense money paid by producers to performers and other personnel required to remain at a shooting location for one or more nights, as opposed to a reimbursement for actual expenses incurred.
  See also PER DIEM.

living newspaper *Hist.* Improvised sketches based on the events of the day; a popular form of **political theater** during the 1930s. The living newspaper plays produced by a **Federal Theater Project** troupe were the occasion of controversy, and led to the disbanding of the FTP.

living through [Translation of Stanislavsky's Russian term, and central concept, *perezhivanie* (pyeh' ryeh' zhih vah' nyeh): to experience] Experiencing the character's life from **moment to moment**.

load in To bring scenery and equipment into a theater for use in a production. Hence, *load-in*: the process of bringing equipment into a theater, and the time period during which this is done; *loading dock*: the place where everything is loaded in. Also called *take in*. *Brit.* Get in.

load out To remove scenery and equipment from a theater; e.g., on a tour. Hence, *load-out*: the process of doing so, and the time period involved. Also called *take out*. *Brit.* Get out.

lobby *n.* The front area of a theater, leading to the auditorium; the foyer, where the box office and concessions are located.

local spot A television or radio commercial that is broadcast only in a limited area and advertises products or stores for that locale only.

location *n.* Any place, aside from a soundstage, used as a set for a film or television shoot. A *location permit* (i.e., a document giving permission to shoot at a particular location) must be obtained from the local government authorities (e.g., the Mayor's Office of Film, Theatre, and Broadcasting in New York). The use of streets requires parking permission for trailers, for placement of the craft services van, and for the trucks that transport sound and lighting equipment. A *location agreement* is signed with the individual owners of a building or other location providing for payment and for certain conditions and responsibilities; e.g., the production company must make sure the location is in the same condition it was in when they arrived, and has a right to show the building or other location in the film. For logistical reasons, all scenes taking place at a particular location are done before moving on, usually necessitating shooting out of sequence.
  See also ACTING IN FILM; ON LOCATION.

location manager The person in charge of finding suitable places to serve as sets for a film and evaluating and photographing the places; and, once they have been chosen by the director, arranging for their use, dealing with budgetary matters involved, and organizing everything regarding the transport of equipment and personnel. The location manager may act as his or her own location scout, or may delegate that responsibility.

location scout A person who finds appropriate interior and exterior places required for a film or television program. The location scout takes detailed photographs and gives the director choices.

location team The crew that works on a location set.

locked-down shot A take in which the camera remains stationary and immobile while the sounds of some event taking place off-camera are heard; used to create suspense.

loge (lohzh') *n.* [Fr. French (lozh'): theater box; actor's dressing room] Another word for a theater **box**.

long shot A take done from a great distance.

long take The shooting of a scene, or a great part of a scene, in its entirety. Also called a *sequence shot*.

loop *v. t.* [Fr. the loops, or sections of film for which dialogue is to be recorded; the loops are played over and over, as much as necessary, to give the actor time to coordinate speaking when lip syncing the mouth movements] To record or **dub** a voice: *She looped the film* (i.e., she recorded dialogue in a studio to be edited onto the film's soundtrack). A procedure rendered virtually obsolete by **automatic dialogue replacement**, although the word looping is still used for the ADR process.

lose *v. t.* **1.** In theater and the media, to get rid of: *lose the chair* (remove it from the set); *lose the light* (i.e., turn it off or unplug it and take it away). **2.** To forget a line. **3.** To fail to elicit the desired, expected, usual audience response or to fail to keep their attention: *losing the audience*. **4.** To allow a moment or action to slip from one's grasp or not to come up to the level of energy and commitment one had previously given it: *to lose the moment*.

losing the light The fading of the natural daylight, or the passing of clouds overhead, during exterior location shooting, requiring that shooting stop.

LORT *n.* Acronym, abbrev., and commonly used short form for **League of Resident Theatres (LORT)**.
See RESIDENT THEATER.

lot *n.* A film studio complex.
See BACK LOT; FRONT LOT.

loupe (loop') *n.* A small magnifier enclosed in a short tube, through which an actor can examine a **contact sheet** of head shots in order to choose which ones to enlarge.

low-angle shot A take done from below the subject being filmed.

low comedian A comic actor whose brand of humor and performance style is crude, unsubtle, tasteless, and vulgar.

low comedy 1. Crude, coarse, tasteless humor. **2.** A vulgar farcical play that includes slapstick, bad jokes, garish costumes and makeup, and a lack of subtlety or sophistication. **3.** As an adjectival phrase, pertains to an actor's unsubtle performance, or to the overdone style in which a production is performed: *a low comedy performance.*

luminaire *n.* A lighting instrument with all its accessories.

Lyceum (lI see' uhm) *n.* **1.** The gymnasium and shaded gardens near Athens where **Aristotle** taught. **2.** A London theater known for productions by **actor-manager** Sir Henry Irving (1838–1905). **3.** A landmark **Broadway** theater, completed in 1903, on 45th Street.

lyric *n., adj.* —*n.* **1.** The words of a song, or part of a song, esp. used in the pl. and esp. pertaining to popular song, musical comedy, operetta, and comic opera: *the lyric to the second verse*; *the lyrics for the first verse*; *song lyrics.* **2.** In the pl., the texts of all the songs in a musical theater piece, taken together: *the lyrics for* My Fair Lady. —*adj. 3.* Musical; melodious; meant to be sung, esp. as pertains to the drama, hence *lyric drama*: the class of plays, such as **opera**, that are sung instead of spoken; *lyric theater*: musical theater. **4.** Light in timbre and register: *a lyric soprano*, or *light soprano*; *a lyric baritone*, or *light baritone*; *a lyric tenor.*

lyricist *n.* A writer of the texts of songs for musical comedy, operetta, or comic opera, or of the words for individual popular songs.

M

MacGuffin *n. Slang* [also spelled McGuffin; Maguffin] Alfred Hitchcock's humorous term for a necessary **plot element** that is of no intrinsic interest whatsoever to the audience, although it can be a matter of life and death to the characters; e.g., the falcon in *The Maltese Falcon* (1931; 1941), the documents in Hitchcock's *North by Northwest* (1959), and the theft of the pocket money in Terence Rattigan's *The Winslow Boy*.

made-for *n. Slang* A film made for television.

magic *n.* The art of doing tricks and creating optical illusions for an audience.

magician *n.* A performing artist who does acts or shows involving tricks, including sleight of hand (prestidigitation, legerdemain), optical illusions, and the appearance and disappearance of objects.
  See also ESCAPE ARTIST; ILLUSIONIST; SMOKE AND MIRRORS.

magic "if" Stanislavsky's term for the actor's basic imaginative tool, **as if**, which enables the actor to project him or herself into the imaginary given circumstances as though they were real.

magic lantern *Hist.* A 19th-c. projector with an oil lamp, a lens, and scenes painted on glass slides; used in the theater for scenery projection, and in a smaller version for home entertainment.

mailing *n.* Sending photos and resumes to agents en masse for the purpose of obtaining representation; or to theaters, soap opera casting directors, or other casting personnel for the purpose of seeking employment.

majors *n. pl. Slang* The principal production studios and distributors of motion pictures.

make an entrance To come into a scene, esp. in a way that commands an audience's attention: *She knew how to make an entrance.*

make it To be successful as an actor; to arrive; to be in the position of being noticed and acclaimed as a performer.

make up *v. t.* The act of applying cosmetics and/or prostheses, false beards, etc. for the purpose of altering the appearance and looking like a character.

makeup; make-up *n.* Greasepaint, pancake, and crème; powder used for setting greasepaint and for blending; eye liner, lining and eyebrow pencils; prostheses; crepe hair beards; derma wax used for prosthetic purposes; wigs and other paraphernalia and materials used to cover and **line** the face, and meant to alter the actor's facial and/or bodily appearance so that he or she looks like the character. Also used to compensate for the effect of hot, bright lighting, which can make the actor look pale and washed out. Today, makeup is less used than formerly in small theaters, but is still used in such venues as large Broadway playhouses or the opera house. In the media it is used, as in the theater, to compensate for lighting effects, or for creating special effects. Paint that brings out skin color and eye liner that permits the eyes to be seen are sometimes all that is required, particularly in intimate theaters. The tubes of greasepaint, etc. are stored in a *makeup box* belonging to a makeup artist or to an individual actor, who leaves them at his or her place in the dressing room.

makeup artist An expert technician who works in film or television applying makeup to actors' faces and lower arms. The makeup artist is usually a licensed union member hired as a freelance worker on the production crew. Makeup used elsewhere on the body is applied by a **body makeup artist**, who is also skilled in the use of makeup prosthetics. In the theater, most actors function as their own makeup artists, except in special instances; e.g., the use of wigs, prosthetics, or other special effects.

makeup call The exact time when an actor must go to the makeup department to be made up.

malapropism (mal' uh prop' ihzm) *n.* [Fr. French: *mal à propos* (ma lah pro po:'); inapposite; inappropriate; poorly timed] The unconscious, unintentional use of a wrong word in place of the right one that was intended; fr. the name of the character Mrs. Malaprop in Sheridan's *The Rivals*: she uses words that are close in sound to those she really means to use, e.g., "She's as headstrong as an allegory on the banks of the Nile."
See also PUN.

male impersonator A woman dressed in male attire who plays a man in vaudeville and club **drag** acts. Cf. **trousers role**.

manager *n.* **1.** The person in charge of a particular theater or acting company. **2.** The boss of an area of the theater and its personnel; e.g., the **box office, house,** or **stage**. **3.** The person in charge of a particular area of a film production; e.g., a **location manager**. **4.** A person who has charge of a particular actor's career. Also called a *personal manager*.

manet (mah' neht) *v. i.* [Latin: he, she, or it remains] A stage direction, meaning that a particular character remains on stage after the others in a scene have left.

manent (mah' nehnt) *v. i.* [Latin: they remain] A stage direction, meaning that a number of characters remain on stage after someone has left.

mannerism *n.* A particular, repeated physical behavior, such as tossing the head back or brushing a shock of hair off the forehead; a clichéd or stereotypical behavior (e.g., the limp-wristed gestures used by fops in Restoration comedies or the simpering giggle of an ingénue). Characters may have specific mannerisms; e.g., the blinking that Nyoukhin, the lecturer in Chekhov's *On the Harmfulness of Tobacco*, points out to his audience, asking them to ignore his nervous tic. Or the actor may have an unconscious physical or vocal mannerism that he or she can work on getting rid of.

manuscript *n.* The complete text of a literary work, play, film, and so forth; abbrev. ms, MS. Always called in the show business world by its shortened form, **script**.

marionette *n.* A full-figure **puppet** that is worked on the miniature proscenium stage from the **bridge** of a marionette theater, by puppeteers working two or more boards to which strings leading to the limbs and head of the marionette are attached.

mark *n., v.* —*n.* **1.** A spot indicated on the set somewhere in front of the camera by **spike tape**, chalk, or other means, where the actor is to stand or move to; hence, to **hit the mark**: to arrive at the correct designated spot. **2.** On a theater stage, the **spike** showing where a piece of furniture or a prop is supposed to be placed. There may be four marks, or spikes, for instance, for the placement of an armchair or sofa. —*v. t.* **3.** To place an indicator of an actor's position on a camera, the floor, or somewhere else on a film set. **4.** To **walk through** a rehearsal without doing everything fully, so as to save energy, particularly if the rehearsal is on a performance day, or if it involves stage combat, which is not done all out, but for which every move is done carefully, sometimes in slow motion. **5.** To sing without using full voice or projection; meant to save the singer's voice; e.g., if the song is to be gone through many times in rehearsal. **6.** To walk through a performance; i.e., to do the performance without conviction and in a desultory manner.

mark a script In the theater, to put all the indications of blocking and other necessary notations into a script during rehearsal. Stage managers mark the script with everybody's moves, and actors mark their scripts with their own moves.

mark copy To underline the words an actor wishes to stress, and write out other indications or notes about actions, intentions, etc., esp. at a commercial **audition** or **voice-over** recording session.

Marker! The word said aloud by the person operating the **clapboard** at the beginning of a take, before banging the boards together.

markers *n. pl.* Small electronic sensors in the form of raised balls or dots, used in **motion capture** shoots; placed on a performer's costume and face.

Mark it! **1.** The instruction of the director or, more usually, the director of photography, to the clapboard operator to bang the boards of the **clapboard** together to make a sound at the beginning of a take, and at the end of a take just after the director has said "**Cut!**" **2.** In the theater, the instruction to indicate in some manner where the lighting and sound levels have been set on the different switches, perhaps by placing a piece of easily seen colored tape on the spot.

marquee *n.* The projecting canopy above a theater entrance, on which the title of the show and sometimes the names of its stars appear; sometimes illuminated at night by a border of still lights, or by a **chaser**.

martial-arts film A genre of motion picture, or an individual movie with numerous fight scenes involving the use of Asian stylized systems of fighting; e.g., kung fu.

mask *n., v.* —*n.* **1.** An artificial, removable facial covering made of any number of materials, from paper to plastic. In the ancient Greek and Roman theater, masks were used to indicate character, whence the *comedy and tragedy masks* symbolizing the drama. Masks are also character markers in some forms of Asian theater, e.g., Japanese **kabuki**; as well as in Italian **commedia dell'arte**, where half masks were also used. And they are used in improvisational classes where acting students are taught how to work with them. Masks set up a particular personality, and give the actor a feeling for character, as well as a sense of freedom. They oblige the actor to use the full body to express the range of the character's emotions. **2.** The area of the face around the cheeks and nasal cavities where actors and singers place the **voice** for maximum effect. —*v. t.* **3.** To hide, conceal, or shield, esp. to set off the backstage area from the stage, so that it will be invisible to the audience: *to mask the stage.* **4.** In performing, for an actor to be in a position on stage partially or wholly hiding another actor, ruining the audience's sightlines.

masking *n.* **1.** The curtains that hide the backstage area from the audience's view; or, on a film set, the devices, including curtains, that prevent anything external to the set from being seen. **2.** The act of concealment of the backstage area.

masque *n. Hist.* An Elizabethan or Jacobean court drama using elaborate costumes and sets, with music and dance as its principal elements.
See ANTIMASQUE.

master *n.* **1.** The original recording from which copies are made. **2.** Short for **master shot**. **3.** [Short for *master switch*] A main, or general central control switch for a system of lights; e.g., a master **dimmer**. Also called a ***grand master***. **4.** The central volume control on a **PA System**.

master of ceremonies; **mistress of ceremonies 1.** A person who introduces people and events to the audience (e.g., the successive acts in a stand-up comedy show). The emcee may frame a show with opening and closing comments. Often abbrev. **emcee**. **2.** A **talk show** host.

master carpenter The person in charge of the theater scenery, of maintaining it, and of the crew members handling it. Also called the *stage carpenter*.

master electrician In the theater and the media, the person in charge of the lighting instruments and the boss of the lighting crew.

master shot The complete take of a scene; done at a medium distance as a wide shot, and including everything and everyone in the scene. Called a *master*, for short.

match cut A shot immediately following another, in which the action in the second shot mirrors that in the first; e.g., the sequence where the bone thrown into the air by the caveman turns into a satellite, in Stanley Kubrick's *2001: A Space Odyssey* (1968). Also called *match-image cut*; *match action cut*.

match dissolve A gradual transformation of one thing into another, achieved through editing together in sequence each separately filmed take of the different stages in the change, which appear to fade into each other seamlessly. Much used in horror films (e.g., in werewolf transformations, achieved by using computers); also used in **time-lapse photography** in nature documentaries to show the passage of time in the development of a flower, or of a baby in the womb.

material *n.* **1.** The contents of a play, vaudeville act, or sketch: *The material was just not funny.* **2.** The play, act, or sketch itself.

matinee *n.* An afternoon or, esp. in children's theater, a morning performance. Most Broadway and Off-Broadway shows have two matinees a week.

matinee idol A handsome, sexy male star who attracts crowds of swooning fans.

matte *n., adj.* —*n.* **1.** A flat black shield cut into a desired shape and placed over a camera lens to mask part of the scene being shot; in the empty space left in the finished filmed image, another filmed image may later be inserted. **2.** [Short for *matte painting*] A detailed, naturalistic painting of a scenic background, done usually on a sheet of glass, and used in film in lieu of the real background. —*adj.* **3.** Dull; not shiny or reflective: *matte finish*; *a matte photo.* Cf. its opposite, **glossy**.

meal penalty Money paid to performers and crew when a proper break for breakfast, lunch, or dinner has not been taken. According to AFTRA and SAG contracts, the first meal break must be six hours after the original call time. A fifteen minute **non-deductible meal (NDM)** may be called at any time before the six hours, and resets the meal clock, i.e., the next meal must be called no more than six hours after the NDM break, or a penalty will be incurred.

mechanical acting Stanislavsky's term for artificial, clichéd, hackneyed, generalized, and conventional ways of performing a character or a moment; e.g., a drunk staggering about the stage, an agitated character pacing up and down.

media *n., adj.* —*n.* **1.** Pl. of **medium**. —*adj.* **2.** Pertaining to entertainment conveyed technologically: *media entertainment.* See also NEW MEDIA.

media personality A television or radio celebrity; e.g., a talk show host, newscaster, or sitcom or soap opera star.

medical checkup A complete physical examination of a performer by a qualified physician; required by the insurance company underwriting the insurance costs of a film.

medicine show *Hist.* A traveling entertainment featuring a quack doctor, or mountebank: a con man who sold fake nostrums, patent medicines, and "vitamin" tonics to gullible crowds from the horse-drawn wagon in which he and an assistant traveled, sometimes with various performers who presented musical or dance routines. Popular esp. in the European countryside (as in Gaetano Donizetti's comic opera, *L'elisir d'amore* (leh lih: zeer' dah mo:' reh:) [Italian: The Elixir of Love]) and in the rural United States from the 19th c. until about 1941.

medieval drama The theater of the Middle Ages in Europe, or an individual play of the period; mostly plays from religious sources, done to inculcate the lessons of religion; there was a tradition of secular theater alongside it.
   See MIRACLE PLAY; MORALITY PLAY; MYSTERY PLAY.

medium *n., pl.* media —**1.** A retentive material vehicle used for making and preserving a **record**; e.g., **film**, videotape, or **compact disc**. In the days of **acoustic** audio recording (1890–1925/26), the medium was the **wax cylinder**, and later, the record. In 1925, the era of **electric** recording began, ending acoustic recording altogether. Contemporary audio media include magnetic **reel-to-reel tape**, the **audiocassette**, and the compact disc (CD), a digital electronic recording medium. Visual and audiovisual media include film, videotape (VHS), laserdisc, and **DVD**, as well as digital registration and playback using a computer. **2.** A venue of entertainment that is conveyed entirely by technological means; e.g., radio, film, television, recording, or the Internet: *the medium of television*. Taken together, these venues constitute the *media industry*.

medium close shot A take of an actor done from the chest up; abbrev. MCS. Also called *medium close-up*, abbrev. MCU; *loose close-up*.

medium long shot A take done from a distance, but not so far away as a **long shot**, and including some of the set and clearly seen characters, photographed from the knees up; abbrev. MLS.

medium shot A take that includes the full figure of one or more characters, or one or more characters from the waist up; abbrev. MS.

megastar *n.* An exceptionally glamorous, instantly recognizable name actor, hugely successful at the **box office** and even bigger than a **superstar**.

Meisner, Sanford (1905–1997) (san' fuhrd mIz' nuhr) Distinguished American actor, member of the **Group Theatre**, and one of the 20th century's most noted acting teachers. He became head of the Neighborhood Playhouse in 1935, after having taught there. "Acting is the ability to live truthfully under imaginary circumstances," he said, and his famous *Meisner technique* focuses on exactly that. Full of sound advice, *On Acting* (Random House Vintage Books, 1987) by Sanford Meisner and Dennis Longwell, presents Meisner's influential work clearly and concisely. To ensure that actors would really be communicating with each other, he devised the *repetition exercise*: its goal is to teach the student actor to listen so that he or she really hears not just the words, but the intentions behind them. Two students face each other, and one makes a remark. The other student repeats it as exactly as possible, without doing an imitation. The first person then repeats what

164

he or she has heard. Gradually, the repetition changes, and something is added; e.g., a change of intonation or an emotion. From this, the students also learn that emotions arise spontaneously from the situations and **given circumstances** in which characters find themselves.

melodrama *n.* [Lit. a play performed with music] Lurid, perfervid 19th-c. well-made plays with stock, one-dimensional character types; e.g., brave heroes, delicate damsels in distress, unscrupulous villains. Usually performed with **mechanical acting**, using every **cliché** in the book. Also sometimes called *sensation drama*.

> See also AHA, ME PROUD BEAUTY!; CURSES! FOILED AGAIN!; GRAND GUIGNOL; LIMELIGHT; NAUTICAL DRAMA; NEXT WEEK, *EAST LYNNE*!;TRANSPONTINE MELODRAMA; WELL-MADE PLAY.

memorizing lines Learning dialogue; committing the words of a part to memory. Ideally, the lines should stay with the actor organically as a result of the rehearsal process: once the objectives, actions, and intentions are determined, and blocking established, the words are more easily retained. But actors are often asked to come in with lines memorized, or to have them memorized at a certain time; it is the actor's professional obligation to comply with these requests. One way of memorizing lines is, first, to understand the actions, objectives, and **subtext**, and then to repeat the lines over and over, either silently or out loud, with proper intentions but without setting line readings, allowing the imagination to swirl around them. Some actors find it helpful to write the lines out, reciting them at the same time. It is also helpful to have a friend **cue lines**, once at least some of them are memorized.

merry-andrew *n. Archaic* A medieval **jester**, esp. one who mocked others and hit them with a **bladder**.

metaphor (meh' tuh fo:r') *n.* An implied or implicit comparison of one thing to another in a non-literal, suggestive way: "the winter of our discontent" (Shakespeare, *Richard III*, act 1, scene 1); "the whirligig of time" (Shakespeare, *Twelfth Night*, act 5, scene 1); "in my flower of youth" (John Milton, *Samson Agonistes*).

meter *n.* **1.** The **rhythm** of a line of verse. See VERSE TECHNIQUE. **2.** The regularly recurring, accented rhythm in a piece of music. Indicated in a **score** by bars that mark off the strong stress (**accent**) at the beginning and by a *time signature* that shows the exact nature of the rhythmic pattern. E.g., 4/4, called common time, is in its most basic manifestation a strong quarter-note **beat** followed by three weak quarter-note beats (a *whole note* has four *quarter notes*). **3.** The rhythm of regular recurring movements in a **dance**.

method acting; the Method Lee Strasberg's innovative version of the Stanislavsky system. Hence *method actor*, a byword for the cliché of mumbling, self-indulgent actors who do not care if their performances are clear to an audience (but this is a misconception of Strasberg's aims and teachings).

method of physical actions The essential Stanislavsky **system**. Its basic premise is that every action taken by a character has a psychological motivation. The core of the method of physical actions is this:

1. Analyze, understand, and define the **given circumstances**, including unconscious motivations, obstacles, and activities.
2. Determine the objective(s).
3. Find the correct action(s), esp. in the course of rehearsals.

metonymy (meh tah' nuh mee) *n.* The replacement of one word with another that is suggested by it, and "with which," as M. H. Abrams tells us, "it has become closely associated because of a recurrent relationship in common experience": *He sets a good table*, i.e., he serves good food. Abrams' example from Shakespeare's *As You Like It* (act 1, scene 4): "Doublet and hose ought to show itself courageous to petticoat." Cf. **synecdoche**, which is similar, and often confused with it.

Meyerhold, Vsevelod (1874–1940) (vsyeh' vyeh lot mI' ehr khawlt') Dynamic, innovative Soviet Russian stage director who split away from the **Moscow Art Theatre** and Stanislavsky, while remaining personally attached to him. He ran afoul of the Soviet authorities for his **formalism** and **symbolism**, and for his abstract productions, which they felt were counter-revolutionary; he paid for his dissidence with his life, when Stalin had him murdered. In his grotesque, stylized, futuristic productions, Meyerhold used masks; **kabuki**; martial arts movement techniques; acrobatics and circus tricks; sets with the look of factories and smokestacks, in the style known as **constructivism**; machine-like assembly line movement; and realistic interpretations of characters, as well as caricature, all mixed together. Meyerhold's principle concept of acting was that the actor of the future should be trained in **biomechanical acting**, concentrating on precise, perfectly timed movements, gestures, and expressions. His student and close associate, Aleksandr Gladkov, kept extensive, detailed notes on everything Meyerhold said and did, and his book *Meyerhold Speaks Meyerhold Rehearses* (Routledge, 1997) is an invaluable compendium of ideas and principles. Meyerhold techniques that we still use today in the theater include working with masks in both the classroom and rehearsal and the **speed-through** rehearsal: he would have his actors do a selective, three-minute version of a play and then list the events they had chosen to include, as a way of zeroing in on what was most important.

See also PRE-ACTING; TRIANGULAR THEATER.

mezzanine *n.* Another name for the **balcony** in a theater auditorium.

microphone *n.* A mechanical device through which sound waves are converted into electrical or electronic signals and transmitted, and then reconverted to sound when sent through amplifying equipment; used for broadcasting or recording, or to amplify the live voice. The digital, computerized recording equipment and the microphones used for commercials, voice-overs, and books are very sensitive; esp. the *condenser mike*, as opposed to the less sensitive *dynamic mike*, which must be plugged into equipment, because it has no built-in power source; e.g., the preamp (short for *preamplifier*: the part of the recording/playback equipment that boosts the signals for the amplifier). The condenser mike, which contains a small battery, has the possibility of using what is called "phantom" power that is built into the mike's preamp (i.e., when the "phantom power" switch is activated); otherwise, like the dynamic mike, it uses power that goes to it from the preamp. The microphone used for recording is usually covered with a cap, made of foam plastic; in front of it is a fine, round wire-mesh screen, called a *pop screen*, mounted on a movable arm. The purpose of both is to blot out or deaden plosive noises, which might record as a popping sound. Microphones are either omnidirectional (i.e., they pick up sound from anywhere) or directional, and must be placed directly in front of, or just to the side of, the reader's mouth; many studio microphones are directional. A personal **body mike** is used for each actor in stage performances of many Broadway musicals and some outdoor theater productions; it is either wireless, or attached by a wire that runs from the microphone to a transmitting device or battery pack that sends signals to a central amplifier. Called a **mike**, for short.

microphone technique The performer's craft used in recording voice-overs, commercial copy, or book narration. Proper professional techniques and procedures in the **recording studio** during a **recording session** include the following:

1. Do not touch the microphone unless given express instruction to do so. Let the sound engineer adjust the microphone for you.
2. Keep about five or six inches from the mike if it is directly in front of you; about three or four inches if it is slightly to the side.
3. Be careful of "p," "t," "s," and plosive sounds generally; they may cause to microphone to **pop**.
4. Learn to breathe silently: everything records, including breathing, which you may think is silent but isn't.

You will be listening to your own voice through the **headphones** as you record into a computer. In the case of **book recording**, you will be seated comfortably with the studio darkened and light shining directly on the book, which you will probably have to hold down on a **reading stand**, if it is not a copy in a three-holed binder or an unbound typed copy, which lie flat. You will not usually be standing, as actors did in the old radio dramas, or as you will when recording a commercial or other voice-over (e.g., a cartoon character's voice).

See also BREATH CUT; LATENCY; LEVEL CHECK; PEAK; PRE-ROLL; PUNCH-IN.

microphone test A check to see if a microphone is functioning as it should: *One ... two ... three ... testing.*

Middle Comedy *Hist.* The later plays of Aristophanes and others, parodying literary figures and social classes.

See also OLD COMEDY; NEW COMEDY.

mike *n., v.* —*n.* **1.** Short for *microphone*; also spelled "mic." —*v. t.* **2.** To equip someone with a microphone.

miked *adj.* Describes a person equipped with a microphone, or a sound that has been amplified using a microphone: *miked sound.*

See also WIRED FOR SOUND.

mike stand [Short for *microphone stand*] An adjustable, standing metal pole steadied on a base, called a **straight stand**, with a clamp at its top for holding a **hand mike**; used by emcees and by comics or singers in clubs or on television.

See also BOOM STAND; GOOSENECK.

milk *v. t. Slang* To play a scene, a joke, or a moment for all or more than it is worth, in order to elicit audience reactions and garner laughter or applause: *to milk a joke; to milk the audience.*

mime *n., v.* —*n.* **1.** Short for **pantomime**. **2.** A *pantomimist*: a person who simulates various situations in silent performance, using movement and gesture. —*v. t.* **3.** To perform silently, without words, using only movement and gesture. **4.** In rehearsal, to pantomime business with props, doors, etc., before the actual props or set pieces are supplied.

minimum *n.* The lowest salary on the pay scale of **Equity** contracts; hence, *Broadway minimum; Off-Broadway minimum.* **Syn.** *scale.*

minimum basic agreement A **Dramatists Guild of America (DG)** contract that playwright members sign with producers, containing royalty provisions, and providing for approval of production elements, the right to be present at rehearsals, and the artistic integrity of the piece; i.e., no changes or alterations without the playwright's permission.

minimum call The minimum amount of time for which IATSE stage crew members or union musicians working or rehearsing in a theater must be paid, exclusive of performance time; usually four hours.

miniseries *n.* A television film divided into several one- or two-hour episodes.

minor role A small but important supporting part.

minstrel *n. Hist.* A medieval poet-musician who recited poems or sang songs, usually of his own composition. They often traveled from castle to castle, offering their entertainments to noble lords and ladies.

minstrel show *Hist.* An American form of variety entertainment with skits and *minstrel songs* purporting to be African-American. The shows were stereotypical and inauthentic, although some of the music was quite wonderful. Popular on both sides of the Atlantic, they were performed mainly by white actors in blackface makeup or, after the Civil War, sometimes by African-Americans in blackface.

miracle play A medieval drama about the life of a saint.

mirror *n., v.* —*n.* **1.** In terms of set dressing and stage properties, a reflective looking glass. Reflections and glare can be avoided using any of several methods.

E.g., in the theater, the **property master** may stretch over the mirror's entire surface a sheer, transparent black or gray cloth that is invisible to the audience and prevents any shine, but allows the actors to see their reflections if necessary. See DULLING SPRAY. —*v. t.* **2.** To imitate as exactly as possible the movements, gestures, and/or intonation patterns of another actor; hence *mirror exercise*: an acting class training exercise in which two students try to imitate each other exactly; also, as in Sanford Meisner's *repetition exercise*, where the actors begin by mirroring each other's tone of voice; *mirror routine*, an act in which two performers reproduce each other's movements as exactly as they can; e.g., the sequence in the Marx Brothers film *Duck Soup* (1933), in which Harpo and Groucho do a kind of quick-time dance using a mirror frame, as if Harpo were Groucho's reflection.

miscast *adj.* Wrong for the part an actor is playing; said of actors who are physically, temperamentally, and/or characterologically unsuitable for a particular role.

miscue *n., v.* —*n.* **1.** An incorrect cue. —*v. t.* **2.** To give an incorrect cue. **3.** To give a cue at the wrong time.

mise-en-scène (mee' zaw*n* seh:n') *n.* [French: lit., put-on-stage] **1.** The finished mounting and **staging** of a play, and the arrangement of all its production elements, including the décors and the movements of the actors. **2.** The completed staging of a film, with the arrangement of sets, properties, lights, and positioning of actors for the camera.

missed entrance 1. Failure to go on stage at the right moment. **2.** Failure to come in with a line, or to begin singing at the right time.
See also COVER; OFF-CUE; STAGE WAIT; STALL.

mix *v. t.* **1.** To combine the separate sound tracks for music, dialogue, effects, and ambient noise into one **sound track** forming the audio portion of a film or television program. **2.** In the theater, to arrange the speakers and other sound equipment for the best effect; a theater **sound designer** often serves as his or her own **sound mixer**.

mixer *n.* Syn. with **sound mixer**.

mixed notices/reviews Critical appraisals of a production, some laudatory, some condemnatory. A single *mixed notice* points out good and bad aspects of one production.

mockumentary *n.* A satirical film that purports to be a documentary and parodies the genre, as well as burlesquing the subject it treats; e.g., the hilarious movies directed and co-written by Christopher Guest, whose performances in them as very different characters are brilliant and supremely funny: *Waiting for Guffman* (1996), *Best in Show* (2000), and *For Your Consideration* (2006).

model *n., v.* —*n.* **1.** A miniature replica of a theater set, made to scale by the designer; it includes working parts representing movable scenery. A set model is usually brought into early rehearsals and shown to the actors, and the scene changes are demonstrated by the designer. **2.** An exact miniature scale replica of an object, creature, animal, person, or entire set that is meant to be filmed for a motion picture; such a model appears life-size and completely real when shot; e.g., trains going through a countryside, ships in stormy seas. Models are often used in the recreation of plane, automobile, or train crashes or shipwrecks, and the takes are intercut with live action sequences. In early film, models were used to create bizarre creatures, which were filmed using stop-motion photography. Adjustments to the limbs, body, and head of the creature were made for changes of position, which were then filmed in sequence; e.g., in *King Kong* (1933). **3.** A person who wears clothing made by a designer in order to show it off either in a live fashion show or in **print work** advertisements, catalogues, or commercials. **4.** A person who poses for a photographer, painter, or other artist. —*v. t.* **5.** To make or construct a small-scale replica of an object, person, or place. **6.** To show off designer clothing at a fashion show or in advertisements. —*v. i.* **7.** To pose for an artist in order to be photographed, drawn, or painted.

See also HAND MODEL.

modern dance Contemporary choreography, free in form and abstract, that explores the possibilities for movement without the set patterns of classical dance or **ballet**. Individual modern dance companies have established their own movement styles, and often, a famous choreographer is at the helm.

modern drama 1. English theater of the mid- to late-20th c., beginning in 1945 after World War Two, following the period of the **Georgian drama**; also sometimes called *post-modern drama*. The absurdist dramas and comedies of Ionesco, Samuel Beckett, and Harold Pinter, and the later realistic plays of Terence Rattigan, as well as the plays of the **angry young men**, and, later, those of Tom Stoppard, David Hare, and Alan Bennett belong to this period. **2.** American theater that begins at the end of World War One and continues to the present. It includes the plays of Clifford Odets, Elmer Rice, Eugene O'Neill, Tennessee Williams, Arthur Miller, Lillian Hellman, and, later, Edward Albee, Lorraine Hansberry, David Mamet, Terence McNally, Lanford Wilson, August Wilson, Wendy Wasserstein, Tony Kushner, and Sam Shepherd.

modern dress A historical or period play that is produced with the actors wearing contemporary clothing; e.g., the 1964 production of *Hamlet* starring Richard Burton, available on DVD.

modulate *v. t.* **1.** To control the level, changes, and variations in tone and pitch of the voice: *She has a well-modulated voice*; *the modulation of the voice*. **2.** To lower the loudness or intensity of the voice. **3.** To regulate and adjust the level and intensity of sound coming through loudspeakers. **4.** In music, to make a transition from one key to another; the transition is called a *modulation*.

moment *n.* In acting terms, the brief duration of time during which something happens; a beat.

See ACTING MOMENT; IN THE MOMENT.

moment of absorption The **Stanislavskian** term for the split second when the actor takes in what has been said or done and assimilates it, just before the moment of reversal, when a beat changes.

moment of orientation The **Stanislavskian** term for the beat that begins a scene: the few seconds or less that a character needs in order to understand what is going on, usually at the beginning of a scene, or to adjust to the entrance of a new character. Leaving out the moment of orientation is immediately unreal, both for the actor and the audience.

moment of reversal The **Stanislavskian** term for the end of a beat, when a character has or has not attained the objective for that beat.

moment to moment Playing a scene without anticipating the next event in it, and allowing it to unfold naturally and organically in the time it takes for each **beat**.
    See also ORGANIC; VULNERABILITY.

money shot The obligatory climactic **pornographic film** take in which the male star ejaculates.

monitor *n., v. —n.* **1.** A television set. Also called a *monitor-receiver.* **2.** A television set without the receiving apparatus inside; used for recording or playback; e.g., in an on-camera commercial audition. **3.** Such a set attached by a long cable to a video camera and placed well away from the set, so that the director and other personnel may watch a take as it is being recorded, in order to check or verify the framing or composition of a shot, the audio quality, and the actors' performances; between takes, the director may call actors over to show them something in a replay of the take. **4.** A small loudspeaker through which an actor and other personnel can hear and follow a show in progress; e.g., a **Tannoy**. Hence *monitor system*: a theater's backstage **PA system**. **5.** In **book recording**, syn. with **copyholder**. **6.** The person who oversees the proceedings at an Equity **open call**, making sure actors sign in and are seen in order. *—v. t.* **7.** To follow a take on the screen as it is being shot. **8.** To follow the performance of a show backstage, so as to be ready for an entrance or to be able to prepare for a **cue**. **9.** In book recording, to follow the book or script along with the reader. **10.** To oversee audition proceedings.

monodrama *n.* A one-person show; a play written for one actor.

monologue *n.* A set piece for one actor; or a solo speech in a play; e.g., a **soliloquy**.

monstre sacré (mo:*n*' str*u*h sah kr*é*') [French: sacred or holy monster] A towering, iconic celebrity; e.g., Sarah Bernhardt, Eleonora Duse, Enrico Caruso.

montage (mo*n* tahzh') *n.* [French: assembly; editing; mounting] **1.** Any version of a film's editing. **2.** The final version of a film's editing. **3.** The way in which a film and individual scenes have been edited (i.e., the way shots are assembled to make a scene; the way scenes are edited together to make a film). **4.** The job of assembling or editing a version of a film.

monthly rep *esp. Brit.* A theater where a play is performed for a month, while another one to be performed the following month is in rehearsal.

mood lighting Illumination meant to create a particular **atmosphere** in a scene.

Moore, Sonia (b. 1902) Influential Russian-born American acting teacher, actor, and acting coach. She knew Stanislavsky, and studied with him near the end of his life, just before she emigrated (first to Great Britain, and then to the United States). She wrote *The Stanislavsky Method: The Professional Training of an Actor* (The Viking Press, 1960), *Stanislavsky Revealed: The Actor's Guide to Spontaneity on Stage* (Applause Theatre Books, 1968), and *Training an Actor: The Stanislavsky System in Class* (Penguin Books, 1979). All three are very instructive and informative; the first contains a practical exposition of the Stanislavsky **system**.

morality play A transitional drama between the medieval church plays and the newer secular theater, dealing with situations in which a religious moral was taught, but in a secular setting; e.g., the 15th-c. English play *Everyman*.

morals clause The contract provision that allows the firing of a performer for reprehensible conduct; e.g., sexual harassment or substance abuse, whether on the performer's own time, or on the set.

morgue *n. Slang* **1.** A theater's archive of reviews and other materials pertaining to its productions. **2.** An archive of photographs of faces used to help create makeup: *a makeup morgue.* **3.** In the days of vaudeville, a theater that was not attracting audiences.

MOS; M.O.S. (ehm' oh' ehs') [Abbrev. for *mitout sound*, i.e., without sound; apparently fr. the accent of German Hollywood film directors, who said "mitout" instead of "without"] Shooting a scene without recording the sound: *We'll shoot this MOS.*

Moscow Art Theatre (MAT) The Russian theater company founded in 1898 by Constantin Stanislavsky and Vladimir Nemirovich-Danchenko; famous for its realistic productions, esp. original productions of Chekhov's major plays.

motif *n.* A recurring theme, e.g., in music, a repeated melody; in film, a repeated image.

motion capture Recording an actor's movements on a computer, as the actor goes through blocking and motions that will later be transferred to animated characters in a film. The stage floor is carefully marked on some shoots, and the actors' moves are limited; in other shoots, a more elaborate set is established, and the actor is blocked by the **director** as if for a regular shoot of a scene. The actor is dressed in a form-fitting full-body black suit covered with strategically placed raised dots: electronic sensors, called **markers**. Similar myriad tiny dots or markers are glued all over the actor's face, except when a **head camera** is used, under the supervision of the **performance capture supervisor**, making the sensors unnecessary.

172

Electronic cameras placed all around the set capture every detail of the movement under computer surveillance by technicians. Before and after each take, the actor must do a "T position" for the camera: arms vertically stretched out from the shoulder. In some shoots, dialogue is lip-synced to prerecorded material, but most of the time it is recorded on the spot during the shoot. You can see the process in action on a DVD bonus feature about Andy Serkis playing Gollum, in Peter Jackson's *Lord of the Rings* series. Called *mocap*, for short.

motion picture A continually changing series of images of people and things in action, photographed as negatives in a consecutive series, using a specially designed **camera** through which film constantly winds. When the images on the developed, positive film are projected onto a screen in ultra-rapid succession, they appear as continuous, natural movement, giving the illusion of watching reality in three dimensions. **Syn.** *film*; *moving picture*; *movie*.

Motion Picture and Television Fund Charitable organization devoted to the relief of film actors.

See also ACTORS FUND.

Motion Picture Association of America (MPAA) Organization of movie producers and distributors; responsible for **MPAA ratings**.

motivated lighting In film and on realistic theater sets, illumination that comes from a natural source, or appears to do so. Cf. its opposite, **unmotivated lighting**.

motivation *n.* The psychological desire, want, or need that causes someone to do something; i.e., to perform a particular action. An essential concept in the Stanislavsky system: the actor must find the character's motivations and make them his or her own.

motley *n.* **1.** Parti-colored; a combination of colors. **2.** A jester's parti-colored costume. Hence, *to wear motley*; i.e., to be a professional **jester** or buffoon.

motor *n. Slang* **1.** Something that drives a play along: character, theme, or a particular plot device. **2. Motivation**, which drives a character to take action.

mountain film A German film genre of the 1920s and early '30s, with stories about intrepid, hardy travelers making their way through perilous mountains.

mouse *n. Slang* **1.** The shadow of a microphone. **2.** A handheld, sliding computer input device; used for moving a cursor around on the screen when working with documents, accessing and working on web sites, etc.

mouth *v. t.* **1.** To **declaim** one's lines, as opposed to acting them. **2.** To mumble one's lines.

mouth noise A speaker's or book narrator's extraneous vocal sounds; if recorded during a session, they must be edited out.

move off To **cross** away from center stage.

move on To **cross** toward center stage. Also called *move in*.

move(s) *n.* **1.** The physical action(s) of going from one place to another that an actor performs on stage: *A move to get away from something always involves a move to go to something.* **2.** In the pl., syn. with **blocking**.

movement *n.* **1.** The action of going from one place to another; or of using a body part to gesture. **2.** The physical technique involved in getting from place to place and in assuming positions when in place: *movement technique*. Movement exercises designed to create flexibility and control are part of all actor training, so that the actor can respond physically to the demands of any role, and to directors' instructions. **3.** In music, a discreet, self-contained division of a longer instrumental work; e.g., a symphony. In performance, each movement is separated by a pause, except when a composer gives the specific direction not to do so; there is no applause between movements.

movie *n., pl.* movies **1.** A motion picture; a film. Hence *moviemaking*: the art and job of producing, directing, working, or performing in motion pictures; *moviemaker*: a film producer or director. **2.** In the pl., the motion picture industry as a whole: *He works in the movies.*

movie commercial A thirty- or sixty-second television **trailer** for a motion picture.

movie palace A grand, elaborately decorated, spectacular cinema, often with a themed decor; built mostly in the 1920s, e.g.,. Radio City Music Hall. Few still exist.

moving picture Syn. with **film**, **movie**, and **motion picture**.

moving shot Any take done while the camera is in motion, following the action in some way (e.g., using a handheld camera, or using a dolly for a **tracking shot**).

Moviola *Trademark Archaic n.* A projection machine with a viewer that allows a film to be seen in miniature by a single person, who can also control the film's speed; used in film editing, and in preparing credits and titles.

MPAA ratings Categories suggesting what audience a movie is suitable for; determined by the Code and Rating Administration board of **The Motion Picture Association of America**, which devised a system of categorizing movies by their content and suitability for audiences in different age ranges. Reasons for the particular rating are usually given when the rating is shown on the screen; for the last four categories of restriction, they include sexual content, violence, and "language." The categories are as follows:

> G: General; suitable for all audiences.
> PG: Parental Guidance Suggested; it is suggested, but not required, that children be accompanied by an adult.
> PG-13: Children under the age of thirteen not admitted unless accompanied by a parent, guardian, or other adult.

R: Restricted; children under the age of seventeen not admitted unless accompanied by a parent, guardian, or other adult.

NC-17: No children seventeen years of age or under admitted.

Some films are NR: not rated, either before they have been given a rating, or are made in a version that includes material that would cause them to be given a restricted rating, which used to be called an X rating. DVDs of such films can often be purchased in both their rated and NR versions; the rated version is often the one released theatrically. Movie trailers are rated in two categories: "All Audiences" and "Restricted." A Restricted trailer may be shown only when R-rated or NC 17–rated movies are screened.

mug *n., v. Slang* —*n.* **1.** Face: *Get a load of the mug on that guy!* **2.** A man: *See that mug over there?* —*v. i.* **3.** To make faces on stage or for the camera, using outlandish, exaggerated expressions meant to provoke laughter.

multiform theater A theater, usually a **theater in the round**, that may change the location of the **acting area** from one production to the next, thus also changing the location of the audience's seating areas, giving them a different view of the stage each time. Such a theater may also allow a change of audience perspective in the course of a performance, when different parts of the house may be used for different scenes; hence, *multiform staging*. Cf. **environmental theater**.

multimedia *adj.* Pertains to a presentation or show that employs different media in combination; e.g., when live actors appear in a film with animated figures, or when a theater presentation uses projected films or television screens as part of a show. Hence, *a multimedia project*. Also called *mixed media*.

multiple-image shot A take in which the same object appears simultaneously several times; e.g., an object that someone who is drunk sees revolving before his or her eyes.

multiple roles Three or more characters played in one project by the same actor: Alec Guinness played eight roles magnificently in *Kind Hearts and Coronets* (1949).

multiplex *n., adj.* —*n.* **1.** A movie house with several auditoriums for the simultaneous showing of different motion pictures. Also called a *cineplex.* —*adj.* **2.** Describes such a movie house: *a multiplex cinema.*

multi-set show A production requiring several completely different décors that must be shifted between acts.

mummer *n.* **1.** A clown. **2.** A performer; hence, mummery: clowning or performing.

mummers' play *Hist. Brit.* In medieval England, a play dealing with death and resurrection, put on locally by amateur players (called mummers) wearing masks and performing partly in mime, or **dumb show**.

muscular memory Stanislavsky's term for the recollection of movement and gesture learned in rehearsal and mechanically repeated.

See also INDICATE; MECHANICAL ACTING.

175

music and opera festivals Gala, celebratory events taking place periodically and seasonally, often during the summer at a particular place, during which concerts, recitals, operas, and other musical performances are given. Among the well known summer festivals are the Spoleto Festival in Italy; the Avignon Festival in France; the Caramoor Festival of classical music in Katonah, NY; the Chautauqua and Lake George Opera Festivals in upstate New York; the Mostly Mozart Festival at Lincoln Center in New York City; the Glyndebourne Opera Festival in England; the Salzburg Festival in Austria, devoted mostly to Mozart; and the Bayreuth Festival in Germany, which presents the works of Richard Wagner.

music business The branch of the **arts and entertainment industry** devoted to creating, performing, teaching, recording, and distributing for public consumption all kinds of instrumental and vocal compositions.

music conductor The person who leads the orchestra by rehearsing and performing with them and giving them his or her interpretation of the music, showing them the beats (usually with a baton) and indicating the proper tempo and dynamics (loudness or softness) of the music. Also called an *orchestra conductor*; *conductor*, for short.

music contractor The person whose job is to hire soloists or choristers for concerts, musicians for an orchestra or band in theaters (e.g., a Broadway **pit orchestra**) or the media (e.g., to hire instrumentalists and **jingle** singers for a **commercial**); or the orchestra that records a film score.

music cues Indications to a film or television music editor as to how to handle the music. E.g., *music down*: lower the volume; *music fade*: lower the volume gradually until it is out altogether; *music in*: start the music; *music in and under; music up and under*: start the music, then lower the volume; *music out*: stop the music; *music up and out*: raise the volume, and then stop the music.

music director The person in charge of all aspects of the music in a film or theater project; he or she may function as a conductor, as well. Also called a *musical director*.

music drama An opera through-composed without many clearly separate arias differentiated from recitatives, and with the drama therefore continuous; e.g., the operas of Richard Wagner (1813–1883).

music editor 1. The person who edits the music soundtrack of a motion picture. **2.** The person who edits recordings of any kind of music. An editor of a classical vocal recital may put high notes from one **take** that sounds wonderful into another take that was better overall, and so produce a seamless take that sounds as if the song were actually performed that way. On a day when they feel they are **in voice**, opera singers may go into a studio to record high notes and ornamented passages for use in editing their recordings.

music hall *esp. Brit.* A theater where variety entertainment was presented, up through about the 1960s; similar to American vaudeville theaters.

music rights Legal entitlement to present or perform a piece of music, obtained from the copyright owner(s), who give the performer or producer clearance; e.g., for those wishing to use a copyrighted song in a movie or television show. Royalties or a fee must be paid. Also called *musical rights*. Cf. **performance rights**.
    See also AMERICAN SOCIETY OF COMPOPSERS, AUTHOTS AND PUBLISHERS (ASCAP); BROADCAST MUSIC INCORPORTATED (BMI).

music stand An adjustable pole resting on three steady feet and holding at its top an adjustable, flat, metal, rectangular shelf with a lip at its bottom to hold a score. Used during music rehearsals and performances, or as a **reading desk** during play readings, or to hold copy during a **voice-over** audition or recording session.

music tent/circus A **summer theater** that presents **arena** stagings of musical comedies under a circus tent; e.g., St. John Terrell's Music Circus, now defunct, in Lambertville, NJ.

music video A film of a **number**, usually by a star singer or singing group.

musical comedy; **musical** A stage play or film in which vocal and instrumental music are an essential part of the show, with spoken dialogue in between the numbers; an American, esp. **Broadway**, variant of the **operetta**. Its musical idioms include popular song, jazz, folk music, gospel, and rock. Many Broadway shows have been adapted for the screen, and many musical comedies were written directly for the movies, esp. in the 1930s and '40s, the "golden age" of the Hollywood musical.

musicalize *v. t.* To turn a spoken play or other material into a musical theater piece.

Musical Stock/Unit Attraction Agreement (MSUA) The **Equity** contract originally meant for productions in large outdoor amphitheaters, but now also used for some indoor theaters presenting musical productions.

musical theater Any form of **drama** in which vocal and instrumental music are an essential part of the entertainment, including musical comedy, opera, and operetta; **lyric** drama.

musician *n.* A person who makes a living as a creator, teacher, or performer of instrumental and/or vocal music, practicing the art of expressing feelings and evoking emotions using sound arranged in an inseparable combination of rhythm, melody, and harmony.

mystery film A motion picture revolving around the solution to a crime.
    See also DETECTIVE FILM; FILM NOIR; THRILLER.

mystery play Medieval drama about some religious event, often in the life of a saint. Similar to the Italian *sacra representazione* (sah' krah reh' preh zehn tah tsee o:' neh; holy or sacred performance) and the Spanish *auto sacramental* (ow' to: sah' krah mehn tahl'; sacred act); hence *mystery cycle*: a series of such plays.

N

name *n.* A star actor whose name is recognizable, as in the phrase *household name*; i.e., one that is recognized in every home. Hence, used as an adj.: *a name actor*, who may play a *name part*; i.e., a leading role such as Hamlet, Othello, or Juliet.

name change Taking a different appellation to the one a person was born with, as when assuming a *nom de théâtre* [French (no:*n'* duh té ah' truh): theater name; **stage name**].

name protection The performing arts unions' policy of allowing only one actor to bear a particular name. Anyone who has the same name as a member must change it when joining one of the unions.

name in lights A star's name on the illuminated theater **marquee** of a Broadway show; by extension, celebrated, esp. as a performer: *Her name is in lights* (i.e., she is famous).

narration *n.* **1.** Story; tale. **2.** The voice-over script of a film; e.g., a running explanation of what the viewer is seeing in a documentary. **3.** The telling or reading of a story, or of the script of a documentary. **4.** The act and job of recording a book.

narrative film 1. A movie that tells a story. **2.** Another term for a **feature film**.

narrative technique Another term for **reading technique**.

narrator *n.* **1.** A performer who tells a story or reads it aloud. **2.** A performer who reads the voice-over text in a documentary or fiction film. **3.** A performer who records books; a **reader**. **4.** The character who tells the story in a first-person novel or short story.

National Academy of Recording Arts and Sciences (NARAS) An organization of recording industry professionals based in Santa Monica, CA. It presents the annual Grammy awards for outstanding recordings.

National Academy of Television Arts and Sciences (NATAS) A New York City–based organization of professionals in the television industry. NATAS presents the annual Emmy awards, recognizing achievement in daytime television programming, including news, sports, and local programs (excluding Los Angeles, which receives its awards from ATAS).
See also ACADEMY OF TELEVISION ARTS AND SCIENCES (ATAS).

National Board of Review of Motion Pictures A New York City organization of film professionals that promotes the interests of movies as an art form.

national network 1. A major commercial television broadcast company that has affiliated stations throughout the country—ABC, CBS, NBC, Fox—as opposed to unaffiliated, independent, usually local stations; **cable television** stations; or educational, noncommercial, public TV stations. **2.** [Short for *national network commercial*] A commercial that is shown throughout the country at the same time, broadcast through a national network's affiliated stations; e.g., during national primetime shows and major sports events. A national network is the most lucrative commercial, because a **residual** payment is made for every showing on a graduated, cyclical **scale**; i.e., when the scale has reached bottom, it starts again at the top. Even a seasonal national network spot (e.g., one made for the Christmas season) can prove very lucrative. Also called a *national commercial*; *national spot*; *national network spot*; *network spot*.

national tour A theatrical production that travels to major cities around the United States. **Equity** contracts cover various kinds of national tours.

natural light Daytime illumination (i.e., from the sun) or real indoor illumination, as opposed to that arranged by lighting technicians. Natural light is used as much as possible when filming out of doors; shooting can only take place during certain hours to ensure lighting consistency. But any kind of effect can be obtained by adding artificial lighting to natural light, as well as by computer enhancement.
  See DAY FOR NIGHT; LOSING THE LIGHT; NIGHT FOR DAY.

naturalism *n.* A late 19th-c. school of literary and artistic thought that went beyond **realism** and concentrated on depicting the unpleasant, seamy aspects of life. Naturalism in the theater meant that every detail would be portrayed without artificiality or whitewashing, and that the squalor and degradation of working-class life and poverty would also be depicted; e.g., in Maxim Gorky's (1868–1936) *Lower Depths* (1902).

nautical drama A popular sub-genre of **melodrama** that concerns the lives and loves of sailors. **Gilbert and Sullivan** parodied **transpontine melodrama** in general in *Ruddigore*, and nautical drama in particular in the character of Richard Dauntless, a stereotypical, boastful, xenophobic seafaring man, who speaks in the typical fake language attributed to sailors (and dances and sings beautifully).

ND [Abbrev. *nondescript*] Pertains to background players of no specific type, as in an urban street or restaurant scene: *ND extras*.

ND stunt performer A stuntperson without outstanding physical characteristics hired for the shoot day of a particular scene to do a specific stunt. The only job the performer may do without an *upgrade* is the stunt for which he or she was hired.

NEAT (New England Area Theater) The **Equity** contract covering salaries and terms of employment in 17 regional theaters; negotiated in 2008.

neoclassical drama Mid-17th- and early 18th-c. plays, many in verse, frequently adapted from Greek and Roman mythological stories such as Euripides' *Hippolytus*, from which Racine took *Phèdre*. The tragedies of Pierre Corneille and the comedies of Molière are neoclassical, but Molière often allowed himself artistic **license** and went beyond neoclassical formalities. The plays are mostly French, but Dryden and other English dramatists wrote *heroic tragedies* in verse in the neoclassic mode. Among the hallmarks of this era is the strict observance of the so-called **classical unities**.

See also CLASSICISM.

net ratings (Nielsen/Net ratings) [Formerly, Nielsen ratings; "net" is short for network] A **scale** on which television shows are listed in the order of their popularity, as determined by a show's number of viewers; monitored by the A.C. Nielsen Company, a leading market research company dealing with the global Internet communications industry. The ratings are published weekly in *Variety*.

network *n., v.* —*n.* **1.** A chain of affiliated television channels with branches throughout the country. **2.** The people with whom one has show business connections. —*v. i.* **3.** To form connections with people in the business in order to further one's career and find work opportunities; e.g., by attending a major theater school, or going to film festivals or gala opening nights.

Network Code AFTRA's agreement with the major television networks covering terms of employment for their members and establishing working conditions, salary levels (including one-day, three-day, and weekly rates; under-fives and background players are covered separately), contributions by producers to pension and health funds, etc.

Network News agreements AFTRA's agreements covering terms of employment for broadcast journalists with the major networks.

Network Radio agreement AFTRA's agreement with radio producers covering employment for its members.

network television The four major channels in the United States, as opposed to cable or public television: CBS, NBC, ABC, and Fox.

neutral angle A position of the camera through which the action is viewed directly, head on, and at the spectator's eye level.

New Comedy *Hist.* The ancient Greek comedies done after Aristophanes. Little has survived, but many were adapted by the ancient Roman writers Terence and Plautus. These comedies used stock characters that were the ancestors of **commedia dell'arte**; e.g., the braggart warrior, the domineering old man.

See also MIDDLE COMEDY; OLD COMEDY.

New Drama *Hist.* An early 20th-c. English theater movement spearheaded by Harley Granville Barker (1877–1946), who wrote iconoclastic realistic domestic tragedies (some of which were censored by the Lord Chamberlain's office) and also mounted innovative productions of Shakespeare and other classics. The movement had to do with freer production styles and the treatment of such taboo subjects as abortion and adultery.

See also CENSORSHIP; DOMESTIC DRAMA/TRAGEDY.

new media Technological, esp. digital, means that have existed since ca. 1980 of conveying entertainment, including (among many other manifestations) the Internet, with its possibilities for streaming audio and video; videogames; MP3 and iPod players that can download entertainment from the Internet. They are the subject of negotiations between producing organizations and unions or guilds representing performing and creative artists, who are making their claims to a deserved residual share of the market; e.g., in negotiations in 2008 by AFTRA on behalf of its members, or by the WGA in 2007, after a strike made the point clear that writers must be paid for their work.

newscast *n.* A television or radio journalism program.

newscaster *n.* The reporter who delivers or announces stories about current events. Also called *anchorperson*, who may also be a *commentator*; i.e., an anchorperson who gives opinions about events or personalities in the news.

newsreel *n. Archaic* A short film that showed some current events in brief, used as part of the program in old-time movie houses before the main feature.

New Wave cinema [Translation of French: *nouvelle vague* (noo vehl vahg')] A post–World War Two French school of filmmaking, using aleatory and **cinéma vérité** techniques. Among its adherents were François Truffaut, whose *Jules et Jim* (1962) was typical of the movement. It derived from the New Wave literary movement, typified by the novels of Alain Robbe-Grillet, who wrote the screenplay for Alain Resnais' *L'Annéee dernière à Marienbad* (lah né dehr nyeh:r' ah mah ree ehn bahd') [Last Year at Marienbad (1961)], a quintessential New Wave film.

Next week, *East Lynne*! *Hist.* **1.** A wry, ironical **catchphrase** used by early 20th-c. American actors on a tour that was doing poor business and losing momentum; i.e., maybe we would do better business if we put on that old **warhorse** *East Lynne*, a late 19th-c. perfervid melodrama adapted from Mrs. Henry Wood's novel of the same name. The piece was immensely popular, but by 1920 the play had become a byword for the ludicrous and the overdone. **2.** Said sarcastically of a melodrama; i.e., "If you think this is overdone, wait until you see the next production, which will be even more lurid—if possible" or of someone's over-the-top performance; i.e., "Next week he or she will be overacting even more—if that's possible."

nightclub *n.* A public establishment where people go for dancing, drinks, and live entertainment by singers and stand-up comics.

night filter A special blue light filter placed on a camera during **day for night** shooting.

night for day **1.** In film, the technique of shooting a daytime exterior scene during nighttime hours, using artificial light that allows it to seem as if the scene is taking place during the day. **2.** The shooting itself: *night for day shooting.*

3. The shoot or shot using such extra light to simulate daytime: *a night for day shoot*; *a night for day shot.*
See also DAY FOR NIGHT.

night light A bright bulb on a stand, left burning on the stage after a theater has closed. Also called a *ghost light.*

night shoot Filming beginning in the evening, and possibly going until dawn.

nighttime drama Hour-long television programs, often part of a **series**, that are broadcast in **prime time**; e.g., police and courtroom dramas such as *Law and Order.*

Noh theater [Also spelled "Nō"] A traditional form of Japanese dance-drama, originating in the 14th c., using classical Japanese music and performed on a bare wooden stage by masked actors.

noises off Sounds issuing from backstage and meant to be heard in the auditorium.

non-air commercial; non-broadcast commercial A television or radio commercial not meant to be broadcast, but made for **in-house** or **demo** purposes.

non-broadcast contract An AFTRA contract covering educational and industrial material not meant for public broadcast, but made for **in-house** or **demo** purposes.

Non-Broadcast/Industrial agreement AFTRA's agreement with producers of industrials covering terms of employment for its members and establishing working conditions, salary levels, etc.

non-deductible meal (NDM) A minimum fifteen-minute food break that may be called at any time on an AFTRA or SAG shoot. It resets the meal clock; i.e., when the break is over, the required six-hour period before a regular, full meal break begins again. The original six hours leading up to a meal break start at call time.
See MEAL PENALTY.

nondirectional microphone A microphone that captures sound from any direction. Also called *omnidirectional microphone.*

non-disclosure agreement Syn. with **confidentiality agreement**.

non-exclusive contract A written legal agreement that allows someone to do similar jobs for different organizations.

nonprofit theater Playhouses and companies that are publicly funded by government and other grants, have no private investors, and present performances without the intention, or the legal right, of earning profits from them. Such theaters are free to accept charitable donations from individuals and foundations. Many **LORT** theaters are nonprofit. Also called *noncommercial theater*; *not-for-profit theater.*

nonsignatory *n., adj.* —*n.* **1.** A producer who is not a participant in union agreements or contracts made with producing organizations. —*adj.* **2.** Not participating in union agreements with producing organizations.
See GLOBAL RULE ONE; SIGNATORY.

nonspeaking part A role in which the actor has **business**, but no lines, esp. in film or television.

nonstop action Sequence of events that appear continuous; achieved by such techniques as **accelerated montage**.

nonunion *adj.* **1.** Pertains to a person who is not a member of a performing artists' or other workers' organization. **2.** Characterizes a play production or film that is done without the benefit of a union contract or agreement.

normal angle A positioning of the camera so that it sees approximately what the eye would usually be expected to see. Cf. **neutral angle**.

not a dry eye in the house Said of a weeping audience at a **tearjerker**; sometimes archly changed to "not a dry seat in the house," esp. when a joke has been uproariously received.

notation *n.* A written, interpretable system of symbols for recording and preserving music or dance, enabling artists to reproduce a piece. *Musical notation* is standardized, but there are several systems of *dance notation*.

notes *n. pl.* Brief instructive communications given after rehearsals to actors by a director and other members of the directorial staff (e.g., a dialect coach, fight director, or, in musical theater productions, a vocal coach or choreographer) or after performances by a stage manager. Directors' notes concern specific moments, blocking, lines, or matters of interpretation; they can be artistic, or disciplinary; comments, or suggestions. Actors who misunderstand or disagree with a note are usually free to discuss it with the director. Dialect coach's notes concern problems with the accents. Notes from a vocal coach deal with voice, intonation, or projection problems. During performances, notes are taken and given to actors by the stage manager, often in written form. Notes are also given to members of the running crew about problems with scene changes, lighting, and so forth.

notice *n.* **1.** A review of a piece by a critic. **2.** Advance written warning given by the management of a theater production and posted on the callboard that it will close: *closing notice*. It may be rescinded from week to week. **3.** A letter of dismissal from management to a performer, providing for a sufficient amount of time for the actor to be replaced, and giving the actor a contractually agreed amount of compensation. **4.** Advance written warning given by a performer to management that he or she intends to leave a show. Two weeks' notice, or more, depending on the contract, is required; no such requirement applies to non-paying venues such as showcases, which the actor may leave at any time, without giving written notice. **5.** Advance written warning given by a performer to management that he or she intends to take the contractual vacation time allowed (subject to approval by the management) or to leave a show for one or more days in order to accept more lucrative employment, such as a television commercial (again, subject to approval by the management, who usually must allow the actor to accept the employment if sufficient notice is given). Lack of sufficient notice on either side may require payment of a penalty.

nude scene A film or play scene in which one or more actors perform wearing very little or no clothing. Some contracts include a *no-nudity clause* or rider, which is a provision that the actor not be required to perform naked; others include a *nudity clause* or rider, which details the conditions under which the actor agrees to perform in the nude, e.g., in scenes involving sexual activity. Auditions in the nude for roles requiring nudity are supposed to take place under strictly controlled conditions, according to union rules.

number *n.* An individual song in a musical theater piece or musical film.

nut *n.* The minimum costs and expenses needed to run a show, including the cost of theater rental; water and electricity; salaries for all personnel; upkeep and maintenance of the plant and equipment, including the stage floor, dressing rooms, lights, and scenery; wardrobe maintenance; production office expenses; and so forth.

O

object *n.* **1.** A person, place, or thing that is part of a character's world: an **object of attention**. Objects can be external (such as a cup of coffee or a chair) or internal (such as a person one loves or someone from the character's past, who is not present in the play). **2.** Also sometimes used to mean *objective*: *What is your object in that scene?*

objective *n.* What a character wants; the character's **goal**; the character's aim; the **problem** the character has to solve; that towards which the character's motivation compels him or her to go; that which galvanizes the character into action. There is an objective for a beat (*beat objective*); for a scene (*scene objective*); and for the play as a whole (*play objective*). Alice Spivak has innovatively and helpfully provided further categories of objectives: for a situation (*situational objective*); for a relationship (*relationship objective*); and for the character as a whole (*character objective*; or *life objective*).
See also SUPER-OBJECTIVE; ZADACHA.

objective camera angle A shot taken from the point of view of an imaginary spectator, as opposed to one done from the point of view of one of the characters. Cf. its opposite, **subjective camera angle**.

object of attention Anything on which an actor focuses his or her concentration, whether internal or external.

obligatory scene The part of a film or play necessitated by the nature of the **story** or the **plot**, and expected by the audience; e.g., the love scenes in a **romantic comedy**, the delivery of the verdict in a **courtroom drama**.

obligatory take A film shot necessitated by the nature of the story or the plot, and expected by the audience; e.g., a **close-up** of the kiss in a love scene or the **medium shot** in a swashbuckling sword fight scene, intercut with close-up shots of the duelists.

oblique angle The positioning of the camera at a diagonal tilt in order to create an unusual or startling effect. Also called an *oblique frame*.

obstacle *n.* Something that is in a character's way, preventing the character from accomplishing an **objective**. It may be physical, another character, emotional, external, or internal.

obstructed view Characterization of a theater seat from which the entire stage cannot be seen; often sold for less money than those that afford a clear view.

odeum (oh dee' uhm) *n.* **1.** A recital hall, concert hall, or theater. **2.** *Hist.* An ancient Greek or Roman small, roofed theater building where plays with music were presented.

off *adv., adj.* —*adv.* **1.** Away from **stage center**: to **move off.** —*adj.* **2.** Forgetting lines or business, or doing the wrong thing, or not being in stride during a performance: *I felt off tonight.*

off book Having learned the lines of a part.

Off-Broadway A New York City theater venue, with theaters widely scattered throughout the city, where new plays, small-scale musicals, or revues are produced. Off-Broadway employment is covered by **Equity** contracts.

off-camera *adj.* Not within the parameters or view of what is being filmed or photographed; unseen, but present nonetheless, e.g., the noise of a car starting.

off-camera dialogue Words spoken by unseen characters, e.g., lines heard during reaction shots of somebody listening.

off-camera turn An on-camera actor's movement away from the camera.

off cue 1. Speaking, or doing something at the wrong time; beginning an action or saying a line early or late. **2.** Responding to a cue incorrectly, with the wrong line or the wrong action.

Offenbachian *adj.* Pertaining to the kind of sparkling, rhythmically effervescent and melodically fertile music, and to the iconoclastic, satiric wit, exemplified in the comic operas and operettas of the French composer Jacques Offenbach (1819–1881), the father of 19th-c. operetta, with nearly a hundred works to his credit.

Off-Off-Broadway The New York City theater venue for shoestring productions of new plays. For some serious theatergoers, this venue is the place to see "real theater," where the concentration is on the plays and the acting. Off-Off-Broadway productions are unpaid showcases for the actors, who invite agents and other theater personnel to see them in the hope of moving on to a paying job in the theater, or even to booking a film or television show. Equity's **showcase code** covers terms and conditions for such performances when union actors are involved.

off season Summer, particularly in New York and London, after the end of the old **season** and before the beginning of a new one. Theater attendance is usually high because of the tourist trade.

offstage *n., adj.* —*n.* **1.** The area not on the set; that part of the stage that is invisible to the audience. —*adj.* **2.** Not in view of the audience: *the offstage area.*

offstage character A person mentioned or talked about in the dialogue, but who never appears onstage; e.g., Protopopov, the school supervisor with whom Natasha is having an affair in Chekhov's *Three Sisters.*

off the air Not being broadcast: *We're off the air* (i.e., "Broadcasting has stopped and you can relax.").

Old Comedy *Hist.* The satirical plays of Aristophanes, with their extravagant parodies of other ancient Greek dramatists and of political and literary figures.
See also MIDDLE COMEDY; NEW COMEDY.

oleo; olio *n. Hist.* **1.** Esp. in vaudeville, a painted rollup backdrop just above **plane** 1, used as a set for a sketch or routine, or painted with advertisements seen by the entering audience, and rolled up for the beginning of the show. Also called an *ad curtain*; *ad drop*; *drop curtain*; *oleo curtain*; *oleo drop*; *roll curtain*. **2.** In vaudeville, an act done in front of the oleo, as the scenery for another was being set up behind it. Also called an *oleo act*; *oleo scene*. **3.** The heterogeneous mix of songs and brief skits sometimes performed as an **interlude** between the acts of a **melodrama**.

omnidirectional microphone One that captures sound from any direction. Also called a *nondirectional microphone*.

omnies *n. pl. Slang* **1.** The general mutterings, occasional comprehensible words, and bits of half-heard and virtually indistinguishable dialogue uttered by **background players** in a crowd scene. Also called *rhubarb*; *rhubarb, rhubarb* (because those words are actually sometimes said by the extras); *walla*; or *walla walla*. **2.** The background players who make these sounds.

on *adv., adj.* —*adv.* **1.** Towards **stage center**: to **move on**. —*adj.* **2.** To be performing well, and very much in stride; to do a good performance: *I was on tonight.* Cf. **cook**.

on a bell; on the bell In the process of doing a take. Once the bell in a studio has sounded, signaling the beginning of shooting, everyone is enjoined to be as quiet as possible and to make no extraneous, unnecessary movement until the bell sounds again twice, indicating that shooting is over for the moment.

on book Following along in the script; e.g., during rehearsals where the actors are expected to have memorized the lines, a stage manager or assistant is on book in order to **feed lines**.

on call Put on notice to be available at any time to be summoned to work; said of media performers and crew members who may not have been given a specific **call time**, but who are nevertheless obliged to hold themselves in readiness to go to work whenever their presence is required: *She's on call for tomorrow.*

on-camera *adj.* **1.** Within the range of what is being filmed or photographed. **2.** Pertains to a taped audition for a television commercial, or to a television commercial as distinguished from a radio commercial: *an on-camera audition*; *an on-camera commercial*.

on-camera turn An actor's movement of the face in the direction of the lens.
See also ON-SCREEN TURN.

on cue Responding to something, speaking, or doing an action at the exact, correct moment: *The telephone rang on cue.*

on deck 1. Backstage, on the stage level of a theater. **2.** Waiting to go on stage. **3.** Next to be seen for a commercial or other audition: *You're on deck.*
See DECK.

one-act play A drama, farce, or comedy lasting from about twenty minutes to an hour, and concentrating on a single event, occurrence, conflict, or crisis in the life of the few characters represented; e.g., Chekhov's one-act farces or Noël Coward's *Tonight at 8:30*, a collection of one-act plays of various descriptions. Also called a *one-acter*.
   See also CHAMBER THEATER.

one-liner *n.* A quick, pointed joke, complete in itself, that requires no feed line, since it usually contains both its own feed and punch lines; e.g., Groucho Marx's joke: "I never forget a face, but in your case I'll make an exception."

one-man show; **one-person show**; **one-woman show** A monodrama; a play performed by only one actor.

one-night stand A performance that takes place once only in a particular theater during a **tour** of a play or musical; a term also used by vaudevillians who traveled on the **circuit**.

one-reeler *n.* A short film of about ten minutes in length; often, a **featurette** before the main showing of a feature film.

one-shot *n.* A take of an individual actor.

one-week stock Summer theater in which each play is given between six and eight performances, while the next play is being rehearsed during the day. After the last performance of the week, the set is struck, and the new décor installed.

on hold Reserved; set aside for future use. Said of an actor who is **on call** for a shoot, or on **first refusal** for a commercial; hence, *on hold for*: waiting to hear about a booking for which a date has been reserved: *I've been put on hold for that spot.* This is no guarantee that one will book it. Also said of a commercial or television show that is not yet released; hence, a commercial's **holding fee**, paid when the commercial is not shown during a **use cycle**.

on its feet Rehearsal of a scene or a play with the actors standing and moving about: *Let's get that scene on its feet!*

on location At a real place that is being used as a set for a film or television show. A set may also be constructed at a location; e.g., 19th-c. Paris streets built in a town in southern France for Raymond Bernard's film adaptation of Victor Hugo's *Les Misérables* (1934).

on-screen *adj.* Seen in a shot.

on-screen turn A movement by an actor toward the camera.
   See also ON-CAMERA TURN.

on the air In the process of being broadcast.

on the lot In the back, open-air part of a studio complex: *If you want to see him, you'll find him on the lot.*

on the road Touring with a production.

on your mark Said of an actor located in the exact spot where the actor is supposed to be. A director might instruct an actor to "stay on your mark" until the director cues the actor to move, usually with a hand signal, if the scene is in the process of being shot.

open *v., adj.* —*v. t.* **1.** To begin the run of a show: *The show opened to rave reviews. We opened the show last night.* **2.** To premiere a film. **3.** To face towards the audience: *open it out*; i.e., to adjust the actor's position so the audience gets a better view. —*adj.* **4.** Available, in a state of vulnerability; an ideal condition for an actor rehearsing or performing: *to remain open.* **5.** Facing out (or partially out) towards the audience.

open call 1. An audition which any performer may attend without a special appointment or agent's submission. Upon arrival, actors, dancers, or other performers must sign up and await their turn to be seen. Some open calls for dancers are group auditions. **Equity** open calls, which in New York take place in the Equity building on 46th Street, are run by monitors who call out the numbers on the **sign-in sheet** and tell people where to wait. For the sake of fairness, producers must hold open calls for all Equity projects, but many plays and musicals have already been cast by the time the open call is held, except for chorus and dance positions; the situation is difficult, if not impossible to control. **2.** A **casting call** for background players in a motion picture. Also called a **cattle call**.
    See also GROUP AUDITION.

open cold To start the run of a Broadway play or musical without having out-of-town tryouts, or in some cases even preview performances.

open film Spontaneous shooting of a sequence or scene, often used in live situations such as a political rally.
    See also ALEATORY TECHNIQUE.

open-ended run An unlimited number of performances of a theater production, which plays as long as there is an audience for it, e.g., most Broadway musicals and plays. Cf. its opposite, **limited run**.

opener *n.* The first act on a **vaudeville** or music hall **bill**.

open rehearsal A play rehearsal which visitors are allowed to attend, usually near the end of a rehearsal period.

opening credits The list of performers and other personnel shown at the beginning of a film or television program.

opening night 1. The first official performance of a play after previews; its **first night**. Critics are allowed to review the piece at its opening performance. There is usually a gala party afterwards. **2.** The first showing of a major feature film, usually attended by its director, stars and other personnel, and well publicized; a film **premiere**.

opening night nerves The **stage fright** experienced by many performers at the premiere performance of a play or musical. Also called *opening-night jitters*.

opening number The first song performed at the beginning of a musical theater piece; the number may be a solo or an *opening chorus*.

opera *n.* [Latin: works; pl. of *opus*: a single artistic work] A form of **musical theater** consisting of a dramatic and musical composition meant to be sung and acted on stage with orchestral accompaniment; a play set to music: a *lyric drama*. Most operas are *through-composed*; i.e., almost every word is set to music, and includes solo and ensemble singing, with the dialogue being sung in **recitative**. But in many operas, the dialogue is spoken. In France, those with spoken dialogue fall into the genre called *opéra comique* (o pé rah ko meek'), which includes some very serious pieces and is not to be confused with *comic opera*, which is also called *light opera*; i.e., charming pieces that deal with light, amusing, romantic situations. *Opera buffa* (o:' peh rah boo' fah) is the Italian term for comic opera; *opera seria* (seh:' ree yah) is the Italian term for serious opera: it is usually applied only to 18th-c. spectacle operas, which were often on classical and mythological themes. The term *grand opera*, now used of almost all productions in any of the great opera houses, really applies to the great 19th-c. spectacle operas, such as those produced at the Paris Opéra: the productions included obligatory lengthy ballet sections—called *opera ballets*—and huge choruses. There have been many notable opera films, where the opera is made directly for the cinema and is not simply a filmed stage performance. Among them are Franco Zefirelli's *La Traviata* (1983) and two Soviet films: Tchaikovsky's *Eugene Onegin* (1958) and *The Queen of Spades* (1960).

See also ARIA; LIBRETTO; RECITATIVE.

opera glasses Small binoculars, sometimes ornate or jewel-encrusted, sometimes mounted on a stick handle, used for viewing the stage, originally only at the opera, but now at any theater.

operetta *n.* [Italian: little opera] A musical theater piece that includes spoken dialogue and is comic or seriocomic, and often romantic in nature, with lush ballads and sprightly dance tunes; e.g., those of the Viennese school by Johann Strauss, Franz Lehar, and Emerich Kalman, and the French operettas of Charles Lecocq and Jacques Offenbach.

operating crew The backstage workers who run a show. Also called *running crew*; *production crew*.

orangescreen process The same as the greenscreen or **bluescreen process**, but with orange as the background color; used when blue or green are already prominent.

oratory *n.* The art of public discourse; e.g. making speeches, speaking in public or in a political arena. In ancient Rome, the art of **acting** was seen as a branch of oratory, and such famous public speakers as Cicero studied with actors in order to add verisimilitude to their emotional legal appeals and persuasive political speeches.

See also SPOKEN ARTS.

orchestra *n.* **1.** The downstairs seating section of an auditorium in an American theater. **2.** A band or group of professional musicians who, in theaters and opera houses, play for a performance. **3.** A group of student, amateur, or trained professional musicians who play large works, such as symphonies or concertos, under the direction of a conductor or **music director**; e.g., the Philadelphia Orchestra. A temporary orchestra may be hired for a particular project, such as a film. **4.** *Hist.* In ancient Greek theaters, the area in front of the stage, where the chorus performed.

orchestra dress [Short for *orchestra dress rehearsal*] A dress or tech-dress **rehearsal** of a musical theater piece, with the full orchestra playing in the pit.

orchestra pit The sunken well in front of a theater stage where the musicians play for a musical theater performance. Called the *pit*, for short. *Brit.* Orchestra well.

orchestra rail/railing The bar or barrier that separates the orchestra pit from the rest of the auditorium.

orchestra stands The music stands in the orchestra pit, with lights attached to the top rim, shining down onto the music.

orchestrator *n.* The person who scores and arranges the instrumental parts for music that has already been composed, hence *orchestrations*: the musical arrangements; *orchestrate*: the act and job of writing the arrangements. Composers may be their own orchestrators, taking their skeleton or outline scores, adding ornamentation, and filling in which instruments are to play what parts. In the contemporary **musical theater**, a **score** is often orchestrated from a composer's piano version by someone hired especially for that purpose. Cf. **arranger**.

organic *adj.* Spontaneous, unanticipated, real behavior resulting, after careful rehearsal, from living **in the moment** and proceeding as the character would from one moment to the next: *organic acting*. Cf. **spontaneity**.

orientation shot Syn. with **establishing shot**.

original *adj.* Pertains to the newly created story of a play, film, or other performance piece, as opposed to one adapted from another source: *an original screenplay*; *an original musical comedy*.

original cast The first group of actors to create the roles in a play or other project.

original production The first presentation of a play or other project.

Oscar®. See AWARDS.

outdoor set 1. A specially constructed exterior décor for a film. **2.** A **location** used as the setting for a film scene that takes place outside.

191

outdoor theater 1. A place for performances that is outside, and open to the sky. The theater may be set into a hillside, like the amphitheaters of ancient Greece and Rome, or in an open area like Central Park, where the Delacorte Theater, home of the New York Shakespeare Festival, is located. There are **Equity** outdoor drama contracts for certain venues. **2.** The productions presented in such a space.

out front In the theater auditorium.

outgrade *n., v.* —*n.* **1.** The elimination of an actor from a job in a SAG or AFTRA venue of employment. —*v. t.* **2.** To eliminate an actor from a production, film, or commercial. Once the actor has been hired for a commercial, signed a contract, and shooting has begun, he or she must be paid a **session fee**, even if outgraded.

outline *n.* A brief schematic sketch of the plot of a story in the order in which the events occur. The outline is sometimes used when pitching a project proposal. It is also a useful and necessary writer's tool, and can help to clarify the story in the writer's mind.

out of character Not in keeping with the established parameters of a person's behavior or way of gesturing, moving, or speaking. Cf. its opposite, **in character**.

out of sequence. See SHOOTING OUT OF SEQUENCE.

out of sync Not synchronized: said of the picture and sound in a film when they are not coordinated so as to be simultaneous (e.g., when an actor's lips do not move in time to the words, or when words are heard before the actor opens his or her mouth).
   See also SYNCHRONIZATION.

out of town Not in New York City; said of all venues where actors perform that are not in New York: *an out-of-town tryout. He's out of town on tour. Brit.* Not in London.

outside-in approach. See EXTERNAL TECHNIQUE.

out-take *n.* In film, a deleted scene or part of a scene that has been preserved; out-takes are sometimes used as one of the bonus features on a DVD: *an out-take reel.*

ovation *n.* Acclaim and **applause** for a live performance; e.g., a **standing ovation**.

overacting *n.* Exaggerated, indicated, histrionic playing. Stanislavsky said that there is no such thing as overacting: there is good acting, and there is bad acting.
   See also INDICATE; MECHANICAL ACTING; MUG.

overhead shot A take done from above a scene.

overlap dialogue Lines that are spoken before another line is finished, as when two people in a passionate argument speak at the same time.

overmodulation *n.* Excess amplification, the result of which can be **feedback** or distorted sound; or, in a radio broadcast, a distorted signal.

overscale Syn. with **above scale**.

oversized prop A large-scale replica of an object; e.g., the household items and furniture used in *The Incredible Shrinking Man* (1957), to give the impression that he was incredibly shrinking.

over-the-shoulder shot A take of an actor, object, or scene that is done from behind the actor, and includes one of the actor's shoulders; abbrev. OSS.

over the top Exaggerated; overdone; hammy. Said of an actor's whole performance, or of specific moments in it.

overtime *n.* **1.** Paid hours or paid portions of hours worked beyond the designated amount of time allowed contractually, which is usually eight hours plus meal breaks. **2.** The monetary compensation for working such extra hours or portions of them.
    See also GOLDEN TIME.

overture *n.* A musical **introduction** to the evening's festivities, usually played before the rise of the curtain; it sets the mood for the audience.

own *v. t.* **1.** In acting terms, to be so identified with a particular role, because of a seemingly definitive performance, that it is difficult for others to play it without reminding the audience of it; e.g., Marlon Brando as Stanley in the film of Tennessee Williams's *A Streetcar Named Desire* (1951): *He owns the role.* **2.** To incorporate a moment or emotion into one's acting **score**, as in the director's instruction to an actor, "Own it!"; i.e., make it yours, incorporate it into your acting score, and perform it with confidence and assurance (e.g., when something has been found in rehearsal that the actor is not yet particularly comfortable with). Cf. **internalize**.

P

pace *n., v.* —*n.* **1.** The speed at which something is performed; e.g., the **tempo** of a scene. —*v. t.* **2.** To time something so that it has the desired tempo: *to pace a scene*; *to pace it up*; i.e., to do a scene faster.

package *n., v.* —*n.* **1.** An entertainment project prepared esp. for touring, usually to summer theaters; hence, *package show*. It may include a star and a few cast members in key roles, an entire company, or a **star** alone; hence, **star package**. The package show will add cast members and production elements when it arrives at the various theaters **on the road**; it is accompanied by an **advance stage manager**. —*v. t.* **2.** To put together such a show.

package house A summer theater that books packages or star packages.

packager *n.* A producer who puts together and sells a prepared production that is booked into theaters **on the road**.

packed house A theater or cinema that is filled almost to capacity.
See also FULL HOUSE.

pad *v. t. Slang* To add extraneous bits of business or dialogue to one's role, in order to lengthen and enlarge it; to **ad lib**.

padding *n.* **1.** Stuffing sewn into a garment. **2.** A stuffed garment to be worn underneath a costume, to add to an actor's girth. **3.** Filler: extra material, inserted into a television or other show, when its running time is too short. **4.** Adlibs or unauthorized extra bits added to an actor's part in performance.

pageant *n.* **1.** A spectacle involving parades and crowds, music, and dancing. **2.** *Hist.* In medieval theater, a play and the huge traveling wagon on which it was performed: the lower part was used as a dressing room, and the upper part as a **wagon stage**.

page count The number of script pages or portions thereof to be shot in any particular take, or day. For convenience, script pages are divided into eight sections, or eighths. An entire page or only part of it is listed on the **call sheet** and shooting schedule, so that the actor knows how much to prepare. On average, a page, once shot, takes one minute of actual film time. The listing "2/8" indicates that two sections of eighths on a page will be shot; "4/8" indicates that half a page will be shot, and so forth. Each eighth may involve a complicated setup of lights and camera angles, much action, and only a few spoken lines. The number of pages shot in a day varies tremendously, and depends on how complicated the setups are, how many different kinds of shots there are, and how many takes need to be done for each eighth of a page.

paint shop Syn. with **scene shop**.

pan *n., v.* —*n.* **1.** *Slang* A terrible review of an entertainment project or of an individual performance. **2.** [Short for *panorama shot*] A sweeping camera move that films a wide swath of scenery. Also called a *pan shot.* —*v. t.* **3.** *Slang* To give a highly critical review of a performance or production. —*v. i.* **4.** During filming, to sweep across a scene with a camera.

See also FLUID CAMERA.

pancake apple box A two-inch-high flat **riser**. Also called *pancake riser*; *eighth apple box*; *pancake.*

panel show 1. A radio or television program on which a group of broadcast journalists conduct a public discussion; e.g., *Meet the Press.* **2.** A **game show** or **quiz show** on which a group of personalities appear; e.g., *What's My Line?*, *Hollywood Squares.*

pan titles Credits that move horizontally across a screen.

pantomime *n.* **1.** Silent acting, using gesture and movement. Called **mime**, for short. **2.** A theater piece that is performed silently. **3.** A popular British entertainment incorporating music, dialogue, and such diverse elements as comic turns, acrobatics, and special magical effects; usually seasonal, e.g., the Christmas pantomime. Called a *panto*, for short.

paper the house To invite people to a performance in order to fill the seats. A house largely filled with such comped invitees is said to be *mostly paper.*

paradoi (pah' rah doy) *n. pl.* In an ancient Greek theater, aisles through which the audience entered, as well as actors playing messengers or returning travelers.

parados (pah' rah dos) *n.* The entrance of the **chorus** in an ancient Greek **tragedy**.

paradox *n.* A contradictory statement or situation that seems ridiculous or absurd, but that may actually be true. "How quaint the ways of paradox,/At common sense she gaily mocks," wrote W. S. Gilbert in *The Pirates of Penzance*, whose plot hinges on a paradox.

See LESS IS MORE.

parallel film editing Assembling two scenes that take place either simultaneously or at different times, but at two different locations, and alternating takes from each; e.g., when someone is waiting to be rescued, and the search party and victim are shown alternately. This is a basic filmic narrative **technique** and **convention**. Also called *parallel cutting*; *parallel editing*; *cross-cutting.*

paraphrase *v. t.* To say lines that are close to the actual lines, but using some or all of the actor's own words.

parley *n. Hist.* A trumpet call: an Elizabethan term.

parody *n., v.* —*n.* **1.** A mocking, satirical work that imitates the style and characteristics of an existing piece or genre; e.g., a parody of *Swan Lake* or a parody of

Shakespearean tragedy, as in the 1960s British comedy revue *Beyond the Fringe*. Hence, *parodist*: one who writes or performs a parody. —*v. t.* **2.** To write or perform such a **spoof** or **burlesque**.

part *n.* **1.** A role in a play, film, television program, commercial, etc. **2.** The music for an individual instrument in an ensemble; e.g., **band part**, *orchestra part*. **3.** Another word for **sides**; i.e., a copy of the lines and cue lines for part of a script.

parterre (pahr tehr') *n.* [Fr. French: *par terre*: on the ground] **1.** The ground floor, or orchestra section, of a theater. **2.** The section of the orchestra over which the balconies hang. Also called *parquet circle; orchestra circle*. **3.** At the Metropolitan Opera, the first tier of box seats.

participation *n.* Profit-sharing arrangement; e.g., the contractual division of the profits among star actors, director, and producers for a film.

particularization *n.* In acting, making each given circumstance and object specific and individual.
    See also ENDOWMENT; SUBSTITUTION.

passing shot A take in which the camera remains fixed while a performer walks past in front of it; or, alternatively, in which the camera moves while the performer either remains stationary, or else walks very slowly past the camera as it, too, continues to move.

passion play A medieval drama depicting the story of Jesus Christ's last days.

pastoral play A mainly 17th-c. genre of drama set in the countryside, with shepherds and shepherdesses as its principal characters.

PA system [Short for *public address system*] In the theater, a set of loudspeakers placed in the auditorium and backstage, so that announcements can be made to the audience, and the play monitored in the greenroom and dressing rooms in order for the listening actors to arrive **on deck** in time for their entrances.
    See also MONITOR; TANNOY.

patch *v. t.* To **plug** lighting, sound, or other equipment together into electrical circuits. Hence, *patch bay*: the board on which audio connectors are attached for the routing of sound; *patch panel*: the board on which dimmers or other light wires are connected; *to patch into*: to interconnect different circuits.

patent theater *Hist. Brit.* A playhouse operated under a royal grant, called a *patent*; e.g., the Restoration theaters under King Charles II.

pathetic fallacy [English aesthetician John Ruskin's (1819–1900) term] The attribution of human emotions, qualities, or intentionality to inanimate nature, natural phenomena, or animals; sometimes as if nature were sympathetic to human fate. Constantly used in **metaphor** in verse drama: *Good things of day begin to droop and drowse* (Shakespeare, *Macbeth*, act 3, scene 2); *Blow, winds, and crack your cheeks!* (Shakespeare, *King Lear*, act 3, scene 2).

pathos *n.* In drama, the powerful, distressing, tormenting quality of the protagonist's plight that allows the arousal of **pity and fear**, empathy, and identification with the suffering; hence, the adj. *pathetic*: capable of arousing tender feelings of sorrow.

patter *n.* Words meant to be spoken or sung quickly, as in the patter songs in **Gilbert and Sullivan**. Hence, *patter-song roles*; i.e., those played by the **leading comedian** in G & S, although patter songs are sung by other characters as well. Part of the effect of the complicated lyrics depends on their rapid-fire delivery; more important, however, is keeping the rhythm steady.

patterning *v. t.* In a **costume shop**, cutting cloth by following a designer's patterns.

pause *n.* A brief suspension in the middle of dialogue. A pause is an **action** as much as if the actor spoke, or did something physical: it is an internal action, and may also represent a change of beat or a transition in thought. It must be filled: a pause is never inactive and never a suspension of the material being performed.

pay and play Provision in a motion picture contract, usually only for high-level performers and other personnel, guaranteeing that a project will be made and that the performer, writer, or director will be paid.

paymaster *n.* An accounting corporation providing payroll services for a producer of radio and television commercials or other projects; it pays residuals to performers for commercials, and salaries or fees for such jobs as **book recording**. The paymaster deducts taxes and social security payments, pays contributions to the union's health and retirement fund, and may deduct an agent's commission. A nonunion book recording job can be turned into an AFTRA one if the company is willing to do so, and if they are paying minimum union rates, by going through a paymaster that pays the required percentage to the union's retirement pension and health insurance fund. The paymaster in such a case must be a **signatory** to AFTRA's **Sound Recordings Code**. A signatory producing company may use a paymaster for the sake of convenience. The paymaster takes a commission for its services, usually ten percent, directly out of the actor's paycheck. In the case of book recording, either the paymaster or the recording company may be union signatories, but this is not true of commercials, where the producing company must be a signatory. Also called *paymaster company*; *talent payment company*.

pay or play Provision in a motion picture contract, usually only for high-level performers and other personnel, guaranteeing that the producer will pay the person even if he or she is not used on the project.

pay-off *n.* The desired audience reaction that results from the actors having built a joke, a scene, or a whole play up to a climax.

peak *v. i.* To speak so loudly when recording that the sound is distorted, and exceeds the level set during the **level check**.

peanuts *n. pl. Slang* Very low pay: *to work for peanuts*.

197

pear-shaped tones Particularly elegant diction and elocution, with sounds that are resonant, mellifluous, and beautiful; also said sarcastically of an actor's **speech** that is too refined, and overdone. In fact, pear-shaped tones may be used to great comic effect, as they were in the episode "Sense and Senility" in the television series *Blackadder III*, with two hammy actors hired to teach elocution to Hugh Laurie as a dimwitted prince.

peep hole A small opening in the front curtain of a proscenium stage through which the **house** may be viewed.

peep show 1. A sex spectacle with one or more performers, viewed through a window by a spectator, who cannot be seen by the performer(s). **2.** *Archaic* A presentation of a play in a miniature toy theater, seen through a small eyehole, sometimes using a magnifying glass. In the 19th c., exhibitors traveled with these theaters, which were placed inside a building or tent; the box had several eyeholes, so that several spectators at a time could see the show. Also called a *raree show*.

penalty *n.* Money paid by a producer to compensate for violation of a contract provision. Also called a *penalty fee*; e.g., a **meal penalty**.

per diem (puhr dee' yehm) [Latin: for the day] An allowance for certain daily expenses; e.g., hotels and meals **on the road**.

perform *v. t.* To appear as an entertainer in public: *to perform a play*; *to perform a concert*; *to perform a role*.

performance *n.* **1.** The public presentation of an entertainment. **2.** The act, presentation, and nature of an artist's work before an audience; an actor's playing of a character.

performance anxiety A performing artist's worry over how he or she will be received by the audience or critics, leading to a fear of going on stage. Also called *stage fright*.

performance art Presentation for an audience by an individual or a group of an ephemeral, prepared event that is often seen one time only. It may take place in a street, or in some other unexpected venue (e.g., a **happening**) or be a piece of conceptual art, such as living sculpture.

performance capture The recording of an actor's dialogue, movements, and facial expressions onto a computer during a **motion capture** shoot.

performance capture supervisor The person on a **motion capture** shoot in charge of overseeing the head cameras, ensuring that they are at the correct angle, and making sure the actors are recorded on the computers attached to the display monitors.

performance marks Symbols, words, annotations, and abbreviations used in a music score to aid and guide a musician in interpreting a composition.

performance practice 1. The skills and knowledge of agreed, generally accepted conventions necessary in interpreting and presenting a work of dramatic, choreographic, or musical art. **2.** The way in which a work of entertainment is presented or performed. **3.** The way in which a work of entertainment was presented to the public in its historical period. Also called *performing practice*.

performance rights The legal permission and entitlement to perform a piece of music in public; e.g., on obtaining a license from ASCAP or BMI. Also called *performing rights*.
　　See also AMERICAN SOCIETY OF COMPOSERS, AUTHORS, AND PUBLISHERS (ASCAP); BROADCAST MUSIC INCORPORTAED (BMI).

performance rights organization An association of copyright holders that protects copyright owners' legal rights and serves as a clearinghouse for payment of royalties and the licensing of works to producers and others; e.g., **American Society of Composers, Authors and Publishers (ASCAP)**. Also called *performing rights society*; *PRO* (pee' ahr' oh'), for short.

performance space An area where entertainments are presented. Also called *performance area*.

performance theory Ideas about how work in the theater should be presented; e.g., Brecht's ideas on the **alienation effect** and **anti-culinary theater**, Grotowski's ideas on **environmental theater**, Boal's ideas on **political theater**.

performer *n.* An artist who entertains the public by participating in the presentation of an amusement.

performing arts Those aesthetic crafts, professions, and occupations practiced in live or recorded presentations before an audience; e.g., acting, singing, playing a musical instrument, dancing. Also called *interpretive arts*, as opposed to creative arts, because performing artists are given material to interpret: such artists are also creative in the way they interpret and present that material, whether engendered by others or by themselves; e.g., an actor is given the sketch or blueprint of a character by the writer, and at the same time creates the character out of him or herself.

period *n.* **1.** A historical epoch; a length or interval of time noted for certain characteristics and conditions: *the medieval period*; *the Victorian period*; *the period of the 1920s, when flappers danced the Charleston, and speakeasies served bootlegged liquor*. **2.** The historical era in which a play or film is set; part of the given **circumstances**, requiring much **research** by actors, director, and designers. **3.** An elegantly constructed and balanced sentence; e.g., Oscar Wilde's epigrams.

period film A movie set in an era other than the contemporary one.
　　See also HISTORICAL FILM.

period play A drama set in an era other than contemporary (i.e., one written in a particular historical time) or a contemporary play set in another epoch. Also called a *period piece*.
　　See also HISTORY PLAY.

perishables *n. pl.* Stage properties that must be replaced for every show; e.g., food and drink consumed on stage or a **breakaway prop**; hence, *perishable props.*

perk *n.* [Short for *perquisite*] *Slang* A nonobligatory extra privilege or benefit given to someone doing a job.
See FRINGE BENEFITS.

personality actor A performer who plays him or herself, living through the situations, so that every character has the same traits and mannerisms; esp. true of some star film actors, whose appealing personalities constitute one of the reasons such actors are stars.

personal assistant A person employed by a busy star actor as a general factotum, or hired as such by the producer to help an actor on a particular project, or employed to work as a general factotum to a director or producer.

personal manager Someone who has charge of an actor's career, and can get clients seen by producers, directors, agents, and casting directors. Many actors have both managers and agents. Personal managers usually collect fifteen percent **commission**.

personal props Objects such as watches, snuffboxes, canes or fans, used by a particular actor for a role; usually kept in the dressing room under the actor's care.
See also HAND PROPS.

personalization *n.* Identifying intimately with circumstances in a script by relating them to aspects of the actor's own life, so that they become real and visceral.
See also ACTOR'S SECRET; ENDOWMENT; SUBSTITUTION.

personify *v. t.* To embody an abstract characteristic, such as virtue or knowledge, in a theatrical character; e.g., in medieval drama.

phonation *n.* The way in which a speech sound is formed, produced, and uttered; i.e., by the vibration and the oscillatory opening and closing of the vocal folds, which is caused by sending air from the lungs upward through them, and by directing the air to a particular part of the vocal apparatus: *vowel phonation*; *consonant phonation.* The study of phonation patterns is very important when working on an **accent**.
See also DIALECT; VOCAL CORDS; VOCAL TECHNIQUE; VOICE.

phone it in *Slang* To walk through a role in a detached, desultory manner, giving a perfunctory performance.

phonetics *n.* The scientific study of human vocal sounds, esp. speech sounds, including the analysis of their source, production, and manner of utterance. The classification of sounds into various categories, as well as the transcription of the classified sounds into the symbols called letters, refined in the *International Phonetic Alphabet (IPA)* to reflect sound as accurately as possible.
See ACCENT; DIALECT.

photo call A **session** in which the actors are photographed both for publicity purposes and to preserve a record of a production. Actors are usually expected to appear in full costume and makeup, so a photo call is often set for directly after a dress or tech-dress rehearsal. Some members of the crew may be required to work a photo call, especially when a change of set or costume is required. Photographers may also take pictures of rehearsal sessions, and actors and crew must be notified ahead of time.

photogenic *adj.* Having features that appear attractive in a photograph or on film.

photograph *n., v.* —*n.* **1.** A still picture of an image, developed from film used in a camera. —*v. t.* **2.** To take a still picture using a camera and film. **3.** To film a motion picture.

photographer *n.* A professional artist-craftsperson who takes still pictures for many kinds of jobs: travel or cooking magazines, newspaper reports, advertisements, actors' head shots, preserving a photographic record of something, rehearsals and performances of theatrical productions, pictures of models for **print work**, etc. Many photographers work through agents, and may leave their **book** at the agent's office for showing to prospective employers.

photography *n.* The act and job of taking pictures. Also the resultant work; e.g., a collection of photographs: *Matthew Brady's (1822–1896) Civil War photography.*

photoplay *n.* Syn. with **screenplay**. Also called a *photodrama*.

photo scan The electronic, digital photographing of an actor during a specially scheduled **session**, from head to foot and at various angles; e.g., for purposes of a **video game** done by **motion capture**, in order to **upload** the photos to a computer for editing them into the game. A kind of photo session.

photo shoot 1. A **session** in which an actor's head shots are taken, or in which still pictures of fashion models, products, places, clothing, etc. are taken, for purposes of **print work**. **2.** Photographing a theater rehearsal, fashion show, photo scan, or other event.

phrase *n., v.* —*n.* **1.** A group of two or more words in grammatical sequence that have a meaningful connection with each other; such a group forming part of a sentence. **2.** A group of musical notes that form an inseparable melodic and rhythmic pattern, usually extending over several measures; a discreet section of a melody. **3.** A choreographed pattern of steps in a dance that form a discreet, separable section of a larger dance, such that it may be worked on separately. —*v. t.* **4.** To group word sequences together for purposes of expression, style, or sense. **5.** To interpret a piece of music by grouping melodic patterns together in an expressive way. **6.** To devise, choreograph, or arrange a pattern in a dance.

phrasing *n.* **1.** The act, style, and way of grouping words together for meaning, and clarity of expression: *an actor's phrasing of Shakespearean lines.* See also ARTICULATION; VERSE TECHNIQUE. **2.** The act and way of grouping the phrases in a musical piece for expressive and stylistic purposes: *a singer's phrasing of an* **aria**. 3. The act and way of arranging choreographed patterns of dance steps.

physical action An undertaking, proceeding, movement, or activity carried out by an actor/character for a particular purpose.

piano dress [Short for *piano dress rehearsal*] A dress or tech-dress **rehearsal** of a musical theater piece, with piano accompaniment only.

piano rehearsal A **run-through** or **work-through** of a musical theater piece in a rehearsal studio or on stage, with piano accompaniment only.

pic *n., pl.* pix *Slang* Short for **picture**; e.g., in **biopic**, a biographical movie. Also used for **head shot**: *I sent the agents my pix*.

pick up **1.** To speed things up: *Pick up the pace! Pick it up! Pick the scene up!*; i.e., play the scene with more energy. *Pick up your cues!*; i.e., be prompt in your response, and speak immediately upon the termination of a speech, without pausing before speaking. Picking up cues is of paramount importance in creating the impression of real, ongoing conversation and in keeping up the tempo and rhythm of a scene. **2.** To hire extra musicians, dancers, or actors for particular performances of a play, concert, or ballet recital, usually when out of town. **3.** To hire and bring in an actor from out of town to perform with local actors. **4.** To transfer an **Equity showcase** to a commercial venue; e.g., **Broadway** or **Off-Broadway**: *The producer picked up the show.* **5.** To bring a successful regional theater show into New York for a commercial run. **6.** To order that a television **pilot** purchased by a network **go to series**. **7.** To continue from where one left off; e.g., to begin recording a book from the place where one stopped.

pick-up *n.* **1.** In book recording, a correction that has to be done after the recording has been listened to and a reader's mistake discovered. See also CORRECTIONS SESSION. **2.** A musician, actor, dancer, or other performer hired to fill out the orchestra or cast of an **out-of-town** entertainment project.

pick-up shot A take of a scene that begins where the previous take stopped.

picture *n.* **1.** [Short for motion picture] A film; movie; hence, *picture palace* (movie theater); *picture show*; *pictures*: the movies. **2.** A stage **tableau**, in which the actors take fixed positions: *stage picture*.

picture-frame stage Syn. with **proscenium** stage.

piece *n.* **1.** An individual speech, song, or other written or musical composition or selection meant for performance. **2.** A play: *The piece was a great success.* **3.** An investment share in a production: *He owns a piece of the show.* **4.** A three-dimensional unit of scenery. Also called a ***set piece***; e.g., an artificial tree, a **practical** fountain.

pilot *n.* **1.** A television program that is meant to sell a series to producers and to find potential sponsors. **2.** The initial program of a television series.

pilot season January through April in Los Angeles, when television pilots are made for new sitcom and nighttime drama series. Many actors go to L.A. hoping to land roles. But the idea of a special season may soon be obsolete: new productions and pilots are now made all year long.

pin spot A spotlight with a narrowly focused beam of light.

piracy *n.* **1.** The crime of the unauthorized use of copyrighted or patented material; copyright or trademark infringement. On a DVD or VHS tape, this can sometimes be prevented by an **anti-piracy signal**. **2.** The act of stealing or plagiarizing such material. **3.** The crime of robbery on the high seas; e.g., 16th- through 18th-century piracy, the subject of many movies.

pirate film A motion picture genre that portrays piracy, usually in past centuries. Mostly fictitious, or based loosely on the lives of real pirates; e.g., *Blackbeard the Pirate* (1952), about the notorious Edward Teach, who terrorized the Carolina coasts in the early 18th c., starred Robert Newton, who also hammed it up delightfully as Long John Silver in Walt Disney's 1950 version of Robert Louis Stevenson's *Treasure Island*, adapted many times for film and television.

pit *n.* **1.** Short for **orchestra pit**. **2.** An area on the ground that is prepared especially for stuntpeople to fall on during the rehearsal and filming of a stunt. **3.** *Brit.* The rear part of the orchestra section of a theater auditorium; the seats located there are called *pit stalls*.

pitch *n., v.* —*n.* **1.** The highs and lows of the voice, and its basic tonality and timbre. **2.** Each level in the entire range of musical notes. Some people have *relative pitch*; i.e., the ability to hear mentally and reproduce a note in relation to another note at the correct interval. And some people have *perfect pitch*; i.e., they can hear mentally and reproduce any note that is desired. **3.** The level at which the tonality of a musical instrument is set, or tuned. **4.** The sales presentation of a project to a film producer. **5.** The presentation of an advertising campaign to the ad executives in charge of a project, or to clients. —*v. t.* **6.** During a performance, to speak by placing the voice at a particular basic level; e.g., in its middle **register**. **7.** To try to sell a film project or an advertising campaign.

pit orchestra The group of instrumentalists playing in the orchestra pit.

pity and fear The two emotions aroused in the audience to a **tragedy**, according to **Aristotle**.

place *n.* Where one is located in space; the location where each scene in a script unfolds. Place is an important given circumstance and conditions behavior; e.g., we behave differently in a public place than at home.

placement *n.* **1.** In voice work, directing the air carrying sound to a resonator (e.g., the **mask**) for maximum vocal resonance and effectiveness of voice projection: *forward placement*. Some opera singers consciously place the voice in a particular area of the mask even when speaking dialogue, so that they sound artificial.

Actors unconsciously place the voice in various areas of the mask as they speak, so that they can sound as natural as possible even when projecting the voice from a stage. **2.** In dance, the alignment of the body.

plane *n.* One of several divisions of the **acting area** on a proscenium stage, from downstage to upstage: plane 1 is the furthest downstage, sometimes below the curtain line, and is divided into downstage right, downstage center, and downstage left. Plane 2 is the next one upstage, sometimes just behind the curtain line; plane 3 is above it. The planes are located downstage of the wings: *a scene in two*; i.e., one enacted in plane 2.

plant *n., v.* —*n.* **1.** An actor who is seated in the audience as part of the show. See SHILL. **2.** A plot point mentioned in passing in a script. **3.** In acting, a gesture, mannerism, or some other character trait that will be seen again and assume importance. **4.** A theater building and all its facilities. **5.** A film studio complex. —*v. t.* **6.** To put an actor in the audience as part of the show. **7.** In playwriting, to **establish** a plot point in passing by hinting at what will later be made clear. **8.** In acting, to make a gesture, mannerism, or the like that will later be significant.

plastic *n.* The physical, external aspects of the actor's embodiment of a character; i.e., appearance, gait, gestures, movement, and voice quality.

play *n., v.* —*n.* **1.** A prose or verse composition written in **dialogue** that tells a story about one or more characters, and is meant to be acted for an audience; a **drama**. —*v. t.* **2.** To act, to perform: *to play an action*; *to play a moment*. **a.** To perform in a drama: *to play a show*. **b.** To act a role in a stage production or other entertainment project: *Edwin Booth played Hamlet many times*. **3.** To perform on a musical instrument. **4.** To perform a musical composition, or participate in a musical performance: *to play a sonata*; *to play a concert*. **5.** To exhibit or show a motion picture: *They played the movie around the country*. —*v. i.* **6.** To be performed, shown, or broadcast: *The tour plays major cities. The sitcom played for a wide audience*. **7.** To perform music: *The band played well*.

play against 1. To do the opposite of what the material might suggest; e.g., to play a tragic scene in a light-hearted or antic manner. Cf. **playing opposites**. **2.** To act as a **foil** for another character, providing a contrast in personality.

play agent A playwright's representative, who tries to get client's work placed with a producer. Also called a *play broker*.

playbill *n.* **1.** A theater **program**. **2.** A one-page broadsheet advertising a play, handed out or posted for publicity purposes.

Playbill.com An informative web site with Canadian and American theater news and listings for Broadway, Off-Broadway, LORT, and London productions.

playbook *n. Hist.* A script, in the Elizabethan theater.

play construction The art of telling the story of a drama by building it into a coherent whole, using the tools of **dramatic structure**.

play doctor A professional writer who is usually brought in late in the process of putting together a project (e.g., when a play or a musical is on its out-of-town try-outs) in order to fix problems by doing some rewriting. Called *doctor* for short. Cf. **dramaturge**.

play down 1. To perform in a condescending manner for the audience. **2.** To **throw away** a line by deliberately giving it no emphasis. **3.** To act a scene in an understated way: *play it down*.

player *n.* **1.** Actor. **2.** Instrumentalist. **3.** Participant in a game or other activity. **4.** A member of a team. Hence, *team player*; i.e., a cooperative, subordinate member of a group or organization who does what is demanded, and has the group's interests at heart.

Players' Guide A book with actors' head shots and contact information, listed by such categories as leading men, leading women, character actors, and comedians. The guide, used for casting, is updated yearly, printed as a bound volume, and available online.

play for a laugh To point up a line vocally, perhaps using gestures or mugging as well, in order to elicit hilarity from the audience. Cf. **milk**.

playgoer *n.* **1.** A habitual attendee at theatrical events. **2.** Someone who goes to the theater.

playhouse *n.* Another word for a **theater** designed and built for the presentation of stage dramas.

playing opposites 1. Acting in a way contrary to what would be expected when expressing a character's feelings, thus adding reality and depth to the playing of specific moments; e.g., a person who is full of rage may smile and speak softly. **2.** The playing of characters as a whole in a way that recognizes a character's ambivalences; i.e., appearing to be the opposite of what the character is, so that a villain, for instance, may be a charming, urbane, well-mannered psychopath, not easily detected by the other characters. In Oscar Wilde's *An Ideal Husband*, Lord Goring poses as a superficial, if witty, man about town, but is in reality a modest, deeply moral person capable of great acts of kindness and friendship. Cf. **play against**.

playing space 1. The particular part of an **acting area** where a scene is played. **2.** Another word for acting area.

playing them out In vaudeville, performing instrumental music while the audience is exiting at the end of a show, after having seen a slide with the words "good night" printed on it, underneath the picture of a child dressed for bed.

playing to the haircuts Performing the last act on a vaudeville bill, when the audience was already leaving the theater in droves, with their backs to the stage.

play it straight To perform simply and without commenting or overdoing.

playlet *n*. A short dramatic or comic piece in one act; a sketch or skit.

play off To react and respond to what the other actor in a scene is giving. Cf. **take it off**.

play opposite To act on stage or screen with another actor, esp., in the leading roles of antagonists or partners: *William Powell and Myrna Loy played opposite each other in the* Thin Man *series*.

play out 1. To face front, or partially front, when acting on stage. **2.** To project a stage performance with energy. **3.** To perform music vigorously and loudly: *The pit orchestra played out*. **4.** To finish; to **run** through completely, e.g., a scene in a rehearsal: *to play out a moment; a beat*. **5.** To exhaust, or be exhausted utterly: *The joke was played out*. **6.** To run a line or unwind a cable gradually and carefully, so as to avoid danger; e.g., to run the line from a **decelerator** during a **wire flying** stunt.

play reader 1. A person who evaluates scripts for a theater, with a view to possible future productions. **2.** A person hired by a literary agent or play agent to evaluate scripts.
    See also LITERARY MANAGER; READER.

play the lead To perform the principal part.

play to the audience During a stage performance, to act a moment or a scene in order to arouse the maximum reaction from the spectators. *Brit*. Play to the **gallery**; play to the **gods**. Cf. **ad lib**; **milk**; **play for a laugh**.

play to the camera During a film shoot, to perform in the most favorable place and position to be photographed, without looking directly at the camera.

play within a play A dramatic **piece** or entertainment presented within the context of a drama, e.g., the play presented at court in *Hamlet* to "catch the conscience of the king."

playwright *n*. A dramatist; a person who writes dramas for the stage.

pleasure garden *Hist*. In 18th-c. England, a popular outdoor landscaped resort, used for assignations as well as entertainment. Sometimes partially or fully roofed over and providing dancing, refreshments, and performances by musicians or acrobats; e.g., Ranelagh or Vauxhall in London, two of the most famous.

plot *n., v.* —*n*. **1.** The storyline of a play or film: *the plot line*. **2.** The outline of the story. **3.** A list and plan for lights, costumes, shoes, or props in a theater production, in the order in which they are needed. —*v. t.* **4.** To plan the outline of a story. **5.** In the theater, to write down an orderly, detailed plan for the uses of lights, costumes, etc.

plot device A useful contrivance, plan, trick, invention, or scheme in storytelling, used to advance the story. In Lewis Carroll's *Alice's Adventures in Wonderland*

and its sequel *Alice Through the Looking-Glass*, the plot devices of Alice falling down the rabbit hole and going through the looking-glass to emerge on its other side enabled Carroll to recount the fantastic occurrences in the fantasy worlds he had invented.

plot element An essential part of a story, without which it would not exist; e.g., the enmity between the Montagues and the Capulets in *Romeo and Juliet*. Cf. **MacGuffin**.

plot hole A gap or inadvertent omission or inconsistency in a storyline, such that certain elements of the story, or even the story as a whole, become unbelievable to its audience.

plot point An important, pivotal event or incident in a story.

plot resolution 1. The outcome of a story, and the moment when it is clear. **2.** The **denouement**, during which the story is brought to a conclusion.

plot thickens, the In the 19th c., a serious phrase describing the developments and complications in the story of a **melodrama**; hence, *plot thickener*: a plot device that adds complications. But the phrase is now an ironical allusion to a transparent, obvious story development. Sometimes sarcastically changed into "the plot thins."

plot twist The device of an unexpected, surprising, often sudden turn of events in the unfolding of a story; e.g., those frequently seen in mystery films.

plug *n., v.* —*n.* **1.** *Slang* A promotional advertisement, esp. for a film or other entertainment project. **2.** *Slang* A laudatory mention and promotion of an entertainment project, often done by one of its stars on a **talk show**. **3.** A pronged male electrical connector. —*v. t.* **4.** *Slang* To talk about a product or entertainment project for publicity purposes. **5.** With *in* or *into*, to connect a piece of equipment to an electrical outlet.

plum *n. Slang* A small, but memorable and outstanding character role; a **cameo**; a sweet and juicy part: *a plum role*.

Plush family *Brit. Archaic* Pertains ironically to empty, plush-covered seats in a theater; i.e., those occupied by nobody: *I see the Plush family has purchased tickets.* Also called the *Bare-stall family*.

podcast *n.* A series of audio or audiovisual files uploaded to and distributed by syndication on the Internet, whether free or to be paid for by the user, such that the files can be downloaded into a personal computer or directly into a media player; e.g., an Apple iPod, the trademarked media player for which such material was first developed. Hence, *podcasting*: the process of uploading and disseminating a podcast; *podcaster*: the person or persons in charge of the podcast.

podium *n.* **1.** A small platform. **2.** The small riser on which an orchestra conductor stands during rehearsals and performances. **3.** *Archaic* Short for *lycopodium*, a 19th-c. flash powder used to create a lightning effect.

poetic drama 1. A play written in verse. **2.** Verse plays, collectively.

poetic justice 1. Originally, a neutral description applying to the distribution of rewards and punishments in a dramatic or literary work; now used to mean the meting out of retribution and vindication in an artificial, unrealistic, literary manner; e.g., the automatic defeat of the **villain** and the triumph of the **hero** in a **melodrama**. **2.** Used as an ironical phrase, when a nasty character gets his or her comeuppance: *It's only poetic justice!*

point of focus The place on the stage to which the director wishes to direct the audience's attention.

point of origin The place from which a show departs to begin its **tour**. It is the producer's obligation on an **Equity** tour to pay for the actors' return to the point of origin when a tour or a **leg** of it is over.

point of view Particular physical perspective; e.g., an individual's position in relation to a physical setting or to another character. Abbrev. POV: an indication in film or television scripts that tells the director and cinematographer from whose perspective a shot is to be taken.

point-of-view shot A take of scenery, an object, or another person, as seen from a particular character's perspective.

point up In acting, to stress or emphasize a line.

political theater Drama that deals with sociopolitical issues, often with the purpose of galvanizing the audience into taking action.
See also AGITPROP; ALIENATION EFFECT; ANTI-CULINARY THEATER; BOAL, AUGUSTO; BRECHT, BERTHOLD; GROWTOWSKI, JERZY; LIVING NEWSPAPER; STREET THEATER.

poor theater Grotowski's idea that theater should use an economy of scenic and histrionic means to present a point of view to the audience, as opposed to presenting a story with rich production values; i.e., gorgeous décors, costumes, and scenic effects.

pop *n., v.* —*n.* **1.** In recording, a sound made when a speaker utters plosives, such as "p" and "t," by expelling the air so forcefully that they cause the **diaphragm** of a **microphone** to smack against another part of the mike. **2.** Short for *popular music*: tuneful, easily accessible vocals and light instrumental pieces. —*v. i.* **3.** To make plosive sounds that are too forceful, causing a recording problem.

popcorn movie A film the whole family can enjoy, while munching on that ubiquitous cinema snack, hot buttered popcorn; a motion picture that is light, entertaining fare, esp. a summer **blockbuster**.

pornographic film A movie that graphically portrays sexual acts, and little else. Also called a *blue movie*; *porno*; *nudie*; *skin flick*; *sleaze*. *Hard porn* is completely graphic; *soft porn* shows sex, but without showing penetration or certain acts in outright detail.

See also EXPLOITATION FILM; FLUFF; FLUFFER; MONEY SHOT.

porta-pit *n.* A soft foam-rubber crash pad that can be transported from place to place, as needed; used in stunt work.

See PIT, def. 2.

position *n.* **1.** In film, the place where a camera or light is set up. **2.** In film, the location of an actor; e.g., **first position, last position**. See INTO POSITIONS!; MARK. **3.** The angle on stage or on a film set at which an actor sits, stands, or faces; e. g, three-quarters profile, full front. **4.** A stage area (e.g., stage left) referred to when placing scenery, set pieces, furniture, or lights. **5.** The place where an actor is supposed to be when playing a scene. **6.** In **ballet**, the direction, body attitude, and stance of a dancer.

poster *n.* A large placard or piece of paper on which an advertisement is printed; e.g., for a play or film.

post-modern drama Another name for **modern drama**, referring esp. to English theater after World War II.

postproduction *n.* All the processes that take place after a film is completely shot, including the editing, dubbing of dialogue, and insertion of **foley** sound effects.

potboiler *n. Slang* **1.** A song or play written to be popular and to sell well, whatever its value or merits as art. **2.** In film, a lurid pulp crime **thriller** full of sex and gore.

practical *n., adj.* —*n.* **1.** A functional stage **set prop**, such as a table lamp, sink faucet, or door or window that can be opened or closed, as opposed to those that are there just for show: *That door stage left is a practical.* —*adj.* **2.** Practicable; operable; able to be used; functional: *a practical stage property.* Cf. *non-practical*: pertaining to a set prop that looks real, but cannot be used.

pratfall *n.* A fall onto an actor's rear end, or *prat*—a word that dates from Elizabethan times. Often done with exaggeration and calling attention to itself; e.g., those in the films of W.C. Fields.

pre-acting *n.* Meyerhold's term for the actor's preparation of the audience by acting out situations in pantomime before actually beginning to play the character, so that the dramatic situation would be clear to the audience before it hears the words. A technique he used in staging his productions.

prebreak *v. t.* To prepare a **breakaway prop** for use by severing it partway in strategic places, in order to facilitate its coming apart.

pregnant pause A short, silent break in the dialogue; one full of suspense and possibilities: every **pause** should ideally be pregnant.

prelude *n.* **1.** An action or event that is preliminary to the main dramatic action, and a harbinger of it; e.g., the meeting of Macbeth and the three witches at the opening of the play. **2.** A brief musical **introduction** or **overture** to a musical theater piece, or to a fugue, or to the movement of a longer piece. **3.** A brief, free-form musical composition.

premiere *n.* The heralded **opening night** of a play, film, opera, or other show; often the occasion for a **gala** first night party.

premise *n.* The main idea, supposition, or assumption that forms the basis of a story.

prepare *v. t.* In acting, to get ready for a **rehearsal**, **performance**, or individual **entrance** or **moment** during a performance.

prepared audition A monologue, speech, or song that an actor has rehearsed and that is ready for use when required; e.g., for a **musical comedy** casting session or for a **LORT** audition (where actors are often asked to come in with two monologues: one contemporary, the other classical).

preparation *n.* The act and/or **process** of getting ready, whether for a **rehearsal** (when the preparation includes the actor's **homework**), for a performance (for which the actor might **vocalize** or physically **warm up**), or for an **entrance**.

preproduction; pre-production *n.* **1.** The stage of preparation for a film shoot after the casting has been completed and all the personnel hired, and when the set is being designed and built, or locations firmed up; costumes designed and constructed, or clothing purchased; and the actors are studying the script before rehearsing. **2.** The stage of preparation for a theatrical production after casting but before rehearsal, when designs are being made and approved and other personnel hired.

prequel *n.* In film, a second or third movie that is part of a series and shows events made before the first movie; e.g., the later films in George Lucas's *Star Wars* series.

prerecorded *adj.* Pertains to audio recorded at one time and used later: *She lip-synced a prerecorded song.*

pre-roll *n.* A small portion of prerecorded material played just before the **punch-in**; e.g., that heard by a **book recording** artist, in order to enable the artist to capture the same tone and tempo when continuing the recording.

presence *n.* **1.** Charisma; the natural ability of the actor to attract the audience's attention. Also commonly called *stage presence*. **2.** Involvement in the time and place where one is supposed to be; i.e., being present **in the moment**.

presentational *adj.* Describes the old-fashioned, external, technical, non-organic approach to acting, in which the character is "presented" or shown to the audience by the actor, who does not feel any of the character's emotions but rather imitates, simulates, or counterfeits them.

presentative blocking Positioning an actor within the direct purview of the camera so that the performer can talk into the camera lens, as if talking to the audience directly. E.g., in the BBC trilogy *House of Cards*, where Ian Richardson as a Machiavellian politician turns to the camera while walking down a flight of stairs in the House of Commons and makes a remark to the audience.

presenter *n.* **1.** A television or radio **announcer** whose function is to introduce a program or program **host**, event, and so forth; e.g., Ed McMahon on the *Johnny Carson Show*. **2.** A person who hands an award to its winner at an **awards** ceremony.

preset *n., v., adj.* —*n.* **1.** The advance establishment or setup of light or sound cues that can then be activated on time. **2.** The machine in a light console that allows the advance setup of light cues. Also called a *controller.* **3.** The placing of props and/or furniture or other set pieces prior to their being needed on stage. **4.** The entire advance setup of everything needed for a show, esp. everything needed at the **top.** —*v. t.* **5.** To set up light cues in advance. **6.** To place props or set pieces in position in advance of their being needed. **7.** To place props, set pieces, etc. in position, in preparation for the beginning of a show. —*adj.* **8.** Pertaining to what has been placed or arranged in advance of its being needed: *a preset prop.*

press agent The publicity person who handles advertising and promotes a show, arranges interviews, and so forth.

press book The collection of reviews and articles regarding a particular production; usually bound into a scrapbook.

press kit An assemblage of printed promotional materials about a performance project given to journalists for publicity purposes.

press pass A complimentary ticket given to a journalist, usually a critic or reviewer.

press release Information given out to journalists for informational and publicity purposes; e.g., an announcement that a star will participate in a certain project.

preview *n., v.* —*n.* **1.** A public performance that takes place before the official **opening night** of a theatrical production. Critics sometimes attend final previews of Broadway or Off-Broadway shows, but they do not release their notices until after the opening. **2.** The showing of a film before its release for the general public to a selected audience, so as to gauge their reactions from questionnaires they fill out. **3.** A **trailer** for a movie. —*v. t.* **4.** To present a play in public performances before its official opening date. **5.** To show a film in advance of its official release date.

prima donna (pree' mah do:' nah) [Italian: first lady] Originally, a neutral term meaning the opera singer who had the principal female role; now also a derogatory term for an egotistical, demanding star, whether male or female. Cf. **diva.**

prime time; primetime *n., adj.* —*n.* **1.** The hours between 7 and 11 p.m., when the maximum number of spectators may be expected to be watching television

211

programs; network primetime **nighttime drama** begins at 8 p.m. Programs compete for primetime viewers, so that their sponsors can sell products and they can stay on the air. But the Internet may be eliminating the entire idea of prime time, because viewers can see programs on their computers at any time, on a channel's **web site**. —*adj.* **2.** Pertaining to broadcasts transmitted between 7 and 11 p.m.: *primetime viewing.*

principal *n.*, *adj.* [Short for *principal actor*; *principal performer*] —*n.* **1.** The actor who plays the leading part. **2.** A leading dancer in a ballet company. **3.** A film actor with a leading role. —*adj.* **4.** That which is the most important, leading, prominent, or outstanding: *a principal role.*

principal boy The young lady who plays the **trousers role** of Prince Charming in a British **pantomime**.

principal girl 1. The young heroine in a British **pantomime**. **2.** In **vaudeville** and **burlesque**, the **comedienne** who plays roles in skits; e.g., the nurse in a **doctor act**.

principal photography The stage of film production during which all the scenes involving the **first unit** and all actors with speaking parts are filmed, including scenes requiring the use of **background players**. Also called *principal shooting.*

print *n.* A copy of a finished photograph, motion picture, or taped television show. A *release print* of a movie is one ready for distribution.

Print it! The instruction from a director to the camerapeople to save a particular, satisfactory take that may be used in the **final cut**.
    See also KEEP TAKE.

print work 1. Photographed advertisements that appear in magazines and newspapers, for which models and/or actors are sent by their agents to **audition**; *print*, for short. The audition for a *print job* consists of being photographed, either standing or sitting, or following the directions of a casting person, who may instruct the actor to move in certain ways. **2.** An advertising job or jobs for models; actors; wardrobe, makeup, or lighting personnel; and photographers and their assistants.

prison film A genre of motion pictures, or an individual film that take place mostly in a jail or penitentiary setting and deals with the prisoners' lives; e.g., *The Shawshank Redemption* (1994), *The Rock* (1996).

privacy *n.* The feeling of being unobserved during a performance; helped by the fact that the audience is in darkness, so that the actor on a lit stage cannot see them, and by the concepts of the **fourth wall** and **public solitude**.

private eye film A **detective film** in which the crime is solved by a PI (private investigator); e.g., the Sherlock Holmes films.

private moment One of a series of Lee Strasberg Method class exercises, in which the actor performs an action that usually demands complete privacy.

private performance The presentation of a play or other project, seen by invitation only, in a residence or other venue.

pro *n.* [Short for *professional*] *Slang* A tried and true professional, in the best sense of the word: accomplished, talented, reliable, responsible, disciplined, and courteous: *a real pro.*

problem *n.* Another term for the Stanislavskian word **zadacha**, usually rendered as **objective** by Elizabeth Reynolds Hapgood in her original translations of Stanislavsky's books: Characters have to solve problems concerning their objectives.

problem play A drama that presents a dilemma—or more than one—that perturbs and upsets the characters, and that must be and usually is resolved by the end of the play. The solutions to the problems may, however, be incomplete and might even give rise to further problems, as they do in the plays of Henrik Ibsen, George Bernard Shaw, and Sam Shepherd or the **cup and saucer drama** of Tom Robertson. The term is usually reserved for some of Shakespeare's plays that are neither comedies nor tragedies, but used to be called "dark comedies"; e.g., *Measure for Measure, All's Well That Ends Well.*
See also THEATER OF IDEAS; TRAGICOMEDY.

process *n.* The actor's or director's way or system of working through a role or a script, including the order of steps taken while doing the work, and the series of changes that occur and are absorbed while heading towards eventual performance: *the rehearsal process.* The process is continuous and involves the cumulative amalgamation into a performance of everything that has been discovered in the course of **rehearsal**.
See also ACTING PROCESS; TOOLKIT.

process shot A take done on a studio soundstage in front of a background image projected on a screen that is behind the actors.
See REAR PROJECTION.

prochronism (proh' kruhn ihzm), *n.* A chronological anomaly consisting of placing a historical character or event much earlier in time, or of using colloquial language or expressions that could not possibly have been used at the time a play or film is set.

produce *v. t.* To bring together and hire the personnel for a play, film, television show, or other entertainment project; to oversee their work; and to present the finished product to the public.

producer *n.* **1.** The individual responsible for overseeing either all aspects of a theater, film, television or other project, and the personnel involved in it, or of a particular area of production in the media; e.g., a **line producer**. **2.** The production company that is producing a particular project. **3.** *Archaic Brit.* A stage director.

production *n., adj.* —*n.* **1.** An entertainment project and everything connected with it: presentation, producing, directing, performing, designing, etc. **2.** The stage of filmmaking during which a film, commercial, or television program is actually being made: *the production stage.* **3.** *Slang* A big deal: *Don't make a production out of it!* —*adj.* **4.** Having a connection to an entertainment project: *production company*; *production manager.*

production assistant A person who helps on various film crews (e.g., sound or lighting), doing odd jobs as necessary for them or for the producer or director; abbrev. PA. The PA is a novice, intern, or entry-level member of the production team.
    See also GOPHER.

production company In the media, a business outfit, with all the necessary facilities, that develops and produces projects and then releases them for distribution.

production coordinator The person on a film shoot who handles all the paperwork, including correspondence; facilitates logistics; and works with an *assistant production coordinator* on large projects. Similar to a *production secretary.*

production contract The contract covering principal actors and stage managers working on Broadway, and on national tours, negotiated by **Actors' Equity Association (AEA)** and the **League of American Theatres and Producers (LATP)**. Also known colloquially as a "white" contract, it is the most lucrative theater contract in the business. Disney Theatrical Productions has an individual version of it, negotiated with Equity.
    See also CHORUS CONTRACT.

production designer The person in charge of the various design staffs working on a project. He or she is responsible for the overall look of the production, and must coordinate the work of the set, costume, and lighting designers, following instructions from the **director**.

production manager The administrative head of a film project actually **in production**. Takes care of the logistics of studio and location shoots, scheduling and budgetary matters (on which he or she must report to the **line producer**), arranging for craft services, transportation, and so forth. A production manager may also serve as line producer.

production meeting A periodic gathering of director, design staff, and other key production personnel during the preproduction or production phases of a theater or film project to discuss problems, logistics, and ways and means of carrying out plans, and to check on progress in various design areas. Cf. **concept meeting**.

production number A lavishly staged ensemble song and dance routine for principals and chorus in a musical theater piece or film.

production sound mixer The person in charge of recording sound during a film shoot, selecting the microphones to be used, operating the audio equipment along with the rest of the sound crew, and keeping accurate, detailed reports on everything that has been recorded. Also called *production mixer*; ***sound mixer***; *floor mixer*; *recording supervisor.*

production still 1. An enlarged frame from a film, made into a still photograph for publicity purposes. **2.** A photograph taken by makeup or wardrobe people for purposes of **continuity**.

production values The perceived aesthetic, satisfying qualities of costumes, décor, lighting, sound, and other physical or technical elements of an entertainment project; in a film or television program, the production values include the quality of professional cinematography and editing.

product placement The prominent positioning, for publicity and marketing purposes, of a recognizable brand-name item in a film or television shot; e.g., a particular cereal in a breakfast scene. The placement is paid for by the manufacturers, and arranged for by a *product placement agent* who works for them. According to a report in the *Backstage* issue of February 21–27, 2008, advertisers are expected to spend upwards of $40 billion on product placement by 2012.

professional actor A person who earns a living by embodying and playing characters, and is a member of one or more of the performing arts unions: a **working actor**.

professionalism in acting A combination of abiding by the rules, standards, ethics, and norms of responsible conduct expected of those who earn their living in the business as actors, and the background, training, craft, knowledge, and skills required for the art of creating and performing characters for the paying public. Professional behavior consists of a common-sense code of conduct that actors are duty-bound to abide by, and that the discipline of show business requires. The first rule is to be courteous, considerate, and respectful to everyone, whether backstage, on stage, in the studio, in rehearsal, or in performance. From that, all else follows:

1. Know, understand, and abide by the terms of your contract.
2. Remember that you are there to serve the play, film, or whatever project you are involved in.
3. Always be on time, which means being a bit early, for all calls, auditions, and appointments.
4. Always sign in for theater rehearsals and performances, so the stage manager knows you are in the house, and for auditions, when required. Nobody may sign in for another actor: the actor must sign in personally.
5. Do your homework. Be prepared.
6. When you are rehearsing, it is part of your job to follow directions and make adjustments as the director requires, even if you disagree. The director has the vision of what the overall play should be like.
7. Have your lines memorized when you are supposed to; i.e., when the director of a project requires them to be memorized.
8. When rehearsals begin on stage, do not leave the set or backstage area until you are told you may do so, when it is certain that the scene you are in will not be repeated, and the next scene will be happening.

9. Do not give directions to your fellow actors. If you have a problem with what another actor is doing in a scene, go to the director or stage manager.

10. Ask the stage manager's permission to leave rehearsal, if you have to do so at any time for any reason.

11. As soon as you have your costume, take care of your wardrobe, and continue to do so once the show opens. Do not make more work for the already overworked wardrobe people. Keep your costumes neat and in their proper location, so that both you and the wardrobe people can find them immediately.

12. Keep your dressing area and your dressing table clean and neat.

13. Always say "thank you" to whoever gives the calls before a theater performance (unless, of course, they are only given over the **PA system**), to acknowledge that you have heard and understood them.

14. Be absolutely quiet backstage during rehearsals and performances, or in a film or television studio when a shoot or taping is in progress.

15. Never miss an entrance.

16. Do not interrupt an actor backstage or on a film or television set when he or she is preparing for an entrance, unless it is absolutely necessary to do so.

17. Always replace props where they are supposed to be, and where you have presumably found them: on the backstage prop table or elsewhere.

18. Do not upstage your fellow performers (or yourself) or steal scenes. Do your job: play your role as you rehearsed it, bearing in mind that your organic performance will cause you to experience the role slightly differently every time you perform. But you have no right to throw your fellow actors off by doing something startling, new, and completely unrehearsed, because you supposedly "felt it." A severe reprimand from stage management usually follows such uncouth behavior.

19. Be there for the curtain call, even if your part had only one scene at the beginning of the performance, unless you are specifically excused.

20. Never appear in costume or makeup outside the theater: to do so shows a lack of respect for the profession and the project.

21. Remember, acting is acting: at no time do you have the right to hurt your fellow performer or put him or her in any danger.

professional organizations Guilds, unions, societies, associations, and companies to which those earning their living in the **arts and entertainment industry** belong. See the index of subjects for a listing, p. 366.

program *n., v.* —*n.* **1.** A handout of a printed sheet or small booklet about a show, including credits for cast, crew, and staff as well as necessary information about the play and intermissions, if any; given to the audience as they enter the theater. In some European theaters, the program is an elaborate book that the spectator must purchase. **2.** A radio or television broadcast or show. —*v. t.* **3.** To make up a radio or television schedule; i.e., to arrange the order of the shows broadcast on a radio or television station: a job done by a *programmer*.

program seller The vendor of a show's **souvenir program** in a theater lobby.

progressive shots Successive takes of an object or person, focusing closer with each take. The series of shots usually ends with a **close-up** or **extreme close-up**.

project *n., v.* —*n.* **1.** In show business, a planned entertainment that may or may not ever be produced: there are always many projects "in development" by film studios. —*v. t.* **2.** To throw the voice. **3.** To show or screen a film.

projection *n.* **1.** Throwing the voice and making the intentions of the lines clear to the audience. **2.** An image thrown onto a stage to create an effect, such as moonlight or forest trees. **3.** The showing of a film. **4.** Prediction of future earnings from a motion picture or other project.

projection booth The room at the back of and above the auditorium of a movie theater, from which a motion picture is shown on the screen.

projectionist *n.* The operator of a film projector in a movie theater.

projector *n.* A machine or device used for the showing of a film or photographic slides, or for throwing an image onto a surface.

prologue *n.* **1.** The section of a play that precedes the main action, giving the audience background information or introducing the main action; e.g., the Prologue in Shakespeare's *Henry V*. **2.** The character who gives an introductory speech.

promo *n.* [Short for *promotion*; *promotional commercial*] A commercial made by a television station or for a television program, to publicize that station or program. Hence, *promo announcer*: one who reads or recites the copy for such a commercial, on radio or television. Some television stations advertise their own news coverage; hence, *news promo*.

prompt *n., v.* —*n.* **1.** The words, lines, or cues fed to an actor. —*v. t.* **2.** To give an actor lines, either during a rehearsal or during a performance, when the actor has had a lapse of memory. The **prompter**, who was always **on book**, was once a permanent member of any production. In the theater, the stage manager would prompt the actors from the stage right side where the stage manager's desk is located: stage right was therefore also called the *prompt side*.

prompt book 1. The stage manager's copy of a play script, prepared with lighting, scenery, and sound cues; furniture and set prop placement plans; and actor's moves, used to call a show. Also called *prompt copy*; *prompt script*. **2.** The prompter's prepared copy of a stage play or opera, with certain cues and moves written into it.

prompt box The sunken, recessed compartment at the front of the stage where the prompter sits during a performance. It is concealed from the audience, and its opening faces the actors. Still used in the opera, it is seldom to be found anymore in other forms of theater. Also called the *prompter's box*.

prompter *n.* **1.** The person who gives actors their lines when they have forgotten them during a rehearsal or performance. **2.** The person who gives opera singers their cues and who follows and conducts the score along with the conductor for the singers' benefit. **3.** [Short for *videoprompter*] A machine with a screen down which a script rolls; it faces performers or newscasters during a broadcast so they can read their lines.

prompt table The desk or table placed at the front of the stage during rehearsals for the director, stage manager, and assistants.

prop *n.* [Short for *stage property*] Any movable object on a set.

propaganda film A motion picture, whether a fictional dramatization or documentary, that is biased in favor of a particular point of view.

prop designer The person who decides what properties will be used (in conjunction with the set and costume designers), purchases props, and makes the plans and drawings for those that must be manufactured.

properties *n. pl.* [Short for ***stage properties***] Movable objects used by an actor or placed on a set, except furniture and set pieces, which are called **heavy properties**. Called *props*, for short.
    See HAND PROPS; PERISHABLES; PERSONAL PROPS; SET PROPS.

property basket; prop basket. See BASKET.

property maker The skilled artisan who manufactures stage properties, and who can sculpt them, carve them in wood, paint them, etc.; sometimes a staff member in charge of a prop shop, esp. in large theaters or opera houses.

property master The chief member and boss of the crew in charge of properties, in both the theater and the media. The property master is also an artisan with the craft and skills to make some props, to deal with the reflection from a **mirror**, to provide realistic **perishables** for stage or film, or to distress furniture or set pieces by painting them so that they look cracked, worn, or shabby.

prop plot The list of props in the order in which they are used, and where each one is placed.

props *n. pl.* **1.** Short for **stage properties**. **2.** The personnel of the props department or the department itself: *We need props on stage now to fix the broken door. Is somebody from props available?*

prop shop The room, atelier, or factory where **properties** are manufactured.

prop table The backstage table on which hand props are set out in carefully labeled places, usually separated by tape delineating the spaces where they are to be put in preparation for a performance. They are picked up by the actor just before they are needed in a scene, and, if the actor exits with them, should be returned to their assigned places immediately.

proscenium *n., adj.* The large framing archway set into the wall that separates the stage from the auditorium. Hence, *proscenium arch*: the framed opening through which the audience sees the play; *proscenium wall*: the full partition that separates the stage and backstage from the auditorium; *proscenium stage*: the framed performance space, often ending just downstage of the proscenium arch.

proskeniun. See SKENE.

prosthesis *n.* An attachment used to alter the appearance of an actor so that he or she resembles a character physically; e.g., Richard III's humpback.

protagonist *n.* The principal character in a play or film, around whom the story centers.

provinces *n. pl.* In theatrical terms, any place where one performs outside of New York or London; also known as "the sticks," and by various other unflattering names.

psychodrama *n.* **1.** A form of educative, improvisational theater dealing with psychological themes: the audience asks actors to act out situations and to play certain roles. **2.** A kind of psychotherapy in which a patient acts out his or her situation under the guidance of a psychotherapist.

psychological gesture Michael Chekhov's term and technique for finding a way into the character by inventing or finding a particular physical movement that awakens in the actor the overall feeling the actor associates with the character. In *Lessons for the Professional Actor* (Performing Arts Journal Publications, 1985), based on classes he gave in 1941, he suggests this way of working with the psychological gesture:

> Take a certain gesture, such as "to grasp." Do it physically. Now do it only inwardly, remaining physically unmoved. As soon as we have developed this gesture, it becomes a certain "psychology," and that is what we want. Now on the basis of this gesture, which you will do inwardly, say the sentence, "Please, darling, tell me the truth." While speaking, produce the gesture inwardly.... Now do them both together—the gesture and the sentence. Then drop the physical gesture and speak, having the gesture inside only.

psychology. See CHARACTER PSYCHOLOGY.

psychophysical action Stanislavsky's term for something the actor/character does and/or says as the result of a psychological motivation; all actions are psychologically motivated, and can therefore be characterized as psychophysical.

public *n.* The audience for a performance event, or for any artistic work.

public access Cable television channels available for rent to individuals or organizations who wish to broadcast a program.

public domain, [in the] Free to be exploited by anyone. Said of an artistic property that does not enjoy **copyright** status; e.g., a play that anybody may produce: *Chekhov's plays are in the public domain, but most of the translations are not.*

publicist *n.* The person who does the job of promoting a product, project, service, or individual; e.g., a **press agent**, public-relations consultant, or publicity manager.

publicity *n.* **1.** Another word for **advertising**. **2.** Advertisements and commercials. **3.** Talking about, advertising, constantly mentioning, or otherwise ensuring fame or notoriety for a product, project, service, company, or individual; hence, *publicizing*, the act of doing all this. Also called *promotion*.

publicity hound Someone who seeks fame and notoriety and takes every opportunity to get noticed by the public.

publicity-shy *adj.* Pertains to a **star** who avoids the **limelight** as much as possible, and who prefers to keep his or her private life private.

public rehearsal A **dress rehearsal** to which the producers, director, designers, cast members, and other personnel may invite guests; it takes place before previews begin.

public relations Ensuring a positive image and good relationship with the community at large or with a segment of the population, by means of advertising, publicized charitable contributions and activities, and the like.

public service announcement A television or radio **commercial** made under government auspices to advise the population on safety developments or regulations, health care concerns, and the like, or to advertise for purposes of tourism; abbrev. PSA. Such commercials are made by union actors under special public service rates of pay.

public solitude The feeling of being alone and private on stage or in front of the camera.
See also CONCENTRATION; FOURTH WALL; PRIVACY.

public television Stations, audiovisual broadcasting, and broadcasts that are funded partly by donations from viewers; e.g., WNET in Newark, NJ; WGBH in Boston, MA. Many public television stations are part of the Public Broadcasting Service (PBS), a national network.

pull *n., v.* —*n. Slang.* **1.** Box office drawing power: *She has pull.* **2.** Influence: *He had pull with the producer.* —*v. t.* **3.** To attract audiences; to be a **box office draw**: *The star really pulled them in.* **4.** To eliminate an act or number from a running order; e.g., in vaudeville or a revue. **5.** To take an actor away from a rehearsal: *The actor was pulled for his costume fitting.* **6.** To take a piece of scenery, stage prop, or costume out of storage, for immediate use in a production.

pull-back shot A take during which the camera withdraws, either slowly or rapidly, distancing objects from the viewer and sometimes widening out the view horizontally.

pun *n.* A joking play on words that deliberately exploits their similarity. Shakespeare's *Richard III* begins with a pun: "Now is the winter of our discontent made glorious summer by this sun [son] of York."

Punch and Judy show *Brit.* A puppet show for children, starring the characters of the odd, irascible, hunchbacked character Punch, based on the **commedia dell'arte** character Punchinello, and his long-suffering but aggressive wife, Judy.

punch *v. t.* To emphasize particularly strongly; e.g., when giving the last line of a joke, by pointing it up.

punch-in *n.* **1.** The sound engineer's commencement of a book recording, pressing the buttons on the sound console that enable an artist to record, continuing immediately after the **pre-roll**; or at the very beginning of a recording, when the engineer points at the artist to give a starting **cue**; hence, *to punch in*: *The engineer punched him in.* **2.** In music recording and editing, the insertion of the **take** of a good line in the middle of a song, replacing a flubbed line; markers are set before and after the flubbed line, and the good take is then punched in over it. **3.** In book recording and editing, the insertion of a good take replacing a flubbed reading, using the method just described for music editing.

punch line The last words of a joke; the **laugh line**. Also called a *gag line.*

puppet *n.* A handheld doll representing a person or animal, often with workable jaws and movable arms; also called a *glove puppet.* Puppet shows are put on for children on some children's television shows or are done live in parks, where a special theater with an opening at the top is used, while the *puppeteer* who works the puppet is concealed behind and below the opening, projecting his or her voice while moving the arms and/or workable jaw of the doll.
 See also BUNRAKU; HAND AND ROD PUPPET; GRAND GUIGNOL; MARIONETTE; PUNCH AND JUDY SHOW; ROD PUPPET; SHADOW PLAY.

put across To communicate and project a performance.

put-in *n., adj.* —*n.* **1.** [Short for *put-in rehearsal*] A rehearsal for new cast members, in order to integrate them into a show, in preparation for their first performance. —*adj.* **2.** Pertaining to such a rehearsal.
 See also REPLACEMENT REHEARSAL.

put on 1. To present or produce an entertainment project. **2.** To **indicate**; to fake or counterfeit feeling or emotion; i.e., to "put an antic disposition on" (*Hamlet,* act 1, scene 5). **3.** *Slang* To tease; to kid someone along; to pull someone's leg; e.g., by pretending that something is true when it is not: *Are you putting me on? Brit.* To have someone on.

put up 1. To install or mount; e.g., a stage set: *We put up the scenery.* **2.** To produce or mount a show.

pyrotechnic supervisor The federally and locally licensed expert technician in charge of explosive substances and devices used in motion pictures; e.g., in an **explosion scene**. Also called *powder person; pyrotechnic operator; pyrotechnician; pyrotechnist.*

Q

Q *n.* Abbrev. for **cue**; seen in stage managers' scripts, but not usually used by actors.

quartz-halogen lamp. See HALOGEN LIGHT.

queer theater Plays and theater companies devoted to the LGBT community.
See GAY AND LESBIAN THEATER, FILM, AND TELEVISION.

quick change 1. Rapidly putting on another costume and/or makeup during a performance, either over the one already being worn or replacing it, so as to be able to enter immediately. Also called *fast change*; *lightning change*; *wing change*. **2.** Substituting one set or set piece for another during a performance in as little time as possible.

quick-change artist 1. A performer who is an expert in changing costumes rapidly. **2.** A vaudevillian who does a specialty act requiring the fast changing of costumes, playing one character after another, and shifting back and forth between characters.

quick-change room A small enclosed space or booth, curtained off from the rest of the backstage area, where the actor, sometimes with the help of a **dresser**, can effect the required quick change of costume or makeup. Also called a *quick-change booth*; *onstage dressing room*.

quick cut Rapidly changing images in a film; used to create suspense in action scenes.
See also ACCELERATED MONTAGE.

quickie *n.* *Slang* A rapidly made, low-budget film, often of poor quality.

quick study An actor who can memorize lines in a very short period of time.

Quiet on the set! Direction to be absolutely silent, preparatory to the beginning of shooting.
See also ON THE BELL; RED LIGHT; SETTLE!; WARNING BELL.

quiz show A variety of **game show**. A radio or television program on which the knowledge of competing contestants, who hope to win a prize, is examined by a quiz show **host** (also called a *quizmaster*), e.g. *Jeopardy*, or on which an individual's knowledge is tested for prize money (e.g., *The Sixty-Four Thousand Dollar Question*), or on which a panel of invited personalities has to guess the identity of a contestant; e.g., *What's My Line?*

quoth the raven *Brit.* The answer to a question from one touring actor to another about whether to stay at particular **digs** where that actor has lodged: the line in Edgar Allan Poe's poem concludes, "Nevermore."

R

radiate *v. t.* To send energy out to the audience; Michael Chekhov's term for what the actor does when performing.

radio *n.* **1.** A device or machine that sends and receives **audio** broadcasts. Radio programs are broadcast in two modes: AM (amplitude modulation) and FM (frequency modulation). **2.** The branch of the **entertainment industry** involved with live, recorded, or prepared commercial and public audio broadcasting for home consumption.

radio announcer A broadcaster or presenter who works in the radio industry.

radio engineer The expert technician who runs the equipment involved in radio broadcasts, handles sound levels, adjusts microphones, and so forth; a **sound engineer** who works in a radio station.

radio play A script that is acted vocally for a broadcast. In the early days of radio, such plays were very popular and there were weekly programs, including everything from mysteries and horror stories to sitcoms. Also called *radio drama*.

radio readers' service A volunteer public service organization found in many localities, which uses actors to read newspapers or magazines to blind listeners; available free, using a special radio supplied by the service.

rain cluster In film, a group of sprinklers arranged above a location or studio set on poles called *rain standards*; used to simulate a shower or storm.

rain drum A hollow, enclosed, round container containing dried peas or lead shot; they rattle against the bottom and sides of the drum when it is rotated, and create the sound of rain. Used in the theater, often in conjunction with a **thunder sheet** and/or a **wind machine**, and as a sound effect on the **radio**; similar to a *rain and sea box*, which also creates the sound of waves.

rain effect In film and television, a storm, thundershower, or other watery precipitation, produced either by computer generation or by the actual sprinkling of water from a rain cluster. In the theater, a special **effects light** may be used.

rain hat A protective cover for a microphone used in outdoor location shooting.

rain pipe A long, hollow, perforated cylindrical tube hung horizontally high above a stage set, into which water is pumped from backstage, creating the onstage effect of rain as it falls through the holes in the pipe; the water is caught in a *rain trough* placed underneath it.

raked stage An inclined playing area that is higher at the upstage end than at the front.

ramp *n.* **1.** An inclined platform that may be used as part of a stage or stage set. **2.** An inclined platform used to roll equipment up and down during a load-in.
See also ESCAPE STAIRS.

223

range *n.* **1.** The extent or span of vocal or instrumental pitch. **2.** The number of different kinds of roles an actor is suited for: *He has a broad range.* **3.** The extent and width of a camera's view: *in camera range*; *out of camera range.*

raree show *Hist.* **1.** A popular 19th-c. street entertainment, featuring novelty acts or strange people or creatures. Also called a *rarity show.* **2.** Syn. with **peep show**, def. 2.

rant *n., v.* —*n.* **1.** A declamatory, uncontrolled speech. —*v. i.* **2.** To **declaim**, esp. in an uncontrolled manner.

raspberry *n. Slang* A rude sound expressing disapproval and made by sticking the tongue through compressed, protruded lips and allowing air to escape loudly. **Syn. *Bronx cheer*.**

rave *n.* **1.** *Slang* A review that praises a play or film enthusiastically. **2.** To **declaim** in a mad, uncontrolled way.

reaction *n.* The actor's emotional **response** to something that happens or is said.

reaction pan A shot that sweeps from one character or happening to show another character's immediate responses, all in one take, as opposed to a simple reaction shot.

reaction shot A take of an actor's nonverbal or vocal responses to something another character says, or to some event or happening.
See also CUTTING ON THE REACTION.

read *v. i.* **1.** To appear a certain way from the audience's point of view: *He reads older than he is.* **2.** To audition: *She will read for a part in a new play.* **3.** To record a book.

reader *n.* **1.** A performer who records books; narrator. **2.** A person who assists the casting personnel at an audition by reading lines with an auditioning actor. **3.** A **story analyst** who evaluates and critiques scripts for a film production or theater company.
See also LITERARY MANAGER; PLAY READER.

reading *n.* **1.** Any rehearsal of a play in which the actors sit and read the script aloud, as opposed to performing it **on its feet**; a **read-through** rehearsal. **2.** The first rehearsal of a play, at which the actors read the play aloud, or the author or director reads the play to the assembled cast: a common practice in Victorian theater. **3.** The particular, distinctive interpretation of a role: *Booth's reading of Hamlet.* **4.** The particular interpretation of a line or speech: *Olivier's reading of "To be or not to be."* **5.** A book recorder's interpretation of the text. **6.** An audition: *She had a reading for a play.* **7.** A public or private presentation of an entire script in progress that is read aloud for the benefit of the writer or for potential producers. The actors may be seated around a table for a private event, or on chairs in front of an audience for a public one. See also BACKERS' AUDITION; STAGED READING. **8.** Public performances or recitations of poetry, short stories, and the like.

reading desk A small table or lectern used to support a script or other material during a public reading. Charles Dickens had one specially designed for the famous programs of readings from his novels.

reading edition A published version of a play meant for the general public. Cf. its opposite, **acting edition**.

reading stand 1. A small, adjustable support resting on a table, large enough to hold a book or script during a book **recording session**. **2.** A **music stand** used to hold a script during a public reading of a play, or copy at a **voice-over** audition or recording session.

reading technique The performer's art, craft, and skills used in making the text clear in live **spoken arts** entertainments, **book recording**, voice-overs, documentary narration, and other audio performances. First, the actor must analyze the text as a script, with its objectives and actions, so as to be able to act it vocally (e.g., in the case of book recording or a live public reading) or, with nonfiction, to make the author's points. Always, the book recorder must tell a story, with its beginning, middle, climax, denouement, and resolution. There are also some purely technical aspects involved in reading aloud. E.g., when recording books, read ahead as you are speaking: your eye must take in the next line or lines, and you must unconsciously prepare to say them, concentrating on what you are reading at the moment, while always staying aware of what is coming next; this technique will make the reading smooth. And don't drop your voice in volume or pitch at the ends of sentences. For more information, see my book *Acting with the Voice: the Art of Recording Books* (Limelight; 2004).
    See also COLD READING; MICROPHONE TECHNIQUE.

read-through *n.* **1.** An early rehearsal in which the cast of a play reads through the entire script aloud in the presence of the director and other production personnel, producers, and author. Done sitting around a table, or in chairs set in a circle or other convenient pattern, and involving discussion and **table work**. **2.** A film or television rehearsal in which the cast and director read through the script aloud; a **script rehearsal**.

real time The actual duration of an event depicted on a film or television program, as opposed to a condensation or other distortion of that duration; e.g., the sinking of the *Titanic*, compressed in time in several films, but shown for about the last two hours of the 1997 movie—more or less the amount of actual time it took.

realism *n.* A mid-19th c. school of artistic and intellectual thought, literature, and theatrical presentation that came about as a reaction against **romanticism** and attempted to portray life and people in as real, objective, and detailed a fashion as possible. The iconoclastic plays of Henrik Ibsen in Norway and August Strindberg in Sweden, and Ivan Turgenev's and Anton Chekhov's realistic Russian comedy-dramas all belong to this school, as do the cup and saucer plays of Tom Robertson. Realism is still the prevailing mode in theater, film, and television.

reality television Shows that use actual people, usually in competitive situations, rather than performers in dramatized fictions.

rear car mount Support structure for holding a camera or cameras fastened securely onto the back part of a vehicle, so that the vehicle's interior can be filmed.

rear projection An image thrown from behind by a projector onto a translucent screen, to create the effect of a particular background; e.g., in a film scene of actors driving in a car. The actors perform in front of the screen, on a theater stage or film studio set. Also called a *back projection*.

receive *v. t.* Herbert Berghof and Uta Hagen's term for understanding and absorbing a line that is delivered to an actor.
  See also LAND; SEND.

recital *n.* **1.** An intimate, small-scale **concert** of vocal music with a simple accompaniment, usually on the piano, or of instrumental music performed by individual artists: *a violin recital*. Recitals may take place in large concert halls, as well as in smaller theaters or rooms. **2.** A dance performance. **3.** A student presentation of vocal or instrumental music, to demonstrate the student's accomplishment in a particular field. **4.** A **spoken arts** entertainment featuring prose or poetry readings: *a dramatic recital*.

recitative (reh' sih tah teev') *n.* Sung dialogue or soliloquy in an opera; the musical setting is supposed to mirror a conversational tone. Some recitatives are underscored with dramatic music. Called *recit* (reh' siht) for short.

recognition scene The moment in a tragedy where a character makes a major breakthrough in understanding the situation and the character's own **tragic flaw**; e.g., Oedipus's realization in Sophocles' play of his true identity. **Aristotle** saw the recognition scene (*anagnorisis*; an ag no:r' ih sihs) as an essential component of a tragedy.

record *n., v.* —(rehk' uhrd) *n.* **1.** Saved data, which may be preserved in public or private archives or by individuals and is kept in writing, or stored on a computer or on an audio, visual, or audiovisual retentive, preservative medium. **2.** A retentive **medium** for preserving music, spoken pieces, films, sound effects, etc. so that they can be played back and listened to or viewed. The medium is altered by the recording process either physically (as in impressing sound signals into grooves in a vinyl disc), magnetically (as in making a tape), or photographically (as in imprinting light signals on film). **3.** A round, flat shellac or vinyl disc containing **analog** audio material, playable in several speeds over the course of its historical development; e.g., at 78 or, later, 33 RPM (revolutions per minute) for a long-playing (LP) record. Played on a turntable with a needle, on a *gramophone* or *phonograph*, also called a *record player*. (ree kawrd') —*v. t.* **4.** To create a saved account or file of data. **5.** To register, impress, put down, or photograph audio, visual, or audiovisual material using retentive, preservative **media**.

recorded rehearsal A filmed repetition of a scene, used afterwards to help the actors change or improve their performances, as they watch it under the guidance of the director.

recording *n.* **1.** An **audio** version of a spoken piece (books, plays, poetry, speeches, and so forth) or of music. **2.** A visual or audiovisual version of a film, television program, or event. **3.** The act, process, and work of registering material on a retentive, preservative **medium** or on a computer.

recording artist An actor, book reader, singer, instrumentalist, or other performer who records audio entertainment material.

recording engineer An expert who handles the equipment and registers the sound for any kind of audio material; a **sound engineer** who works in the recording industry. Also called a *recordist*.

recording industry The business devoted to making, distributing, and selling recorded music and spoken pieces, involving performers, sound engineers, marketers, salespeople, and retail and Internet outlets, together with all the personnel involved, including such unions as AFTRA, which represent the interests of performers.

recording session Scheduled period of time during which projects are registered on a preservative audio **medium** or computer by a sound engineer working with other personnel, such as a director or conductor, who supervise a performer or performers.

recording studio 1. The place where an audio project is put down using a preservative medium or computer. **2.** The soundproof booth in a complex containing several such studios. The booths are small, to avoid a lot of extra "air" in the sound being recorded, and usually lined with soundproof materials, which can also deaden the sound as the artist is recording (hence the necessity of being close to the microphone).

recording technique See MICROPHONE TECHNIQUE; READING TECHNIQUE.

recurring role A part that is intermittently played in a television series, but not in every episode. E.g., in *Will and Grace,* Grace's mother, played by Debbie Reynolds in nine episodes; Will's mother, played by Blythe Danner in eleven episodes.

red lights The red glass lamps that are hung above the door of a **soundstage** and that are lit and flashing when shooting is in progress, as a warning not to enter or leave, and to be as quiet as possible.

redress; re-dress *v. t.* To change the appearance of a set by putting different props and decorations on it; e.g., window curtains or paintings.
See DRESS.

reel *n.* **1.** A round, wheel-like frame or spool on which an audiotape or motion picture film is wound. **2.** A roll of audiotape or movie film. **3.** *Slang* An audiovisual **demo**.

reel-to-reel tape An analog audio recording **medium** consisting of audiotape wound on one reel and threaded onto another reel, called a *take-up reel*, onto which it will be continuously wound as a recording is made. Also called *open-reel tape*.

reenactment *n*. The recreation of a historical event. E.g., a trial, using the actual transcripts; a Civil War battle, performed by hobbyists in the place where it occurred; or in a film, e.g., the television docudrama, *Culloden* (1968), which recreates the final battle of the 1745 Scottish uprising. Hence, *reenacter*: one who participates in a reenactment.

reflector *n*. A shiny or dull surface either attached to or built into a lighting instrument to help expand and diffuse the light.

refrain *n*. **1.** The final, regularly recurring section of each strophe in a poem, or verse in a song; e.g., the **chorus** of a number in a musical theater piece. **2.** The melody or music of the regularly repeated section, which may be a memorable tune that becomes as popular as a **catchphrase**.

regional theater A **LORT** theater. Also called a *resident theater*.

régisseur (*ré* zhih: suh*r*') *n*. [French: stage manager; assistant director; *Archaic*: **actor-manager**] **1.** The **stage manager** of a **ballet** company, who rehearses the company and maintains or restages the choreography. **2.** The **assistant director**, in French film and television. **3.** The stage manager, in the French theater.

register *n., v.* —*n.* **1.** The particular pitch or **range** of a singer's **voice**: *the soprano register*; *the bass register*. **2.** One of the pitch levels of any voice: *the high, middle, and low registers*. —*v. t.* **3.** To make known, and to put on record: *to register a complaint with the union*. **4.** To exhibit or show: *to register anger*. **5.** To perceive something: *The audience registered the character's anger*. **6.** To **record**.

registration shot A film take that begins as a drawing, painting, or photograph and that suddenly comes to life; e.g., the opening sequences in *Meet Me in St. Louis* (1944) and Orson Welles's *The Magnificent Ambersons* (1942).

regressive angles A series of takes using different positions of the camera that bring the action closer to the viewer by demagnifying the point of view; e.g., in *Vanilla Sky* (2001), the panoramic view of New York City seen from on high, and then the window of Tom Cruise's apartment, and then its interior.

regressive shots A series of takes during which the camera withdraws or pulls back further on each take, making whatever is being filmed appear to grow smaller, sometimes quite suddenly and dramatically. Cf. its opposite, **progressive shots**.

rehearsal *n*. **1.** The organized, progressive **process** of practice and repetition used in preparing a play, film, television program, commercial, or any kind of show or entertainment project for performance. In the **media**, rehearsals are of very short

228

duration: soap operas usually rehearse for half a day before the actual taping of the episode. Sitcom episodes rehearse for several days before the taping. Prime-time nighttime television drama scenes are rehearsed just before they are shot. Rehearsal time for films varies, depending on the director's requirements and budgetary considerations. Rehearsals for plays in the theater usually last for several weeks. Due to commercial considerations, less and less time is spent on theater rehearsals, but public readings and workshops often take the place of what would otherwise be lost weeks and insufficient rehearsal time. **2.** An individual practice session for an entertainment project.

See the index, p. 368, for a list of the different kinds of rehearsals.

rehearsal call The time at which actors and other personnel must report during the preparation process of a stage play, film, or television taping. In the case of stage managerial staff, the call is much earlier than it is for the actors, because the staff must prepare whatever is necessary for the rehearsal to begin: props put in place, the floor of a studio properly taped to indicate acting areas, and so forth. Actors should report for rehearsal before the actual call time, in order to be ready to start on schedule.

rehearsal pay Monetary compensation paid to actors during the rehearsal period of a play, which used to be less than pay for performances, but has now been mostly equalized by **Equity** agreements with producing organizations.

rehearsal procedure in the theater The first rehearsal after a *meet and greet*, at which the actors and various personnel make each other's acquaintance, is usually a **read-through**, during which the stage managerial staff, director, actors, and perhaps designers sit around a table or in a circle of chairs. At an early rehearsal, the designers show costume plans and set plans, often in the form of a working model, to the actors. During the **table work**, the director talks about the play, the period, and other germane matters. Stanislavsky would have the actors do various scenes as improvisations using their own words instead of the text. But nowadays, rehearsals often continue with general preliminary **blocking** (i.e., blocking rehearsals, also called staging rehearsals) and then with individual scene rehearsals, until an entire act is ready; then the next act is worked through. The acts are then rehearsed as acts. Then the play as a whole is rehearsed in work-throughs, walk-throughs, and run-throughs. Costumes may be added for final run-throughs. Finally, there are technical rehearsals using lights, scenery, and costumes; adjustments are made as the "techs" proceed. Then come the tech-dress rehearsals in full costume, and ten-out-of-twelve days; and the dress rehearsals. There is usually a final **dress rehearsal**; perhaps two or three, the last often being an **invited dress**, to which the actors and other personnel are allowed to invite guests. Finally, there are preview performances for commercial productions before the play officially opens for the critics. Daytime rehearsals may be called during the preview period, since the play has not yet opened. During the run of a play, understudy and replacement rehearsals are regularly called; there may be rehearsals for the regular company at the discretion of the management, e.g., for putting in replacements. The actors may be called for periodic **brush-up** rehearsals, or for a line-through or **speed-through** rehearsal, esp. after a day off, where this is not prohibited by **Equity rules**.

rehearsal studio A large room used for play, dance, or other kinds of rehearsals.

rehearsal technique 1. The actor's methods and ways of practicing a performance project, memorizing lines, dealing with director's **notes**, and taking direction. **2.** A particular tool used in rehearsing; e.g., **improvisation**; **substitution**.
See JUSTIFICATION; SENSORY PROCESS; STAGE TECHNIQUE; TAKE DIRECTION.

rehearse *v. t.* To prepare and practice a performance project.

rehearse around To rehearse in the absence of one or more performers. Moments and scenes not absolutely requiring the performer's presence are done.

relate *v. i.* In acting terms, to listen and respond to another actor/character.

relationship *n.* The nature of the character's connection to other characters, as well to inner and external objects, to place, and to time, involving how and why the character relates.

relatives in the ice business A vaudevillian's ironical description of an unresponsive, hostile, cold audience, who were said to have had such family relations, in the days when there was an ice business and the iceman was seen carting his blocks of ice into every home for use in the family's ice box (an early form of refrigerator).

relaxation *n.* The absence of extraneous tension or anxiety, allowing the actor to be loose and flexible and to react spontaneously and organically.
See also CONCENTRATION.

released *adj.* **1.** Pertaining to an actor who is not hired to do a commercial for which he or she was on **first refusal**. **2.** Permitted to do a commercial for a product, once a commercial made for a similar product is no longer being broadcast. **3.** Allowed to leave at the end of a rehearsal, shoot, or other job session. This usually involves getting permission from a stage manager or director, if the actor leaves early; it includes the process of signing out. **4.** Describes a film available for distribution, showing, or broadcast.

religious film A genre that includes biblical epics and stories about the lives of saints, and movies about members of the clergy and situations involving religion.

repartee *n.* Quick-witted, clever rejoinders and banter; e.g., in a conversation where the interlocutors try to score points, as in the exchanges between Beatrice and Benedict in Shakespeare's *Much Ado About Nothing*.
See also STICHOMYTHIA.

repertoire *n.* **1.** The collection of plays or other pieces that a theater has done or is prepared to do; also, any such collection: *the Shakespearean repertoire*. **2.** An actor or singer's prepared roles or pieces: *Her repertoire included many bel canto roles*. **3.** The operas or ballets that a company has done, or is prepared to do.

repertory theater A theater that produces several plays in a season, and may repeat them in what is called **rotating rep**. Usually applied to provincial English theaters, as opposed to American regional theaters that do discreet production after discreet production. Repertory companies may develop a repertoire of plays that they can revive season after season. Called a *rep theater*, for short.

repetition exercise. See MEISNER, SANFORD; MIRROR.

replacement *n*. An actor who joins the cast of a play to take over a role from someone who has left the production.

replacement rehearsal A **put-in** for someone who is taking over a role. Replacement cast members are rehearsed individually, usually by the stage manager; the full company is then called for a put-in before the actor's first performance.

representation *n*. Work done on behalf of a performer by the performer's **agent**, helping the performer to secure work and negotiating contracts once employment is offered.

representational *adj*. Contemporary acting practice, in which the actor "represents" the character by living through the character's life moment to moment.

repression *n*. The Freudian concept that certain ideas and emotions, in which guilt and shame are associated, have been pushed out of and excluded from consciousness and forgotten, because they are threatening for some reason to the individual. The repressed emotions of a fictional character can play an important part in an actor's interpretation.
    See also SUPPRESSION; UNCONSCIOUS.

reprise (ruh preez') *n., v.* [French: taken again] —*n.* **1.** In musical comedy, the repetition of a musical number, in part or as a whole, that has been heard earlier in the show. —*v. t.* **2.** To repeat a musical number that has been heard earlier in the show. **3.** To perform a role again that an actor has previously done, esp. in musical comedy: *Ethel Merman reprised her stage role as the ambassadress in the 1953 film of* Call Me Madam.

re-recording mixer In film, the person who is responsible for the final mixing and balancing of a soundtrack, combining all the elements from the different recorded tracks: dialogue; music; and effects. Also called a *dubbing mixer*.
    See also SOUND MIXER.

rerun *n., v.* —*n.* **1.** The broadcast of all or part of a television series after its initial run is over; usually in **syndication**. Reruns often entitle the actors to **residuals**. **2.** The individual program being broadcast: *a rerun.* —*v. t.* **3.** To broadcast a series or a program some time after its initial broadcast.

research *n*. Investigation for the purpose of obtaining information; e.g., the historical and behavioral investigation done by a director or actor when preparing a period piece, the study of period dances by a choreographer, looking up the pronunciations of words in preparation for a book recording, or consulting with the **technical adviser** on a film.

reset *n., v.* —*n.* **1.** The preparation for a **retake**. —*v. t.* **2.** To put things on a film set back where they were at the beginning of a take; to make sound equipment ready to roll; to place camera equipment back in its opening position; and to get actors into first positions, preparatory to doing a retake. Cf. **restore**.

Resetting back to one! The director's instruction to a film crew and actors to prepare immediately for another take of the same scene; also heard as "**Back to one!**"

reshoot *n., v.* —*n.* **1.** A take or shot that has been done again because the original was unsatisfactory in some way. —*v. t.* **2.** To film a take, scene, or part of a scene again, usually on a different shoot day. Cf. **retake**, which is a reshoot done immediately after a take.

residence *n.* An engagement as a **guest artist** on a university campus or other school; hence, *to be in residence.*

Resident Musical Theatre Association (RMTA) Agreement The **Equity** contract covering employment in both non-profit and commercial musical **stock** theaters. A resident company of at least four Equity actors, one stage manager, and one assistant stage manager must be maintained.

resident theater A regional theater company that hires actors either for an entire season, or for an individual show; the actors are said to be "in residence"; a member of the **League of Resident Theatres (LORT)**. Often called *regional theater.*

residuals *n. pl.* Royalty payments made to actors for the showing of a commercial, television program, or televised feature film, or for some other project. Residuals can also be paid for DVDs sold, or for the Internet use of a project. Residual payments for the use of a project in contemporary new media venues are the subject of ongoing discussion, controversy, and negotiations when contracts with producers come up for renegotiation with writers' and actors' unions. In 2007, after a three-month strike, the **WGA** won the right to a share of Internet revenues. For commercials, actors usually receive residual checks directly from the agent who handled the project, and whose financial or accounting department has the actor's power of attorney to deduct the agent's ten per cent **commission**. Commercial residuals are paid to actors on different scales, depending on the kind of contract under which they were made (**national network, wild spot**, and so forth). For **book recording**, narrators in the U.S. do not receive residuals, but they do in Great Britain, where, however, the initial recording fee is much lower. Book recording, not completely unionized even there, is covered by **British Equity** contracts.

resonance *n.* The reverberation and enrichment of sound, amplified when the sound waves bounce off some solid object.
See ACOUSTICS; PLACEMENT; VOCAL TECHNIQUE.

resonator *n.* A surface off of which sound waves bounce, providing reverberation, enrichment, and texture; e.g., the bones in the **mask**.

response *n.* **1.** The actor's reply to a line or action from the other character in a scene. Perhaps the most important acting technique is to **listen and respond. 2.** The actor's emotional **reaction** to what is happening in a scene.

resting *adj. Slang, esp. Brit.* Unemployed as an actor; between engagements.

Restoration drama English plays written after the restoration in 1660 of King Charles II to the throne, until ca. 1700. The period is esp. known for the Restoration comedies of Colley Cibber, William Wycherly, William Congreve, Sir George Etherege, and others, and for the early plays of John Dryden.

restore *v. t.* To put things on a set back the way they were; i.e., to place everything where it was at the beginning of a scene or part of a scene, so that it may be rehearsed again, or, in film, so that another take can be done. Cf. **reset**.

result *n.* The way of playing a moment, arrived at through rehearsal; hence, *to go for results*: to try to achieve them technically without working up to them organically. They should never be predetermined, although they often are, esp. in short rehearsal periods. Still, as Stanislavsky advised, "Never begin with results"; i.e., with an advance decision about what they should be.

résumé *n.* In acting terms, a one-page outline listing of a performer's career credits by category and venue; voice category, esp. if the person is a singer; education; other experience; and special abilities or talents, as well as personal information (height, weight, hair and eye color), contact information, union affiliations, and agents. The résumé is usually accompanied by an 8" by 10" glossy photograph of the performer, called a **head shot** or a résumé shot. A theater actor's credits are generally listed just below the personal information under the following categories, in order: Broadway, Off-Broadway, Regional. Each theater credit includes the name of the theater, and may include the director's name. This is followed by a listing of film and television credits. Commercials are usually listed on a separate résumé that is "available upon request," as the main résumé states. Education, special abilities (e.g., dialects and stage combat), and awards are listed at the bottom. A different résumé is required for each field; e.g., a **book recording** résumé, a **motion picture** résumé.

retake *n., v.* —*n.* **1.** A shot that has been done over again. —*v. t.* **2.** To shoot a scene, part of a scene, or a particular shot again, either for safety or because it is unsatisfactory in some way; or to film variations in performance moments that will give the director choices. Usually done immediately after an initial take.

retire *v. i.* **1.** *Archaic* A stage direction, meaning to withdraw from a scene by walking a short way away from it: *He retired upstage.* **2.** To cease to work in a particular job or profession. See also EARLY RETIREMENT.

return engagement Coming back to a theater to perform the same play again.

returns *n. pl.* **1.** Box office receipts. **2.** Unsold tickets given back to a production company by a ticket agency.

revenge tragedy A Jacobean genre of bloody melodrama involving vengeance; e.g. John Webster's *The Duchess of Malfi.*

reverse angle The opposite **point of view** from what the viewer has just seen: if we have been looking over a character's shoulder at an event taking place, we will now see the character's face and reactions.

revised pages Rewritten dialogue or scenes that may be given to the actor and other personnel at any time during a shoot; they are dated, and each successive set of revised pages is printed on differently colored paper.

revival *n.* A production of a play or musical after its **original production** has closed for some time.

reviewer *n.* A broadcast, newspaper, or magazine journalist who gives a critique of a performance project.

revolving stage A turntable platform that goes round, stopping to reveal different sets or turning partially to show a different view of the same set.

revue *n.* A prepared variety entertainment of sketches, songs, and dances that runs at a theater or cabaret; sometimes thematic (e.g., the series of *Forbidden Broadway* revues).

rhubarb. See OMNIES.

rhythm *n.* **1.** The arrangement or pattern of alternating slow and fast beats in music, depending on the length of each note. **2.** The pattern of slow or fast movement and dialogue in the playing of a character or a scene. An actor standing still can have a fast internal rhythm of thoughts. Conversely, an actor might move quickly and think slowly.
   See also METER; PACE; TEMPO.

rialto (ree al' toh) *n.* [Fr. the shop-lined Rialto bridge in Venice] *Slang* The Broadway theater district: *See you on the rialto!*

rider *n.* An extra clause appended to an actor's standard contract regarding specifics that have to do with a particular production; e.g., a clause regarding a **nude scene**, or rental of the actor's **wardrobe** for costume purposes.

rigging *n.* The backstage system of weighted ropes and pulleys that holds fast or releases flats, flies, and other pieces of scenery.

right *n.* **1.** The side of the stage to the actor's right as he or she faces the audience: **stage right**; abbrev. R. To make a right second entrance, or a right third entrance, is to come onto the stage from the stage right side, in the second or third planes. **2.** The side of a movie or television set seen to the right from the camera's point of view: **camera right**.

right-to-work state A state that has a statutory legal provision, which may be part of its state constitution or passed as a separate piece of legislation, prohibiting anyone from requiring a worker to join a union as a condition of employment, although unions are still allowed to function. Voluntary membership in a union is permitted; by union rules, union members are not allowed to accept nonunion employment. Union partisans often call the "right to work," "the right to work for less." The twenty-one right-to-work states are Alabama, Arizona, Arkansas, Florida, Georgia, Idaho, Iowa, Kansas, Louisiana, Mississippi, Nebraska, Nevada, North Carolina, South Carolina, South Dakota, Tennessee, Texas, Virginia, and Wyoming.

In states with no such legal provisions, such as New York and California, the producing organizations and unions negotiate agreements and contracts without government intervention, except when arbitration is asked for in the case of an impasse. The agreements must be in accordance with the provisions and requirements of the federal Labor Management Relations Act of 1947, known as the Taft-Hartley Act from the names of its sponsors in Congress. In New York, actors who work in certain venues (such as Broadway or Off-Broadway theaters) must be members of Equity, but there are contract provisions that have been negotiated allowing producers of large shows to use a certain number of non-union actors, just as there are in the media industry, where a percentage of the background players may be non-union.

rim shot A drummer's hitting of the drum's edge and/or the cymbals attached to the drum with the drumstick, making three sharp rhythmic sounds that point up a bit of comic business: *buh DUM bum*; used esp. in **vaudeville** and **burlesque**.

ring down [the curtain] [Fr. the 18th-c. custom of ringing a bell to signal the end of an act] To close the **house curtain**.

ringmaster *n.* The **master of ceremonies** at a **circus**, and the troupe's leader; usually dressed in a top hat and red tailcoat, and carrying a whip and sometimes a **hand mike**.

riser *n.* A small raised platform, with various uses (e.g., to raise an actor higher). Usually called an **apple box**.

road company A theatrical touring group that travels with its production of a play or musical; e.g., a **bus and truck** tour.

road house A theater that books touring productions.

road manager The administrator who deals with logistics and travels with a road company, making sure that lodgings are satisfactory and schedules observed.

road show A touring production of a play, musical, or other live entertainment; e.g., the **circus**.

roam Syn. with **wander**.

rock opera A through-composed musical theater piece with rock music; e.g. the Who's *Tommy* (1969; filmed in 1975), the first of the genre to be so called.

rockumentary *n.* A documentary that follows a rock band on tour, shows excerpts from its concerts, and usually contains interviews with members of the band and others connected with it.

rod puppet A three-dimensional doll with long, thin metal sticks or poles attached to its arms, which are worked from below by a concealed puppeteer; e.g., one used in southeast Asian puppet shows. Cf. **hand and rod puppet**.

role *n.* The part an actor plays; character.

roll *v.* —*v. t.* **1.** To start the camera and sound equipment for filming or taping. —*v. i.* **2.** To be working or functioning; said of a camera when a scene is being taped or filmed: the cameraman's or cinematographer's announcement "Rolling!" or "We're rolling," means, "We're ready to film! The camera is on and the tape or film is winding on its spools." For the sake of convenience, the same word is used for digital shoots or computerized **book recording**, when there is no actual film or tape involved: "Rolling" is the signal that the director can give the cue "**Action!**" or, in the case of book recording, the **cue** from the sound engineer that the narrator may begin reading.

Roll 'em! "Start up the camera and sound equipment!" Also heard as "Roll it!": *Roll camera! Roll sound!* When all is in order, the camera operator says, "Rolling!" and the sound recordist says, "**Speed**."

romantic comedy A play or film dealing in a light-hearted, humorous, amusing way with love and its complications.

romantic drama Late 18th-c. and early to mid-19th-c. prose and verse plays, written without using the **classical unities**. The plays of Victor Hugo, and **melodrama** in general, are typical. At its premiere in 1830, Hugo's hugely successful verse drama *Hernani* was the occasion of riots in Paris between advocates of romanticism and adherents of **classicism**.
    See also NEOCLASSICAL DRAMA; STURM UND DRANG.

romanticism *n.* A late 18th-c. and early to mid-19th-c. school of artistic and intellectual thought, literature, and theatrical presentation that reacted against **classicism** and portrayed passionate, overwrought, heightened emotional stories of aspiration, love, and betrayal, with overwrought heroes and heroines to match, emphasizing the imaginative and the individual.

romantic lead(s) The principal male and female protagonists in a story about love.

room tone Ambient sound that is recorded on a separate *ambient (atmosphere) sound track* for a film or television program, in order to be able to use it as necessary to maintain the sound **atmosphere** of a scene. While it is being recorded, immediately after a take, everyone remains absolutely silent. Room tone is also taken during **book recording** sessions, immediately after the session, for the same reason. Also called *background presence*.

Ross Reports A booklet published several times a year with updated listings of agencies and agents; casting directors; producers of commercials, motion pictures, and television programs; and production houses in both New York and Los Angeles.

rotating rep [Rep: short for *repertory*] The system of alternating presentations of plays, comic operas, operas, or musicals in a company's repertoire. **Gilbert and Sullivan** was done in rotating rep by the D'Oyly Carte Opera Company: they might do *The Mikado* for two nights, *H. M. S. Pinafore* for the next two, and so on. And the practice is ubiquitous in **opera** seasons worldwide.

rotoscoping *n.* **1.** The process, act, and job of tracing a live-action film scene frame by frame, for use in an animated **cartoon**; largely superseded by the computer digital process for which the same name is used. The drawings were projected on a glass panel using a projector called a *rotoscope*, and then redrawn by an animator. **2.** A **special effects** process used in **compositing**, e.g., making a **matte** painting of a scenic element, which will be part of a composite background; superimposing cartoon figures on a background.

rough blocking The director's preliminary working plan of actors' stage movements; hence, *to rough out the blocking*.

rough cut A preliminary edited version of a film, assembled from finished takes used in the order in which they may eventually be edited together to make the **final cut** (finished version). Also called *rough edit*.

   See also ASSEMBLE.

routine *n., adj.* —*n.* **1.** An **act**, esp. in a variety show: *a comic routine*; *a dance routine*. **2.** A dance number, or the danced part of a number, in a musical: *the dance routine in act two*. **3.** A habitual way of doing an appointed task; e.g., the steps gone through when setting up before a particular show: *the stage manager's routine.* —*adj.* **4.** Pertains to a habitual way of carrying out an appointed task: *the actor's routine preparation*.

row *n.* A line of audience seats, usually with each place numbered.

royal box The private seating area reserved for members of the ruling family, and their elite invited guests; usually the center rear box in the tier of boxes.

royalty *n.* Payments to the owner of a copyrighted artistic property for its use, sale, or licensing.

run *n., v.* —*n.* **1.** The duration of time during which successive performances of a play are presented: *a short run*; *an eight-month run.* —*v. t.* **2.** To go through lines, a scene, or part of a scene. **3.** To rehearse a scene, or a whole play, all the way through, without stopping. —*v. i.* **4.** To take a certain amount of time: *The play runs for two hours. That scene runs for five minutes. The show ran for a year.*

run lines 1. To help an actor by going through a role with him or her, reading the cue lines and correcting errors in the actor's own lines. **2.** To go through a role or part of a role, usually once it has been memorized, with the actor one is playing opposite, mostly without a director being present and often without doing the blocking. **3.** To rig the ropes backstage; to set up the rigging.

running crew The backstage staff and the technicians who handle lights and/or sound from the front-of-house booth, who work under the stage manager's direction during a performance; usually referred to as the **crew**, for short. Also called the *operating crew*.

running gag A joke or bit of comic business that recurs periodically in the course of a play or film, designed to get the biggest laugh the last time it is played; often in a series of three. Also called a *running joke*.
See also CAPPER.

running lights The low-level backstage illumination kept on during a performance, so that actors and crew can find their way.

running order 1. The sequence of acts in a vaudeville or music hall show. **2.** The sequence of numbers in a musical comedy.

running time 1. The temporal duration of a particular performance: *The running time this evening was two hours.* **2.** The amount of time a performance usually takes, or is expected to take: *The play ran fifteen minutes over its running time.*

run-of-the-play contract A contract that commits an actor to doing a play for its entire run. There are provisions for giving sufficient notice if an actor has to leave the production permanently. And if an actor books a more lucrative job (e.g., a day's shoot on a television commercial), the actor, having given sufficient notice, may be allowed by the management to leave for the necessary amount of time.

run-through *n.* **1.** A complete rehearsal performance of a play, with or without costumes and other technical aspects of the production. A run-through may or may not be interrupted by the director on a **stop and start** basis. **2.** A complete rehearsal of a film or television scene, often just before shooting.

runway *n.* A long, narrow, or wide extension proceeding from a stage into the auditorium; used in burlesque houses and fashion shows.

rush *v. t.* To hurry through a scene, a moment, or an entire play, instead of taking the proper amount of time and doing it at the proper **tempo**.

rush call 1. A last-minute **casting call** either to replace someone or to hire more **background players**, because not enough showed up on the set. Also called *rush casting*. **2.** A last-minute audition; e.g., when an agent calls a client at noon, and says, "I have an audition for you today at three. Can you make it?"

rushes. See DAILIES.

S

SAG Acronym, abbrev., and usual appellation for **Screen Actors Guild**.

sandbag *n., v.* —*n.* **1.** A sack, usually made of canvas, filled with sand, and attached to ropes as a balance or counterweight for a piece of scenery or flat that must be raised and lowered. —*v. t.* **2.** *Slang* To decide not to do a project; to squash or squelch a project.

Sardoodledum *n.* The mythical kingdom where the subjects of French playwright Victorien Sardou (1831–1908) reside; a term coined by George Bernard Shaw, who rather unfairly crowned the witty, astute playwright King of Sardoodledum. The term is meant to characterize popular melodramas and well-made plays, esp. those of Sardou, which, according to Shaw, exemplified the false, the facile, the mindless, the nonsensical, and the overdone; e.g., *La Tosca*, which Sardou wrote for Sarah Bernhardt.

satellite television Broadcasts transmitted into a dish receiver—a *satellite dish*—using the microwave technology of satellites (electronic communication machines) located in space. The transmissions are then transferred through the dish to the home television monitors of subscribers. Satellite TV is particularly useful where it is impossible to lay the cables necessary for cable television.

satire *n.* A piece that mocks or makes fun of social customs, mores, habits, and ways of behaving.

satyr plays Lewd ancient Greek comedies that were part of the religious rites involved in the worship of the lubricious god Dionysius. According to **Aristotle**, these rites were the origin of comedy. Later, such plays were preformed after the tragedies at the **Dionysia**.

Savoyard (sa vaw' yuhrd) *n.* [Fr. London's Savoy Theater, built by producer D'Oyly Carte esp. for the production of **Gilbert and Sullivan** comic operas] **1.** A member of the company that performed in the original productions of G & S. **2.** A performer in G & S operas. **3.** A Gilbert and Sullivan fan.

Savoy operas The fourteen Gilbert and Sullivan comic operas, even though the first five were not produced at the Savoy Theater.

scale *n., adj.* —*n.* **1.** Basic fixed minimum pay; the lowest rate of pay on the contractual listing of graduated pay levels; base pay for any particular job or category of work. Many actors doing a play, commercial, television show, or film work for scale. All union agreements with producers have listings of minimum salaries to be paid for any particular job. **2.** A graduated, progressive series of steps; a listing of such steps or levels: *pay scale*. **3.** In music, a graduated, progressive series of tones ascending or descending in specific steps; i.e., in fixed intervals. **4.** Magnitude: *the scale of a production.* —*adj.* **5.** Pertaining to pay: *a scale actor*; i.e., one who works for scale. **6.** Pertaining to magnitude: *a large-scale production.*

239

scale plus ten [Short for *scale plus ten per cent*] A clause in a commercial contract providing that commission be paid as part of the actor's salary; written up as "scale plus ten per cent." On commercial jobs where the actor works for **scale**, agents are not permitted to take a ten per cent **commission**, hence the clause.

scalper *n.* **1.** An unscrupulous individual who gouges the public by selling hard-to-get tickets to hit shows or other events at a price much higher than that marked on the ticket. Also called a *ticket scalper*. **2.** A management that sells tickets at an exorbitant price.

scan *v. t.* To go through a line or lines of verse, for instance in a verse drama, analyzing the meter and rhythm; hence, the n. *scansion*: the analysis of a line or lines of verse.

scenario (sih nar' ee oh), *n.* **1.** A summary of the plot, main points, and episodes of a story or play. **2.** A detailed summary of a teleplay or screenplay, including a synopsis of the story and a listing of the main shots and locations.

scenarist (sih nar' ihst), *n.* A writer of scenarios for screenplays and/or teleplays.

scene *n.* **1.** A convenient subdivision of an act in a play or screenplay. *French scenes* are so called because in published versions of French plays, a new scene begins every time a new character enters. **2.** The unit of a play or screenplay that entails a particular kind of event: *a love scene*; *a death scene*; *a sex scene*. **3.** The place where something happens: *the scene of the duel*. **4.** *Hist.* The stage of an ancient Greek or Roman theater.

scene change The shift of scenery, props, furniture, etc., at the end of a scene in a play, to the next one. In a proscenium theater, the curtains may be closed; or left open, with the auditorium in darkness, in an **avista** situation.

scene dock The backstage area of a theater where flats and other scenery are stored. Also called the *scene bay*.

scene in one A brief section of a play performed in the front downstage **plane** (plane 1), in front of a scrim or curtain, usually while another scene is being set up behind it. Called *in one*, for short.

scene master A switch to which a number of lighting circuits, all used in a particular scene, are connected, so that all the circuits can be activated at once.

scene painter An expert artist who paints the scenery for a film or play. Also called a *scenic artist*.

scene plan Schematic outline drawing of a stage set. Also called *floor plan*.

scene shop The atelier or factory where theater scenery is constructed and decorated.

scene stealer **1.** An actor who inappropriately draws the audience's attention, when the focus should be elsewhere. **2.** An actor whose performance is so good that it virtually eclipses those of the others on stage.

scene study 1. A teaching method used in acting classes, which consists of learning and presenting individual scenes from plays. **2. Homework** on the individual subdivisions of the act in a play one is rehearsing.

scene work A director's in-depth rehearsal with actors on movements, moments, motivations, and ways of playing actions, in both theater and film.

scenery *n.* Another word for **set**: the **décor** showing the place(s) in which a story unfolds. In some productions, there is no scenery beyond the bare stage floor and the back wall of the theater.
See also SET.

scenery wagon A rolling platform on wheels or castors used for carrying set pieces onto the stage for scene changes. Also called *stage wagon*; *stage dolly*; *wagon*, for short.
See also AVISTA; SEGMENT STAGE.

scenic *adj.* Pertaining to the stage or its décor: *scenic life*; *scenic beauty*.

scenic designer Syn. with *set designer*.

scenic truth The illusion of reality and of spontaneous life being lived from moment to moment created on stage. As Stanislavsky said, "Scenic truth is not the truth of life; it is peculiar to itself."

schlock (shlahk') *n., adj.* [Yiddish; German (spelled Schlag): blow or whipping; hence also, whipped cream] *Slang* —*n.* **1.** A film, play, or other entertainment that is frothy, superficial, inferior junk. —*adj.* **2.** Pertaining to such an entertainment: *a schlock film.*

schmaltz (shmahlts') *n.* [Yiddish; German: rendered, solidified chicken fat, used for frying] *Slang* Tearjerking sentimentality or melodramatic emotion, laid on with a trowel; hence, the English adjective *schmaltzy*: *What a schmaltzy performance!*

schmatte (shmah' tuh) *n.* [Yiddish: rag; also spelled "shmatte"] *Slang* **1.** Any garment, particularly one that is worn out and ragged, but kept out of affection as an old favorite; sarcastically or admiringly said of a new, possibly somewhat garish outfit: *So where did you get that schmatte?* **2.** Derogatory or affectionate term for a costume: *Time to put on the schmatte!*

school act *Hist.* A vaudeville **routine** that takes place in a classroom, with a ludicrous teacher, adult actors playing students, and inane jokes in answer to silly questions.

science fiction film A motion picture genre or individual film that centers around the use of technology and technological devices; usually a futuristic **fantasy film**, often one set in an alien world or galaxy. Called a *sci-fi film*, for short. Also called a *space opera*.

score *n., v.* —*n.* **1.** The music for a composition. **2.** The music of a composition written out using musical **notation**. **3.** In acting, the order of the actions in a scene, or in the script as a whole, and the order of the beats, each of which betokens a change of action; the score is personal to each actor. —*v. t.* **4.** To write out music for a composition. **5.** To orchestrate a musical composition. **6.** In acting, to make a list of the beats and actions in the order in which they occur: *to score the beats.* — *v. i.* **7.** *Slang* To be a **hit**: *That play scored with the critics.*

screen *n., v.* —*n.* **1.** A large flat surface onto which an image or a film may be projected. **2.** The front surface of a television set, on which the picture appears. Also called a *video screen.* **3.** A standing panel or folding panels used as part of a set, behind which actors may hide in such scenes as the "screen scene" in Sheridan's *The School for Scandal.* **4.** A **synecdoche** for the film industry: *star of stage and screen.* —*v. t.* **5.** To show a film. **6.** To adapt material for filming: *to screen a novel.* **7.** To film; to make a motion picture.

Screen Actors Guild (SAG) The Los Angeles–based performing artists' union, founded in 1933, that covers employment in motion pictures, filmed television programs, filmed television commercials, and other entertainment venues and provides such benefits as health insurance and pensions for its members. In order to become a member, an actor must have been offered a principal contract for a SAG motion picture, commercial, or other project, which immediately makes the actor eligible for membership. This first job may be done on a **waiver**, without the actor being a member. An actor may also join if he or she is a member of one of the unions in the **Associated Actors and Artistes of America (4-As)** and has dome a principal job under the auspices of any of those unions. Background actors may join SAG if they have had at least three shoot days on a SAG film, for which they receive three waivers, sometimes also called vouchers; they must have been paid SAG scale as well. Proof of employment must be presented by both principals and extras, and an initiation fee must be paid.

    See also BACKGROUND PLAYERS; COMMERCIALS; FORCED CALL; MEAL PENALTY; THEATRICAL FILM CONTRACTS; TRAVEL ALLOWANCE; TRAVEL COMPANION ALLOWANCE; RESIDIUALS.

screen direction The path of a performer's movement across the camera's field of vision during a take, from left to right or vice versa, including a change of path. It must be consistent in every take.

Screen Extras Guild (SEG) *Hist.* A Hollywood-based labor union of background actors working in motion pictures; dissolved in 1992 and amalgamated with SAG.

screening *n.* **1.** The showing of a film: *an invited screening.* **2.** Projecting a film.

screenplay *n.* The text of a film or television program, written by a screenwriter.

screen test A filmed or taped audition for a motion picture; also sometimes called a **camera test**. Screen tests for the stars who wanted to play Scarlett in *Gone with the Wind* (1939) are included among the bonus features of some DVD editions.

screen-test *v. t., i.* To **audition** actors for a film: *He screen-tested twenty actors for the role. She screen-tested for a film.*

screenwriter *n.* A person who pens film or television scripts.

screwball comedy An esp. popular genre in the 1930s of outrageously farcical motion pictures with eccentric characters and situations; e.g., *Bringing Up Baby* (1938), *My Man Godfrey* (1936).

scribe *n. Slang* A dramatist, esp. a screenwriter.

scrim *n.* A transparent, gauzy curtain that may have scenic elements painted on it and that hangs in front of a stage set in a proscenium theater; it may appear opaque, and scenes may be performed in front of it. But when it is lighted from behind, it becomes transparent, and the audience sees the rest of the set through it; it is then usually raised and the action continues. Its opacity may be further ensured by the use of a **blackout drop** positioned behind it.

Scrim coming down! A warning to everyone on stage that the transparent curtain is being lowered.

script *n., v. —n.* **1.** [Short for **manuscript**] The complete text of a play or film; hence, *playscript; filmscript. —v. t.* **2.** To write a play or film; hence, *"scripted by."*

script analysis Breaking down the text of a play or film into convenient smaller parts so they can be studied separately before being put back together. The actor must first understand the particular genre of the script; e.g., action-adventure, comedy, tragedy, murder mystery. Following Stanislavsky's **system**, the actor divides the play into smaller units, for study. The actor also analyzes the themes: why the play was written in the first place. Having understood genre, theme, and structure, the actor must then begin to understand how his or her character fits into the story, what role he or she plays in it, and the shape of that story: the **journey** the character takes, where it begins and where it ends, and what happens along the way. Also called *text analysis*.

script approval The contractual right of an actor engaged to play a part to accept or veto the text or parts thereof for an entertainment project, esp. a film; a privilege usually reserved for stars.

script rehearsal A **read-through** of a film or television script, held prior to a stage rehearsal or taping of an episode (e.g., for a sitcom) or just before shooting a film scene; usually a sit-down rehearsal, with the actors, director, and writers seated around a table, and design and technical staff sitting in chairs around the rehearsal studio.

script supervisor A usual term for **continuity supervisor**.

scrub *v. t. Slang* To remove something from a set. **Syn.** *eighty-six; kill; lose.*

season *n.* The duration of time during any part of a year when performances take place. Hence, *seasonal*, pertaining to venues where performances take place only at certain times of the year; e.g., seasonal **stock**. On television, the season for the broadcast of new programs usually begins in the fall and continues through the following spring. On Broadway, when the first new shows open in the fall, the season begins, and goes officially until summer, which is considered **off season**. In repertory theaters, the season may last for several months before the theater closes temporarily between seasons.

seasonal commercial A television or radio spot made for showing during a particular limited time period; e.g., a **national network** Christmas commercial.

season finale The last show in a television series for that particular season; usually broadcast with much hoopla, particularly if the series will be continuing the next season.

season ticket A yearly **subscription** to all productions in a particular theater.

seat *n., v.* —*n.* **1.** The place where an audience member sits. —*v. t.* **2.** To show or usher a spectator to his or her place. **3.** To have places for; capacity to accommodate: *The theater seats 600 people.*

seating *n.* **1.** Places for the audience in a theater or other venue. **2.** The act of showing someone to their places: *There will be no seating once the curtain is up.*
　　See also AMERICAN-PLAN SEATING; CONTINENTAL SEATING.

seating chart The plan of the seats in a theater auditorium, showing the layout of the rows and the location by number of each individual place. It is posted in a theater lobby to help spectators purchasing tickets decide where they might like to sit.

second act, to To sneak into a theater to see the latter half of a show without having purchased a ticket, by mingling with the crowd of audience members returning from intermission before the second act begins and finding a vacant seat.

second banana. See BANANA.

second team Stand-ins for the principal actors. They take the place of the **first team** when scenes are being set up, and the camera and lights positioned and focused.

second unit The film crew that shoots scenes not involving **principal photography**, such as extra location shots, crowd scenes, or scenes with **subplot** elements.

segment producer The producer in charge of various individual portions and special feature stories on a television news broadcast.

segment stage A small, round platform on wheels or castors used for shifting set pieces in a theater, esp. during a quick **scene change**.
　　See also SCENERY WAGON.

segue *n., v.* —*n.* **1.** In film and music, a smooth transition from one thing to the next. —*v. i.* **2.** In film, to make a smooth transition to the next scene. **3.** In music, to move smoothly from one section of a piece into the next.

selections *n. pl.* Wardrobe choices provided by a performer on a SAG or AFTRA project (e.g., the several differently colored suits or dresses a background player is asked to bring to a shoot, from which the **stylist** will choose) or the choices provided by the stylist from rented clothing.

self-direction *n.* The actor's instructions to him or herself in the absence of a director; e.g., when preparing a book for recording, a monologue for a theater **audition** or acting class presentation, or copy for an **on-camera** or **voiceover** commercial audition.

sell *v. t.* To perform in a committed, forceful way, putting an interpretation across so that the audience really "buys" it; esp. said of songs: *She really sold that number.*

sell-out *n.* A hit show or performance for which all the tickets have been sold; hence, a *sold-out house.*

semidocumentary *n.* A film of seemingly real events that appear to be taking place for real, and in real time, but that are staged and filmed in a naturalistic way, often like a newsreel. E.g., Costa-Gavras's *Z* (1969), the television movie *Culloden* (1964), and *The Battle of Algiers* (1965). Like the latter two, the film may be based on real events.

semiprofile shot A take of an actor's face in three-quarters' view.

send *v. t.* Uta Hagen's term for delivering a line to another actor with the intention of eliciting a response; sending involves **expectations** and **speculation** as to the outcome.

sennet *n. Hist.* A fanfare—an Elizabethan stage direction.

sense memory. See AFFECTIVE MEMORY.

sensory process The actor's way of working with **substitution**, sense memory, **endowment**, and emotional recall. The actor visualizes whatever **object** or person is being used, and asks relevant questions pertaining to it that will recall the physical nature of the object, or the physical appearance of the person, and the emotions connected with them. This allows the actor to experience the substitution or endowment viscerally.

sequence *n.* **1.** A series of related takes that are edited together to compose a single, coherent incident or event; e.g., a chase scene in an **action-adventure** film or the riot on the Odessa steps in Serge Eisenstein's *Battleship Potemkin* (1925). **2.** In the theater, a series of related, continuous actions in a particular scene.

serial *n.* A story told in a series of individual short films that were shown in movie houses every week; the **cliffhanger** ending of each **episode** was resolved shortly into the new one. Popular from the days of silent films through their demise in the 1930s.

series *n.* A running set of television programs that may last for more than one season; e.g., half-hour sitcoms, hour-long nighttime **episodic television** programs.

series finale The final show of a television series that has lasted several seasons.

service charge A handling fee paid for using a credit card to purchase a theater ticket by phone or computer.

session *n.* **1.** The delimited period of time scheduled and used for rehearsal, coaching, recording, filming, or taping during any one day. It may consist of an hour or more, or of an eight-hour workday. **2.** The delimited period of time during any one day when a casting call is held. **3.** Time set aside for working on a project; e.g., for writing or conferring.

session fee The amount of monetary compensation paid for each scheduled time period during which work on a media project, such as a commercial, is supposed to take place.

set *n., v.* —*n.* **1.** Décor; scenery, in the theater and the media. **2.** A radio or television monitor-receiver. —*v. t.* **3.** To place permanently; e.g., to put a prop in a certain position on stage. **4.** To fix the permanent level for a lighting cue: *to set a cue.* **5.** To prepare or arrange a stage for a performance or during a rehearsal: *to set the stage*; *to set up*; *to be set*: *Are we set stage left?* (i.e., "Are we ready to proceed with the rehearsal?") **6.** In acting, to **keep** or preserve business, a line reading, an acting moment, or the way a scene is played, insofar as that is possible. **7.** To solidify, fix, and **gel** a performance, which will be repeated more or less as it has been staged, even though an emotional moment cannot be set: it will happen as it happens. **8.** To put words to music. **9.** To schedule a definite date or dates for a performance or entertainment: *The date is set.*

set decorator In film and television, and sometimes in the theater, the person in charge of supervising the set dressers, and of furnishing the set with its overall look through the use of furniture, props, and materials.

set designer The person in the theater and the media who is in charge of planning the scenery and the mechanical logistics involved in making it work. The set designer, a combination of artist, architect, and engineer, draws and makes models of the scenery, drafts the **floor plan**, and oversees construction, painting, and decoration.

set deputy A volunteer SAG or AFTRA representative working on a film, television show, or commercial; he or she makes sure sanitary and safety conditions are adequate, and communicates any problems or concerns on behalf of members to the union. The set deputy, who is found usually only on large-cast projects, is not empowered to resolve problems, but only to report them to the proper authorities.
See DEPUTY.

set dresser A crew member who places props on the set, and removes them as necessary.

set dressing 1. Furnishings and decoration for a décor, including props and furniture. **2.** The act and job of furnishing a décor, and giving it a finished look.

set piece 1. A stationary or standing item of furnishing used on a theater or film décor; e.g., a sofa, a painted or real tree, a fountain, or a bridge over a stream. **2.** A monologue, a song, or other material that has been rehearsed and is ready to be used for a **prepared audition** or a performance.

set props Objects placed as dressing on a film or stage set, except furniture, and not usually employed by actors as hand props or personal props, although some of them may be used by actors at certain moments; e.g., vases of flowers, lamps, or shelves of books. Some are *trim props*: mirrors, paintings, chandeliers.

set the scene 1. In playwriting, **exposition**: to **establish** the locale, time, and other necessary details for a play or film: *Shakespeare sets the scene of Romeo and Juliet in Renaissance Verona*: "In fair Verona, where we lay our scene..." **2.** In the theater, to put the scenery, set dressing, and set props in place. Also called *set the stage*. **3.** In set design, to make decisions on the nature of the scenery, and how and where it will be placed.

setting *n.* **1.** The locale and/or time where a play or film takes place: *The setting of Julius Caesar is ancient Rome at the end of the Republican era.* **2.** The scenery. **3.** The musical composition to which words or lyrics have been fitted, and the act of writing music to fit lyrics: *the setting of the words*; *setting words to music*.

Settle! A command shouted when a **warning bell** has sounded, and shooting is about to begin.

set up 1. To prepare for shooting by arranging the lights, set elements, sound equipment, and camera angles. **2.** To prepare a space for a rehearsal, or a stage for a performance.

set-up *n.* **1.** The necessary preparation(s) for a theater rehearsal or performance; or for a film shoot or television taping. **2.** The carrying out of the preparation(s): *the set-up of props*. **3.** The position of a camera when ready for a shoot: *the camera set-up*.

sex comedy A graphically lascivious comic play or film that revolves around salacious encounters and complicated love affairs.

shadow play A southeast Asian drama, most notably in Bali, Java, and Thailand but also in Chinese and other cultures, largely based on traditional, mythological stories; performed with cut-out puppets in back of a curtain. They are illuminated from behind so only their silhouettes are seen. While the puppeteers manipulate the shadow puppets, the play is chanted by the *kru* (kroo'). [Khmer: master; fr. Sanskrit: *guru*]

Shakespearean (shayk speer' ee uhn) *n., adj.* —*n.* **1.** An actor who specializes in performing the plays of Shakespeare. **2.** A scholar who specializes in the study of Shakespeare's life and works. **3.** An admirer and aficionado of Shakespeare's works. —*adj.* **4.** Pertaining to the works of William Shakespeare (1564–1616), and/or to the style and form of his writing: *a Shakespearean sonnet*.

share *n.* A partial financial interest in a show. In the Elizabethan theater, Shakespeare and other actors were shareholders, or sharers, in the company to which they belonged.

Shavian (shay' vee uhn) *n., adj.* [Fr. Latin for Shaw: *Shavius*] —*n.* **1.** An advocate of the democratic socialist ideas of the Irish writer George Bernard Shaw (1856–1950) or of his **theater of ideas**; hence, *Shavianism*: the ideological following of or adherence to Shaw's ideas. **2.** A scholar of Shaw's life and works. —*adj.* **3.** Pertaining to the kind of incisive wit and penetrating ideas exemplified in the plays and other works of Shaw.

shill *n. Archaic* A performer planted in the audience of a variety show who is there to initiate laughter and applause; a **plant**.

shoe plot In **wardrobe**, a listing of footwear, who uses it, and when.

shoestring production A low-budget play or film.

shoot *n., v.* —*n.* **1.** The making of a film, filmed television program, or filmed commercial. **2.** A particular **session** during which filming takes place. —*v. t.* **3.** To film a project or any portion thereof.

shoot around To film in the absence of one or more performers. Moments and scenes not absolutely requiring the performer's presence are done.

shoot call The exact time when the personnel involved in a film project must report to begin work. Also called a *shooting call.*

shooting in sequence Filming scenes in the order in which they were originally written. Even if this is done (often at some inconvenience) for the sake of continuity in the actors' performances, it entails a great deal of sitting around while lights and cameras are set up, angles determined, and so forth. Shooting close-ups and medium and long shots, and taking scenes from different points of view, also affects the performances.

shooting log The details of every shot and take during a session; kept by the camera operator and crew.

shooting out of sequence Filming scenes not in the order in which they occur in the script, but in the most convenient order, which depends on such factors as location availability or the desirability of using an actor with only a few scenes within one or two shoot days. Most films are made out of sequence.

shooting schedule A list of the scenes to be filmed on any one day, prepared and posted daily. It includes the personnel involved, the sets or locations, and any special equipment. Also called a *production schedule.*

shooting script A screenplay fully prepared for the making of a motion picture, with the scenes arranged in the order in which they will be filmed.

shooting the playback Taking a scene with actors lip-syncing to the prerecorded soundtrack they have made.

shooting wild Syn. with **wild shooting**; i.e., doing a take without simultaneously recording the synchronous sound.

shop *n.* **1.** A place of work: *a union shop* (i.e., a workplace that has been organized by a union); *a nonunion shop.* **2.** The factory, room, or atelier where props, costumes, creatures, etc. are manufactured: **costume shop; creature shop; prop shop; scene shop; wig shop.**

shop manager The expert artist-technician who is the boss of a costume, creature, prop, makeup, wig, or other kind of atelier.

short *n.* A brief film; e.g., a **cartoon, newsreel,** or **travelogue.** Also called a *short subject.*

shot *n.* **1.** The view of an image being filmed: *a clear shot.* **2.** In film or television, a scene, part of a scene, or an individual **take** that has been filmed or taped without stopping, from start to finish. **3.** The basic unit from which films are constructed.

shotgun mike A sensitive unidirectional microphone; i.e., one that will pick up sound only from directly in front of it. Also called *line microphone.*

show *n., v.* —*n.* **1.** A public presentation or performance of a play, musical, concert, dance recital, opera, and so forth. **2.** In the film world, a motion picture: *We're working on a great show* (i.e., movie). —*v. t.* **3.** To exhibit a motion picture.

showboat *n.* A traveling paddle-wheel steamer on which entertainments were presented. The shows could be plays, melodramas, and/or variety. In the 19th c., such craft plied the Mississippi and other rivers in the United States, docking at various landings along the way and presenting spectacles for several evenings before moving on to the next venue. Jerome Kern's (1885–1945) and Oscar Hammerstein II's (1895–1960) Broadway musical *Show Boat* (1927), filmed in 1936 and again in 1951, immortalized the institution.

show business The **entertainment industry**; often shortened to "showbiz," or "show biz"; referred to as "the business" or "the biz" by those who are a part of it.

showcase *n., v.* —*n.* **1.** A union or non-union production of a play or musical in which the unpaid actors display their talents so that agents, casting personnel, and potential employers can see them in action; also, a production that its creators have mounted in order to attract potential backers. **Equity** actors who present their union membership cards at the door of a union showcase must be admitted free, if seats are available. People involved in an **Equity showcase** often hope it will **go to contract**; i.e., that a producer will be interested in picking it up for a commercial production, which very occasionally does happen. —*v. t.* **2.** To display or reveal talent: *That film showcased the actors' talents perfectly.* **3.** To exhibit a project with the intention of attracting potential investors and/or producers: *to showcase a play or musical.*

showcase code The agreement between producers and **Actors' Equity Association (AEA)** that covers the rules and regulations under which non-commercial

performances of plays may be presented. Working conditions, number of performances, size of theater or other performance space of no more than ninety-nine
seats, and compensation if actors are not hired should a play move to a paying
contract are among the aspects dealt with in the code, which also details different
levels of showcase (tier one, etc.).

show folk; show people Theater professionals.

showgirl *n. Archaic.* A young lady member of the chorus in a musical comedy,
esp. one dressed in a showy costume, as in the *Ziegfeld Follies*, where crowds of
gorgeous, gaudily dressed young ladies proceeded slowly down long staircases.

showman *n. Archaic* A producer, impresario, performer, or playwright, esp. in the
19th and early 20th centuries.

showmanship *n.* The craft, skills, and qualities necessary and desirable in performing, or in producing or directing an entertainment.

show must go on, the An old saying, and a motto of show folk the world over, that
no matter what has happened, and no matter what personal grief a performer has
suffered, he or she must perform as scheduled, unless that should be completely
impossible. In any case, a performance must take place in spite of all vicissitudes.

show stopper A hit number in a musical comedy that is received by the audience
with such a thunderous **ovation** that the performance is forced to halt temporarily.

shtick (shtihk') *n.* [Yiddish: piece] *Slang* **1.** A bit of comic business; a comic **routine**.
2. A particular intonation pattern, **catchphrase**, gesture, **gimmick**, or distinctive
movement that an actor or comic has made his or her personal trademark.

shutters *n. pl.* Two to four hinged flaps attached to the sides, top, and bottom of
lights that can be opened and closed to control the amount and direction of the
light; also colloquially called **barn doors**.

sick chair *Hist.* In Elizabethan theater, an armchair in which an ill character was
carried onto and off the stage.

side announcement In **book recording**, the opening and closing information
recorded for each side of a **tape**; e.g., for the Talking Books made for the American
Foundation for the Blind.

sidekick *n.* The partner of the hero, esp. in a **western**.

side lighting Illumination of objects from the right or the left.

sides *n. pl.* Pages of selected excerpts of a script given to actors for auditions, or
sometimes for actual filming or taping: an actor playing a small part will often be
given sides, instead of the entire script.

sideshow *n.* A secondary entertainment alongside the principal one, which is usually
a **carnival** or **circus**. Fire-eaters or sword-swallowers, contortionists, tumblers,
jugglers, weight-lifting strongmen, mind readers, hypnotists, fortune tellers, and

exhibits to which admission is paid, such as a **freak show**, may all be included, as well as games of chance, target shooting for a prize, and foods and refreshments.

sight gag A visual joke or bit of funny business that requires no words.

sightline(s) *n.* The visual field of view of the stage in a theater auditorium; they must be taken into account when staging a play.

sight-read; sight-sing *v. t.* To look at music for the first time, and play or sing it accurately without prior acquaintance with the score; esp. applied to vocal music sung without the help of an instrumental accompaniment. Hence, *sight-reading*, *sight-singing*. Useful and necessary in many fields; e.g., choral singing, **jingle** singing for commercials, or rehearsing a new number for a show.

signatory *n., adj.* —*n.* **1.** A producer who is a party to union agreements and contracts. —*adj.* **2.** Pertains to such a producer.

signature tune A melodic theme associated with a particular individual performer, usually played just before he or she enters, esp. in old television programs.

signed *adj.* **1.** Contracted to work exclusively with one **agent** or agency: *He is signed exclusively for commercials, but he freelances legit.* **2.** Engaged or booked for a show.

sign in 1. To put one's initials next to one's name on the list of actors posted on a theater callboard, so that stage management is aware that the actor is in the house; the actor must sign in personally. **2.** To put one's name or initials on the form provided at a film, commercial, or other **shoot. 3.** To write one's name and other information on the form set out at a commercial or other **audition**.

sign-in sheet 1. A list of cast members posted on the callboard of a theater on which they put their initials when they arrive for work. **2.** A form, required by union rules, to be filled in by actors auditioning for a project such as a television or radio commercial. It includes the actor's name, social security number (actors often write "avail." or "available"), agent's name, time of arrival, actual call time, time of departure, and whether it is the actor's first, second, or third audition. These sign-in sheets are necessary in case the casting personnel keep the actor over the allotted time allowed (in which case the actor must be paid a penalty fee) or if the actor is called for more than two callbacks, in which case the actor must be paid a fixed rate per callback. **3.** A form, required by union rules, that is partially filled in by an actor doing a commercial, film, or other media project when the actor reports for work, so that the number of hours worked can be noted at the end of the day and any overtime or penalties accrued can be added to the actor's check. The actor initials the form at the end of the workday, after the assistant stage manager in charge of dismissing actors for the day has filled in the final times. This is usually a separate form from the regulation **time sheet**.

sikkinis (sih kee' nihs) *n.* The **chorus** dance of ancient Greek satirical **comedy**; it imitated animal movements in such plays as Aristophanes' *Frogs*.

251

silent bit 1. A piece of business that is performed without speaking by an actor, whether a principal or background player. **2.** *Hist.* A category in SAG contracts, eliminated in 1994; meant for a background player who was given business to do, and could therefore be upgraded.

See also SIGHT GAG; UPGRADE.

silent film Motion pictures made before the introduction of sound in 1927.

Sills, Paul (1927–2008) American author, teacher, and stage director. His background was in the improvisational theater of Chicago's Second City, which he co-founded and directed. He also co-founded the Compass Players, but was best known for **story theater**, which combined creative **improvisation** with **animal exercises** to bring to life and create the world of famous fairy tales in an innovative way that also reflected the political relevance of theater to current events.

silver bullet [Fr. the horror story idea that only a silver bullet could kill a werewolf] Esp. in film, a perfect and simple plot resolution device that solves all problems; a kind of **deus ex machina**. Also called a *magic bullet*.

silver screen A characterization of the screen on which a motion picture is projected that implies the glamour of the movie business: *to appear on the silver screen*.

simile (sih' mih lee) *n.* A direct comparison using the words *like* or *as*: "My love is like a red, red rose"—Robert Burns.

simulcast *n.* The simultaneous broadcast of a sports contest, opera, or other program on television and radio, esp. of a **live** event, in order for listeners to be able to hear the sound as well as possible; or of a program on several channels at the same time; or of a program broadcast in several languages at once on different channels.

Singspiel (zihng' shpeel') *n.* [German: sing-play] A musical theater piece, esp. one with spoken dialogue; e.g., a comic opera or operetta (a popular 18th-c. form).

Sit into the shot! "After you hear the cue 'Action!' move in and sit down on the designated mark!" A direction to actors to move from off-camera into camera range, and to sit down in the place on which the camera is focused as the take begins; e.g., a sofa.

situation *n.* **1.** The **circumstances** in which characters find themselves at any given moment. **2.** Part of the plot of a story; e.g., the circumstances in a particular scene.

situation comedy Half-hour episodic television series that are meant to be funny. Done for a season or more using the same regular cast of characters and various guest stars; broadcast weekly during primetime evening hours, or rerun on late-night television. Sitcoms are rehearsed for several days in front of live audiences and taped or filmed at the end of the work week. They are actually between twenty and twenty-five minutes long, in order to allow time for commercials. Called *sitcom*, for short.

Sitzprobe (zih:ts' pro:' buh; -prohb') *n.* [German: sit-rehearsal] **1.** The first rehearsal of an opera with singers and orchestra, usually after the singers have memorized their parts; the piece is played through, with no stage movement or action. **2.** Any sit-down **rehearsal** of an opera without movement or action.

size card A small rectangular piece of cardboard that actors fill in when they go for a **commercial** audition, with lines for the actor's name, address, agent, phone numbers, eye and hair color, clothing sizes, etc. It is used by wardrobe people if the actor books the commercial, so it is best to be accurate. Usually, a Polaroid® photo taken by an assistant is attached to the filled-out card.

skene (skeh:' neh:) *n. Hist.* In ancient Greece, a building at the back of the raised stage, where dressing rooms were located; it was behind the *proskeniun* (pro skeh:' nee *oo*n), which, so it is conjectured, was decorated with painted scenery representing a palace entrance, temple, or other appropriate place.

sketch *n.* A short comic act in a television comedy show, such as *Saturday Night Live*, or in a vaudeville evening or revue. Also called a *skit*.

skill sheet A form that an actor who is signed with an agency fills in, listing the actor's talents and special areas of expertise (which may either be related to acting or completely extraneous to it) and that the agent keeps on file and consults as necessary. For instance, an actor who specializes in dialects will list all the accents he or she can do. If the actor speaks a foreign language; plays a musical instrument; practices a sport; rides horses; handles sailboats or motor boats; can drive a truck; is skilled at welding or other jobs; can cook with professional skill; does acrobatics, magic, juggling or some form of martial arts; or deals cards like an expert croupier, any or all of those things should be listed.

skins *n. pl. Slang* **1.** A listing used on a SAG or AFTRA shoot of the names and call times of all those working for the day; sometimes used by a **production assistant** to call the roll of **background players** before shooting starts. **2. Tights.**

skip a line To leave out a bit of dialogue inadvertently.

slapstick *n.* Broad clowning, involving physical bits of business such as falling, slipping on a banana peel, and the like. The term comes from the stage implement used in **commedia dell'arte**, consisting of a handled flat board to which another flat board is attached at the top by a hinge: when the boards are banged together, the slapstick makes a brief, loud, sharp, cracking sound. It was used to point up a comic line or droll bit of stage business; the bang might be followed by a whistle on a slide whistle.

See also **knockabout; rim shot**.

slasher film A violent, bloody horror film involving murder with such weapons as knives and hatchets.

253

slate *v. t.* [Fr. the **clapboard**, also called a slate, held up to the camera to be photographed] **1.** To record one's name before starting a commercial or other audiovisual or audio audition: *Please slate your name.* Sometimes the actor is also asked to state the agent's name and other pertinent information. At the end of the audition, there may be an **end slate**, and the actor states his or her name again. **2.** To schedule a film or television program's **release** date: *The film is slated for summer release.* **3.** *Brit. Slang* To **pan** a play, film, etc.

Slate it! "Hold the slate up in front of the camera so we can see it clearly!" A direction to the operator of the clapboard given at the beginning of a take.

slice of life Pertains to naturalistic dramas that appear unstructured and drift through the limited stories they tell, providing inessential, myriad realistic details in their presentation of incidents in the lives of ordinary people, as in **kitchen sink drama**, or showing the seamy underside of life, as in Maxim Gorky's *Lower Depths*.

slip stage Syn. with **wagon stage**.

slot *n., v.* —*n.* **1.** A performer's place on a **vaudeville running order**. **2.** A performer's **billing** in the credits of a television program. **3.** A program's place in a television **lineup**. —*v. t.* **4.** To put a performer into a particular place in a vaudeville running order, or in television credits; hence, *to slot in.* **5.** To schedule a television program for broadcast. Syn. with **slate**, def. 2.

slow burn The long buildup of anger that is held back until it can be held no longer and finally explodes (e.g., Jackie Gleason's reactions in his television series *The Honeymooners*). An actor's **technique** used to hilarious or horrific effect.

slow motion Actions and events that seem very slowed down in time, achieved by the cinematic **technique** of running the film through a camera at a speed of more than the standard twenty-four frames a second. Called *slomo* or *slo-mo*, for short.

slow study A performer who has difficulty learning lines.

slow take 1. A delayed reaction involving gradual recognition; used to comic effect in the films of Charlie Chaplin, Laurel and Hardy, and W. C. Fields, and in tragedy; e.g., in a **recognition scene**. **2.** A long turn to look at someone or something, done without hurrying; often used in horrifying situations and horror films.

Small Professional Theater (SPT) agreement A national **Equity** contract covering theaters seating fewer than 350—except theaters in New York, Chicago, or Los Angeles. There are ten salary categories, and the agreement applies to both commercial and non-profit theaters, as well as to seasonal or single productions; tours are not permitted.

smash *n. Slang* A hugely successful play, musical, or other entertainment: *a smash hit.*

smoke and mirrors [Fr. the use of smoke to distract the audience and create a mystic atmosphere, while mirrors are retracted or turned in certain directions during a disappearing act] **1.** A **metaphor** for the creation of an **illusion**; for something illusory; or for an insubstantial, unsatisfactory, but perhaps clever explanation: *It was all smoke and mirrors.* **2.** Illusions meant to deceive the audience, or to create surprises; e.g., the entrances of Dr. Miracle from various seemingly impossible places, in act 3 (or 2, depending on the version) of Offenbach's *The Tales of Hoffmann.*

smoke machine A device for creating artificial fog or hazy, misty effects. Also called a *fog machine*; *smoke pot.*

sneak preview The showing of a film to a paying audience in advance of its release to the general public, in order to gauge audience reactions.

snoot *n.* [Fr. Scots: snout] A cylindrical cone fitted onto a **spotlight** to help eliminate spill, and further direct the beam of light. Also called *cone*; *funnel*; *head.*

snow box A metal canister or other container perforated at the bottom, through which shredded bits of white confetti or soap flakes are allowed to fall, to create the effect of snow on stage. Much used in **melodrama**.

snow cradle A large sack with holes or slits cut into it, suspended tautly between two battens above the stage and filled with white confetti. When it is shaken, the confetti falling slowly through the holes creates the effect of snow. Also called a *snow bag.*

snow machine 1. In the theater, a motorized mechanical device that is hung above the stage and releases wet soap flakes to simulate whirling or slowly falling snow. **2.** A blower that spreads white plastic foam to create artificial snow in winter scenes in motion pictures. Also called a *snow maker.*

soap opera [So called because when they were done in the form of radio plays, their sponsors advertised laundry detergent, as they still do] An hour-long television drama series with never-ending stories about relationships, broadcast during the day. The actors usually memorize the scripts overnight or over a weekend, rehearse in the morning early, and tape in the afternoon after the lunch break. For most scenes, there is one rehearsal in the afternoon for the camera, and then the actual **taping** starts. Also called *daytime drama*; *daytime serial*; *soap*, for short.

socialist realism An artistic movement in painting, literature, theater, and film in the Soviet Union and other Communist countries. Artists depicted or portrayed the working class and its struggles in order to show the reality of their lives and to extol their contribution to human welfare.

Society of Stage Directors and Choreographers (SSDC) A New York City–based organization that negotiates contracts and working conditions for directors and choreographers with theater producing organizations, and provides various other services for its members.

sock and buskin [Fr. the ancient Roman low shoe (Latin: *soccus*) worn by comic actors and the buckskin half boot, the **cothurnus**, worn by tragedians] *Archaic* A **metonymy** for the **drama**: the sock for comedy; the buskin for tragedy.

soft copy Material that can be read on a computer screen, as opposed to hard copy, which is printed out. **Sides** for auditions may be emailed as soft copy, and printed by the actor so he or she has a **hard copy**.

soft focus The achievement in a shot of a gauzy, slightly blurred effect, usually by shooting through **gauze** or some viscous material and/or by using **back lighting**.

soft sell In commercials, a soothing, non-aggressive, low-pressure way of advertising a project with subtle persuasiveness.

soft shoe A jazzy style of dancing in musical comedy or variety shows, using shoes that make a brushing sound during the dance. Cf. its opposite, **tap**.

soliloquy (suh lih' luh kwee) *n.* A monologue revealing inner feelings or ideas, spoken by a character in a play who is alone on stage; hence, *to soliloquize*: to deliver or indulge in such a monologue.

solo *n., adj., adv.* [Italian: alone] —*n.* **1.** A number sung by one singer alone. **2.** A dance number for a single dancer. **3.** A piece, or a section of a piece, for one instrument: *an oboe solo*; e.g., in a symphony movement. —*adj.* **4.** Pertaining to music or dance performed by one person alone: *a solo song.* —*adv.* **5.** To sing, play, or dance alone by oneself: *to sing solo*.

song and dance exercise A two-part Lee Strasberg Method classroom **acting exercise**. In the first part, an actor must choose a simple, easily remembered song, such as "For He's a Jolly Good Fellow." The actor must stand facing the class/audience and maintain eye contact as he or she sings each syllable separately, filling the lungs with air each time and singing as loudly as possible. This part of the exercise helps lead to self-awareness of the tension and inhibition the actor may not be aware of. In the second part of the exercise, the actor takes the same song and sings it again syllable by syllable, doing a dance movement on each syllable. Often, actors will stop and try to think of a movement each time, instead of being spontaneous. The purpose of the dance part of the exercise is to make the actor aware of how much he or she is intellectualizing, instead of **living through** the **moment**.

song and dance man *Archaic* **1.** A male musical comedy performer. **2.** A vaudeville performer with a musical act that included dance routines.

song and supper rooms *Hist.* In the 19th c., special rooms in pubs where variety entertainments took place, for a small admission charge.

song stylist A vocalist who sings in an intimate way; a nightclub singer who uses various techniques, esp. crooning and half talking, half singing to **put across** a **number**.

song writer A composer of popular tunes.

soubrette (soo breht') *n.* **1.** The light **ingénue** role in a play, opera, or operetta of a pert, perky, lively, clever, and sometimes impertinent young lady, esp. a lady's maid or serving girl. **2.** The actress or singer who plays such a role.

sound bite An audio excerpt considered striking or newsworthy, taken from an interview, news program, or other source.

sound booth 1. The small, enclosed, soundproof room in a studio where the engineers run the equipment and record the performers in the enclosed other half of the studio. **2.** The small, enclosed, soundproof room or separate section of the **lighting booth** in a theater from which sound cues are run.

sound camera A motion picture camera capable of simultaneous filming and audio recording.

sound check 1. A test of the acoustics in a theater, often done by orchestras before a concert, and always by actors arriving in a new theater when on tour. Actors stand on stage and recite lines while other actors (who will afterwards take their turn on stage), or a stage manager move around the auditorium making sure the lines are audible and comprehensible. **2.** A test of the sound atmosphere in a film shoot or recording studio.

sound crew The team that deals with microphones and recording equipment and records dialogue and ambient noise on a film or television shoot.

sound cue A signal for something to happen or for an actor to speak, given by using a noise; e.g., the ringing of a doorbell or telephone.

sound design 1. In the theater, the strategic placement of microphones, amplifiers, and loudspeakers in order to create the desired audio effect, and to have the actors and/or musicians heard evenly all over the auditorium. **2.** In motion pictures, another term for **sound effects** design.
    See also ACOUSTICS; AMPLIFICATION; BODY MIKE; HEAD MIKE; GENERAL AREA MIKE; MICROPHONE; MIKED; WIRED FOR SOUND.

sound designer The person who decides what audio equipment to use and where to use it for a theatrical production, and places microphones and speakers strategically in a theater auditorium in order to ensure the best acoustic and audio effect. He or she checks the level and quality of the acoustics and deals with actors' personal body or head mikes. The sound designer is also responsible for such special effects as the rumbling of thunder in a storm scene, and may work as his or her own **sound mixer**.

sound effects Specially created or naturally occurring noises that recreate certain natural or man-made phenomena (e.g., rain in a storm, birds singing, or a church bell ringing) and that provide audio background and/or atmosphere in a scene. In the theater, they may be recorded sounds played over a loudspeaker, or manually done backstage by a technician, as they were in an old-time **radio play**. In radio and the theater, machines were created to reproduce certain sounds; e.g., a **wind machine**; **thunder sheet**; rain and sea box; or **rain drum**. The sound of horses' hooves galloping was made by a technician rhythmically banging two coconut shells on a board. In radio, there were constantly used *sound effects records* containing every sound you could think of, including those for all kinds of transportation,

257

from cars and trains to boats and planes; fires and fire engines; whistles, bells, and clocks; animals and birds; and breaking glass. They are designed for theater, film, and television by a *sound effects designer*, who is a specialist in creating them.

See EFFECTS; FOLEY; THUNDER SHEET.

sound engineer 1. The person responsible for recording in a recording studio; he or she handles and maintains the recording equipment and microphones, adjusting levels and monitoring the recording. **2.** The person who works the recording equipment in a book recording session. **3.** The recordist, esp. the chief recordist (called a **production mixer**) on a film shoot.

sound film Another word for talking picture; **talkies**.

soundie *n. Hist.* Three-minute featurette films of vaudeville sketches and musical numbers, similar to contemporary music videos, that were specially made to be played in bars, diners, and other public places on a projector called a *Panoram*: a jukebox with flashing colored lights and a monitor screen at the top. They lasted from the early to mid-1940s, and customers paid a nickel for each showing.

sound man 1. A sound engineer, sound technician, or sound designer. **2.** In the theater, the technician who installs and adjusts the actors' body mikes.

sound mixer 1. In film, an expert sound engineer or sound technician who is a specialist in using an audio mixing console to combine audio that has been recorded live and/or in a studio, making the combination seamless and undetectable, and in combining the different kind of sound tracks (music, dialogue, etc.). Hence, *sound mixing*: the job and act of combining sound. Sound mixers usually specialize in a particular area: *dialogue mixer*; *music mixer*. **2.** In the theater, the person who assists the **sound designer** in placing the speakers, arranging at the audio console what sounds go through what speakers; often syn. with sound designer. **3.** An audio **console** or **board** at which sound can be mixed: *an audio mixing console*.

See also MIX; PRODUCTION SOUND MIXER; RE-RECORDING MIXER.

Sound Recordings Code AFTRA's compilation of fees, salaries, terms of employment, and working conditions for the audio recording of music, books, and other projects, negotiated with producing organizations on behalf of its members.

soundstage *n.* **1.** The interior area of a film **studio** building where shooting takes place, containing a fully dressed and lit set; so called because it is more or less soundproof (although one sometimes has to stop shooting while a loud airplane passes overhead), and because actors' dialogue and other sound is recorded as part of the shoot. Also called *production sound stage*; *shooting stage*. **2.** The studio building containing such a stage.

soundtrack; **sound track** *n.* The audio portion of a film or television program.

souvenir program An elaborate, lavishly illustrated booklet sold in theater lobbies before and sometimes after a performance as a memento of the show.

space stage An **abstract set** or décor that is minimal, and consists of platforms, levels, and stairways. It can be used for any or all plays in a repertory season, or may be designed for a single production.

space-through *n.* [Short for *space-through rehearsal*] A rehearsal in which the performers, on stage for the first time after having rehearsed elsewhere, go through their moves and blocking for spacing (i.e., to feel what the space is like) and to time entrances. Also called a *spacing rehearsal*.

spaghetti western A film set in the American west and made in Italy, Spain, or Yugoslavia. Actors from those countries as well as Americans are used; the films have to be dubbed, and the lip-syncing is not always terribly successful.

spear carrier An extra in a play or opera; so called because the background player is often called upon to play a spear-carrying guard.

special *n.* A spotlight used for a particular performer: *the lead actor's special.*

special-ability extra A background player with a particular skill, which should be listed with an agent or casting company on a **skill sheet**. The pay for the use of such skills is higher than for ordinary extra work. The skills do not include **stunt** ability, which involves a separate category of performer altogether.

special agreement Equity's term for any individual contract for a particular project or venue not covered under other **Equity** contracts.

special effects Artificially created illusions of reality; abbrev. SFX in screenplays. There seems no end to the possibilities of creating vast computer-generated armies, incredible battles in space, raging tempests, overflowing volcanoes, exploding buildings and vehicles, dinosaurs, strange creatures, and horrifying monsters.
See also EFFECTS.

special makeup effects Prostheses and other devices meant to create the particular look of a character, or to recreate a well-known person's face. Sometimes very difficult for actors to wear and perform in, the special makeup may require hours to put on.

specialty *n.* **1.** An actor's particular ability or field of expertise: *Her specialty is dialects.* **2.** A vaudeville act that uses a performer's unusual skills and talents, such as magic, juggling, contortions, performing a **fan dance**, and the like.

specificity *n.* In acting, detailed, precise, and particular knowledge of a character's life, and of every moment in that life as it appears in the play, as well as the application of that knowledge when performing, giving reality to the playing.
See also HERE, TODAY, NOW, THIS VERY MINUTE.

spectacle *n.* An elaborate show, such as a **pageant** or **extravaganza**.

speculation *n.* Uta Hagen's term for the character's internal ruminations and thoughts on the possible outcome and consequences of expressing an intention or carrying out an action, or of not doing so.
See also EXPECTATIONS; INTERIOR MONOLOGUE; SEND; RECEIVE; LAND.

speech *n.* **1.** Communicative vocal utterance and/or communicative gesture: *Deaf sign language is a kind of speech.* **2.** The act of speaking; i.e., of communicating in language, by uttering meaningful words vocally, or by using linguistic gesture. **3.** The art of speaking well, with good diction and vocal technique, taught in acting schools and by coaches. **4.** A group of lines of dialogue spoken by an actor. **5.** A particular group of lines: *Hamlet's "To be or not to be" speech.* **6.** An oration or public discourse delivered by an individual speaker: *Lincoln's Gettysburg Address.*

Speed! The cue called out by a sound technician to inform the director that the sound equipment is functioning, and ready to record.
See ROLL 'EM!

speed-through rehearsal A particular kind of brush-up in which the actors recite their lines at top speed, without pausing; in some speed-throughs, they also hurry simultaneously through their moves.
See BRUSH-UP REHEARSAL.

spell it out To make a point clearly and succinctly by emphasizing important words and speaking fairly slowly, making sure it sinks in; sometimes necessary, esp. in verse plays involving complicated language, but usually to be avoided.

spike *n., v.* —*n.* **1.** A small, easily seen **mark**, usually made with a piece of spike tape. —*v. t.* **2.** To place an indicatory mark on a set. The instruction from a director to a stage manager, or from the stage manager to an assistant, is, "Spike it, please!"

spike tape A narrow version of **duct tape** in various colors, used to **tape the floor** of a rehearsal studio or stage, or to indicate where something is to go on a set (e.g., a light switch on a wall; a prop, such as a vase, on a table; or a couch on the stage floor) or placed as an actor's or cameraperson's **mark** for a shoot or taping.

spill *n.* Partial illumination of an area that is not supposed to be lit. Also called *bounce.*

spin *n.* A single playing of a song on a radio show.

spine *n.* The core (or **throughline**) or main thrust of a scene, or of the play as a whole; also, the main life drive or objective of a character.

spin-off *n.* A derivative television show, usually a sitcom, starring an actor whose popular character was a supporting role on another sitcom and who was so well received that the character was considered deserving of his or her own series.

spit-take *n.* A **technique**, esp. in **farce**, involving a person drinking a liquid and, being shocked or surprised while the liquid is still in the mouth, forcibly expelling it and spraying it all over the place, usually with a loud spluttering sound; e.g., when being clapped on the back by someone entering a room.

split screen 1. A film editing technique in which two actions filmed separately are spliced onto the same negative: in the finished movie the actions appear to be happening in the same place; e.g., in scenes with actors playing a **dual role**. **2.** In television, the division of the screen into two halves, with two different but related scenes on each half; e.g., when a broadcast journalist is reporting on a storm, seen on the other half of the screen.

spoken arts The public reading or recitation of poetry, books, short stories, and so forth; oratory and public discourse: *spoken-arts recording*.

Spolin, Viola (1906–1994) Influential, innovative American teacher of self-expressive improvisation. She devised a number of **theater games**, about which she published several books, among them the well known *Theater Games* (Northwestern University Press, 1986) and *Improvisation for the Theater* (Northwestern University Press, 1963).

sponsor *n., v.* —*n.* **1.** An organization, company, or person who pays to advertise products or services on a television or radio show. —*v. t.* **2.** To advertise a product or service on a broadcast. **3.** To help underwrite a show, or support a particular person or endeavor.

spontaneity *n.* The actor's feeling of **freedom** during a performance or rehearsal, allowing unpredictable, unrehearsed moments to happen naturally, without pre-meditation, and on a sudden impulse. Cf. **organic**.

spoof *n., v.* —*n.* **1.** A **parody** or lampoon of a person, film, opera, other entertainment, or institution, in which the object of the mockery is imitated, along with an exaggeration of typical characteristics; e.g., the fake TV news program on *Saturday Night Live*. —*v. t.* **2.** To perform or write a **parody** or lampoon.

sports industry That branch of the entertainment industry devoted to athletic games and contests, both amateur and professional, live or broadcast, and employing a vast number of people in various positions.

sports agent A business representative working on **commission** for an athlete, handling the athlete's career and negotiating contracts.

sportscast *n.* A television or radio broadcast of a sporting event.

sportscaster *n.* The television or radio **broadcaster** who announces the sports news or who gives a running commentary and blow-by-blow description on radio or television of a live sporting event. Also called a *sports announcer*.

spot *n.* **1.** Short for *spotlight*. **2.** A television or radio commercial. **3.** *Archaic* An engagement to play a theater role; and the role itself: *I did a spot on Broadway*; *I had a spot on Broadway*. Hence also, *to make a spot*: to secure an engagement.

spot announcement In radio, a commercial read by an announcer.

spotlight *n.* A light that focuses narrowly on a particular area. A *pin spot* is one that focuses a particularly narrow beam of light on a particular place. A *baby spot* is a small spotlight. Called a *spot*, for short.

See also DIAPHRAGM; ELLIPSOIDAL REFELCTOR SPOTLIGHT; FOLLOW SPOT; LIMELIGHT; XENON ARC SPOT.

spotting *n.* The act and process of narrowing the light beam emanating from a **spotlight**, esp. a **fresnel**, in which the lamp inside the housing can be moved forward and backward. Cf. its opposite, **flooding**.

Sprechstimme (shpr*eh*' shtih' muh) *n.* [German: speak-voice] A way of half singing, half speaking without using exact pitches, similar to **recitative** (which does use pitches), used in opera; or the delivery of a song by an actor who does not really sing it, but who half speaks it. Also called *Sprechgesang* (shpr*eh*' guh zahng') [German: speak-sing].

spy film A motion picture that tells a story of international intrigue and espionage, either real or fictitious; e.g., the James Bond **action-adventure** films.

squawk box 1. A loudspeaker that is part of a theater's **PA system. 2.** A loudspeaker that is part of a stockbrokerage house's intercom system; hence the use of the phrase to mean a morning television show that discusses financial investments.

squib *n.* **1.** A remotely detonated, small explosive charge that simulates the explosion of a bullet hitting a target; used in gunfight scenes in films. The squib's wiring is concealed, and the squib hidden underneath actors' clothing; the actor is protected by the metal plate on which the squib is mounted. Squibs are often attached to *blood sacks* that burst simultaneously with the charge, creating the naturalistic effect of someone being shot. **2.** *Archaic* In Renaissance Italian theater, a small flare rocket set off to simulate lightning.

stable *n.* The group of actors, esp. the character actors, under contract to a film **studio** in the days of the **studio system**. Steady work was provided by each studio for these stalwarts of the industry, and many appeared in **plum** character roles in quite a few films every year. They were often on a weekly *retainer salary*.

stage *n., v.* —*n.* **1.** A playing space or **acting area. 2.** The raised platform used for performances in a theater. **3.** A **synecdoche** for the theatrical industry or the theatrical profession, esp. the acting profession: *to go on the stage* (i.e., to become an actor); *a star of stage and screen.* —*v. t.* **4.** To put on, produce, or direct a play. **5.** To **block** actors.

stage band A group of instrumentalists that performs in costume on stage, acting the role of musicians as part of a show. E.g., the uniformed martial band that precedes the entrance of the peers in act 1 of Gilbert and Sullivan's *Iolanthe*, or the band of *klezmorim* (klehz mo:' rihm)—east European Jewish musicians who played *klezmer* (klehz' mehr) music; i.e., Yiddish secular folk music—referred to nostalgically and affectionately by Madame Ranevskaya in Chekhov's *Cherry Orchard*. They appear briefly on stage to play music, and she gives them some money.

stage box A seating area partitioned off on three sides, containing a few semi-private places next to the stage. In the 17th c., such boxes were on the stage proper, just inside the proscenium arches.

stage brace A sturdy, thick rod for supporting flats and other scenery and making sure they stay steady and fixed in place. The length of the brace is adjustable; one end is fastened using a **stage screw** to the stage floor, while the other end is fastened to the back of the piece of scenery. Also called *brace*; *extending brace*; *extension brace*.

stage business Any physical **activity** performed as part of the action in a play. Called **business**, for short.

stage center The middle **acting area** of a proscenium or arena stage, divided into three playing areas: downstage center (abbrev. DC), center (abbrev. C), and upstage center (abbrev. UC).

stage clamp A metal fastener shaped like the letter "C" and used to secure two flats and hold them together as tightly as possible. Also called a *C-clamp*.

stage combat Arranged and carefully rehearsed and choreographed fights, fencing, boxing, knock-down brawls, or other forms of pugnacious behavior. There are experts in different fields of stage combat: some specialize in swordplay, some in fistfights.

stagecraft *n.* Skill in the arts of the theater. Also called *theater craft*.
  See also STAGE TECHNIQUE.

stage crew The backstage staff of stagehands and technicians that work a show.

stage crew chief The boss of the stage crew, who assigns the jobs and also determines how the scene changes will be effected; e.g., in what order the **flies** will be handled, or furniture shifted, and where it will be moved.

stage directions That part of a written play script that informs the actors, directors, and designers where and when a scene is taking place, and also details other aspects of the activities in a scene. Stage directions for actors are the author's instructions that may tell them with what emotion the author envisions the delivery of a particular line, or what the writer thinks the actor should do physically; e.g., sit, make a cross. It is best for the actor to ignore such directions until things have been worked out in rehearsals, when the delivery of the line may turn out to conform to the author's stage direction, or not. Some authors, such as George Bernard Shaw, write stage directions so extensive as to be almost novelistic. Others, such as Harold Pinter, leave more to the interpretive powers of the actors and director.

stage director 1. The person in a theater in charge of all aspects of a production's **mise-en-scène. 2.** *Archaic Brit.* Stage manager.

stage door The backstage staff entrance to a theater.

stage doorman The porter (doorkeeper) at a theater's backstage staff entrance.

stage-door Johnny A man who waits outside the theater's staff entrance for an actress whom he is pursuing or courting or wishes to meet.

stage fall A tumble that looks real, but that is carefully arranged and rehearsed, so as to avoid injury; actors learn the elementary technique of how to **break a fall**. See also PRATFALL.

stage fight A combat in a play; e.g., fencing, boxing, or other physical conflicts. Carefully staged and rehearsed so as to avoid injury.

stage fright A state of agonizing, panicky nervousness, more or less severe, brought on by the dread of appearing on stage in a performance or other event; e.g., the delivery of a speech. Symptoms may include perspiration, trembling, loss of appetite, and "butterflies" in the stomach. Usually, once the actor steps out onto the stage and begins performing, stage fright disappears. Also called **performance anxiety**.

stage left The side of the stage to an actor's left. The abbreviation used by actors and staff in noting moves or positions in a script is L. UL is up, or upstage left. DL is down, or downstage left. XL means cross left. XDL means cross down, or downstage left. XUL means cross up, or upstage left.

stage machinery All the paraphernalia and mechanical, electric, and electronic devices used on a theater stage to deal with the technical aspects of a production, including the system of levers, lines, ropes, and pulleys; wagon stages; trap elevators; etc.

stage manager The official in both the media and the theater responsible for overseeing a production in all its aspects. In the theater, the stage manager's duties include running rehearsals, including observing proper breaks, and, once the show is up and running, conserving the performance as it was directed; calling the show: giving cues for the lighting and scenery changes; and sending an assistant to give the actors their calls. At the half hour **call**, or a bit later, the stage manager sends an assistant to collect the actors' valuables for safekeeping during the performance; they are returned at the end. Stage managers' contracts are handled by **Actors' Equity Association**; some stage managers or assistant stage managers may understudy, or play a role.

stage manager's desk The raised backstage table from which the stage manager calls the show; equipped with a light that shines on the prompt script, and often located near the downstage right entrance onto the stage.

stage money Fake currency used in a production.

stage movement The actors' moves from place to place; i.e., **blocking**.

stage name An actor's professional appellation. The term is more usual when the name is different from the actor's real, legal given name, which may of course also be used as a stage name. One of the performing arts union rules is that no two actors may have the same name: **name protection**. Actors change their names for several reasons: the union rule, euphony, memorability, and ethnicity. In the old Hollywood days, for instance, Jewish actors would often change their names, so that they would not limit or stereotype themselves and could play a wider variety of roles.

stage parents The mothers and fathers of child actors. They have terrible reputations (sometimes deserved; mostly not) as domineering and exploitative monsters.

stage picture 1. The director's positioning and grouping of performers, presenting a particular vision to the audience; a **tableau. 2.** The look of the stage setting: *a beautiful stage picture.*

stage pocket One of a series of metal boxes placed in the backstage floor or on the wall, containing electrical outlets for lighting cables.

stage presence An actor's ability to draw the audience's attention, arising from a sense of being centered and concentrated, and thus able to project emotion and passion.

stage properties Objects other than furniture used in theatrical productions. Also called *properties*; *props*, for short.

stage right The side of the stage to an actor's right; abbrev. R. UR is up, or upstage right; DR is down, or downstage right; XR is cross right; XDR is cross downstage right; XUR is cross upstage right.

stage right(s) 1. The copyright of a theatrical work. **2.** Legal entitlement and permission to produce a play; e.g., permission from a playwright's estate to produce a drama to which they own the copyright.

stage screw A large, winged, grooved metal rod or threaded peg with a handle used for fastening stage braces or other devices, such as iron supports for scenery, to the stage floor. Also called a *stage peg*.

stage setting 1. Scenery, in general. **2.** A specific décor: *the stage setting for scene 1.*

stage slap A forceful, resounding hit that looks real, but is done by the actor clapping one hand against another (sometimes with his or her back to the audience), or one hand against a thigh, while the hitting arm completes its motion, rather than by actually striking the other actor, who reacts as if struck. A light slap might, however, be done for real, as would a light *stage punch*. Punches and slaps depend for their realistic value on the reaction of the actor being hit. Also called a *stage hit*.

stagestruck *adj.* Enamored of the theater; **bitten by the bug**; all but incurably obsessed with the world of show business; victimized by *stage fever*: that hectic, overheated desire to be a professional actor.

stage technique The technical skills that are part of an actor's craft. Aside from good **vocal technique** and **acting technique**, they include the following:

1. How to prepare for a **cross**: a short time before the cross, anticipate it by putting a slight amount of weight on the leg that will remain stationary

when the other leg moves to begin the walk: on the left leg if you cross right; on the right leg if you cross left.

2. When turning to cross, always turn downstage, not upstage.
3. How to sit: feel the seat with the back of the thigh and sit down smoothly without looking around.
4. How to gesture with one hand: use the upstage hand, so as not to conceal the face or body.
5. Always **cheat** out as much as possible, so as to be facing downstage; do not **upstage** yourself.
6. When a character crosses past you, do a slight **counter-cross** to adjust the stage picture automatically and unobtrusively.
7. Always **find the light**.
8. In a **theater in the round**, turn slightly as you speak to include automatically all areas of the audience, without making an obvious point of doing so.

stage time The **convention** of the condensed duration of events in plays or films; e.g., a story that may span many years takes two or three hours to tell. Also called *dramatic time*.

stage wait An unforeseen, unintentional pause during a performance; caused by a missed **cue** or a missed entrance.

stage whisper The hoarse sound made by forcing air over the vocal cords, without making them vibrate, or causing them to vibrate minimally, while using diaphragmatic support to project the voice so as to be audible to the audience, but conventionally unheard by characters who are not supposed to know what is going on.

staged reading A public presentation of a play that includes elementary blocking, and in which the actors, not required to have memorized the dialogue, carry their scripts.

stagehand *n.* Generic designation for any member of a **crew** working in a theater, or film or television studio. Professional stagehands, who often have particular specialties, such as props, are members of **IATSE**.

staging *n.* **1.** Mise-en-scène; the way in which a play is mounted, blocked, choreographed, and presented. **2.** The act and process of mounting a play. **3.** Another word for blocking.

staging rehearsal A rehearsal in which the actors are staged; i.e., told when and where to move. Also called a *blocking rehearsal*.

stagy *adj.* Exaggeratedly theatrical; overdone; histrionic.

stall *v. i.* To play for time during a **stage wait**.

stalls *n. pl. Brit.* The front rows of **orchestra** seats in a theater auditorium, and the seats themselves.

See also PIT.

266

stand *n.* **1.** A stop on a tour, and the amount of time the road company stays in a particular place; e.g., a **one-night stand**. **2.** The theater where a touring production performs. **3.** A large easel for holding a stiff cardboard theater **poster**, placed at a theater entrance. **4.** A tailor's **dummy**, used in a **costume shop**.

Stand by! "Get ready!" A warning direction or instruction from the stage manager or assistant film or television director to technicians or actors to be prepared on the command "Action" or "Go" to do what comes next; e.g., the instruction to a lighting technician, "Stand by for cue one!"

stand-by *n., adj.* —*n.* **1.** Similar to an understudy, the stand-by is in readiness to go on stage and play a rehearsed role; hence, *standing by*. One of the differences between a stand-by and an understudy is that the stand-by is required to phone the stage manager to find out if he or she has to go on that evening, but is not required to be physically present in the theater (although this is not always the case), whereas the understudy must show up, sign in, and remain in the theater during the entire performance, leaving only during the curtain call. Stand-by status is arranged contractually. —*adj.* **2.** In readiness; describing actors who are standing by; equipment that is available immediately to replace the equipment being used, should it develop technical problems; and props (e.g., **sugar glass**, ready to be used for another take).

stand-in *n.* An actor who resembles a **principal** physically and, as a member of the **second team**, replaces the principal for purposes of setting lights, marks, camera angles, and so forth; hence, *to stand in*.

standing ovation Acclaim and applause at the end of a live performance, accompanied by the audience getting to its feet as a special manifestation of appreciation.

standing room Places at the back of a theater auditorium or, sometimes, at the back of a theater balcony, where spectators, called *standees*, stand to see a performance. Sometimes, when a house is sold out, only standing room places are available: the initials SRO mean *standing room only*.

standing set **1.** In film, a décor that has been constructed on a studio **back lot** and left as a more or less permanent set to be used in any number of films. **2.** In television, a permanent set used for a recurring key place in a series; e.g., the interior of the Miami house in *The Golden Girls*.

stand-up comedy Humorous routines and solo acts performed by an individual comic who tells a series of jokes or does a turn in various venues; e.g., nightclubs, cabarets, comedy clubs, television, or, sometimes, in a Broadway theater; e.g., Jackie Mason's or Dame Edna's Broadway shows. In clubs where they perform, the comics stand and deliver their jokes, often using a **hand mike**. Called *stand-up*, for short.
    See also BORSCHT BELT.

Stanislavskian *adj.* Pertaining to the art, theories, ideas, methods of actor training, and realistic, organic acting that Constantin Stanislavsky advocated.

Stanislavsky, Constantin (1863–1938) (kon' stuhn teen sta' nih slahv' skee) Russian actor, stage director, acting teacher, and the most important theorist of modern acting. Known for the creation of his **system**, which, in its numerous transmogrifications, remains the basis for teaching acting in the United States. Born in Moscow, Constantin Sergeyevich Alexeyev (sehr gay' uh vihch ah lyik syay' yihf) was the scion of one of the richest merchant families in Russia. He was an amateur actor at an early age, and later a professional, changing his name to Stanislavsky. He and Vladimir Nemirovich-Danchenko (1858–1943) (vlah dee' myihr nyehm yee ro:' vihch dahn' chyehn ko), a well known theater critic, teacher, littérateur and playwright, founded the **Moscow Art Theatre** in 1898, in order to fulfill their ideal of what theater and acting could be. The MAT became known for its original productions of Chekhov's major plays. Stanislavsky would spend the rest of his life there, teaching, directing, and acting.

Around 1906, Stanislavsky began to work on and evolve the system, suggesting an exhaustive, all-inclusive method for rehearsal, which he later modified considerably, since it proved impractical. Between 1911 and 1923 he devised a series of exercises for his Moscow Art Theatre Studios—the first of which was founded in 1912—where he had begun to teach the system. "Literally hundreds were tried and either incorporated or discarded," as Mark Gordon tells us in his useful, informative book *The Stanislavsky Technique: Russia—A Workbook for Actors* (Applause, 1987).

Stanislavsky wrote several books about acting. Although largely concerned with actor training in elementary techniques, *An Actor Prepares* (Theatre Arts Books, 1936; 23rd printing 1969)—Stanislavsky's original title actually translates as *An Actor Works on Himself*—covers in semi-novelistic form the necessary terms and topics needed for character creation. His next two books, *Building a Character* (Theatre Arts Books, 1949) and *Creating a Role* (Theatre Arts Books, 1969), detail his system of working methodically on characters. They were actually compiled from his notes; he did not see them published, as he had *My Life in Art* (Foreign Languages Publishing House, n.d.) and *An Actor Prepares*. The main principle they espouse, as does *Stanislavsky on the Art of the Stage* (Hill and Wang, 1961), is to build a character from the inside out.

stanza *n.* **1.** A verse; i.e., a discreet division of a poem, hymn, or song. **2.** *Archaic* An episode of an old-time radio serial drama.

star *n.* A famous performer who is very much in the public eye.

star dressing room The most desirable one, occupied by the leading man or woman; usually nearest the stage for easiest access and sometimes quite spacious.

starlet *n.* A promising novice movie actress who plays leading parts and is perhaps bound for future stardom.

star package A production that has been prepared ahead of time for a name actor who plays the lead, often in a musical comedy, and mostly during the summer. The star travels from one star package theater to another with his or her own costumes, joining a resident company that has rehearsed the project.

star-studded *adj.* Pertains to an event, such as a film premiere or gala opening-night party for a Broadway show, attended by a great many celebrities, especially luminaries from the show business world: *a star-studded evening.*

star system The handling and grooming of principal motion picture performers, esp. promising actors with distinctive good looks, voices, talent, and personalities, made into stars through the use of publicity in the days of the **studio system**, when the studios were run by their founding moguls.

star turn A vaudeville or variety act done by a well known, popular performer.

star vehicle An entertainment project meant to showcase or feature the talents of a name performer.

stasimon (stah' see mon) *n. Hist.* A choral ode sung and danced by the **chorus** at the end of each episode of an ancient Greek **tragedy.**

state theater 1. A government-subsidized playhouse. **2.** The system of government-subsidized playhouses in a particular country.

static camera shot A take in which the camera does not move. Used a great deal in early movie-making, such shots can give the audience the impression they are watching a staged play, rather than a motion picture. Static camera shots are still used for certain effects, such as still establishing shots; e.g., the stifling effect of the desert in David Lean's *Lawrence of Arabia* (1962).

station *n.* **1.** A radio or television **channel. 2.** The building(s) where a radio or television channel's broadcasting equipment and facilities, offices, studios, etc. are located.

Steadicam *n. Trademark.* A **handheld camera** with a balancing, stabilizing device that permits it to remain steady throughout a shoot.

steal a scene 1. To **up-stage** other actors, and so bring oneself to the audience's attention at an inappropriate moment, or in an inappropriate way. **2.** To give such a noticeably good performance in a scene that it eclipses those of other actors.

stellar role A rich, demanding leading part for a star actor.

step *n.* **1.** A dance move. **2.** In music, the interval between two notes. **3.** One of the raised levels in a staircase, at a door sill, etc.

step on a laugh To **kill** a laugh (i.e., not to allow the audience to laugh) inadvertently and ineptly, by coming in too soon with the next line or bit of business before the audience has finished laughing, or, sometimes, even started.

step on a line To come in with one's next words **off cue**; i.e., to cut off another actor's line by speaking too soon, as a result of not really listening. A kind of **anticipation.**

stichomythia (stih' kuh mih' thee uh) *n.* [Greek; fr. *stichomythein*: to speak in alternating lines of dialogue] Rapid-fire exchanges of sharp, pointed dialogue, as in some of Noël Coward's plays (e.g., *Private Lives*), or Tom Stoppard's *Rosencrantz* *and Guildenstern Are Dead*, or in Shakespeare's *Richard III*, act 4, scene 4, in the confrontation between Richard and Queen Elizabeth. Each line of dialogue here is a *hemistich* (heh' mih stihk'), which is half a line that ends in a *caesura* (sih zhoo' ruh; a rhythmic break for sense in the middle of a verse), and continues metrically into the next line of dialogue:

K. RICH.:   Now, by the world—
Q. ELIZ.:   'Tis full of thy foul wrongs.
K. RICH.:   My father's death—
Q. ELIZ.:   Thy life hath that dishonor'd.

See VERSE TECHNIQUE.

still *n.* [Short for *still photograph*] A printed photograph taken from a frame of a motion picture; used for lobby displays in movie theaters or for publicity purposes in print media.

stitcher *n.* The person in a **costume shop** who sews the clothing together and assembles the finished outfits.

stock *n., adj.* —*n.* **1.** Usually, summer theater; short for *summer stock*, although winter stock also exists; productions are seasonal. Actors who regularly do summer stock are called *stock actors*. In **one-week stock** theaters, a resident company is hired for the season, and rehearses a musical comedy or play for a week while performing another in the evening or at matinees. Some summer stock theaters are **star package** houses. And there are festival stock houses that present classic plays with star casts. Contractual salaries and conditions vary tremendously, especially between union and nonunion theaters. **2.** Raw material; e.g., unexposed negative film. —*adj.* **3.** In common use; standard; expected; used repeatedly: *a stock scene; stock film footage*.
   See also COUNCIL OF RESIDENT STOCK THEATERS (CORST); COUNCIL OF STOCK THEATERS (COST) AGREEMENT; MUSICAL STOCK/UNIT ATTRACTION AGREEMENT (MSUA); RESIDENT MUSICAL THEATRE ASSOCIATION (RMTA) AGREEMENT.

stock character An obligatory person in a particular kind of story; e.g., the younger sibling in a teenage romance, the gallant knight and his squire in a medieval tale of chivalry, or the sidekick to the hero of an old-fashioned western.
   See also TYPE; TYPE CASTING.

stock response A mechanical reaction that is predictable, standard, and expected.

stock scenery Standard painted flats, set pieces, and units stored and reused in any number of productions; e.g., in **rotating rep** or **one-week stock**.

stock shot A take using archived **film footage** to show a location, such as the streets of New York or the Houses of Parliament in London.

stock situation An obligatory, standard event or scene in a story; e.g., the clandestine meeting of two lovers whose love for each other has met with opposition.

stooge *n.* The **straight man** in a vaudeville **comedy team**: he often played the role of a put-upon chump, the comic victim of manipulation.

stop and start The usual method of working through material in **rehearsal**, esp. in early read-through and blocking rehearsals, and in later work-throughs. The director will stop the actors to give blocking or a direction, or an actor will stop to make a point or ask a question; then they will proceed, incorporating the new blocking or direction.

stop-motion Syn. with **freeze-frame**.

stop the show To provoke such prolonged laughter or applause (or both) that the performance is temporarily halted.

Stop thinking! The direction to an actor in rehearsal when the actor is too much in his or her head; i.e., is intellectualizing instead of allowing things to happen organically. Also heard as *Stop thinking; start acting!*

See IN YOUR HEAD.

story analyst A person who evaluates and critiques scripts for a film production company. Also called a *reader*. Cf. **story editor**.

storyboard The schematic visual presentation of the plot of a commercial or film, done by a *storyboard artist* as a series of cartoon drawings, much like a comic strip in a newspaper; used as a guide during shooting. It shows camera angles and characters, and usually has dialogue and/or stage directions printed underneath each drawing; dialogue sometimes appears in comic-strip balloons. At **on-camera** commercial auditions, a storyboard is posted near the **sign-in sheet** for actors to look at in conjunction with the **copy** they are supposed to read.

story conference A meeting of screenwriters, the film director, producers, and other personnel to discuss the writing of a script, possible alterations, and other details.

story editor The film studio executive who functions as a **story analyst**, and may rewrite scenarios or presentations to producers.

story theater A form of play devised by the American director Paul Sills in the 1960s that was based on improvisations in rehearsals, which were then **set** so they could be repeated in performance. The plays were based on Grimm's fairy tales, seen as politically relevant because of their timeless psychological and sociocultural themes.

straight makeup Theatrical makeup that brings out an actor's facial features, and prevents stage lights from washing them out. Cf. its opposite, **character makeup**.

straight man The person in a comedy or comedy act who feeds, or sets up the comedian's jokes; the **stooge**.

straight stand A rigid, upright, adjustable pole on a steady base used for holding a microphone; a kind of **mike stand**.

straight theater Spoken plays, as opposed to musical theater; hence, *straight play*.

straight time The standard eight-hour workday.

Strasberg, Lee (1901–1982) American actor and acting teacher; began his career with the **Group Theatre**; head of the **Actors Studio**, where he taught his innovative Method—which has been much misunderstood—based in the Stanislavsky **system**. Strasberg's books *A Dream of Passion* (Penguin Plume Books, 1987) and *Strasberg at the Actors Studio: Tape-Recorded Sessions*, edited by Robert H. Hethmon (Theatre Communications Group; 5th Printing, 2000) show exactly what he taught. His core belief about character interpretation is based on the idea of truthfulness on stage: the actor is him or herself always, and the character can therefore really be none other than the actor who infuses him or herself into the role by means of asking the question, "How would I behave and feel in these circumstances?" as opposed to simply asking, "How does the character behave in these circumstances?" But both questions must be asked. The actor's aim is to be organic, and that implies using the self as the character: "It is I who live through the play, not some preconceived, inorganic conception of the character." At the same time, the actor has to behave as the character. Contrary to popular misconceptions, Strasberg taught that actors must be disciplined and have good vocal and acting technique.
    See also METHOD ACTING; PRIVATE MOMENT; SONG AND DANCE EXERCISE.

straw hat theater Another term for **summer theater**; hence, *straw hat circuit*; *straw hat trail*.

stream of consciousness The term of American psychologist and philosopher William James's (1842–1910) for the constant river of thoughts that arise from the unconscious and fall back into it; some of the thoughts are dwelt on, and some simply pass by unnoticed.
    See also INTERIOR MONOLOGUE.

streaming *n.* The continuous transmission of an audiovisual entertainment over the Internet, so that the viewer can begin watching it even before the complete project has been transmitted. Sometimes this entertainment can be downloaded permanently, as a **download to own**; sometimes it is in the form of a **download to rent**.

street theater Performances done outdoors for a public that may gather and disperse as the play or presentation goes on; usually political in nature. Often, the presentations are improvisational, although they may be at least partially scripted, or based on a scenario. Sometimes called *gorilla theater*, perhaps a misnomer or **malapropism** for guerilla.

Stretch it out! A **hand cue**, given to a television or radio performer during a broadcast. It consists of miming with both hands, drawn slowly apart as if stretching a rubber band or piece of gum, thumbs and forefingers out, other fingers folded down.

strike *n., v.* —*n.* **1.** Refusal to work until working conditions and/or salaries are improved. **2.** The removal of objects, furniture, etc., not needed in the next scene during a performance. **3.** The dismantling of a set, lights, or other equipment once their use is no longer required; e.g., at the end of a **one-week stock** production. —*v. t.* **4.** To take action on job issues by refusing to work until they are settled. **5.** To remove everything from a set not needed for the next scene in a performance, or for a film take. **6.** To take apart a set. At the end of a run, which can be as short as a week in one-week summer **stock**, the set is struck and disposed of, on *strike night*; a *strike party* may follow.

Strindbergian *n., adj.* —*n.* **1.** An admirer of the works of the "Shakespeare of Sweden," playwright August Strindberg, or an adherent of his pessimistic philosophy. **2.** A scholar devoted to studying Strindberg's life and works. —*adj.* **3.** Pertaining to the pessimistic, misogynistic view of life exemplified in some of Strindberg's works.

strip lighting A row of attached lights, each in its own individual metal housing; used in theater and sports stadiums.

striptease artist A performer who slowly and provocatively removes articles of clothing until she or he is naked; e.g., a young lady in a **burlesque** show; an **ecdysiast.**

strobe *n., adj.* —*n.* **1.** [Short for *stroboscope*; *strobe light*] A blinking, pulsating lamp that flashes on and off very quickly on a set timer. —*adj.* **2.** Pertains to such a light: *a strobe effect*. The strobe effect creates a sense of the discontinuity of an object or person, who appears to be moving jerkily from place to place, or staying jerkily in one place. Strobe effects are used in horror films or dream sequences, as well as in discotheques and in some Broadway musicals and plays.

strolling player *Archaic* An itinerant actor. In the 18th and 19th centuries, such actors wandered the countryside in groups, presenting plays in various venues, from country fairs to small town squares. Called *strollers*, in Elizabethan days.

stub *n.* [Short for *ticket stub*] The small part of a ticket torn off and kept for accounting purposes by the **ticket taker** at the entrance to a performance.

student rush The custom at some theaters and opera houses of reserving discounted tickets that are sold to young people and others who line up outside the theater a half hour or so before **curtain time.**

studio *n.* **1.** A place for learning and practicing the elements of one's art; e.g., the **Actors Studio.** Hence, *acting studio*: a small-scale establishment or school where the art and craft of acting are taught; e.g., the HB Studio. **2.** A large building where a film, television program, or commercial is made. Sets can be constructed inside these vast halls, and there are often dressing rooms and other facilities either in the studio building, or, more often, in adjacent buildings. **3.** A large room where a television program is taped or broadcast; e.g., a **game show** or **talk show**; a *television newsroom*; or where a soap opera set is located: *television studio*. **4.** A room that is used for teaching acting, for rehearsing a play, or for presenting a live performance; or a complex containing such rooms. In New York City, for example, there are a number of rehearsal studios, which have separate rooms (studios) that can be rented for such purposes: *a rehearsal studio complex*. **5.** A film production company; e.g., Warner Brothers, Paramount, or MGM, as in the adjectival phrases **studio system** or *studio chief*: the head of one of the major studios.

studio audience The spectators at the taping of a television talk show, sitcom, comedy show, or other program; or at a live radio broadcast, in the days of radio drama, quiz shows, and comedy in the early part of the 20th c.

studio complex A movie production company's lot, with all the buildings that serve various purposes on it, including production offices, storage depots, and soundstages.

studio floor manager A television studio stage manager; the liaison between the **floor** and the **control room**.

studio set Film or television décor on a soundstage or **back lot**.

studio system *Hist.* A method of autocratic, dictatorial rule of motion picture companies with actors under contract to them, run by founding moguls. It lasted roughly from 1925 to 1960, and gave way eventually to the freer system of independent productions that put actors under contract for a particular project, done under the auspices of the studio. After the demise of the studio system, actors were all **freelance**, with talent agents representing them. The tradeoff was considered worth it by many, if not most actors, but others regretted the old studio system that had kept them under general contract. Even Bette Davis, who notoriously decried it and had her problems with the studio bosses, ultimately came to think it was better for most actors than the newer freelance system. The producers of the studio system provided classes and training for actors, dancers, and singers, aside from making over their images and, often, changing their names. And, most importantly, they gave a **stable** of character and other actors steady work, putting them under contracts that could last for a year or more, and were renewable, often on terms more advantageous to the studio than the actors. Actors could be assigned roles they did not really want to do, for instance, or be loaned to other studios without their being able to do much about it, unless they wanted to be in breach of contract.
See also STAR SYSTEM; THREE-PICTURE DEAL.

studio tank A large, artificial, enclosed pool filled with water and placed on a soundstage for filming various kinds of sequences.
See also TANK SHOT.

studio theater An establishment, such as the **Actors Studio**, where actors, directors, playwrights, designers, and other theater personnel are trained, and where they present productions. Also called a *laboratory theater*.

studio zone The delimited area around a building or complex where SAG shooting takes place; within this "local studio zone," negotiated by each branch of the union, the management is not obliged to pay transportation costs to get the actors to the set, as it is outside the zone. In New York, for instance, the zone is an eight-mile radius from Columbus Circle to whatever studio or set (which may be on location), is being used.

stunt *n.* Special business that requires great physical skill and dexterity; esp. used in film and television. Stunts, which are often very dangerous, include car chases, falls from great heights, burn gags (also called fire gags), and choreographed combat. They are sometimes done by the actor playing the character, but more often by a stunt double.

stunt casting The practice, not unheard of in **Hollywood** or on **Broadway**, of hiring a star film or television actor to do a part for which he or she is not necessarily ideally suited, in order to garner maximum publicity and attract customers.

stunt director The person who coordinates and arranges stunts. Also called a *stunt coordinator*.

stunt double A stuntperson who resembles another actor physically, and replaces that actor in the filming of stunts.

Stuntmen's Association of Motion Pictures A Hollywood-based organization that represents male stunt performers.

stuntperson *n.* A specially trained, highly skilled, adept actor who performs stunts in films, television programs, commercials, outdoor shows and, sometimes, in the theater.

Stuntwomen's Association of Motion Pictures A Hollywood-based organization that represents female stunt performers.

Sturm und Drang (shtoorm' *oo*nt drahng') [German: storm and drive, or stress] German romantic melodrama of the 1760s to the early 19th c., often featuring a noble, soul-searching hero fighting against all the odds nature and nurture can provide; e.g., the plays of Friedrich Schiller (1759–1805), such as *Don Carlos* (1787).

style *n.* In acting, a distinctive, characteristic way or mode of behaving or comporting oneself in accordance with the requirements of a particular play, such as a farce, as opposed to a drama; or a realistic modern prose play as opposed to an Elizabethan verse tragedy: *acting style*. Also, the characteristic way of behaving in a particular historical epoch: *period style*, which includes how the actor wears costumes, makeup, and such special hairpieces as wigs; how one moves and gestures, bows, curtsies, or otherwise shows deference; uses accessories such as a fan, handkerchief, or sword; and behaves to those of different rank and station. Acting and period styles are inextricably connected. Style has to evolve organically from the rest of the work on character, and to be personalized and internalized. For more on the subject, see my book *Using the Stanislavsky System: A Practical Guide to Character Creation and Period Styles* (Limelight, 2008).

stylist *n.* The person on a film, commercial, or television set in charge of wardrobe selection and purchasing or renting clothing, as opposed to a costume designer, who draws costume designs and selects materials that are then tailored and sewn. The stylist selects, puts together, and fits the actor into his or her clothing, with the ultimate approval of the director. Usually, the price tags are left on purchased clothing until it is used, with the understanding that clothing not used may be returned to the merchant for a full refund. Used clothing may sometimes be purchased by the actor, by special agreement with the production company.
  See also COSTUME DESIGNER; COSTUME FITTING; SELECTIONS.

subjective camera angle A shot taken from the point of view of a particular character.

submission *n.* **1.** The action taken by the agent of an actor, model, or other performer of communicating a performer's name, or a list of names, to casting personnel, in order to help secure employment for clients. **2.** The actors' names sent to casting people.

submit *v. t.* To communicate a list of performers' names to casting personnel, directors, or others in a position to offer employment.

subplot *n.* A secondary story that may mirror or contrast with the main story and that provides complications and interest to what might otherwise be an unrelenting, unrelieved single plot.

subscription *n.* **1.** Season tickets to a series of plays, operas, or other musical or theatrical events. Many theaters, opera houses, and concert halls rely on the money they make from subscriptions, and may offer discounts and other perks as inducements to subscribe. **2.** A monthly fee paid to receive the broadcasts of premium channels on **cable television**. **3.** A yearly fee paid to receive magazines, newspapers, and other periodicals.

substitution *n.* The actor's conscious replacement of the fictitious objects, emotions, events, people, relationships, or places with objects from the actor's private life. Substitution is one of the most important tools used to bring reality to character portrayal. In performance, the actor must relate directly to the other actor: substitution is therefore a rehearsal (rather than a performance) tool, and should be forgotten by the time the actor gets to the performance stage.
  See also ACTOR'S SECRET; AFFECTIVE MEMORY; ENDOWMENT; SENSORY PROCESS.

subtext *n.* The underlying meaning of the lines in a script; i.e., the **intention** of the character, conditioning the way in which a line is said or an action carried out. As Stanislavsky succinctly stated, the subtext is what causes us to say the words.

subtitles *n. pl.* **1.** Superimposed on-screen captions of translations of spoken dialogue in a foreign film. **2.** Superimposed on-screen captions of dialogue in the same language as the spoken dialogue, for the benefit of the hearing-impaired.

subway circuit New York City theater, especially theater that is not in the **Broadway** district.

succès d'estime (sük seh: deh steem') [French: lit. success from esteem; i.e., success because of esteem for a person] A play that is a polite critical success, but not a commercial one; born of consideration for the past achievements of a playwright, rather than of respect and admiration for the play being reviewed.

succès de scandale (sük seh:' duh skaw*n* dahl') [French: lit. success from scandal; i.e., success by reason of being scandalous] A play that is a popular success because of some juicy gossip connected with one or more of its stars, or because it has nudity, or outspoken sexual or politically outrageous scenes or dialogue.

sugar glass Clear or tinted, hardened sugar and water syrup product, used to make breakaway glass; e.g., in sheets used in windows shattered during action takes.

summer blockbuster. See BLOCKBUSTER.

summer stock 1. Plays presented at theaters that are open for the season from June to early September. **2.** Seasonal theaters that operate under **Equity** stock contracts.

summer theater 1. A playhouse that operates from around June to early September; often the venue of a summer festival. **2.** Collectively, the plays and musicals performed at summer playhouses.

superimposition *n.* In a motion picture, the printing of one image over another, so that both appear on screen at the same time; a technique used to create ghosts and also for the playing of dual roles, such as those of twins, or the two cousins in *The Prisoner of Zenda* (1937; 1952). The **bluescreen process** allows the superimposition through **compositing** of actors against a background that will be supplied after scenes are shot. Superimposition is used all the time for subtitles and for the opening credits of films and television programs.

supernumerary (soo' puhr nyoo' muh reh:' ree) *n.* Extra; background player. Called a *super*, for short.

superobjective *n.* **1.** The main thrust or aim of the play as a whole (i.e., where the arc of the story leads); the main theme and subject of a play or film; its **spine**. **2.** A character's main, overall **objective** or life drive.
    See also THROUGHLINE.

superstar *n.* A glamorous, wealthy name actor so well known as to be instantly recognizable, more so than a simple **star**, but less rich and powerful than a **megastar**.

superstition *n.* An irrational belief, one not founded in reason or requiring any kind of proof of its veracity, in omens and portents of future ill or good luck, and in the efficacy of some form of "magical" behavior to ward off ill luck. In *Julius Caesar* (and in many other Shakespearean plays), superstition plays a major role, and nearly all the characters pay attention to prophecies. Caesar himself claims to

277

discount such things as augury or the prophecy of the Soothsayer to "beware the Ides of March," but he is assassinated. And don't forget Calpurnia's prophetic dream! There are many theatrical superstitions, among them the phobia about not quoting from *Macbeth* in the precincts of a theater, or elsewhere. It is always called "the Scottish play" and is considered extremely unlucky. If anyone in the dressing room or any other part of a theater accidentally quotes from the play, he or she must go through a kind of magic ceremony in order to ward off ill luck. One version: leave the dressing room, turn around three times, and ask permission to reenter. Among the many theatrical superstitions is the idea that whistling backstage brings bad luck. In the 19th c., when British sailors were often hired as stagehands—hence, such nautical terminology as **deck** and **on deck**—and the signal for lowering flats from the flies was a whistle, this might have made some sense, since whistling could result in being hit on the head by a sandbag. But the superstition is actually much older, and whistling was considered a way of summoning the Devil.

    See also BREAK A LEG!

supertitles *n. pl.* Screened overhead projections, seen just above the proscenium arch, of written translations of lyrics or dialogue performed in a foreign language; or transcriptions of lyrics or dialogue in the language used for performance; esp. used in opera houses.

supporting cast The actors in any parts other than the leading roles; they "support" the leading players in telling the story. Also called *supporting players*; *supporting actors*.

suppression *n.* A defense mechanism that consists of the conscious damping down of emotions, feelings, and impulses the mind considers harmful, but not threatening enough to repress into the **unconscious**. Suppressed emotions, which add dimension to a character, have an important part in playing actions, and in **playing opposites**.

surround *n.* A **cyclorama** or other extensive backcloth that conceals the back wall of a stage in a theater.

suspense *n.* Psychological uncertainty as to what will happen next, accompanied by a sense of excitement and the desire to know what will happen. The creation of suspense is part of the writer's art, to begin with; and in a film or play, depends upon the ability of all the people bringing a story to life.

suspension of disbelief The temporary pretense that something artificial is real: characters are real people who are doing real things; and events are taking place and unfolding spontaneously. The audience and the actors, each in a different way, are asked to participate in this fiction, without which they might as well all stay home.

sustain *v. t.* **1.** To keep something going. **2.** To remain **in character** throughout an entire performance, living each moment with the requisite constant level of energy: *to sustain a character*; *to sustain a performance*; *to sustain a moment*.

Suzuki, Tadashi (tah dah' shee soo zoo' kee) Influential Japanese theorist and theater director who bases his ideas on ancient Greek theater, as well as on traditional Japanese **noh** and **kabuki**, with their stress on physical control and stylization. He works not only in Toga, Toyama, Japan, but also in Saratoga Springs, NY, where he co-founded an acting and training company. He has written twelve books, including *The Way of Acting* (Theatre Communications Group, 1986), probably his most popular book in English. For Suzuki, the physical life of the character is its most important manifestation, and to that end his methods emphasize finding the correct **action** to play, correctly carried out. The whole body must speak, and must be involved in the character, even if nothing is being said. The Suzuki method of actor training concentrates on each important individual part of the body: feet, tongue, eyes, and so forth, so that each is alive and involved. Acting requires a great deal of natural animal energy. The contemporary theater is replete with such non-animal energy as electricity, used in lighting and special effects, and this vitiates the power of the actor to communicate. Suzuki tells us that in his training he emphasizes first and foremost the use of the feet, "because I believe the consciousness of the body's communication with the ground leads to a great awareness of all the physical junctions of the body."

swallow-take *n.* A comedic technique of audibly gulping while swallowing saliva, often accompanied by bulging eyes and a gesture of loosening a shirt collar, followed by dropped jaws, as a reaction of fright or surprise; effective in film, e.g., when the camera can focus on the victim's prominent Adam's apple going up and down.

swashbuckler *n.* A film genre that features a daring, show-off, sometimes rather naughty albeit sympathetic swordsman hero who casually romances women with supreme self-confidence and fights duels, esp. in medieval, Renaissance, or 17th- and 18th-c. romances; e.g., in pirate films, where the hero is usually a loveable scapegrace. Errol Flynn, Tyrone Power, and Douglas Fairbanks Sr. and Jr. are among those who played some of the heroes in such films. The hero himself is also called a swashbuckler.

swan song An actor's final performance. Chekhov's one-act play *Swan Song* takes place after a final **benefit** performance for a retiring actor, who has fallen asleep in his dressing room and been abandoned by everyone, except the impoverished old **prompter** who sleeps in the theater and is awakened by the actor coming onto the stage.

sweat out a mike To perspire so that the perspiration gets onto or into a **body mike**, rendering it inoperable.

swing *n.* **1.** A member of a musical comedy chorus who covers the dance tracks of different members, and substitutes for any of them if someone is absent, often earning extra pay for each track. **2.** A kind of jazz with a smoothly rhythmic beat that admits of dancing, very popular in dance halls during the 1930s.

sword-and-sandal epic A motion picture set in the ancient world of Egypt, Greece, or Rome. Many a **religious film** is also a sword and sandal epic.

symbolism *n*. A 19th-c. European movement in the arts that used things, objects, people, animals, etc. to stand for certain aspects or qualities of life: a clock for the passage of time; a tree for all of stolid, unresponsive nature. But the symbolists went beyond this simple reductionist idea, and refined it into a system or way of making art using symbols. The movement was a forerunner of the contemporary academic study called *semiotics*, whose principal theory is that everything is a sign or symbol for something else.
　　See also MEYERHOLD, VSEVELOD.

synchronization *n*. The coordination of voice and lip movement in a film, so that the sound is synchronous with the perceived movement. Called *sync*, for short.
　　See also ADR; DUB; LIP SYNC; LOOP; OUT OF SYNC.

syndication *n*. The practice of selling pre-recorded television shows for broadcast in any number of markets throughout the United States, often first-run series that are then seen as reruns on local stations. Actors are paid **residuals** for these syndicated showings.
　　See also BICYCLE.

synecdoche (sih nehk' duh kee) *n*. The use of one word substituting a whole for a part, or a part for a whole; e.g., Hollywood, for the film industry; the theater, for the entire industry and everything connected with it. Or to substitute the specific to mean the general, and vice versa; e.g., tragedian, for actor; theater, for auditorium. Cf. **metonymy**, with which synecdoche is often confused.

synopsis *n*. A plot summary; used in printed programs of plays and operas, and essential in presenting a project to a film production company.

synthesis *n*. A principle advocated by various theoreticians, such as Edward Gordon Craig (1872–1966)—the designer of Stanislavsky's experimental production of *Hamlet*—that all the elements in a production should be in complete harmony and function together.

system, the Stanislavsky's way of preparing a part, his methods of script and character analysis, and his way of teaching acting. The deterministic theory underlying the Stanislavsky system is that every action the character takes has an emotionally based psychological reason. The system's basic **technique** is to break down a play and role into their elements, followed by the process of putting the elements back together. One of the system's basic premises is that an actor can only carry such analysis so far on his or her own: the actor must discover the true nature of the **subtext** and intentions, and what he or she has to do, in the course of rehearsing with other actors and entering imaginatively into the given circumstances.
　　See METHOD OF PHYSICAL ACTIONS; SCRIPT ANALYSIS; STANISLAVSKY, CONSTANTIN.

T

tab *v. t. Slang* To pull a theater curtain.

tableau *n.* [Fr. French; short for *tableau vivant* (ta blo:' vee vo:*n*'): living picture] A **stage picture** formed by actors freezing in poses or attitudes, singly and in groups; often utilized in 19th- and early 20th-c. staging, esp. at the beginning or end of a scene or act.

table work Discussion of a project during sit-down **read-through** rehearsals, including **stop and start** reading of the text, some character analysis, and details about **given circumstances**; e.g., historical background information for a period piece.

tabs *n. pl.* [Short for *tableau curtains*] **1.** Any **masking** curtains. The proscenium arch curtain is sometimes called a *house tab.* **2.** *Travelers*: curtains drawn across the stage from one side to the other.

tag line 1. The final announcement about the product in a radio or television commercial. Called a *tag*, for short. **2.** The final line of a stage performance. **3.** A **catchphrase**, or catchword.

tail-away shot A take in which actors or an object, such as a vehicle, move directly away from the camera in a straight line.

tail slate Syn. with **end slate**.

take *n., v. —n.* **1.** In acting, a sudden, surprised serious or comedic reaction resulting in a fixed stare, involving recognition of someone, some thing, or some circumstance; hence, *to do a take*. See also DOUBLE TAKE; SPIT-TAKE; SWALLOW-TAKE; TRIPLE TAKE. **2.** In film or television, each continuous filming or taping of a scene or part of a scene, from the moment the camera begins photographing it to the moment it stops. **3.** In audio recording, each continuous recording of someone's voice from start to finish. **4.** Box office receipts. Also called *takings*. *—v. t.* **5.** To film a scene or part of a scene: *Let's take the first three lines of that speech, and that will be all for this take.* **6.** To record someone speaking into a microphone, from the moment the person begins until the moment the person stops, or is stopped. **7.** To perform: *Let's **take it from the top!*** **8.** To assume a prominent position: *take stage*; i.e., to make oneself the center of attention during a performance.

take direction To accept and carry out instructions given by a director to an actor regarding the playing of a character, or the acting of a scene or moment; one of the skills an actor must learn. When a director demonstrates a move or an action, the actor must stand **downstage** of the director and observe the demonstration from the same position the audience would be in. The actor must also be skilled enough to make an instantaneous **adjustment** when the director instructs the actor to change a **motivation** or an **action** or the nature of an emotional **moment**,

281

or even gives the actor a particular **line reading**: such adjustments call for immediate **justification** by the actor. The initial stages of blocking also call for justification: if an actor is told to cross to a certain place on stage, the move must appear natural and logical. Although the actor may question or continue to disagree with a director's instruction, the actor must ultimately do as the director wishes.

Take five! "Begin your five-minute **break**!" Also, "Take ten," "fifteen," etc. This is an official notification from the stage manager that a break is beginning.

take in Syn. with **load in**; hence, *take-in*: the act and process of bringing scenery and equipment into a theater, and the period of time during which this is done.

Take it away! 1. "It's your turn, partner!"; e.g., in a vaudeville dance act, where the dancers take turns doing solos, as well as dancing together. **2.** "Open the curtain!" A stage manager's direction to the stagehand running the curtain.

take it down 1. To lower the intensity or level of light, or of a particular lighting instrument: *take it down to five*, six, etc. **2.** To lower the intensity or level of sound.

Take it from the top! "Let's do the line, speech, scene, or the part of the scene we were working on again from the beginning!" This direction is heard often in the theater during rehearsals; also heard: "Take it back!" or "Take it back to ___!"

take it in 1. To lower a fly into position on the stage; the instruction is given to the flyman: *Take it in!* Cf. **Fly coming in! 2.** To make part of a costume smaller: *take it in at the waist*.

take it off 1. To respond to what the acting partner is doing (i.e., being alive in the scene) and following the principle **listen and respond**, as opposed to acting with predetermined reactions: *to take it off the other actor*. **2.** To get and respond to a **cue** from a particular source: *Take it off the lights*.

take it out To raise a fly to the fly gallery from its position on the stage; the instruction is given to the flyman: *Take it out!*

take it up 1. To raise the intensity or level of light, or of a particular lighting instrument: *take it up to five*, six, etc. **2.** To raise the intensity or level of sound.

take-off *n.* A **parody**, imitation, or impression of a work or person.

take out Syn. with **load out**; hence *take-out*: the removal of scenery and equipment from a theater (e.g., on a tour) and the time period during which this is done.

talent *n.* **1.** That indefinable quality that, in actors, is the sensitive, imaginative ability to fuse their own minds and bodies with the character they are bringing to life and to perform that character. **2.** The media industry term for performer(s): *Is the talent ready to shoot?*

talent payment company An independent show business accounting and payroll company to which jobs are farmed out by production companies. **Syn.** *paymaster*.

talent representative Performer's **agent**. Also called a *talent agent*.

talent scout 1. Someone working for a performing artists' agency, production company, or sports organization whose job is to seek out and recruit exceptional performers or athletes to represent. **2.** A person who looked for and recruited exceptional performers and future stars for one of the major studios in the days of the **studio system**.

talkies *n. pl. Archaic Slang* Movies that talked, after decades of silence; talking pictures; sound films.

talking heads Close-up faces viewed on a screen that speak and do nothing else; e.g., in some soap opera scenes or newscasts.

talk show A radio or television interview program emceed by a *talk-show host*, who converses with invited guests. The interviews on television talk shows are often interspersed with variety entertainment; e.g., acts by stand-up comedians, musical groups or solo performers. When a film is released, its stars will publicize it on a talk show; they may appear on several such shows on late-night television: *the talk-show circuit*. Some talk shows are devoted exclusively to a particular area of interest; e.g., books, politics, or theater. Most TV talk shows are **prerecorded**; i.e., recorded in front of a studio audience earlier on the day of their broadcast.

tank shot A take of a scene in a water-filled studio pool, called a **studio tank**. This may involve actors, or scenes of ships in a storm (the ships being models that appear to be real when the tank shot is edited into the film). An actor required to do a tank shot may be wrapped in a towel and given brandy to drink between takes: one can get cold and shivery after only a few minutes of doing such a scene.

Tannoy *n., pl.* Tannoys *Trademark* Small professional loudspeakers with adjustable levels used in backstage areas, greenrooms, and dressing rooms to monitor a performance; e.g. by actors listening to it. Used generically for any such loudspeaker.

tap *n., v. —n.* **1.** [Short for *tap dance*] A jazzy style of dancing in shoes with metal attachments to heel and toe that make a rhythmic clickety-click sound. Cf. its opposite, **soft shoe**. —*v. i.* **2.** To tap dance in a variety show, musical comedy, etc.

tape *n., v. —n.* **1.** A specially coated plastic ribbon used as a preservative medium for recording audio or video projects: *audiotape; recording tape; videotape.* **2.** A plastic, vinyl, or paper ribbon of varying width and heaviness coated with adhesive on one side; e.g., **duct tape; spike tape**. —*v. t.* **3.** To record an audio or audiovisual project or any portion thereof on videotape or audiotape; e.g. a **soap opera**, a live **concert**. **4.** To attach or **spike** something using adhesive ribbon.

tape around To put down a scene or part of a project on videotape in the absence of one or more performers, doing scenes in which they are not involved.

tape the floor; tape the stage To prepare a studio or stage for rehearsal by laying strips of colored adhesive vinyl ribbon, called **spike tape**, out on the floor to delineate areas of the set, placement of furniture, and so forth. The job of the stage managerial staff.

taping *n.* **1.** The **session** during which a program is done for a television video-camera using recording tape; or a sound project recorded on audiotape. **2.** The act of recording a project or any part thereof on videotape or audiotape.

task *n.* **Objective**; one of several translations of the **Stanislavskian** term **zadacha**.

team *n.* **1.** Two or more performers who do an act together. **2.** The cast of an entertainment project. **3.** All the personnel involved in putting together and performing a project.

teamwork *n.* **Ensemble** playing; a very important aspect of performing in the theater.

tearjerker *n.* A film, television program, or play designed to elicit weeping from the audience.

teaser *n.* **1.** The brief sequence, usually lasting a minute or two, that opens a television show just before the first commercials. **2.** An advertisement for a play or film that has a tantalizing aspect to it: *Don't tell anyone who did it!* **3.** The long banner curtain just inside the top of the proscenium arch, masking the flies; it is the top half of the framing curtains, the two sides being the tormentors. **4.** *Hist.* Business in a 19th-c. melodrama meant to titillate and tantalize the audience; e.g., an **act curtain** in which the villain has the heroine cornered.

techie *n.* *Slang* Any worker on the technical staff or crew of an entertainment project.

technical adviser An expert in a particular field who is employed as a consultant on a film; e.g., Lucie Aubrac (1912–2007), the technical adviser for the film based on episodes in her life story, *Lucie Aubrac* (1997). Also called *production adviser*; *production consultant*; *special consultant*; *technical consultant*.

technical approach to character creation Working on a role's **plastic** before working on internal motivations; an approach that deals first with **external technique**.

technical coordinator The director's assistant on a taping or shooting using more than one camera and done before a live studio audience. The TC supervises the camera movements and checks to make sure that everything is being taken correctly. Called a *TC*, for short.

technical director The person in charge of a theater's lighting and sound equipment and of stage machinery, and the personnel who maintain and run it; usually a staff position in LORT theaters and some major summer theaters. The TD oversees the construction of scenery, the hanging of lights, the installation of sound equipment (including the theater's PA and monitoring systems), and the preparation of costumes. Called a *TD*, for short.

284

technical rehearsal One in which the lighting, sound, effects, and scenic aspects of a production are worked with and adjusted. Usually called a *tech*, for short. Techs are often conducted as **cue-to-cue** rehearsals, meaning that after a lighting, sound, or effects cue, the dialogue is largely skipped to get to the next one. Each cue may also be extensively worked on in a **dry tech**. A *tech-dress rehearsal* is a run-through, **stop and start** technical rehearsal in which the actors wear their costumes; one or more tech-dresses are held before a full dress.

technician *n.* Anyone working in the entertainment industry on a crew as a stage-hand, electrician, lighting person, sound person, carpenter, scene painter, costume maker, cameraperson, or in any other related job.

Technicolor *n., adj. Trademark —n.* **1.** A three-color dye transfer system used for printing movies in color: *a film in Technicolor. —adj.* **2.** Pertaining to a film made using this system: *a Technicolor film.* **3.** Used generically to mean any **color film**.

technique *n.* **1.** A general system, method, or way of working in a particular field: **acting technique**; **stage technique**. **2.** The ability to employ the special skills required in a particular field of endeavor: *That ballet dancer has good technique.* **3.** A particular kind of skill, such as the technique of comic **timing**, or of bel canto singing. **4.** A specific technical skill, such as **holding for a laugh**. **5.** A particular procedure; e.g., the **three-camera technique**, used in shooting films and esp. television programs.

telecast *n.* A television broadcast.

teledrama *n.* A play or film written for television. Also called a *teleplay*; *telefilm*.

telegraph *v. t.* To convey information to the audience before it should be conveyed; e.g., by anticipating a reaction.

telephoto lens One that can focus on far-away objects and bring them into perspective as if they were close.

TelePrompTer *n. Trademark* A **videoprompter** that scrolls scripts during a television broadcast, so that the announcer or performer can read his or her lines. Often used generically to mean any videoprompter.

telescope *v. t.* To speed up the action of a scene or play.

telethon *n.* A television marathon program presenting stars, variety acts, musical acts, etc. in aid of a charity. Viewers may call in to make contributions.

televangelist *n.* A preacher who appears on television.

televise *v. t.* To broadcast a show or film on television: *The TCM (Turner Classic Movies) channel televises many old films.*

television *n.* [*TV*, for short] **1.** [Short for *television set*] A monitor-receiver set for broadcasts of audiovisual programs. **2.** The programs that can be viewed on a monitor's **screen**. **3.** A **synecdoche** for the audiovisual broadcasting industry.

285

television commercial foreign-use fee. See FOREIGN DISTRIBUTION.

television industry The business of making programs and commercials for audiovisual broadcasts and of broadcasting daytime drama, nighttime drama, sitcoms, films, news, sports events, etc., involving personnel in engineering and other technical jobs, production, performing, advertising, distribution, and sales.

television ratings Categories of audience suitability for television programs; similar to film ratings, and serving the same censorial purpose: who may appropriately see what? The ratings are: TV-G (suitable for everyone; for general consumption), TV-MA (for mature audiences only), TV-PG (suitable for general viewing by everyone, with parental guidance suggested), TV-Y (suitable for young children), TV-Y7 (children's program appropriate for age seven and older), and TV-14 (not appropriate for children under fourteen years of age, because of sexual content or bad language, drug use, and the like).

temp *n., v., adj. Slang* —*n.* **1.** A person who has been hired on a short-term basis to do office or other work. Many actors are forced by economic necessity to have such a **bread-and-butter job**. —*v. i.* **2.** To work at such a job. —*adj.* **3.** Short for temporary: *a temp job*.

tempo *n.* **1.** The **pace** at which a scene is played. Tempo includes rhythm: the rhythm of the scene as a whole, and of each character in it. Even if one character's rhythm is slow and the other's fast, the rhythm of the scene as a whole may be either. It is up to the director to determine tempo, if necessary. In the old days, there were directors who used a drum to beat time during early rehearsals of a scene, once it was **on its feet**. **2.** The pace of a piece of music; set and indicated by a conductor in rehearsal and performance.

ten out of twelve The number of hours actors may rehearse in the last period of technical and dress rehearsals, contractually arranged between **Equity** and theater management organizations. Actors may rehearse ten hours out of a twelve-hour workday during this period, perhaps for several days in a row, and any overtime must be paid and proper breaks taken, or penalties will be due. Ten-out-of-twelve days, as they are called, are grueling and taxing for everybody involved.

tentpole *n. Slang* A motion picture that is expected to or does actually make a great deal of money, so that it is an economic mainstay for its producers; hence, *tentpole season*: summer, when summer blockbusters are released.

text *n.* **1.** The complete written script of a play, film, or television program. **2.** The words of a song. **3.** The words of a written work.

tetralogy *n.* A rarely used word for a series of four literary or musical works, plays or films that tell related stories; e.g., Richard Wagner's *Ring* cycle.

text analysis Syn. with **script analysis**.

theater *n.* **1.** A building housing a stage, a backstage area with dressing rooms, scenery and costume storage, etc., and an auditorium where an audience can sit and see a live show. **2.** Any public **performance space** or building for the presentation of live or recorded entertainments; e.g., a movie theater, an open-air amphitheater. **3.** A **metonymy** for the acting profession: *He went into the theater at an early age.* **4.** The collectivity of a playwright's works: *the theater of George Bernard Shaw.* **5.** The business of writing, directing, producing, designing, presenting, and performing plays: *the theater business.*

Theater Communications Group (TCG) An organization based in New York City whose purpose is to promote professional theater. It publishes a monthly magazine and sponsors scholarship and other programs.

theater festival A gala, celebratory event taking place periodically and seasonally, often during the summer, at a particular venue where plays and/or musicals are performed. Among the well known festivals are the Edinburgh Festival in Scotland, which presents a great variety of works; the New York Shakespeare Festival, which presents plays at the Delacorte Theater in Central Park; and the Ontario Shakespeare Festival in Canada.

theater games Exercises and improvisations used in actor training; e.g., the *trust exercise*: an actor stands with his back to another actor and then falls back, and trusts that the second actor will catch him or her. Another game: actors run around in a group, and the instructor yells "**Freeze!**" The actors hold their positions, and analyze how they feel.

theater in the round A flat, open acting area that is at the bottom of tiers of seats surrounding it on three or four sides: *three-quarters round.* Aisles between groups of tiers may allow for actors' entrances and exits. The **acting area** may be delimited by light, or the entire area may be used. When a performance takes place **in the round**, a special technique of delivering lines is required: the actors must make it a habit to turn about slightly, making sure all sides of the audience hear them; but this technique must in no way be intrusive, or destroy whatever illusion is being created.

theater of the absurd An artistic movement in playwrighting lasting from the late 1940s through the 1960s that took as its starting point the nihilistic and existentialist ideas that life is basically meaningless and impossible to understand: life has only the meaning we choose to give it. In other words, taken by itself, life is an absurdity. Its seminal authors were Samuel Beckett and Ionesco, and its present practitioners include Edward Albee and Tom Stoppard.

theater of cruelty Antonin Artaud's (1896–1948) (aw*n* to na*n*' ahr to:') term for the deliberate shattering of the illusions of our present existence so as to awaken the spectator to the realities of life during a theatrical performance: this awakening could be cruel, but without it, for Artaud, there was no meaningful theater. A writer and film scenarist, as well as an actor and director, Artaud published his most famous book, *The Theatre and Its Double*, in 1938; he attacked convention and stressed the sensuous, direct experience of both the actor and the audience as being of primary importance.

theater of fact Semi-documentary plays based on actual documentation and other evidence, arranged for dramatic effect; e.g., Jessica Blank and Erik Jensen's play *The Exonerated* (2002), about stories of real people released from death row once their innocence was proved.

theater of ideas Plays containing intellectual arguments and debates; e.g., the plays of George Bernard Shaw and Henrik Ibsen. Ideas may not be directly stated, but are always implied. Shaw's characters indulge in intellectual arguments, but in Ibsen, the social or sociological context is the background for the conflict. Also called *thesis plays*, esp. when a particular point of view is advocated.

theater of sources Jerzy Grotowski's term for the deep, unconscious origin of personal healing and well-being, which the actor must use in the creative **process** in order to create authentic theater that will move the spectators.

theater party 1. A group of audience members who have purchased a block of tickets, and attend a play together. **2.** A **benefit** evening in the theater.

theater schools Educational establishments where actors, directors, designers, and other theater personnel receive an education and basic training in stagecraft and the arts of the drama. Also called *acting schools*; *drama schools*.

There are a number of very well known establishments in both Great Britain and the United States, and acting students may also study with noted teachers (such as Alice Spivak in New York City; she began her teaching career at the HB Studio) who rent studio space where they hold classes.

British schools include The London Academy of Music and Dramatic Arts (LAMDA), The London Central School, The Royal Academy of Dramatic Arts (RADA), the Bristol University Department of Drama, and the Manchester School of Theatre.

American schools include The American Academy of Dramatic Arts, with New York and Hollywood locations; The New Actors Workshop, founded by Mike Nichols; HB Studio, founded by Herbert Berghof, whose wife Uta Hagen was its most famous teacher; the New School for Drama, presided over by Robert LuPone; the Neighborhood Playhouse; the Stella Adler Conservatory, with connections to NYU; The Acting Studio, founded and run by James Price; the William Esper Studio; the Michael Howard Studio; the T. Schreiber Studio, run by Terry Schreiber; Hollywood Stunts, a New York City–based professional stunt training center; and The Linklater Center for Voice and Language, presided over by the noted teacher and innovative voice expert Kristin Linklater—all in New York City. In Los Angeles, the schools include the American Musical and Dramatic Academy (AMDA), with a New York City location as well; Hollywood's New York Film Academy, which also has branches in New York City and international venues such as Paris and London; the California Institute of the Arts, located in

Valencia; and the Dell'Arte International School of Physical Theatre, located in Blue Lake, which includes courses in its curriculum on masks, mime, clowning, and commedia techniques. Schools where actors can learn the specialties of film acting include the New York–based American Film Institute (AFI).

Among the many wonderful American universities with outstanding drama departments are various branches of California State University, as well as The University of California at Berkeley, CA; Rutgers University's The Mason Gross School of the Arts in New Brunswick, NJ; New York University in New York City; Northwestern University in Evanston/Chicago, IL; Carnegie Mellon University's School of Fine Arts in Pittsburgh, PA; and the Yale University Drama School in New Haven, CT.

All of the schools have web sites that include descriptions of their philosophy and acting courses, a listing of faculty members, and admissions procedures.

See also STUDIO THEATER.

theatrical community The collectivity of people professionally involved in the theater. Also called *theater community*.

Theatrical Film contracts Agreements by **Screen Actors Guild (SAG)** with producing organizations covering employment on the east and west coasts for its members working in motion pictures meant for release in cinemas; establishing working conditions, salary levels, contributions to the union's health and pension funds, and so forth.

theatrical gauze A stiff, heavy, cotton or linen open-mesh, semi-transparent material used in scrims, and in some costumes.

theatricals *n. pl.* **1.** Amateur performances. **2.** *Archaic* Professional actors: *an eminent theatrical.*

See also DRAMATICS.

theme *n.* The underlying and governing idea or ideas in a play or film, presenting the author's point of view about an aspect of life.

theme music Melody associated with a particular film, television project, or performer. Called a *theme*, for short.

thespian *n., adj.* [Fr. the ancient Greek composer and innovative performer of dithyrambs, Thespis, said to be the first person to respond to the **chorus** with individual lines, thus beginning the practice of playing a part] —*n.* **1.** An actor. —*adj.* **2.** Pertaining to acting, esp. in the theater: *thespian anger*; *thespian artistry*.

third banana. See BANANA.

three-act structure The division of a **screenplay** into three major sections, called acts; a usual form in screenwriting. Act 1 sets up the story and its major problem(s) by introducing the protagonists, secondary characters, and, by the end of the act at the latest, the antagonist. Act 2 goes through the vicissitudes and complications of the story, and ends with the hero's lack of success in solving the problem(s). In act 3, the problem is resolved.

three-camera technique Shooting a scene from three different angles or vantage points at the same time. This technique, so useful for editing purposes, is often used in television, esp. in soap opera.

three-day player An actor hired for three days of shooting on a film project; an AFTRA and SAG category that stipulates the base salary to be paid for a three-day job.

3D film [Short for *three-dimensional film*] A motion picture that appears to be taking place on the spectator's own solid spatial plane, with actual depth, height, and width, as if the actors were live on a set. The rarely used *3D process* employs stereoscopic cameras, photographing the images simultaneously and slightly to the side of each other, with the actors performing such stunts as **wire flying** for the **bluescreen process**, as in *Journey to the Center of the Earth* (2008). Special viewing glasses converge the projected double images to create the rounded, three-dimensional effect. Also spelled *3-D*; *three-D*.

three-picture deal A typical contract between an actor and a studio in the days of the **studio system**, giving the studio the right to assign roles to the actor, who would play **as cast**; the first role was often specified, the others up to the producers' discretion.

three-shot *n.* A take of three performers at the same time.

three-wall set A film décor with one interior partition missing: the camera is placed where the missing wall would be located.

thriller *n.* A suspense-filled movie that is designed to rivet the audience to the screen (figuratively, of course), and to make them tremble and shudder as they follow the vicissitudes of the protagonists through perilous situations.

throughline *n.* The thrust of the story in a play, leading to its resolution. Each scene has its own throughline, or **spine**. So does each character, with her or his story's arc, and life objective. The throughline of the actions leads to the fulfilling of the **super-objective**.
　　See also COUNTER-THROUGHLINE.

throw *v. t.* **1.** To **project** the **voice**. See also VENTRILOQUIST; VOCAL TECHNIQUE. **2.** To cast a beam of light; e.g., from a luminaire.

throw away *v. t.* The **technique** of treating something, esp. a line, as unimportant, casual, or not worthy of notice or emphasis; used for comic or dramatic effect.

throwaway *n.* **1.** A line that is delivered in a casual offhand way. **2.** A flyer advertising a play, esp. one handed to a passer-by.

throw distance The length in space to which a beam of light reaches; e.g., the distance from a luminaire to an actor being illuminated, determining where the actor will be blocked and where the light will be positioned. Cf. **focal length**.

thrust stage A playing area that goes beyond a simple proscenium design and is extended into the auditorium.

thunder sheet A large, rectangular, flat, flexible piece of sheet metal with a handle at the bottom, hung backstage and shaken to create the sound effect of thunder, often used in conjunction with a **rain drum**; also used on the **radio**.

ticket *n.* A small printed card, slip of paper, numbered tiny plastic rectangle, or other indication of the right to be admitted to an event or to retrieve a coat from a cloakroom.

ticket agency/broker An office where tickets on consignment from a theater or producing organization may be purchased.

ticket taker The person who collects admission cards or slips at the **door**.

tights *n. pl.* A skin-tight, form-fitting garment, covering the body from the waist down, worn by gymnasts, actors, and dancers, sometimes with a **leotard**. Worn by male actors as part of a costume in a period play (e.g., in Shakespeare); often worn with a **dance belt**. There is also a full-body version, from the neck down.

time *n.* The day, hour, and exact moment when a scene takes place. Time—past, present, and future—is an important given **circumstance**, as is the amount of time a character has to perform a certain task. The historical era in which a play is set is also of paramount importance. Stanislavsky, an expert in producing period pieces, wanted actors to immerse themselves in the play's epoch as much as possible: reading its literature as well as secondary sources, such as biographies; viewing its art; listening to its music, etc.

time a laugh To hold (i.e., to remain silent and stationary, temporarily suspending the action of the play) while the audience laughs, until the laughter is subsiding and the right moment for delivering the next line arrives. In film, a laugh can be ruined by poor editing: the director can be as responsible as the actors in ensuring that the audience has time to enjoy itself by allowing silence, but not too much, after a laugh line instead of immediately coming in with the next line—the equivalent to timing a laugh in the theater.

time an entrance 1. To figure out in an on-stage rehearsal or **space-through** how long it will take to get on stage at the exact right moment. An actor who has to go through a door, walk down steps, and end up at center stage on cue must time the **entrance**, which often involves beginning to prepare it, and moving towards the entryway earlier than the actor might have originally thought necessary. **2.** To appear on stage at the exact right moment: *He timed that entrance perfectly.*

time it out 1. To wait for the proper moment to come in with the next line when holding for a laugh. **2.** To determine the amount of time business takes in order to coordinate it with the action. **3.** To determine the amount of time an entrance takes in order to be there at the correct moment. **4.** The instruction to an actor to do any of these things: *"Time it out!"*

time-lapse photography In film, takes of a subject done at precise intervals and then matched together and shown as a **match dissolve**, giving the viewer an accelerated version of an occurrence; e.g., a desert blooming, as in some nature documentaries.

time sheet 1. In AFTRA and SAG jobs, a form on which hours worked, breaks for meals, and all other matters relating to scheduling are recorded, to keep track of what was done when and to help in determining if any penalties are due for a contract violation. It is a union requirement that a time sheet be kept for all film, television, and commercial productions, and that actors initial the time sheet before they leave at the end of the workday. Also called a *time report*. **2.** In the theater, the stage manager's timekeeping records for the running time of a show, and of each act in it, as well as the length of intermissions; notes on audience reactions may be included.

See also SIGN-IN SHEET.

timing *n.* The **technique** of making something happen at the exact carefully rehearsed moment when it is supposed to happen. Timing is essential in music and dance and in an actor's making an entrance or an exit; it is an elementary comedy technique, as well as being an essential of stage combat. Correct timing depends on setting up the right **tempo, rhythm,** and **pace**.

Tin Pan Alley; **tin-pan alley** *Archaic* **1.** A nickname for the then somewhat seedy district of New York City where most publishers of popular music had their offices from ca. 1885 to 1930, on West 28th Street between Sixth Avenue and Broadway; by extension, the music publishing district of any city. **2.** Collectively, the publishers and composers of popular music working in that era: *tin-pan alley musicians*.

tiring house [Short for *attiring house*] *Hist.* The dressing room area of an Elizabethan or Jacobean theater.

title role The character for whom a play, film, etc., is named; e.g., Hamlet; Hedda Gabler.

title song A short piece of vocal music, the lyrics of which include the name of the project; e.g., the opening **number** of Rodgers and Hammerstein's *Oklahoma*.

titles *n. pl.* Another word for film or television **credits**.

tits and ass A burlesque show or musical revue that features women in scanty costumes revealing a great deal of female anatomy, and doing particularly provocative bumps and grinds. Also called *t and a*, for short.

See BUMP, def. 3.

tone it down To reduce the emotional energy or histrionics in a scene or performance: a direction to an actor. Easier than telling an actor to do more when he or she is not doing enough. Cf. **less is more**.

tongue *n.* The mount for a camera on a **dolly**, allowing it to swing in either direction; hence, the directions, "Tongue left!" or "Tongue right!"

Tony®. See AWARDS.

toolkit *n. Slang.* The actor's set of techniques, tools, and tricks of the trade acquired through study and experience. Among the contents of the actor's toolkit are a knowledge of drama and **stagecraft**; the ability to apply **makeup** and to deal with the **plastic** aspects of a role; knowing how to **take direction**; the **method of physical actions**; **playing opposites**; **rehearsal technique**; and **stage technique**. Also called *toolbox.*

top *n., v.* —*n.* **1.** The beginning of a play, act, scene, section of a scene, line, or speech. See TAKE IT FROM THE TOP! —*v. t.* **2.** In comedy, to say a punch line that gets even more laughter than the previous joke. **3.** In musical theater, to come in with the next line after a **number** at a greater peak of energy than that with which the number finished.

top banana The leading comedian in an act, esp. in burlesque and vaudeville, but also sometimes in a play or musical.
    See also BANANA.

top billing The first actor's credit listed at the beginning of a film, television program, or in a theater program, poster, or advertisement.

top liner; topliner *n.* **1.** The star of a film; the actor's name appears in first place **above the title**. **2.** *Archaic* The headline act; i.e., the main **attraction**, in a vaudeville or music hall show; the **headliner**.

top of the bill The first act in a vaudeville or music hall show.

topper *n. Slang* **1.** A joke that gets the climactic laugh in a **running gag**; or one that elicits a greater response than the previous joke. **2.** A cylindrical top hat.

torch singer A vocalist who performs in nightclubs and cabarets and croons songs that are full of misery, bemoaning the fate of unhappy lovers; the songs are called *torch songs.*

tormentor *n. Slang* One of two long, narrow curtains just inside either side of the **proscenium** arch, masking the wings and, usually, light trees that are hidden behind them. Together with the **teaser**, the tormentors form a frame for the stage, inside the proscenium arch.

tour *n., v.* —*n.* **1.** The travels that actors and crew (the *touring company*) make with a production—called a *touring production*—going from theater to theater, usually for a predetermined, limited period of time: *a six-month tour.* **2.** The **circuit** that a production makes when traveling from theater to theater. —*v. t.* **3.** To take a show **on the road**.
    See also BUS AND TRUCK; NATIONAL TOUR.

track *n., v.* —*n.* **1.** In a musical comedy, the order of each chorus member's dance moves, the dance routine, and the positions on stage with each move, for each number: *dance track*. The **dance captain** is usually in charge of keeping these records. A **swing** has rehearsed and can perform more than one track. **2.** A **channel** on which a portion of the audio or visual takes of a film are recorded, to be combined later into a whole. —*v. t.* **3.** To note the moves and positions of each dancer for each number. **4.** To go through a scene mainly for its blocking. **5.** To trace the **score** of physical moves and blocking in a scene. **6.** In acting, to go through the **score** of beats and actions, tracing the vicissitudes of a particular relationship, or characterological theme. **7.** To trace a character's journey.

tracking shot A take of a scene where the camera travels on special dolly rails laid down for it, following the actors as they move along. Also called *traveling shot*; *dolly shot*.
See also FLUID CAMERA.

trade papers Periodicals and newspapers that are concerned particularly with show business. Among the most useful for actors are the *Hollywood Reporter*, *Variety* and *Daily Variety*, *Backstage East*, *Backstage West*, and the ***Ross Reports***. The first five trade papers on this list have audition notices, regular informative news columns, articles of general interest to the show business community, and advertisements for all kinds of services: coaching, photographers who do actors' head shots, medical or clinical services, classes, and acting schools.
Trade papers have their own delightful lingo, and in any issue of *Variety* you are more than likely to see all the following slang:

aud; auds: audience; audiences.
biz: business, particularly show business
Blighty; Old Blighty: the United Kingdom
crix: critics
distribs: distributors
fest: festival
Gotham: New York City
hyphenate: fulfilling more than one function, or practicing more than one profession; e.g., an actor-director
helmer: film or stage director
indie: independent film
kidvid: children's television programs
legit: legitimate, meaning theater
Oz: Australia
perf: performance
pic: motion picture
scribe: writer
syndie: syndication
unspool: to release a film for public showing

In the 1930s, you could work in the "pix biz" [pictures business] (i.e., the movie industry) and read such headlines as "Sticks Nix Hick Pix," i.e., moviegoers in the provinces are rejecting and not going to see corny, old-fashioned comedies and sentimental romances meant originally just for tasteless, unsophisticated them.

tragedian *n.* **1.** An actor who performs in tragedies. **2.** An author of tragedies.

tragedienne n. An actress who performs in tragedies.

tragedy *n.* [Fr. Greek *tragoidia* (tragedy); lit. "goat song," from the prize of a goat given to the winner at the **Dionysia**] A play with an unhappy, indeed catastrophic ending for the protagonists. For **Aristotle**, this ending resulted from error and guilt.

tragic flaw A blind spot in a character's self-perception that leads him or her to disaster; Aristotle's word is **hamartia**. The fault or flaw is often that of **hubris**: god-defying pride. Oedipus's tragic flaw is his belief that by taking certain actions he can escape the fate that Apollo has decreed for him—this is hubris, for no mortal can contravene the gods' unalterable decrees; only the gods themselves can change what they have set in motion.

tragic hero; **tragic heroine** A protagonist of a tragedy.

tragicomedy *n.* A hybrid genre of drama that began in the Elizabethan theater, and that crosses **comedy** and **tragedy** and emphasizes the ironic and the humorous in human destiny; sometimes called a *heroic comedy*. Such plays often have a rueful ending: not tragic, but not happy either. Scenes of **low comedy** are interspersed with serious dramatic scenes; e.g., in Shakespeare's *The Merchant of Venice*, in which characters of different social classes mingle and interact, or Chekhov's bittersweet play *The Cherry Orchard*: the Ranevskys lose everything they have held dear, but their lives are not threatened, and Lopahin, the former serf, has triumphed over his adversity.

trailer *n.* **1.** An approximately three-minute-long commercial of excerpts from a film artfully put together, showing what it is about, and meant to attract the viewer. Shown in a movie house, and cut down to thirty seconds for a television **movie commercial**. **2.** A large mobile camper used on location shoots, where there are a number of such vehicles serving various purposes: actors' private dressing rooms, with their names on the doors; wardrobe; makeup; toilet facilities; administrative offices; the director's office; etc. A specially designed trailer used for movies is the *cinemobile*, which can transport equipment to locations and also contains dressing rooms and other accommodations. See also HONEYWAGON.

train call *Hist.* The appointed time for actors on tour to meet at the station in order to leave for the next **stand**, esp. in the early to mid-20th c.

training film A movie made for educational purposes; e.g., for driver education.

transceiver *n.* The device in a microphone that transmits the sound signals; in a **body mike**, it is an exterior device; in a **hand mike**, it is inside the microphone.

transcription *n.* **1.** A recording of a radio or television broadcast. **2.** An **arrangement** or adaptation of a musical composition that alters the original in some way; e.g., by adding ornamentations or changing instrumentation.

transformation scene *Brit.* The obligatory climactic scene in a **pantomime**, in which the set collapses in some way, to be replaced by another, even more marvelous decor.

transition *n.* **1.** The change from one **beat**, or from one **moment**, to the next. See also MOMENT OF REVERSAL. **2.** In film, the smooth change from one scene to another. 3. In music, a **bridge**, often including a modulation from one key to another.

translate *v. t.* Alice Spivak's term for the way in which an actor can understand and justify a director's instructions, by turning them into his or her own acting terms. For example, if the director's instruction is to **pick up** the **pace**, the actor can justify this by telling him or herself that there is a more urgent need to accomplish an objective.

transpontine melodrama (tranz pon' tihn, —tIn) [Transpontine: across, or on the other side of the bridge; in this case, the bridges over the Thames] *Brit. Hist.* 19th-c. melodramas presented in theaters on the south bank of the Thames, in Southwark.
    See also NAUTICAL DRAMA.

transportation department The division of a film studio production office that deals with everything regarding the logistics of moving people and equipment around in vehicles.

transpose *n.* To change the key in which a musical composition was written to a higher or lower one; sometimes necessary to accommodate the **range** of a particular singer.

trap *n.* [Short for *trapdoor*] An opening in a stage floor through which actors can make an entrance or an exit, or scenery can be lifted up to the stage level. It usually has either a removable top or one or more flaps.
    See also GRAVE TRAP; VAMPIRE TRAP.

trap room The space underneath the stage where the machinery that works the traps is to be found, and where the actors who use them wait for their entrances.

travel allowance Money for travel, lodging, and food expenses paid to an actor on tour with a stage production, or on a film shoot when the actor must make his or her own way to a distant location.
    See also PER DIEM.

travel-companion allowance Money for transportation, lodging, and food expenses for a spouse or relative who accompanies an actor on a film shoot on location.

travel day 1. On a stage production tour, a day when the company must go to its next theater; no performance is scheduled for that day. **2.** On a motion picture shoot, the day set aside for travel to a location distant from the point of origin of the production.

traveler *n.* A curtain that can be drawn along an upper track. The black curtains or **tabs** that often mask the back and sides of the stage are travelers. Also called a *French tab* (tableau curtain).

traveling shot Syn. with **tracking shot**.

travelogue *n. Archaic* A **featurette** about faraway places; used to be a regular part of cinema programs, shown before the main **feature**.
  See AND SO WE SAY FAREWELL.

travesty *n.* **1.** A **parody** or exaggerated **spoof** in imitation of a well-known play, film, opera, ballet, or other entertainment. **2.** Used figuratively, a contemptible, pale, grotesque imitation of the real thing: *a travesty of justice. His presidency was a travesty.*

treatment *n.* **1.** A synopsis version of a script with sample dialogue interspersed with story narrative and outline, meant for presentation of a film project to potential producers after the project has gotten beyond the one-page presentation stage. The treatment may also be used as an outline when the screenwriter is writing the full script. **2.** Syn. with **adaptation**: *the movie treatment of a novel.*

triangular theater Meyerhold's idea that theater consists of a pyramid, or triangle, with the director at the top, the actors at the bottom on one side, and the audience at the bottom on the other, all controlled by the director, who tells the audience what to look at and the actors exactly how to make things clear to the audience.
  See MEYERHOLD, VSEVELOD.

trilogy *n.* A series of three plays that tell one story; e.g., Eugene O'Neill's *Mourning Becomes Electra*, based on Aeschylus's trilogy the *Oresteia* (o:' rehs tI' uh).

trims *n. pl.* **1.** The tops of the flats, **flies**, and **masking**. **2.** The ends of film rolls cut off during editing.

triple take A comic bit in which a look of neutrality or blank incomprehension is instantly followed by a second, and then a third look of surprised comprehension: it involves turning away from the object of attention, turning back, turning away again, and finally turning back and fixing the attention—all done in a twinkling.
  See also DOUBLE TAKE.

triple threat An actor who speaks, sings, and dances.

tritagonist *n. Hist.* In ancient Greek tragedy, the third actor after the **protagonist** and **deuteragonist**. He played such minor but important roles as the Shepherd in Sophocles's *Oedipus the King*.

trombone *n. Slang* The device or lever that permits the operator of a **follow spot** to control the narrowness or wideness of the light beam.

troubadour *n. Hist.* In southern France, a wandering medieval **minstrel** and lyric poet.

troupe *n.* Acting company, esp. touring actors, who "troupe" around the country. To "be a trouper" means to be a really good person, and a true professional who knows what he or she is doing as a performer and is able to cope with the unexpected: *She's a real trouper!* An actor who misses an entrance, on the other hand, is eminently not a trouper!

trousers role A male character played by a woman (e.g., Cherubino (keh' roo bee' no:) in Mozart's opera *The Marriage of Figaro*) or the **principal boy** in British **pantomime**. Also called a *breeches role*; *pants part*.
See DRAG.

trust *n., v.* —*n.* **1.** In acting, the faith and confidence an actor has in his or her fellow performers; e.g., to do a script as rehearsed, not to inflict injury in fight scenes, and to be able to cope with such unpredictable circumstances as a **stage wait**. —*v. t.* **2.** To have faith and belief in someone or something; to rely on something or someone.
See THEATER GAMES.

truthfulness *n.* In acting terms, awareness of what is real, and the imaginative leap from that knowledge to the feeling of reality in the fictitious **given circumstances** of a role. For Stanislavsky, the actor had to cultivate this feeling of truthfulness, using his or her imagination, in order to enter into the play.

tryout *n.* **1.** A play or musical production that is done **out of town**, usually at several theaters, to test how it will be received, before coming in to New York. A **play doctor** will sometimes be brought in to fix problems by doing rewrites. Directors or actors may be replaced during tryouts. In the mid-20th c., tryouts in New Haven and other well known venues were obligatory. **2.** An audition; hence *to try out for*, a term usually reserved for community theaters or other amateur companies.

tucket *n. Hist.* A trumpet call—an Elizabethan stage direction.

tune *n., v.* —*n.* **1.** A melody. **2.** A whole song. **3.** The musical setting for words: *the tune for a hymn.* —*v. t.* **4.** To adjust a musical instrument to the standard pitch level: *to tune an instrument.* Hence, *in tune*: correctly pitched; *in tune with*: in harmony with (e.g., with the other instruments in an orchestra); *tuned up*: brought to a harmony of pitches. **5.** To adjust a radio or television set so that it can receive the desired broadcast signal. Hence, *tune in*: to turn to a number on a dial, or press a remote control channel selector button; *tune out*: to turn the radio or television channel off.

tungsten-halogen lamp. See HALOGEN LIGHT.

turn *n.* **1.** In the world of vaudeville, the act put on by a performer; also, the individual performance of that act. **2.** In dance, a vertical rotation or partial rotation of the body.

turkey *n. Slang* A flop show.

turnaround *n.* **1.** The amount of time between the end of one shooting day and the beginning of the next. Call times for the next day's shoot vary, depending on when someone was dismissed for the day. If a performer or crew member is called without a proper amount of turnaround time, which is contractually arranged between producing organizations and unions, the producer must pay a penalty. Depending on shooting schedules, it may in fact be necessary to call an actor without giving him or her the proper rest period; hence the term **forced call**. **2.** In the theater, the changeover from one show to another; e.g., in an opera house that does its shows in **rotating rep**.

turn in In the theater, to move the head and/or the body towards center stage, without moving away from one's spot.

turn out 1. In the theater, to move the head and/or body away from center stage, without moving off one's spot. **2.** In dance, to move the legs outward from the hips, pointing the toes to either side. **3.** To show up to see a film or theater performance, or in support of some cause; hence, *turn-out*: the audience: *We had quite a large turn-out this evening.*

turntable *n.* Syn. with **revolving stage**.

tweak *v. t.* To make a slight **adjustment** to a performance.
See also TONE IT DOWN; TAKE IT UP.

twist ending Surprise conclusion to a story that reverses audience expectations of what the outcome would be.

twofer *n. Slang* [Fr. *two for one*] Two tickets sold for the price of one; i.e., each one for half the price. A promotional deal used by theaters to attract more customers.

two-hander *n. Slang.* A play, film, sketch, or act for only two actors.

two on the aisle Seats that are next to each other, with one on the outside of the row, next to the center aisle, in **American-plan seating**. Such seats are preferred by critics reviewing a production, and they are usually comped for reviewers.

two-shot *n.* A take of two people, who are on camera at the same time.

two-step 1. A dance choreographed in the pattern step-close-step, esp. used in vaudeville soft-shoe routines as an introduction leading into a more complicated dance, or for vamping; i.e., marking time, when used as a **bridge**. **2.** A stage staircase unit with only two risers.

type *n.* A generic representative of a group or class of people. E.g., the dirty, unshaven, ragged tramp; the rubicund, buxom country lass; the warm, comforting,

middle-aged mother; the built-up, muscled athlete; the jolly fat person; the merry widow; the injured husband; the **vamp**; and so forth. Also called a *character type*.
See also CENTRAL CASTING; STOCK CHARACTER.

type casting Assigning roles based on an actor's physical appearance and/or personality; hence, the adj. and v. *typecast*. Some actors feel stuck or categorized as being a certain character type, and some who have done sitcoms and other TV shows are difficult to cast, because they are so well known for the character they played. In one of the most well known examples of type casting, Bela Lugosi (1882–1956), actually a versatile leading man, was always seen as Dracula, or some kind of disturbing character. As a result, he could never get beyond the horror film genre.

typing *n.* The practice of categorizing an actor by physical appearance or personality.

U

unconscious *n.* In Freudian terms, that part of the mind, and its contents, of which we are not immediately aware. Most mental processes take place unconsciously. In acting terms, the unconscious motivations that push literary characters to seek certain objectives and to play actions the way they play them can be more important than conscious motivations.

See also AMBIVALENCE; CHARACTER PSYCHOLOGY; EMOTIONS; IMAGINATION.

uncredited role A small part or walk-on role in a film for which the actor's name is not listed in the **credits**.

underacting *n.* Weak playing that does not fulfill all the requirements of a role. The performer who underacts does not put much emotion or reality into a part. Cf. its opposite, **overacting**.

underdress *v. i.* To wear a costume or part of a costume underneath another costume so as to be able to effect a **quick change** during a stage performance.

under-five *n.* A role that, by SAG and AFTRA contractual terms, has fewer than five lines; also, the actor playing such a role. There are many such parts in soap operas and other television programs. One of a soap opera casting director's jobs is to hire under-fives, and you can always send a picture and resume directly to that person with a letter expressing your interest.

underground film An independent film that has been shown to a select group of devotees, often friends of the filmmaker, and that may develop a cult following. Sometimes the film is political in nature; sometimes it is experimental and plays with different camera techniques and montage effects.

underline *v. t. Slang* In acting, to emphasize or stress a particular line or words in order to make a point; to **spell it out**.

underplay *v. t.* To deemphasize a line or a moment, in order to have the next line or moment stand out; to act in the simplest, most unemphatic manner; not to be confused with **underacting**.

underrehearsed *adj.* Said of a badly prepared, poorly rehearsed performance or of an actor who has not been allowed sufficient time to get ready for presentation.

understudy *n., v.* —*n.* **1.** An actor who learns and rehearses a role in order to be able to perform it when the cast member playing it is unavailable. Also called a *cover.* —*v. t.* **2.** To cover a role or roles.

understudy rehearsal A **session** during which understudies go through their roles on stage under the supervision of the stage manager, once a show has opened. Understudy rehearsals for Broadway and Off-Broadway take place regularly.

union *n.* An organized group or association of workers whose leaders are empowered to negotiate with management organizations on all issues affecting employment, including working conditions, terms of employment, vacations, sick days, time off, salaries, health, welfare, and pensions.

unit *n.* **1.** The **Stanislavskian** term for a short section of a play or scene; a bit; a **beat. 2.** In film, another word for the particular **crew** involved in shooting either principal or secondary photography: the **first unit**; the **second unit. 3.** An individual piece of stage scenery; e.g., a **flat. 4.** A set piece of scenery that fits into a larger setting, e.g., a door with its frame; a window; a fireplace with all its components: *a fireplace unit*. Hence, *unit setting*; i.e., one composed of interlocking sections or parts that can be put together and rearranged as necessary. **5.** A lighting instrument together with its accessories; e.g., a follow **spot** and its attached **diaphragm**: *a light unit; a lighting unit*.

unit director The person in charge of the first or second units; he or she works under instructions from the film's **director**.

unity of action; unity of place; unity of time The three **classical unities** observed by the 17th- and 18th-c. neoclassicists. Also called *the three unities*.

university theater 1. A playhouse located on a campus, and used by students for productions. **2.** Drama presented and performed by students, usually under the direction of a teacher, at an institution of higher learning.

unlimited use cycle The thirteen-week period during which a **commercial** may be broadcast as many times as the advertiser wishes. A fee must be paid for every cycle, and no residuals are paid when such a system of compensation is used. When the commercial is not shown, but may possibly be used again, a **holding fee** in the same amount must be paid for each cycle. A **wild spot** is usually paid for under this system.

unmotivated lighting In film and realistic stage plays, lighting that is either deliberately artificial, or does not look as if it is coming from a natural source. Cf. its opposite, **motivated lighting**.

unscripted *adj.* Not part of the text or rehearsed performance of a play, film, etc., but added by an actor during a performance; e.g., an **ad lib** or improvised moment.

up *adj., adv.* —*adj.* **1.** Unable to remember lines, or what comes next: *I don't know what happened to me out there tonight—I was up.* To be "up in a part," on the other hand, is to know it perfectly. —*adv.* **2.** Short for **upstage**: *The actor crossed up.*
See also BE UP FOR; DRY; GO UP; GO UP FOR.

upgrade *n., v.* —*n.* **1.** A change from a lower to a higher salary category in a SAG or AFTRA venue of employment. —*v. t.* **2.** To raise the category and consequently the salary of an actor in a **commercial**, film, or television program. An actor may be hired as an extra, and either be assigned a bit of important business, or be otherwise

302

so recognizable as to require that he or she be upgraded to principal status, which includes residual payments. **3.** To pay an increased rate beyond what a performer was originally paid, because the producer wishes to take preexisting material and expand its use; e.g., in the case of an **audiobook** recorded as **hard copy** for a non-commercial venue that the producer now wishes to release as a **digital audio download**. The upgrade increases the rate in such a case to the *full code rate*; i.e., to the full commercial release fee stipulated in AFTRA's **Sound Recordings Code**, as opposed to the lower rate originally paid. No residuals are paid when the upgrade is accepted as fair and equitable.

See also DOWNGRADE; OUTGRADE.

up light A lighting instrument that illuminates the actor and set from below; e.g., footlights or a luminaire placed beneath a translucent section of a stage floor.

upload *n., v.* —*n.* **1.** Audio, visual, textual material, or other data sent from one computer or from the **Internet** to another computer, where it is downloaded, i.e., received. —*v. t.* **2.** To send data from one computer or from the Internet to another computer.

upscale *v., adj.* —*v. t.* **1.** To render something more luxurious, and to make it appear higher on the economic ladder; e.g., when decorating an interior location set. —*adj.* **2.** Dressed in chic evening wear, or other rich apparel; e.g., the background players in the embassy ball in Tom Cruise's *Mission: Impossible* (1996). **3.** Pertains to an upper-class milieu.

upstage *n., v.* —*n.* **1.** The back or rear part of the **stage**: the part of the stage farthest away from the audience, and to the rear of the actor, in a proscenium theater, or in a theater in three-quarters round; abbrev. U. —*v. t.* **2.** To face downstage while positioning oneself **above** the actor who is speaking, so that the other actor is forced to turn his or her back to the audience, hence, by extension, to **steal a scene**. **3.** To face **up**, so that one blocks oneself from the audience view: *to upstage oneself* (something to be avoided).

up-tempo *adj.* A number in a musical comedy that is fast-paced and rhythmically rapid.

use cycle The thirteen-week period during which a **commercial** may be shown.

See NATIONAL NETWORK; RESIDUALS; UNLIMITED USE CYCLE; WILD SPOT.

usher *n., v.* —*n.* **1.** The person who shows audience patrons to their cinema or theater seats and gives them theater programs. Ushers in the United States are unionized. In Europe, it is customary to tip the usher, but that is not usually done in the U.S. —*v. t.* **2.** To show people to their seats. Hence, *ushering*; i.e., the job or act of showing people to their seats.

Use it! A direction to an actor to take advantage of the actor's own emotional state, esp. where it might be appropriate for the character, incorporating it into the playing of a moment or scene. But the phrase is often applied in situations where the actor's own emotions or feelings seem inappropriate, but might somehow be of use, as in **playing opposites**. When the actor takes account of what is happening during a performance and goes along with it, instead of forging ahead in a pre-planned, calculated way, he or she is "using" the reality of the situation.

See also LISTEN AND RESPOND.

utility role A small character part that serves a useful purpose; e.g., the butlers in Oscar Wilde's *The Importance of Being Earnest*, the messengers in Shakespeare's plays.

utility stunt performer A stuntperson hired on a weekly contract to do any general stunts required and to double for one or more actors; this is a union classification.

V

Vakhtangov, Eugene (1888–1923) (vahkh tah*n*' go:f) Innovative Russian actor and director, student of Stanislavsky, teacher at the MAT studio, and important dissenter from the strict Stanislavskian approach to creating character. He tried to synthesize Meyerhold's and Stanislavsky's ideas into an approach to the actor's art that he called *fantastic realism*: a style of production in which the actors were "real" within their roles, but performed using stylized movements in sometimes abstract settings. One of Vakhtangov's important, heretical deviations from the Stanislavsky system is his concept of the **object of attention**, which has to do with the nature and the use of **substitution**. For purposes of concentrating, the actor has to have selected an object on which to concentrate his attention, and for Stanislavsky, that object must be connected to the play, the objective, the relationship, or to the time and place of the given circumstances. But for Vakhtangov, the virtual originator of the **actor's secret**, the object of attention is not necessarily required to have anything whatsoever to do with the material being performed. And neither the director, fellow actors, nor the audience need ever know or guess what it is.

vamp *n., v.* [Short for *vampire*] *Slang.* —*n.* **1.** A seductive young lady trying her wiles and ploys on a prospective lover. **2.** The role of such a seductress; a **character type**, esp. in the 1920s and '30s. **3.** A repeated, brief, introductory musical sequence. **4.** *Archaic* The role of a vampire; i.e., a bloodsucking undead character such as Dracula. —*v. i.* **5.** In music, esp. in musical comedy, vaudeville, or burlesque, to play a brief introduction or musical figure repeatedly (e.g., while a strip-teaser makes a slow, seductive entrance, or while waiting for a performer to enter, or until a singer is ready to begin singing); e.g., the repeated notes in the rhythmic pattern tum-ta-ta, tum-ta-ta, played for a **Gilbert and Sullivan patter** song. Hence the direction to "vamp 'til ready." **6.** To improvise a moment during a **stage wait**; to **stall**. **7.** *Archaic* To play a vampire role; or to play such roles regularly. —*v. t.* **8.** To attempt a seduction: *She vamped him.*

vampire trap [So called fr. its use for the entrance of the vampire in *The Vampire*, a 19th-c. melodrama] A stage trapdoor with two flaps that spring open and closed.

variety *n., adj.* —*n.* **1.** Entertainment that includes different kinds of acts, such as stand-up comedy, comic sketches, songs, specialty animal acts, and so forth. —*adj.* **2.** Pertaining to such entertainment: *a variety act.*

varifocal *adj.* Capable of changing or varying focus by lengthening or shortening an apparatus; e.g., a **zoom** lens, a zoom ellipsoidal spotlight.

vaudeville *n.* **1.** Variety entertainment consisting of various kinds of acts, including songs, song and dance acts, comedy skits or sketches, juggling, acrobatics, magic, mind-reading acts, hypnotists' acts, and other specialty performances. American stand-up comedy developed from vaudeville, of which it was a regular feature. Some famous vaudeville artists who toured the United States for decades later went on to make films, as well as radio and television programs; e.g., George Burns and Gracie Allen, Milton Berle, and Jack Benny. **2.** A comic, short theater piece, sketch, or farce. "Vaudeville" was Chekhov's word for some of his one-act plays, such as *The Boor*. **3.** A sarcastic or satiric French **cabaret** song.

vehicle *n.* A film, play, or other entertainment that showcases the talents of a particular performer; e.g., a **star vehicle**.

Velcro (vehl' kroh) *n., v.* [Fr. French: *velours* (vuh loor'): velvet; and *crochet* (kro sheh:'): hook] *Trademark* —*n.* **1.** A plastic fastening ribbon, one side of which is smooth and is sewn onto material, the other side of which is rough and sticks to the rough side placed opposite it. Velcro is used in costumes for quick changes, and to make a convincing ripping sound, e.g., in a **fight scene.** —*v. t.* **2.** To fasten something using Velcro.

velours; velvets *n. pl.* Stage curtains made of velour or velvet, and all of one color; used for **masking**, or as front proscenium legs and borders.

ventriloquist *n.* A performer who projects his or her voice as if it were coming from the mouth of the ventriloquist's **dummy**, doing an act that consists of comic conversations and routines with the dummy. In a live theater or nightclub, the act may involve audience participation.

venue *n.* **1.** The general locality or kind of theater where performance events take place; e.g., **Broadway, Off-Broadway. 2.** A specific individual theater, sports arena, or other **performance space**.

verbal action Speech in furtherance of an objective; usually directed at another character, or at the character's self, in the case of a **soliloquy**. A verbal or vocal action may be anything from a command to the statement "I love you." Speech in general, especially when it is in fulfillment of obtaining an objective, is active on stage and constitutes an action, according to Stanislavsky, for whom correct **vocal technique** was as important a part of his system as internal, psychological technique. Verbal action is a particularly important part of performing Shakespearean and other verse dramas, and of playing comedy. You can use the playwright's punctuation as a guide: it provides clues to intentions and subtextual meaning.

verismo (veh rih:s' mo) *n.* [Italian: realism] Late 19th- and early 20th-c. realism in Italian literature and opera, often dealing with **domestic drama/tragedy**; e.g., Giovanni Verga's (1840–1922) story *Cavalleria Rusticana* (kah' vah leh ree' ah roos' tee kah' nah) [Rustic Chivalry], made into an opera by Pietro Mascagni (1863–1945) in 1899.

verse drama A play, or the collectivity of plays, written in poetry.

verse technique The specialized way of dealing with the lines in plays written in poetry; i.e., by **phrasing** them, and taking their **rhythm** and the rhyme of the verse into account, but (except in rare instances) not dwelling upon or making rhyme or rhythm obvious: they will be apparent to the audience anyway. The actor must deal with given circumstances and subtext, while not forgetting the nature of the rarefied language.

An understanding of meter is essential in doing Shakespearean and other verse plays. Meters (rhythms) alternate strong and weak stresses in a predetermined, recurring pattern, called a **foot**. A metric line of poetry is named after the number of feet it contains: One of the most commonly used meters is *iambic pentameter* (I am' bik pehn ta' muh tuhr), which takes account of the natural rhythm of the English language; it is the primary, but not the only, verse form in which Shakespeare wrote. An *iamb* (I' amb) is a foot containing one weakly stressed syllable followed by one more strongly stressed syllable; there are five iambs (or iambic feet) in a line of iambic pentameter: "Thou *canst* not *speak* of *that* thou *dost* not *feel*"—*Romeo and Juliet*, act 3, scene 3. The lines sometimes include an extra weak (unstressed) syllable at the end: "To *be* or *not* to *be*: that *is* the *question*." Knowing how to break up the verse (i.e., how to **phrase** it so that it sounds real, and yet retains the gorgeousness of its language) is essential. In this excerpt from act 1, scene 2 of Shakespeare's *The Tempest*, Prospero is talking to his daughter Miranda, to whom he has just told the story of the travails that brought them to the desolate shores of the island where they dwell. The double slashes indicate suggested, possible pauses, however brief, for sense and for pointing up the lines so they are clear to an audience:

Know thus far forth. //
By accident most strange, // bountiful Fortune, //
Now, my dear lady, // hath mine enemies
Brought to this shore; // and by my prescience //
I find my zenith doth depend // upon
A most auspicious star, // whose influence, //
If now I court not but omit, // my fortunes
Will ever after droop. // Here cease more questions;

In addition to rhymes and **meter**, playwrights have used *assonance* (a' suh nuhnts) and *alliteration* (uh lih' tuh ray' shuhn) in their verse plays. Alliteration is the repetition of consonants: *three hundred thirty-three*. Assonance is the repetition of vowel and diphthong sounds: *How now, brown cow?*

The actor doing a verse play should also understand the nature of **figurative language**. Figures of speech include the **euphemism**, the **pun**, the **metaphor**, the **simile**, the **metonymy**, and the **synecdoche**.

See also AMPLIFICATION; BLANK VERSE; COUPLET; MALAPROPISM; PATHETIC FALLACY; STICHOMYTHIA.

version *n*. **1.** A particular variant of a story, novel, or other source that has been adapted for another medium, such as the stage or the screen: *There are various versions of Gaston Leroux's story of* Phantom of the Opera. **2.** A translation: *the subtitled or dubbed English version of a French film*. **3.** The particular form of adaptation: *the film version of a novel; the movie version of a stage play; the musical comedy version of a play* (e.g. *My Fair Lady*, adapted from Shaw's *Pygmalion*).

Victorian drama Plays written and performed during the reign of Queen Victoria of England (1837–1901). They include innumerable forgotten melodramas, well-made plays, and farces; Tom Robertson's realistic **cup and saucer drama**; W. S. Gilbert's plays; the verse plays of Edward Bulwer Lytton; and the comedies and dramas of the Anglo-Irish writers Oscar Wilde, Dion Boucicault, and George Bernard Shaw.

See also GILBERT AND SULLIVAN; MELODRAMA; REALISM.

video *n., adj.* [fr. Latin (wee' day oh): I see] —*n.* **1.** The visual, picture portion of a television broadcast. **2.** A film, television show, or other entertainment recorded for viewing on videocassette (VHS) or DVD: **music video**. **3.** The technical elements involved in the transmission and reception of television broadcast images. —*adj.* **4.** Pertaining to the visual aspects of a technological entertainment project.

video game A technologically engineered and produced electronic game played on a computer or television screen, using game controls, or played in a public arcade; it usually involves pursuit and escape situations. Video game producers employ actors under AFTRA or SAG contracts to do voice-over narration and characters, or to do **motion capture** shoots for animated game characters; rehearsals and shoot days are sessions for which the actor receives a **session fee**.

videoprompter *n.* A machine that faces speakers on a television broadcast and scrolls lines down for them to read; e.g., an **Executive Speech Prompter** or **TelePrompTer**.

viewfinder *n.* A device that is either a separate attachment to a **camera** or part of the lens, and that a **photographer** or **cinematographer** looks through as a help in framing or composing a **picture** or **shot**. Also called a *range finder*.

viewpoints *n. pl.* Particular deconstructive areas of focus used by a performing or creative artist to concentrate on aspects of a project for analytical purposes. Originally developed by choreographer Mary Overlie in the 1970s, the idea of viewpoints was an attempt to narrow down the focus of concentration for interpretive dance purposes. The viewpoints were space, story, time, emotion, movement, and shape. These were further refined by Anne Bogart, with an eye to making the viewpoints useful for actors. She eliminated emotion and story, since she saw these as too broad and too pervasive in theatrical presentations, and felt they would be naturally dealt with in the course of dealing with the other viewpoints. In considering space, the actor concentrates on the architectural surroundings of artificially constructed spaces or of natural outdoor spaces, as well as the patterns of movement the character makes in the space. Shape includes the pattern of movement and gesture, and time includes tempo, duration, and the repetition of movement in time.

vignette (vih nyeht') *n.* **1.** An act or monologue for one actor, consisting of a character sketch; e.g., Ruth Draper's monologues. **2.** A **plum** character role in a play of film. **3.** A background that is painted on a scenic drop, suggesting a setting rather than realistically recreating it in detail.

villain *n.* An evil person or character; the bad guy or gal.

violation *n.* Breach of contract; infringement of a contractual provision. Producers, performers, or other personnel who breach a contract are said to be *in violation*.
See FORCED CALL; MEAL PENALTY; TURNAROUND.

virtuoso *n., adj.* —*n.* **1.** An exceptionally skilled, creative, brilliant performer. —*adj.* **2.** Pertains to the outstanding qualities, skilled performance, or brilliant work of such an artist; also, *virtuosic*: *a virtuoso violinist*; *a virtuosic interpretation*.

visual cue A signal that must be seen by a performer or crew member, who then knows when to speak or to perform an action; e.g., a cue light, a hand signal, a nod.

Vitaphone (vI' tuh fohn') *n. Hist. Trademark* An early movie sound recording process, developed under the auspices of Warner Brothers.

vitascope (vI' tuh skohp') *n. Hist.* One of the first film projectors, invented by Thomas Alva Edison.

vocal *n.* [Fr. a shortening of *vocal music*] *Slang* **1.** A song, esp. in musical comedy, vaudeville, or revue. **2.** The delivery of the songs in a musical or revue: *The vocals were terrific* (i.e., the songs and the way they were delivered).

vocal cords The folds of muscle in the larynx through which air is sent in order to produce the voice; called, more correctly, *vocal folds* or, colloquially, the *voice box*, which is the term for the entire larynx, vocal folds, and epiglottis. Sounds are controlled by the opening and closing of the epiglottis and the sub-glottal pressure directing the stream of air to a **resonator**.

vocal energy The force of the voice when projected using the muscles of the vocal apparatus and the diaphragm, and the amount of such force.

vocalist *n.* A singer, esp. in cabaret, nightclubs, or vaudeville.

vocalise (voh' kuh leez') *n.* A singer's exercise using vowels or syllables, for developing agility; e.g., in opera singing.

vocalize (voh' kuh lIz') *v. i.* **1.** To warm up the singing voice preparatory to performing. **2.** To practice vocal technique for singing, using exercises such as vocalises, scales, arpeggios, etc.

vocal score The music of the singers' parts, together with a piano reduction of the orchestral accompaniment, of an opera, operetta, musical comedy, or other musical theater piece.

vocal technique Method or way of producing and using the voice when performing. Good technique and correct habits inculcated through proper training enable the actor to use the voice for its greatest variety and nuance, without injury to the vocal cords, and to sustain the voice with energy not only over an entire performance, but also to maintain it over an entire career. The elements of vocal technique include correct **placement** of the voice in the **mask**, so as to bring out its greatest

resonance; diaphragmatic support for the voice; correct, sustained and sustainable breathing technique; and the fluid use of a voice trained to be variable and flexible, so that it is in the service of the character and is used to express what the character desires to express without conscious, calculated effect.

voice *n.* The sound produced by forcing air from the lungs through the larynx and vocal cords so that it creates **resonance** and sonority when it vibrates against the bones. Voices are characterized and categorized by their **range**. The name of the range is also used to mean the person having that range:

1. Alto: the lowest-pitched female singing voice; short for contralto; and the highest-pitched male voice, called a countertenor. There are also boy altos.
2. Baritone: the medium-range mature male singing voice. A light or lyric baritone has a slightly higher range than a baritone; a bass-baritone has a slightly lower range.
3. Bass: the lowest-pitched mature male singing voice. A *basso cantante* (bah' so kahn tahn' teh) [Italian: singing bass] has a good top **register**, as well as an excellent low range; a *basso profundo* (pro foon' do) [Italian: deep bass] has a fine low register, and not a very high range.
4. Countertenor: an adult male singer with a contralto range. Also called a *male alto.* Many countertenors are experts in baroque music and sing in opera houses, performing roles written in some cases for castrati. A *castrato* (kah strah' to) [Italian: castrated] was a male contralto or soprano singer who was castrated as a boy. The practice of castrating choirboys with unusually beautiful soprano voices, in order to preserve the voice, was fairly common in the late 17th through the early 19th centuries, and was even continued in rare cases through the early 20th. In the early 18th c., castrati were much in demand in opera houses, where they sang the florid, heroic roles specially composed for them in baroque operas.
5. Mezzo-soprano: the medium range mature female singing voice, between a contralto and a soprano.
6. Soprano: the highest-pitched female singing voice. There are also boy sopranos. A lyric or spinto soprano has a lighter voice than a dramatic soprano. A coloratura soprano is one who specializes in the technique of singing the florid ornamentations in the music found, for instance, in early 19th-c. romantic bel canto opera (behl' kahn' to) [Italian: beautiful singing].

The higher end of the range, where singers feel vibrations in the **mask**, is called the **head voice**. The lower end of the range, where singers feel vibrations in the chest, is called the **chest voice**. A *falsetto* is an artificial, unnatural high-pitched male voice, used in speaking and/or singing, sometimes to comic effect. Singers and actors both have a high, middle, and low voice; i.e., they have all three registers. It is the middle **register** of the speaking voice that, when properly supported, carries best in the theater. Good vocal technique will prevent too much *vibrato* (vee brah' toh) [fr. Italian]: shaking of the voice, in any register.

voice coach Someone who works with an actor on vocal matters: diction, production, projection, general technique, and/or accents and dialects. Also called a *vocal coach*.

See also DIALECT COACH.

voice-over *n.* [Also spelled *voice over* or *voiceover*] The recorded voice of an unseen actor in television and radio commercials, documentary film narration, films, television programs, video games, and animated features or short cartoons for which characters' voices are used. The person recording most voice-overs is usually unseen, but in film, the device of having a character's thoughts done as a voice-over while we see the actor thinking is quite common; e.g., in Laurence Olivier's film version of *Hamlet* (1948). There is a great deal of work in the voice-over field, and most actors have a separate, specialist **agent**—often a member of a large agency with which the actor is signed—to handle voice-over employment. Increasingly, voice-over auditions for commercials are done from the actor's home via computer, in a **home studio**. A computer microphone and special software are needed. The actor accesses his or her agent's **web site**, where auditions arranged for their clients are specially listed on an individual basis, downloads the **copy**, rehearses it, records it, and sends the **audition** recording to the agent over the **Internet**. The agent then sends it on to the casting director or other personnel in charge of casting the spot.

See also BOOK RECORDING; IN-HOUSE; READING TECHNIQUE.

voice part 1. The music or melodic line for a particular category of singer in an ensemble piece: *the soprano voice in the "Hallelujah Chorus."* **2.** One of the melodic lines in a musical composition: *the bass voice of a piano sonata*.

voice qualifier The way in which a word is said or a line delivered, having nothing to do with its linguistic content; e.g., in a hoarse, drunken, sick, whining, raspy, loud, soft-spoken, high-pitched, obsequious, or drawling voice, thus communicating a condition or relationship.

voice test 1. An audio audition. **2.** A check of an actor's vocal levels during a recording session. Also called a *level check*.

volume control 1. Adjusting the level of sound in a **PA system**; in a theater production's sound system; or on a radio, television or audio playback machine. **2.** The switch with which sound levels are adjusted.

vomitorium (wo:' mih to:' ree *oom*) *n., pl.* vomitoria (–ah) [Latin] *Hist.* The huge single door or double doors that opened into an amphitheater or stadium seating area, in ancient Rome.

vomitory *n.* An aisle in a **theater in the round** between tiers of seats, allowing audience ingress; sometimes used by actors for entrances and exits. Called *vom*, for short.

vote with one's feet To express disapprobation of a play or other entertainment by leaving at an intermission or while it is being performed.

voucher system Colloquial term for a **Screen Actors' Guild (SAG)** admissions procedure, whereby an actor who has worked as a principal on a SAG project receives a waiver or voucher enabling him or her to apply for membership.

vulnerability *n.* The actor's openness to what is happening during a rehearsal or performance and the availability to deal in an alive way, **moment to moment**, with whatever may transpire.

W

wagon *n.* Short for **scenery wagon**.

wagon stage 1. A mechanized rolling platform the size of the performing area on a theater stage, on which an entire set can be mounted, and which can be wheeled from offstage onto the stage platform. Also called a *slip stage.* **2.** *Hist.* The performance platform on a medieval **pageant** cart.

waiver *n.* **1.** Permission from Equity to use union actors in a non-paying showcase production in the theater in California: *an Equity-waiver production.* If the production is transferred to a paying venue, the actors in the waiver production must be transferred with it, or paid a stipulated number of weeks of salary. See also EQUITY 99-SEAT PLAN; SHOWCASE. **2.** Written permission from SAG to employ union actors in a non-union situation. E.g., in a university film department student film; or for **deferred payment** on a regular SAG project; or for a nonunion actor to do a job as a principal, for which the actor receives a document called a waiver or voucher, such a job being an eligibility requirement for union membership.

walk *n. Hist.* In 18th-c. English theater, the particular kind of role an actor played: *Her walk was the young heroine.*

walk away with the show To triumph as a performer to such an extent as to eclipse the other actors in a production; also heard as *walk off with the show.*

walkie-talkie *n.* A wireless, hand-held, two-way communications device with an antenna. Used on movie sets, esp. on location; e.g., for rapid communication between personnel on the set and an AD who must call actors from their trailers for a take.

walk-in *n., adj. Slang.* —*n.* **1.** A theater patron who buys a ticket at the box office just before a performance. —*adj.* **2.** Describes such a person or people: *a walk-in crowd.*

walk-on *n.* **1.** A small utility role, such as those Shakespearean messengers whose only function is to deliver a communication and then depart. **2.** The actor playing such a role.

walk the curtain To pace along behind a **house curtain** as it is being closed in order to make sure the two halves close completely and properly.

walk through [a performance] To perform in a desultory, uninvolved fashion.

walk-through *n.* **1.** A **rehearsal** of a play that proceeds with as little **stop and start** as possible; a slow **run-through** rehearsal, as opposed to a detailed **work-through**. **2.** The rehearsal of a film or television scene just before it is shot or taped, for purposes of finding the actors' marks and checking camera focus.

walk up a flat To raise a flat lying on the stage floor by starting at its top end, and slowly raising it by walking along, changing the position of hands by lowering them as the flat gets higher, until it is completely upright and ready to be positioned and fastened to the stage floor, or removed from the stage; a job usually done by more than one **grip**.

walla *n. Slang* Background noise, esp. that made by extras on a film shoot. Also called *walla-walla*. **Syn.** *omnies*, def. 1.

wander *v. i.* To move aimlessly away slightly from the position in which one has been blocked, straying gradually and perhaps going back and forth. Also called *roam*; *roaming*; *sneaking*.

wardrobe *n.* **1.** An individual actor's costume(s). **2.** The costumes for an entire cast. **3.** Short for **wardrobe department**.

wardrobe allowance Fee paid to an actor or other performer for the use of items of his or her own clothing, or for the use of an entire outfit.

wardrobe call A summons to a **costume fitting**; a term generally used in the media, whereas "costume fitting" is the term generally used in the theater.

wardrobe department The personnel in charge of maintaining costumes in a theater or on a shoot or taping. In the theater, their jobs include laundering, sending items out for dry cleaning, ironing as necessary, distributing such items as clean socks and tee shirts, making sure costumes used for quick changes are in the right place, and serving as backstage dressers for quick changes or as dressers in the dressing room, particularly for complicated costumes such as soldiers' armor or ladies' corsets and stays. It is the responsibility of the actor to make the wardrobe personnel's life easier by putting his or her costume(s) in the assigned place in the dressing room.

wardrobe supervisor The head of a production's wardrobe department; the person responsible for everything having to do with costumes.

war film A motion picture that tells the story of soldiers' lives in combat.

warhorse *n. Slang* A sturdy, tried-and-true, beloved play, opera, musical, or ballet that always works, and that is often revived with great success; the mainstay of an opera, repertory, ballet, or summer stock company; e.g., operas by Puccini or Verdi, musicals by Rodgers and Hammerstein, Tchaikovsky's ballets. But the term has a certain derogatory connotation as well, referring to a piece that is done so often that it seems hackneyed and is therefore performed half-heartedly by a company that is tired of it.

warm up 1. To prepare for a performance by doing vocal and physical exercises, as opposed to the mental preparation for the role itself. **2.** To tell jokes to the audience before the taping of a television sitcom, and so put them in the mood to laugh when the sitcom is performed; the job is given to a stand-up comedian.

warm-up *n.* **1.** The physical and vocal exercises a performer does before a rehearsal or performance in order to limber up. **2.** The routine a comedian does before the taping of a sitcom.

warn *v. t.* To alert someone that a cue is coming up, e.g., the stage manager's warning to a lighting, sound, or stage technician: "Warn cue one . . . go, cue one!" The word *and* before such cues as "**Action!**" is a warning.

warning bell The clanging instrument that rings once to inform everybody that shooting is about to take place and that everyone had better settle down and be quiet and rings twice to inform everybody that shooting has stopped.

See ON A BELL.

warning light 1. Another term for **cue light**. **2.** Another term for **red light**. **3.** The glowing red or other colored light on a television or movie camera indicating that the camera is on. Also called a *power-on light*; *red eye*.

See also VISUAL CUE.

wash *n.* **1.** General, soft, unfocused lighting. **2.** The illumination of a particular area with a wide swath of such softening light.

washboard weeper Radio **soap opera**; slang from way back when laundry was done in a tub using a washboard: a rectangular, wood-framed, corrugated metal surface on which soapy laundry was scrubbed to get out the filth.

water curtain 1. The sprinkler system meant for fire control, placed directly behind or in front of a theater's **fire curtain**. Also called a *deluge curtain*. **2.** A long, pierced pipe suspended above the front of an **outdoor theater** stage, used to create rain.

wave machine A type of apparatus or powered device used to create waves in water, either in an outdoor location or a **studio tank**. One type uses a huge open cylindrical drum that, when activated, creates a wave with each revolution. The second kind uses a wedge that can be raised and lowered to varying heights, so as to create waves of different sizes; the effect of water growing more agitated and then calming down can thus be created. Actors in shipwreck or storm scenes will often be swimming in artificially controlled turbulent waters. Also called a *wave generator*; *wavemaker*.

wax cylinder Thomas Edison's invention of the earliest preservative **medium** for sound recording, consisting of a hollow tube coated with a wax substance on which the sound was fixed in grooves; used in the early days of **acoustic** recording. It was fitted onto a cylinder, and played on the *gramophone* using a *needle* or *stylus*. Called a *cylinder*, for short.

weak *adj.* **1.** Poorly performed, without commitment, energy or life: *a weak performance*. **2.** Describes an actor who performs in this manner.

weathercaster *n.* The announcer who delivers news of present meteorological conditions, as well as predictions of future conditions (called a *forecast*) on a radio or television broadcast; hence, *weathercast*: meteorological reportage. Also called *forecaster*; *weatherman*; *weatherperson*; *weatherwoman*.

weather day Safety-precaution alternate day of possible location shooting, to be used if meteorological conditions preclude shooting on the regularly scheduled day. Actors are booked for that day as well as for the regular day, and must be duly compensated.

weather delay Necessary, unpredictable, and unspecified period of postponement of location shooting because of meteorological conditions.

webcast *n.* A program or show broadcast on the Internet; e.g., an **Internet film**.

webisode *n.* An episode of a program, serial, or film made for the Internet.

web site A cyberspace place or online destination accessible on the Internet. Agencies; trade papers; unions; groups; television and radio stations; current stage productions; professional organizations of all kinds, including those giving grants; casting people; and individual performing artists all have web sites. There are web sites devoted to various interests, activities, and famous people; e.g., well known writers, classical composers, or film stars. And every actor should have one that includes pictures and resumes, audio and video material, and any other pertinent information about current, upcoming, or past projects, as well as links to other sites, such as the **Internet Movie Database (IMDb)** or the **Internet Broadway Database (IBDB)**. Web masters can design such sites so that they are attractive and colorful.

weekend shoot Filming that may begin on Saturday and go through Sunday.

weekly *n., adj.* —*n.* [Short for *weekly contract*; *weekly player*] **1.** A contract between a performer and the management of a film or television program that provides for the performer to be employed for an entire week; i.e., to be paid by the week, as opposed to the day, even though he or she may not work every day of that week. —*adj.* **2.** Hired for or by the week.

weekly rep *esp. Brit.* A repertory theater that presents a different play each week for its entire season.

weenie *n. Slang* An inorganic plot device, such as a **deus ex machina**, that ensures a happy ending.

well-made play A drama in which every strand and plot thread is neatly and logically tied up at the end. The well-made play was the most popular form of drama from the 19th c. on, exemplified in **melodrama** and in the works of the prolific playwright and opera librettist Eugène Scribe (1791–1861), who practically devised it single-handed. It is still in constant use; e.g., in mystery and courtroom dramas.

We're back! "Break's over!" The stage manager's injunction, often shouted, to everyone to end the break and return to rehearsal.

We're clear! "The cameras are off and we are not broadcasting!" This announcement is made during a live television broadcast, such as a talk show, to the personnel in the studio at the beginning of a commercial break, and at the end of the show.

316

We're on in five ... four ... three ... two ... [one]! The command from the director or stage manager to start acting on a television show: "one" is usually not said. Also heard shortened: **In five ... four ... three ... two ... [one]!**

West End London's main venue of commercial theaters: London's Broadway.

western *n.* A film that takes place in the American Old West, and tells stories involving cowboys, Indians, ranchers, sheepherders, and the settling of the West.

wet-for-wet A scene that takes place during a storm, or in an underwater location, and that is actually shot underwater; or during a rainstorm either real or artificially created. Cf. **dry-for-wet**.

What, never? Hardly ever! An immediately popular **catchphrase** from the **refrain** of the Captain's song in act 1 of Gilbert and Sullivan's 1878 smash hit, *H.M.S. Pinafore*.

wheel *n. Archaic Slang* **1.** A **circuit** of **vaudeville** theaters. **2.** The owner(s) of the circuit: *the big wheel(s)*. **3.** A circuit theater manager: *What did the wheel have to say about the act?*

while life Uta Hagen's term for **activity**, because the activity or activities go on while the conflict of the scene is being played out, yet are secondary to it.

Who am I? The actor's first question about the character, in the Stanislavsky **system**. While certain answers can be given immediately upon reading the script, esp. regarding elementary **circumstances** (age, marital status, profession, nationality, educational background), others, such as the real nature of relationships and motivations, will have to await **exploration** and **discovering through doing** in **rehearsal**.

whodunit *n. Slang* A murder mystery novel, play, television show, or film.

whoop-whoops *n. pl. Slang* In film, extra sounds added to enhance a scene, such as the noise of an explosion, police sirens in a chase scene, or the clanging of fire-engine bells.

wide-angle shot A take using a special *wide-angle lens* that includes a large, opened-out area of scenery, giving greater perspective of view on a horizontal plane than is possible using an ordinary camera lens. Used in filming battle scenes, where a panoramic view of clashing armies alternates with closer shots of individual combatants, and to give the audience a panoramic view of deserts and oceans in such films as *Titanic* (1997) and *Lawrence of Arabia* (1962). Also called a *wide shot*.

wide release Distribution of a motion picture in many markets simultaneously; e.g., a feature film with major stars, expected to generate high box office receipts. Similar to **general release**.

wigmaker *n.* A designer and manufacturer of perruques, wigs, and hairpieces (including sideburns, mustaches, and beards) for specific characters and for period pieces; a perruquier. Actors go for wig fittings to their ateliers, or else the wigmaker goes to the theater or film set.

See also HAIRDRESSER; HAIRPIECE.

wig shop The atelier or workplace where hairpieces, including wigs, beards, and mustaches, are manufactured.

wigwag *n. Slang* Syn. with **red light**; so called because the light flashes continually while shooting is in progress.

Wildean (wIl' dee uhn), *adj.* Pertaining to and characteristic of the epigrammatic wit and charming sense of humor exemplified in the plays and other works of the Irish writer Oscar Wilde (1854–1900).

wild shooting Filming a scene, part of a scene, or an entire motion picture without simultaneously recording synchronous sound, which will be dubbed in later. This may be called for in noisy locations such as city streets, where the traffic noise would interfere with recording the dialogue, which would have to be dubbed anyway. Also called *shooting wild*. **Syn. *MOS*.**

wild sound Noise, such as **room tone**, or shouts or laughter in a crowd scene, recorded for editing purposes immediately after a take.

wild spot A television commercial for a nationally available product shown at different times either throughout the country or else in a specific regional market. The advertiser pays individual local affiliated national network or independent stations for the showings, and may select the times during which the spot will be broadcast. Actors' residuals are calculated according to various scales, and payments vary, depending on the contract.

wild west show *Hist.* A popular 19th- and early 20th-c. circus-like traveling entertainment featuring cowboys and Indians, target-shooting displays, and horse-riding acts. The most famous and spectacular was Buffalo Bill's Wild West (the word "show" was not included in its name), founded and run by William F. Cody (1846–1917) and featuring famed sharpshooter Annie Oakley (1860–1926) as well as horse riders from Turkey, Argentina, Mongolia, and Arabia, all wearing their colorful native costumes and demonstrating particular national skills. In 1885, the show featured Sitting Bull (1831–1890), the Lakota Sioux holy man, and twenty of his braves.

Wind it up! A hand **cue** consisting of rolling the index finger in forward circles, indicating to the performer on a television show that the moment to end that part of the broadcast is rapidly approaching, and that the performer should bring things to a satisfactory conclusion. The hand signal is often followed by drawing a finger across the throat—the hand cue for **Cut!**

wind machine A device for creating the sound of whirling, blowing air; i.e., wind. In film, it consists of a noisy fan over which cloth is draped. In the theater, it consists of a large cylindrical slatted drum turned on its rim, steadied and braced between two stands by an axle, with a canvas cloth draped over it. Its handle is turned at various speeds so that the canvas rubs against the slats to make the sound of anything from a breeze to a storm at sea; e.g., in productions of Shakespeare's *The Tempest*.

See also EFFECTS; RAIN DRUM; THUNDER SHEET.

wing(s) *n.* **1.** The **backstage** area(s) on either side of a proscenium stage set, adjacent to the onstage acting area. **2.** Painted scenery flats that frame a proscenium set, and may be placed on both sides of the stage in planes 2, 3, and 4 of the **acting area**.

wing it *Slang.* To do a performance without having had proper rehearsal or preparation, like a fledgling bird that flies from the nest for the first time.

wired for sound Equipped with a (usually concealed) microphone and its battery pack; e.g., with the **head mike** often used in Broadway musicals.

wire flying In film and on stage, the act of being suspended in the air by cables attached to machinery controlled by technicians so that the performer can seem to be falling through space, or pretend to fly, as in James M. Barrie's *Peter Pan*. On stage, the wires are concealed by being made of semitransparent material and worn attached to hidden harnesses; in a film they are often painted a bright color, so that they can be easily removed digitally in the final **edit**.

See also DECELERATOR.

wire removal The **post-production** deletion by computer technicians of all traces of the cables or wires used in wire flying in film stunts, as well as any shadows they may cast; achieved by digital retouching (i.e., electronically re-coloring the wires and shadows in every frame, so that they blend completely with the background).

wooden *adj. Slang* Inexpressive, stiff, unmoved and unmoving; said of actors who do not appear to experience or live through the emotions of their roles.

word cue A particular word in a line of dialogue that is an actor's signal to speak, or a technician's to do something; e.g., to activate a **follow spot**. For an actor, the cue may be in the middle of a line that must be interrupted. Cf. **line cue**.

word perfect Knowing a part completely and with absolute accuracy.

wordplay *n.* Banter; persiflage; **repartee**; e.g., the punning exchanges between Katherine and Petruchio in act 2, scene 1 of Shakespeare's *Taming of the Shrew*.

work *v.* —*v. t.* **1.** To go through a scene or a part of it, or through an entire act or play, stopping and starting as necessary to make adjustments: *to work a scene*; *to work through a scene*. **2.** To do a job in a stage production: *to work a show*. —*v. i.* **3.** To be what is required and effective for a moment, a line reading, a scene, or a whole play or performance project, in order to be satisfying and perceived as right: *The scene works*. **4.** To have a job in show business; esp. an acting job, as opposed to a **bread-and-butter job**: *He works a lot* (i.e., as an actor).

319

work call A stage crew's time to report for backstage and onstage labor, exclusive of rehearsal or performance; e.g., to put up scenery, hang lights, or install electrical or sound equipment. No actors or other performers are called.

work for peanuts. See PEANUTS.

working actor A performer who is regularly employed, usually in diverse venues, and who is known to people in the business, but is not always a **star** to the general public. For many actors, it is a worthy ambition to be a working actor.

working script The stage manager's copy of a theater play, with complete notations about blocking, lighting cues, and so forth.

working title A proposed, tentative name for a film or other project; used while it is in gestation.

work lights The onstage illumination—except that designed for the production—used for doing the required jobs connected with lighting, scenery, etc. and for rehearsing.

workshop *n., v.* —*n.* **1.** A laboratory production of a play or musical that is worked on during rehearsals by the writer(s), director, and perhaps a **dramaturge**, usually with a future commercial production in mind. The production may or may not be presented to the public; there may be an invited audience for some presentations. After the workshop stage, a play or musical may move on to a **showcase** production, and then perhaps to a paying venue. There are **Equity** contracts for workshops. Also called a *workshop production.* —*v. t.* **2.** To work on a such a performance project in a laboratory situation.

work through To rehearse a scene, part of a scene, or a whole play, stopping and starting for purposes of solving problems, staging, and making adjustments.

work-through *n.* [Short for *work-through rehearsal*] A **rehearsal** in which as much of the play is possible in the time allotted is gone through in order, stopping and starting as necessary. A work-through is usually done about halfway through the rehearsal **process** after the preliminary staging and blocking rehearsals.

See also STOP AND START; WALK-THROUGH.

world premiere The much-heralded first showing of a major feature motion picture or performance of a major play by a well known writer, accompanied, usually, by a star-studded gala opening night reception.

wow *n., v. Slang* —*n.* **1.** A sensational triumph. —**2.** v. t. To triumph unreservedly and heartily in a performance: *We really wowed 'em tonight!*

wrangle *v. t.* [Fr. *cattle wrangling*: herding cattle to make sure they stay together] **1.** In the media and theater, to take care of or supervise any number of diverse kinds of people, animals, or things. **2.** In a **motion capture** shoot, to tend to the cables that are attached to the **head camera** worn by each actor by walking with the actor during a take, making sure the wires are not tangled, and that the actor is free to move.

wrangler *n.* In the film and media world, and sometimes in the theater, a person who is hired to handle, supervise, or take care of any number of diverse people or things.

See ANIMAL WRANGLER; BABY WRANGLER; CELEBRITY WRANGLER; CHILD WRANGLER.

wrap *n., v.* —*n.* **1.** The conclusion of shooting a project, or part of it: *That's a wrap!* The statement is usually followed by cheers, and even champagne, and by a celebratory *wrap party*, which sometimes takes place right there on the set. —*v. t. and i.* **2.** To conclude the shooting of either an entire project or part of it: *to wrap a film.* A director or stage manager might say, "We're wrapped for the day" or "Let's wrap today, if we can." An actor might tell someone, "We were wrapped [dismissed] early" or "We wrapped [finished] early."

writer *n.* A person who authors material to be read and/or performed; an author, e.g., a **dramatist** or **playwright**; a **screenwriter**.

Writers Guild of America (WGA) The organization of screenwriters who work in film and television. There are two branches: Writers Guild East, based in New York City, and Writers Guild West, based in Hollywood. The WGA has bargaining power for its members, and negotiates agreements and contracts with producing organizations.

write-up *n.* A review of or article about a play, musical, film, or other entertainment or about one of the stars involved in it: *a favorable write-up.* Hence, to write up: to review a play, etc.: *He wrote up the play.*

X, Y, Z

X *n.* **1.** Symbol for the actor's move called a **cross**. **2.** Abbrev. for a single frame of film.

xenon arc spot An extremely powerful **follow spot** that uses xenon, a non-reactive gaseous element, inside its **arc lamp**.

xiqu; **hsi chü** (shee' dgoo') *n.* [Chinese: song-theater] Traditional Chinese musical theater. It is a combination of mime, dance, instrumental and vocal music, and spoken lines, all in the service of telling a story, with characters played by individual actor-singers. There are more than three hundred forms of this music theater, sung in different Chinese languages and using different musical systems and structures. Also called *Chinese opera* or *music-drama*.

X-rated A film grade indicating strong, graphic sexual content.

yoke *n.* A U-shaped metal clamp attached to lighting instruments; the yoke is clamped to a **batten**, allowing the light to be maneuvered for focusing.

young leading man; **young leading lady** Actors in their twenties and early thirties who play principal parts in plays and films.

Your back is facing the camera! "Turn around and position yourself so that we see your face!" An indication from a director to actors; also heard as "Your back is to the camera!"

You're off! "You are no longer on the air!" The broadcast has stopped and the performer may move and speak freely.

You're on! 1. In the theater (esp. in burlesque or some other kind of variety show), an instruction or command from the stage manager or an assistant, meaning, "Get out on stage: your turn to perform has come up!" **2.** In the media, the indication that a broadcast is beginning, meaning, "You're **on the air**: start talking!"

YouTube *n.* A web site with astoundingly varied content, including films of famous actors and performers; e.g., silent excerpts of American actor Joseph Jefferson's (1829–1905) performance of Rip van Winkle, songs by Gallagher and Shean; www.youtube.com.

zadacha (zah dah' chah) *n.* [Russian: task; something that must be done] Stanislavsky's term, usually translated as **objective**, but also as **task**, **goal**, and **problem**.

zany *n. Archaic* The miniature head on the end of a stick carried by a court **jester** in the medieval and Renaissance eras; hence, by extension, a jester, buffoon, or

clown (and, later, crazy or odd). The head was often a caricature of the jester who carried it.

zarzuela (sahr sway' lah) *n.* [Spanish; fr. the name of a hunting lodge near Madrid, *Palacio de la Zarzuela* (pah lah' *th*ee o theh lah *th*ahr *th*way' lah), where such pieces were first performed] The musically and dramatically sophisticated Spanish form of operetta or comic opera, often satiric in content; popular in Central and South America as well.

Z-film *n.* *Slang* A low-budget, terrible film, often pornographic, but with such low **production values** that it doesn't even deserve an X rating.

zone shot Filming of a particular section or area of a set, and/or of an actor required to stay on his or her marks in that area.

zoom *n., v.* —*n.* **1.** Quick or slow, in or out movement of the camera lens during a take, focusing closer or farther away from the action by using a special **varifocal** lens that can focus closely on distant objects and make them appear in greater detail, or make them appear smaller by pulling focus away from them; hence, *zoom shot*: a take that uses such lens movements to magnify or demagnify the subject being filmed. **2.** [Short for *zoom lens*] A controllable, varifocal lens, the length of which varies as it is operated. **3.** In film editing, a rapid cut from one kind of shot, such as a close-up, to another, such as a medium shot. —*v. i.* **4.** To use the zoom lens.

zoom ellipsoidal [Short for *zoom ellipsoidal spotlight*] A **spotlight** with an adjustable, varifocal length.

zoom-freeze A shot in which the camera's zoom lens stops its movement suddenly, thus making whatever it is photographing appear to remain motionless and static.

zoom in To use the zoom lens to pull the view towards the action, lengthening the lens tube, which will have been shortened or at its shortest position, without moving the camera itself

zoom out To use the zoom lens to pull the view away from the action, shortening the lens tube, which will have been extended, without moving the camera itself. Also called *zoom back*.

Selected Bibliography

This bibliography constitutes the beginnings of a basic show business library, and the books on acting, drama, film, and theater are among the most useful I consulted for this dictionary. If you begin by reading the works of Stanislavsky, you will readily see that contemporary books on acting are variations on the work of that supreme theorist and practitioner of the art. His approach to finding the *arc* of a role (that is, the linear "shape" of the dramatic character's **journey** from beginning to end) is still useful for plays from every era, from the ancient Greek to the modern *Pinteresque* (a term used to describe the plays of the late Harold Pinter; his plays contain terse dialogue and long pauses full of anxiety and nameless menace, sometimes to great comedic effect). The knowledge in these sources can only enrich the experience of working as a creative, interpretive artist, and will prove a supremely useful supplement to everything actors can only learn on the job.

Abrams, M.H. *A Glossary of Literary Terms*. 7th ed. Boston, MA: Heinle & Heinle, 1999.

Adler, Jacob. *A Life on the Stage: A Memoir*. Translated with commentary by Lulla Rosenfeld. Introduction by Stella Adler. New York: Applause Theatre and Cinema Books, 2001.

Adler, Stella. *On Ibsen, Strindberg, and Chekhov*. Edited and with a preface by Barry Paris. New York: Random House, 1999.

———. *On the Technique of Acting*. Foreword by Marlon Brando. New York: Bantam Books, 1988.

Aristotle. *Poetics*. Edited and translated by Stephen Halliwell. Longinus. On the Sublime. Translation by W.H. Fyfe. Revised by Donald Russell. Demetrius. *On Style*. Edited and translated by Doreen C. Innes, based on W. Rhys Roberts. Cambridge, MA: Harvard University Press, 1999; reprinted, 2005.

Artaud, Antonin. *The Theater and Its Double*. Translated by Mary C. Richard. New York: Grove Press, 1994.

Avilov, Lydia. *Chekhov in My Life: A Love Story*. Translated from the Russian and with an introduction by David Magarshack. New York: Harcourt, Brace, and Company, 1950.

Baily, Leslie. *The Gilbert and Sullivan Book*. New York: Coward-McCann, Inc., 1953.

Barba, Eugenio, and Nicola Savarese. *A Dictionary of Theatre Anthropology: The Secret Art of the Performer*. New York: Routledge, 2006.

Bartow, Arthur, ed. *Training of the American Actor*. New York: Theatre Communications Group, 2006.

Benedetti, Jean. *The Art of the Actor*. New York: Routledge, 2007.

———. *David Garrick and the Birth of Modern Theatre*. London: Methuen, 2001.

————. *Stanislavski: A Biography*. New York: Routledge, 1990.

————. *Stanislavski and the Actor*. London: Methuen Drama, 1998.

————. *Stanislavski: An Introduction*. New York: Routledge, 1982.

————. *The Moscow Art Theatre Letters*. Selected, edited and translated by Jean Benedetti. New York: Routledge, 1991.

Bernhardt, Sarah. *The Art of the Theatre*. Translated by H.J. Stenning and with a preface by James Agate. New York: The Dial Press, 1925.

————. *My Double Life: The Memoirs of Sarah Bernhardt*. Translated by Victoria Tietze Larson. Albany, NY: State University of New York Press, 1999.

Bloom, Harold. *Shakespeare: The Invention of the Human*. New York: Riverhead Books, 1998.

Blumenfeld, Robert. *Accents: A Manual for Actors*. New York: Limelight Editions, 2002.

————. *Acting with the Voice: The Art of Recording Books*. New York: Limelight Editions, 2004.

————. *Tools and Techniques for Character Interpretation: A Handbook of Psychology for Actors, Writers, and Directors*. New York: Limelight Editions, 2006.

————. *Using the Stanislavsky System: A Practical Guide to Character Creation and Period Styles*. New York: Limelight Editions, 2008.

Boal, Augusto. *Theatre of the Oppressed*. Translated by Charles A. Leal-McBride and Maria-Odilia Leal-McBride. New York: Theater Communications Group, Inc., 1985.

Bogart, Anne and Tina Landau. *The Viewpoints Book: A Practical Guide to Viewpoints and Composition*. New York: Theater Communications Group, 2005.

Boleslavsky, Richard. *Acting: The First Six Lessons*. 29th printing. New York: Routledge, 1987.

Boucher, François. *20,000 Years of Fashion: The History of Costume and Personal Adornment*. Expanded edition. With a new chapter by Yvonne Deslandres. New York: Harry N. Abrams, Inc. Publishers, 1987.

Brestoff, Richard. *The Great Acting Teachers and Their Methods*. Lyme, NH: Smith and Kraus, 1995.

Brook, Peter. *The Empty Space: A Book About the Theatre: Deadly, Holy, Rough, Immediate*. New York: Touchstone, 1968.

Caine, Michael. *Acting in Film: An Actor's Take on Movie Making*. New York: Applause Theatre and Cinema Books, 1990.

Callow, Simon. *Acting in Restoration Comedy*. New York: Applause Theatre and Cinema Books, 1991.

————. *Being an Actor*. New York: St. Martin's Press, 1984.

Campbell, Drew. *Technical Theater for Nontechnical People*. New York: Allworth Press, 2004.

Carnicke, Sharon M. *Stanislavsky in Focus*. London: Harwood Academic Publishers, 2003.

Carnovsky, Morris, with Peter Sander. *The Actor's Eye*. Foreword by John Houseman. New York: Performing Arts Journal Publications, 1984.

Chamberlain, Franc. *Michael Chekhov*. New York: Routledge, 2004.

Chekhov, Anton. *The Complete Plays*. Translated, edited, and annotated by Laurence Senelick. New York: W.W. Norton & Company, 2006.

———. *Letters of Anton Chekhov*. Translated by Constance Garnett. New York: Macmillan, 1920.

———. *The Seagull Produced by Stanislavsky*. Production score for the Moscow Art Theatre by K.S. Stanislavsky. Edited with an introduction by Professor S.D. Balukhaty. Translated from the Russian by David Magarshack. New York: Theatre Arts Books, 1952.

Chekhov, Michael. *Lessons for the Professional Actor*. From a collection of notes transcribed and arranged by Deirdre Hurst du Pray. Introduction by Mel Gordon. New York: Performing Arts Journal Publications, 1985.

———. *To the Actor on the Technique of Acting*. Revised and expanded edition. Foreword by Simon Callow. Preface by Yul Brynner. New York: Routledge, 2002.

Cibber, Colley. *An Apology for the Life of Colley Cibber*. New York: Dover Publications, 2000.

Cole, Toby and Helen Krich Chinoy, eds. *Actors on Acting: The Theories, Techniques, and Practices of the World's Great Actors Told in Their Own Words*. New York: Three Rivers Press, 1970.

Craig, [Edward] Gordon. *Henry Irving*. New York: Longmans, Green, and Co., 1930.

Delsarte, François, L'Abbé Delaumosne, Angélique Arnaud, Marie Géraldy, Alfred Giraudet, Francis A. Durivage, and Hector Berlioz. *Delsarte System of Oratory: 1. The Complete Work of L'Abbé Delaumosne. 2. The Complete Work of Mme. Angélique Arnaud. 3. All the Literary Remains of François Delsarte (Given in his own words). 4. The Lecture and Lessons Given by Mme. Marie Géraldy (Delsarte's Daughter) in America. 5. Articles by Alfred Giraudet, Francis A. Durivage, and Hector Berlioz*. 4th edition. New York: Edgar S. Werner, 1893.

Ellmann, Richard. *Oscar Wilde*. New York: Alfred A. Knopf, 1988.

Esper, William and Damon DiMarco. *The Actor's Art and Craft: William Esper Teaches the Meisner Technique*. Foreword by David Mamet. New York: Random House, 2008.

From Russia to Shdanoff: The 100-Year Odyssey of Chekhov and Shdanoff. Burbank, CA: Singa Home Entertainment, DVD, 2004.

Garfield, David. *The Actors Studio: A Player's Place*. Preface by Ellen Burstyn. New York: Macmillan Collier Books, 1984.

Gladkov, Aleksandr. *Meyerhold Speaks Meyerhold Rehearses*. Translated, edited, and with an introduction by Alma Law. New York: Routledge, 1997.

Glavin, John, ed. *Dickens on Screen*. Cambridge, U.K.: Cambridge University Press, 2003.

Gorchakov, Nicolai. *Stanislavsky Directs*. Foreword by Norris Houghton. New York: Limelight Editions, 1991.

Gordon, Mel. *The Stanislavsky Technique: A Workbook for Actors*. New York: Applause Theatre and Cinema Books, 1987.

Gossett, Philip. *Divas and Scholars: Performing Italian Opera*. Chicago: The University of Chicago Press, 2006.

Grant, Gail. *Technical Manual and Dictionary of Classical Ballet*. Illustrated by the author. 3rd revised edition. New York: Dover Publications, Inc., 1982.

Grotowski, Jerzy. *Towards a Poor Theatre*. 1st ed., 1968. New York: Routledge, 2002.

Hagen, Uta. *A Challenge for the Actor*. New York: Charles Scribner's Sons, 1991.

Hagen, Uta, with Haskell Frankel. *Respect for Acting*. New York: Macmillan, 1973.

Hartnoll, Phyllis, ed. *The Oxford Companion to the Theatre*. 3rd edition. London: Oxford University Press, 1967.

Hill, Aaron and William Popple. *The Prompter: A Theatrical Paper (1734–1736)*. Selected and edited by William W. Appleton and Kalman A. Burnim. New York: Benjamin Blom, 1966.

Hindley, Geoffrey, ed. *The Larousse Encyclopedia of Music*. New York: Crown Publishers, Inc., 1971.

Houghton, Norris. *Moscow Rehearsals: The Golden Age of the Soviet Theatre*. With an introduction by Lee Simonson. New York: Grove Press, 1936.

Hull, S. Loraine. *Strasberg's Method as Taught by Lorrie Hull: A Practical Guide for Actors, Teachers, and Directors*. Foreword by Susan Strasberg. Woodbridge, CT: Oxbow Publishing, Inc., 1985.

Irving, Henry. *The Drama: Addresses*. London: William Heinemann, 1893.

Jefferson, Joseph. *The Autobiography of Joseph Jefferson*. Edited by Alan S. Downer Jefferson. Cambridge, MA: Harvard University Press, 1984.

Jones, Ernest. *Hamlet and Oedipus*. New York: Doubleday & Co., 1949.

Joseph, B.L. *Elizabethan Acting*. 2nd ed. London: Oxford University Press, 1964.

Kennedy, Dennis, ed. *The Oxford Encyclopedia of Theatre and Performance*. New York: Oxford University Press, 2003.

Kift, Dagmar and Roy Kift. *The Victorian Music Hall: Culture, Class, and Conflict*. New York: Cambridge University Press, 1996.

Konigsberg, Ira. *The Complete Film Dictionary*. 2nd ed. New York: Penguin Reference, 1997.

Kracauer, Siegfried. *Orpheus in Paris: Offenbach and the Paris of His Time*. New York: Horizon Press, 1983.

Lewes, George Henry. *On Actors and the Art of Acting* (1875). New York: Elibron Classics, 2005.

Lewis, Robert. *Advice to the Players*. Introduction by Harold Clurman. New York: Theatre Communications Books, 1980.

Lichtenberg, Georg Christoph. *Lichtenberg's Visits to England as Described in His Letters and Diaries*. Edited and annotated by Margaret L. Mare and W.H. Quarrel. Orig. ed., Oxford University Press, 1938. New York: Benjamin Blom, 1969.

Linklater, Kristin. *Freeing Shakespeare's Voice: The Actor's Guide to Talking the Text*. New York: Theatre Communications Group, 1992.

Macready, William Charles. *Reminiscences and Selections from His Diaries and Letters*. Edited by Sir Frederick Pollock, Bart. New York: Macmillan and Co., 1875; the Michigan Historical Reprint Series, n.d.

Marowitz, Charles. *The Other Chekhov: A Biography of Michael Chekhov, the Legendary Actor, Director, and Theorist*. New York: Applause Theatre and Cinema Books, 2004.

Meisner, Sanford and Dennis Longwell. *On Acting*. New York: Random House Vintage Books, 1987.

Mekler, Eva. *Masters of the Stage: British Acting Teachers Talk About Their Craft*. New York: Grove Weidenfeld, 1989.

———. *The New Generation of Acting Teachers*. New York: Penguin Books, 1987. (Interviews with Michael Howard, William Esper, Michael Schulman, Terry Schreiber, John Strasberg, Warren Robertson, Ed Kovens, Elinor Renfield, Ernie Martin, Alice Spivak, Eric Morris, Allan Miller, John Lehne, Darryl Hickman, Joan Darling, Jeff Corey, Andrei Belgrader, Bud Beyer, Michael Kahn, Ron Van Lieu, Dale Moffitt, and Mel Shapiro.)

Merlin, Bella. *Konstantin Stanislavsky*. New York: Routledge, 2003.

Merriam-Webster's Encyclopedia of Literature. Springfield, MA: Merriam-Webster, Inc., 1995.

Mikhail, E.H., ed. *The Abbey Theatre: Interviews and Recollections*. Totowa, NJ: Barnes and Noble Books, 1988.

———. *Goldsmith: Interviews and Recollections*. New York: St. Martin's Press, 1993.

———. *Oscar Wilde: Interviews and Recollections*. Two vols. New York: Harper & Row Publishers, Inc., 1979.

———. *Sheridan: Interviews and Recollections*. New York: Macmillan, 1989.

Miller, Pat P. *Script Supervising and Film Continuity*. 3rd ed. Boston, MA: Focal Press, 1999.

Moore, Sonia. *The Stanislavsky Method: The Professional Training of an Actor*. Preface by Sir John Gielgud. Foreword by Joshua Logan. New York: The Viking Press, 1960.

———. *Stanislavsky Revealed: The Actor's Guide to Spontaneity on Stage*. New York: Applause Theatre and Cinema Books, 1968.

———. *Training an Actor: The Stanislavsky System in Class*. New York: Penguin Books, 1979.

Nagler, A.M. *A Source Book in Theatrical History (Sources of Theatrical History)*. New York: Dover Publications, Inc., 1952.

Nemirovich-Danchenko, Vladimir. *My Life in the Russian Theatre*. Translated by John Cournos with an introduction by John Logan, a foreword by Oliver M. Saylor, and a chronology by Elizabeth Reynolds Hapgood. New York: Theatre Arts Books, 1936.

Noccioli, Guido. *Duse on Tour: Guido Noccioli's Diaries 1906–07*. Translated and edited with an introduction and notes by Giovanni Pontiero. Amherst, MA: The University of Massachusetts Press, 1982.

Olivier, Laurence. *Confessions of an Actor: The Autobiography*. London: Orion Books, Ltd., 1982.

Olivier, Tarquin. *My Father Laurence Olivier*. London: Headline Book Publishing PLC, 1992.

Partridge, Eric. *A Dictionary of Catch Phrases: American and British from the 16th Century to the Present Day*. Revised and updated edition edited by Paul Beale. Lanham, MD: Scarborough House, 1992.

———. *Shakespeare's Bawdy: A Literary and Psychological Essay and a Comprehensive Glossary*. New York: E.P. Dutton, 1960.

Pavis, Patrice. *Dictionary of the Theatre: Terms, Concepts, and Analysis*. Translated by Christine Shantz. Preface by Marvin Carlson. Toronto: University of Toronto Press, 1998.

Piches, Jonathan. *Vsevelod Meyerhold*. New York: Routledge, 2003.

Pitcher, Harvey. *Chekhov's Leading Lady: A Portrait of the Actress Olga Knipper*. New York: Franklin Watts, Inc., 1980.

Potter, Helen. *Impersonations*. New York: Edgar S. Werner, 1891.

Radice, Mark. *Opera in Context: Essays on Historical Staging from the Late Renaissance to the Time of Puccini*. New York: Amadeus Press, 1998.

Randel, Don Michael. *The Harvard Dictionary of Music*. 4th edition. Cambridge, MA: The Belknap Press of Harvard University Press, 2003.

Rayfield, Donald. *Anton Chekhov: A Life*. New York: Henry Holt, 1997.

Robinson, David. *Chaplin: His Life and Art*. New York: McGraw Hill, 1985.

Rathbone, Basil. *In and Out of Character*. New York: Limelight Editions, 2004.

Redgrave, Michael. *In My Mind's I: An Actor's Autobiography*. New York: The Viking Press, 1983.

Rudlin, John. *Commedia dell'Arte: An Actor's Handbook*. New York: Routledge, 1994.

Saint-Denis, Michel. Theatre: *The Rediscovery of Style*. Introduction by Sir Laurence Olivier. New York: Theatre Arts Books, 1960.

Schechner, Richard. *Performance Theory*. New York: Routledge, 1988, 2003.

Senelick, Lawrence. *The Chekhov Theatre: A Century of the Plays in Performance*. Cambridge: Cambridge University Press, 1997.

———. *Serf Actor: The Life and Art of Mikhail Shchepkin*. Westport, CT: Greenwood Press, 1984.

Shattuck, Charles H. *The Hamlet of Edwin Booth*. Chicago, IL: The University of Illinois Press, 1969.

Sheehy, Helen. *Eleonora Duse: A Biography*. New York: Alfred A. Knopf, 2003.

Sher, Antony. *Year of the King: An Actor's Diary and Sketchbook*. New York: Limelight Editions, 2003.

Singleton, Ralph, and James A. Conrad. *The Filmmaker's Dictionary*. Edited by Janna Wong Healy. 2nd ed. completely revised and updated. Hollywood, CA: Lone Eagle Publishing, 2000.

Skinner, Edith. *Speak with Distinction*. Revised with new material added by Timothy Monich and Lilene Mansell. Edited by Lilene Mansell. New York: Applause Theatre and Cinema Books, 1990.

Slater, Niall W. *Plautus in Performance: The Theatre of the Mind*. Princeton, NJ: Princeton University Press, 1985.

Spivak, Alice, written in collaboration with Robert Blumenfeld. *How to Rehearse When There Is No Rehearsal: Acting and the Media*. New York: Limelight, 2007.

Spolin, Viola. *Improvisation for the Theater*. Chicago, IL: Northwestern University Press, 1963.

––––––. *Theater Games*. Chicago, IL: Northwestern University Press, 1986.

Stanislavski, Constantin and Pavel Rumantsev. *Stanislavski on Opera*. Translated and edited by Elizabeth Reynolds Hapgood. New York: Routledge, 1974.

Stanislavsky, Constantin. *An Actor Prepares*. Translated by Elizabeth Reynolds Hapgood. New York: Theatre Arts Books, 1936; 23rd printing, 1969.

––––––. *Building a Character*. Translated by Elizabeth Reynolds Hapgood. New York: Theatre Arts Books; 14th printing, 1949.

––––––. *Creating a Role*. Translated by Elizabeth Reynolds Hapgood. New York: Theatre Arts Books (6th printing), 1969.

––––––. *My Life in Art*. Translated by G. Ivanov-Mumjiev. Moscow: Foreign Languages Publishing House, n.d.

––––––. *My Life in Art*. Translated by J.J. Robbins. Orig. pub. Little, Brown and Company, 1924. New York: The World Publishing Co. Meridian Books, 1966.

––––––. *On the Art of the Stage*. Introduced and Translated by David Magarshack. New York: Hill and Wang, 1961.

––––––. *Stanislavsky Produces Othello*. Translated from the Russian by Dr. Helen Nowak. London: Godfrey Bles, 1948.

Strasberg, Lee. *A Dream of Passion*. New York: Penguin Plume Books, 1987.

Strasberg at the Actors Studio: Tape-Recorded Sessions. Edited and with an introduction by Robert H. Hethmon. Preface by Burgess Meredith. New York: Theatre Communications Group, 1991; 5th printing, 2000.

Styan, J.L. *Restoration Comedy in Performance*. New York: Cambridge University Press, 1986.

Suzuki, Tadashi. *The Way of Acting*. New York: Theatre Communications Group, 1986.

Toporkov, Vasili. *Stanislavski in Rehearsal*. Translated and with an introduction by Jean Benedetti. New York: Routledge, 2004.

Uta Hagen's Acting Class. New York: Applause Theatre and Cinema Books, DVD, 2004.

Womersley, David, ed. *Restoration Drama: An Anthology*. Oxford, U.K.: Blackwell Publishers, 2000.

Wood, Melusine. *Historical Dances, 12th to 19th Century: Their Manner of Performance and Their Place in the Social Life of the Time*. Princeton, NJ: Princeton Book Company Publishers, 1982.

Recommended Reading
Books of Actors' Interviews

Of the many sources of information about the way actors go about creating characters, the books of interviews that you will find listed here are particularly helpful. You can learn something from each of the actors—some useful tip, or an overall approach to the work. Ultimately, you will develop your own personalized method or system of working on a role, and you may find it useful to draw on the many available sources, always bearing in mind that it is in the doing, as Stanislavsky thought, that one learns the most. No matter what the theory, it must, after all, be put into practice.

Brown, Dennis. *Actors Talk: Profiles and Stories from the Acting Trade*. New York: Limelight Editions, 1999. (Interviews with Beulah Bondi, Barry Bostwick, José Ferrer, Lillian Gish, Sterling Hayden, Danny Kaye, Stacy Keach, Gregory Peck, George Rose, Jessica Tandy, and Paul Winfield.)

Bryer, Jackson R. and Richard A. Davison, eds. *The Actor's Art: Conversations with Contemporary American Stage Performers*. New Brunswick, NJ: Rutgers University Press, 2001. (Interviews with Zoë Caldwell, Hume Cronyn, Jessica Tandy, Blythe Danner, Ruby Dee, George Grizzard, Julie Harris, Eileen Heckart, Cherry Jones, James Earl Jones, Stacy Keach, Shirley Knight, Nathan Lane, Jason Robards, Maureen Stapleton, Eli Wallach, and Anne Jackson.)

Burton, Hal, ed. *Great Acting*. New York: Bonanza Books, 1967. (Interviews with Laurence Olivier, Sybil Thorndike, Ralph Richardson, Peggy Ashcroft, Michael Redgrave, Edith Evans, John Gielgud, and Noël Coward.)

Funke, Lewis and John E. Booth. *Actors Talk About Acting*. Two vols. New York: Avon Books, 1961. (Interviews with John Gielgud, Helen Hayes, Vivien Leigh, Morris Carnovsky, Shelley Winters, Bert Lahr, Sidney Poitier, Alfred Lunt, Lynn Fontanne, José Ferrer, Maureen Stapleton, Katherine Cornell, Paul Muni, and Anne Bancroft.)

Jeffri, Joan, ed. *The Actor Speaks: Actors Discuss Their Experiences and Careers*. Westport, CT: Greenwood Press, 1994. (Interviews with Alan Alda, Mary Alice, Philip Bosco, Al Carmines, Pat Carroll, Miriam Kressyn, Marcia Jean Kurtz, Susan Nussbaum, John Randolph, Jason Robards, Jr., Mercedes Ruehl, and B.D. Wong.)

Luckhurst, Mary and Chloe Veltman, eds. *On Acting: Interviews with Actors*. New York: Faber and Faber, 2001. (Interviews with Annabel Arden, Simon Callow, Ayan Çelik, Willem Dafoe, Eve Ensler, Danny Hoch, Barb Jungr, Luba Kadison, William H. Macy, Miriam Margolyes, Linda Marlowe, Conrad Nelson,

Ruth Posner, Hugh Quarshie, Liev Schreiber, Michael Sheen, Anthony Sher, Anna Deveare Smith, Elaine Stritch, and Indira Varma.)

Shafer, Yvonne. *Performing O'Neill: Conversations with Actors and Directors.* New York: St. Martin's Press, 2000. (Interviews with James Earl Jones, Jane Alexander, Michael Kahn, Jason Robards, Theodore Mann, Arvin Brown, Len Cariou, Teresa Wright, Gloria Foster, Edward Petherbridge, and Fritz Weaver.)

Tichler, Rosemarie and Barry Jay Kaplan. *Actors at Work: Conversations with Frances Conroy, Billy Crudup, Philip Seymour Hoffman, Kevin Kline, John Lithgow, Patti LuPone, S. Epatha Merkerson, Estelle Parsons, Mandy Patinkin, Ruben Santiago-Hudson, Marian Seldes, Kevin Spacey, Meryl Streep, and Dianne Wiest.* Foreword by Mike Nichols. New York: Faber and Faber, Inc., 2007.

Index of People

Index of Subjects
by Category

345

Commercials

Dance

Directions

Drama

Script and Playwrighting Terms

Expressions, Catchphrases, Idioms, and Slang

Catchphrases

Expressions, Idioms, and Slang

Foreign-Language and British Terms

Jobs and Professions

Lights and Lighting Terms

Media: Radio, Film, Television, and the Internet

Technical and Technological Terms

Genres

Music

Professional Organizations

About the Author

Robert Blumenfeld is the author of *Accents: A Manual for Actors* (Revised and expanded edition, 2002), *Acting with the Voice: The Art of Recording Books* (2004), *Tools and Techniques for Character Interpretation: A Handbook of Psychology for Actors, Writers, and Directors* (2006), and *Using the Stanislavsky System: A Practical Guide to Character Creation and Period Styles* (2008) and the collaborator with noted teacher, acting coach, and actress Alice Spivak on the writing of her book *How to Rehearse When There Is No Rehearsal: Acting and the Media* (2007)—all published by Limelight. He lives and works as an actor, dialect coach, and writer in New York City, and is a longtime member of Equity, AFTRA, SAG, and the Dramatists Guild. He has worked in numerous regional and New York theaters, as well as in television and independent films. For ACT Seattle he played the title role in Ronald Harwood's *The Dresser*, and he has performed many roles in plays by Shakespeare and Chekhov, as well as doing an Off-Broadway season of six Gilbert and Sullivan comic operas for Dorothy Raedler's American Savoyards (under the name Robert Fields), for which he played the Lord Chancellor in *Iolanthe* and other patter-song roles. He created the roles of the Marquis of Queensberry and two prosecuting attorneys in Moisés Kaufman's Off-Broadway hit play *Gross Indecency: The Three Trials of Oscar Wilde*, and was also the production's dialect coach. Mr. Blumenfeld has recorded more than 315 Talking Books for the American Foundation for the Blind, including the complete Sherlock Holmes canon, *The Hunchback of Notre-Dame*, and *The Count of Monte Cristo*. He received the 1997 Canadian National Institute for the Blind's Torgi Award for the Talking Book of the Year in the Fiction category, for his recording of Pat Conroy's *Beach Music*, and the 1999 Alexander Scourby Talking Book Narrator of the Year Award in the Fiction category. He holds a B.A. in French from Rutgers University and an M.A. from Columbia University in French Language and Literature.